Facing Ethnic Conflicts

Facing Ethnic Conflicts

Toward a New Realism

Edited by
Andreas Wimmer
Richard J. Goldstone
Donald L. Horowitz
Ulrike Joras
Conrad Schetter

Published in cooperation with the
Center for Development Research, University of Bonn

ROWMAN & LITTLEFIELD PUBLISHERS, INC.
Lanham • Boulder • New York • Toronto • Oxford

ROWMAN & LITTLEFIELD PUBLISHERS, INC.

Published in the United States of America
by Rowman & Littlefield Publishers, Inc.
A wholly owned subsidary of The Rowman & Littlefield Publishing Group, Inc.
4501 Forbes Boulevard, Suite 200, Lanham, MD 20706
www.rowmanlittlefield.com

PO Box 317, Oxford
OX2 9RU, UK

British Library Cataloguing in Publication Information Available

Library of Congress Cataloging-in-Publication Data

Facing ethnic conflicts : toward a new realism / Andreas Wimmer ... [et al.].
    p. cm.
  Includes bibliographical references and index.
  ISBN 0-7425-3584-3 (cloth : alk. paper) — ISBN 0-7425-3585-1 (pbk. : alk. paper)
  1. Ethnic conflict. I. Wimmer, Andreas.

HM1121.F33 2004
305.8—dc22
                                                                    2004002285

Printed in the United States of America

♾™ The paper used in this publication meets the minimum requirements of
American National Standard for Information Sciences—Permanence of Paper
for Printed Library Materials, ANSI/NISO Z39.48-1992.

Contents

Introduction:
Facing Ethnic Conflicts

Andreas Wimmer

Over the past decades, ethnonationalist conflict has become the dominant form of mass political violence. The overwhelming majority of civil wars in the postwar era were fought in the name of ethnonational autonomy or independence (Scherrer 1994:74)—as was the case during earlier waves of civil wars in the nineteenth and twentieth centuries, such as during the Balkan wars or the dissolution of the Ottoman and Habsburg empires. Since the 1950s, the number of ethnic conflicts continued to increase. The trend reached a peak 1993–1994, as figure I.1 illustrates. Recent examples abound: The intransigence of ethnonationalist politics led to catastrophe in Bosnia; the break-up of the Soviet empire ignited a bushfire of separatist battles at its southern borders; Burundi finds no more respite than does Myanmar's hinterland or southern Sudan.

Parallel to this trend, the desire to understand and to contain these conflicts has grown over the past decades and especially after the end of the Cold War, when governments and international organizations came to regard them as a security problem of global proportions—only recently overshadowed by the U.S. preoccupation with fighting terrorist groups and their supporters. Ethnic conflicts became a testing ground for a new morality of promoting peace, stability, and human rights across the globe. Ethnic chauvinism and hatred were perceived by public intellectuals such as Ignatieff (1997) as the major obstacle for globalizing the Western model of a liberal society based on equality and the respect for cultural differences.

This book offers some of the best research on how to understand ethnic conflicts and on how to prevent such conflicts, settle them by outside

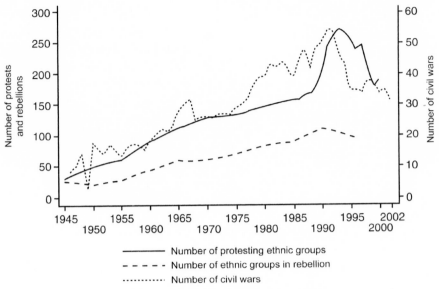

Figure I.1.   Global Trends in Ethnopolitical Conflict, 1945–2002

Sources: For protest and rebellion data, see Bennett and Davenport (2003). Civil war data are from Eriksson et al. (2003), accessed at www.prio.no/cwp/ArmedConflict/. I would like to thank Brian Min for producing the graph.
Note: Protest data are for five-year periods from 1945 to 1985 and annually after 1985. Rebellion data are for five-year periods from 1945 to 1994 with partial data from 1995 to 1998. Civil war data are annual from 1945 to 2002.

interference, and design institutions that reduce the risk of escalation. It combines research-based arguments with the expertise of diplomats, NGO officers, and government advisers. Before I summarize the structure of the book and the content of its chapters, I should like to outline, in broad strokes, four strands of the debate that have unfolded in different institutional environments and their respective discursive spheres: the general discussion about ethnic conflicts in the quality press and media, struggling with understanding the "new world disorder" brought about, as it seemed, by ethnic chauvinism and nationalist fervor; the development of policy thinking over the past decades and its recent diversification into a range of approaches, from heavy-handed military intervention to mediation between grassroots organizations; a new research tradition that is closely tied to these policy debates and mainly rooted in think tanks and consulting firms; and, finally, a much older academic tradition, focused on how to understand the politicization of ethnicity in the developing world and beyond.

There is, as I will argue below, a general lack of communication between these various fields: Journalists are rarely aware of the scholarly debate and the results it has produced; policymakers continue to discuss models that imply an understanding of conflict out of tune with the models that researchers have developed; academics often arrive at policy conclusions that are far off the accumulated experience of ethnic conflict management; scholars that evaluate policy options are sometimes unaware of the decades of research undertaken by their more academically oriented colleagues. This book documents the state of the art in three of these four fields and aims, by bringing them together in one single volume, to establish a basis for future communication between the various communities.

SOME POPULAR VIEWS

Four popular understandings of the post–Cold War surge in ethnic conflicts dominate public reasoning in quality newspapers and foreign policy journals—mostly ignoring the long-term trends that underlie this more recent wave. Many journalists and experts in governmental and multinational institutions attribute the growing political significance of ethnicity to what one may call a "defrosting effect." As the "ice" of authoritarian rule that was preserved through superpower rivalry melts away, "ancient hatred" between ethnic groups (Kaplan 1993) is being revived and fueled by incompatible claims to rational self-determination and political sovereignty (Callahan 1998).

A related view has recently spread, if rarely openly expressed, among Western foreign policymakers disenchanted with the prospects for preventing and settling ethnic conflicts in the Caucasus or the Balkans. The new states that issued from the former communist bloc are seen as being simply too heterogeneous in ethnolinguistic or ethno-religious terms to function as "normal" nation states. The only "solution," cynics maintain, is therefore to give way to the drive for national self-assertion and let it follow its natural course until homogenous nation states emerge (see Jentleson 2001).

Other observers join best-selling sociologists like Beck (1997) in postulating a universal desire for cultural rootedness, accentuated under current conditions of globalization and rapid social change. Globalization makes people search for a secure homestead and produces an aggressive nationalism that threatens existing states where national and political boundaries do not coincide. More recently, Amy Chua (2004) has offered, in another best-selling book, a different version of the globalization hypothesis: The worldwide spread of markets increases inequality between trading minorities and the majority population, while the diffusion of democracy offers demagogues an opportunity to point to these minorities as scapegoats responsible for the downsides of globalization.

The most successful thesis, repeated and debated ad nauseam by the informed public around the world, is Samuel Huntington's clash of civilizations, which he sees replacing the competition between communism and capitalism during the Cold War. The major lines of conflict now run parallel to the civilizational fault lines separating orthodox from nonorthodox Christians, Confucians, Muslims, Africans, and Latin Americans (Huntington 1993).

It is striking how little this popular literature takes notice of the specialized academic literature that has developed over the past decades. Many prominent authors—and with them their replicators in the media—seem to be unaware of the existence of a rich research tradition discussing such popular notions extensively, from the civilizational conflict thesis (Gurr 1994; Russet et al. 2000; Chiozza 2002) to the argument that ethnic heterogeneity itself is at the roots of conflicts and wars (Kasfir 1979; McRae 1983; Vanhanen 1999; Bates 1999; Collier and Hoeffler 2000; Ellingsen 2000; Fearon and Laitin 2003) to the debate on the trading minority hypothesis (Bonacich 1973; Horowitz 1985:113–124).

POLICY APPROACHES

In parallel to this rising public interest in ethnic conflicts, the political assessment has undergone considerable change. As mentioned before, governments and international organizations now regard ethnic conflicts as a security problem of global proportions—exceeded only recently by the potential for terrorist attacks by fundamentalist organizations or pariah states that have acquired (or are assumed to have acquired) "weapons of mass destruction."

The current attention to ethnic conflict contrasts markedly with the approach of previous periods. Since the prehistory of ethnic conflict management is largely forgotten, a digression may be permitted here.[1] The first systematic international approach to the question of ethnonational minorities was developed in the aftermath of the First and Second Balkan Wars and elaborated after World War I (Krasner and Froats 1998). The League of Nations introduced a detailed regime of minority rights, especially in the fields of language, education, and political representation. Sovereign status was given only to those newly independent states that had lived up to the minority protection provisions they had negotiated with the League. The main motive for the League's minority policy was to avoid, after having accepted the principle of national self-determination, claims to statehood proliferating to unmanageable proportions. Seen from today's perspective, it is interesting to note that minority protection was understood as a transitory means for achieving, over the long run, full assimilation into the national majorities (Kovacs 2003). The League even accepted what we nowadays call ethnic cleansings in order to achieve stability and homogeneity, for example the "population exchange," as it was euphemistically called, foreseen in the treaty of Lausanne between Turkey and Greece (Bartsch 1995).

The minority rights regime, however, could not prevent the further politicization of the ethnic question in many mandate areas or other dependent territories that were to achieve full independence. It lacked an effective enforcement mechanism, and the rivalry between the colonial empires made a common stance impossible, which led many mandate powers to take the minority rights provision lightly. Most important, however, the nationalist aspirations of many minority elites could not be satisfied with language and educational rights and reserved parliamentary seats (Arendt 1951). The spiral of ethnonationalist mobilizations and countermobilizations culminated in a new wave of purges and ethnic cleansings all over Eastern Europe, the Balkans, and Russia.

After World War II, the Western policy-making approach changed considerably. The minority rights regime of the League was completely discredited and the new hegemon, the United States, placed greater emphasis on individual human rights as opposed to group rights (Krasner and Froats 1998:244). In addition, the imperial powers of France, Britain, Holland, and Portugal soon abandoned the colonial project and sought to foster a process of "nation building" leading the colonial subjects to independence. "Nation building" (cf. Bendix 1964) was meant to overcome "tribal" or "ethnic" particularisms by creating a community of citizens. It was hardly compatible with the notion of "minority rights" that had prevailed in the interwar period. More often than not, however, the colonial masters saw one particular ethnic group, usually the most Christianized, most literate, politically most reliable, as representing the core group of the nation-to-be and systematically supported them by recruiting members of this group into the army, bureaucracy, and university system of the embryonic state apparatus, thus laying the ground for many of the postindependence ethnic conflicts (Wimmer 2002).

Nation-building was complemented by upholding the territorial boundaries of the new states, usually corresponding to former imperial provinces. There was virtually no Western support for irredentist or separatist ethnonational movements during that period, mostly for fear of uncontrollable domino effects, especially in Africa, where few state boundaries coincided with linguistic, religious, or other cultural dividing lines. Western governments saw the violent conflicts that were unleashed after independence as the birth pains of the new nations and largely a matter to be settled by the elites of the new countries themselves—as long as the winning parties and groups remained loyal to the former colonial power and ensured that the domains of French, British, or Dutch influence did not shrink.

The Cold War reinforced this pragmatic, selective interventionism. As soon as conflicting parties took on different ideological stances along the great divide between communism and capitalism, they were able to marshal support from the superpowers eager to prevent a country from falling into the hands of the archenemy. Peacemaking, democratic stability, or minority rights were non-issues in a time when conflicts were largely seen from a strategic geopolitical and military point of view. Winning the battle was the aim, not settling conflicts and promoting stability and peace. A systematic approach to ethnic conflicts, as had existed in the interwar period, never developed (Brown 1993; Callahan 1998).

The end of the Cold War has brought about a major shift in policy thinking in Western capitals in at least three different ways. First, direct political and military intervention in developing countries now seemed to be a feasible option, since the risk of escalation into a full-scale world war, a threat ever-present as long the nuclear powers watched each other's moves in every corner of the globe, now ceased to exist. Second, with the virtual defeat of the communist countermodel, Western political and economic doctrines became almost globally valid. Accordingly, Western governments felt responsible to help developing countries and especially the countries of the former Eastern bloc on their way to democracy, legal security, good governance, and market economy. Settling ethnic conflicts was important for achieving a politically stable environment conducive to these reforms. Third, the ethnonationalist wars, especially in the Balkans but also in Iraq, Turkey, Sri Lanka, Ethiopia, and elsewhere, triggered a flow of refugees to the West that greatly enhanced the consciousness of living in a unified, interrelated global system. The refugees thus helped to build up the political will for prevention, early action, intervention, and peacemaking and fostered a new discourse of responsibility and morality that complemented the more instrumental power-balance arguments of traditional foreign policy. Seen from a global point of view, the many small-scale wars spreading in the newly independent states of the East or in democratizing societies of the South had replaced the confrontation between East and West as the main threat to global peace and stability— before the terrorist attacks on the World Trade Center and the Pentagon suddenly shifted the perception of threat, at least in the United States, rather dramatically and gave rise to a new doctrine of prevention and intervention driven by a "homeland security" agenda.

In the shadow of these concerns and outside the United States, many governments continue to focus their foreign and security policy on the multiple small-scale confrontations with no clear strategic implications for Western countries. Some governments have developed far-reaching policy plans with the aim of preventing or peacefully settling such conflicts or reconstructing war-torn societies. Perhaps the most ambitious plan was the Canadian Peace Building Initiative, which brought together the Departments of Foreign Affairs, International Trade, and International Development. The Swedish government has also developed a comprehensive approach and has made conflict prevention the foremost goal of Sweden's development policy, acting in concert with the military and diplomatic services. Other such examples abound.

More specifically, several policy approaches to prevent, mitigate, or peacefully settle ethnic conflicts have been formulated during the past fifteen years, both by international organizations such as the UN, NATO, the Council of Europe, and the Organization for Security and Cooperation in Europe (OSCE) and by national governments and various sectors of the NGO community.

These include, first, several options to prevent escalation in the preconflict phase. A number of techniques, including early-action, round-table diplomacy; permanent field missions; and the like now fill the arsenal of governments and multilateral institutions. Preventive diplomacy has acquired particular importance and, at least in the white papers of several Western governments and international organizations, represents one of the foremost priorities of foreign policy and development cooperation.

Second, new techniques for negotiating peace between warring ethnonational factions have been developed and have been combined or alternated with military interventions and peace-enforcing operations. These range from negotiations in secluded places under heavy political and military pressure from the international community (such as the negotiations in Dayton, Rambouillet, or Stormont) to behind-the-scenes talks at the kitchen table organized by nongovernmental organizations, such as the famous Oslo negotiations between PLO and Israel as well as various combinations of official and unofficial diplomatic efforts to bring peace, now generally labeled "multitrack" diplomacy.

Third, a new branch of mostly NGO activities has come to flourish, nourished by the hope that conflicts between ethnic communities can be mediated through peaceful dialogue. Some involve the leadership level; others target civil society organizations or the grassroots. The aim is to overcome entrenched stereotypes and intolerance that are considered to be at the root of the conflicts. Techniques include interactive conflict resolution, conflict transformation, and psycho-political trauma healing.

Fourth, the end of the Cold War has enabled the UN to establish supranational juridical institutions that prosecute ethnocides and other crimes that are not adequately addressed by national juridical systems. The international war criminal tribunals for Rwanda and for the former Yugoslavia are the most prominent examples here. Fifth, new experiences in the field of restorative justice—as opposed to the retributive justice of war tribunals—have been made, such as with the truth commissions of South Africa or of Guatemala. They rely on the idea that revealing the truth will make it possible to heal some of the emotional wounds of past conflict and make a new beginning in conflict-torn societies possible. The more modest international fact-finding commissions, such as the one on Kosovo, also belong to this repertoire of instruments.

Sixth, good governance, rule of law, and democracy are praised—among many other things—for bringing peace and stability to conflict-ridden societies. Many policymakers believe that this trio of institutional reforms will "civilize" political behavior and help de-escalate ethnic conflicts. Seventh, an even larger number of experts is convinced that institutional reforms should specifically address the issue of community relations where these have been characterized by violence and protracted conflict. A set of such institutions has been promoted for their conflict-reducing properties. Many favor federalism and other autonomy regulations as solutions to ethnic conflict, including various national governments (without exceptions and, not surprisingly, all of federalist states) and international organizations. A second prominent and much-promoted institution is power-sharing arrangements at the political center, including various consociational arrangements, in which cabinet seats are distributed among ethnic communities that choose separately among "their" candidates; reserved seats in parliament; various consultative bodies including minority representatives; and the like. A third group of tools includes minority rights, such as those offered by the ILO convention 107—so far mainly ratified by Latin American countries—the Council of Europe Convention regarding minority rights, and the recommendations of the OSCE.

These policy measures have been offered, tested, or implemented with varying degrees of success in a number of ethnic conflicts since 1989: in Ireland, Bosnia, Macedonia, Corsica, Sri Lanka, Indonesia, Bangladesh, the Philippines, Chechnya, Georgia, Turkey, Nagorno-Karabakh, the Sudan, Sierra Leone, Burundi, Rwanda, Nicaragua, Ecuador, Guatemala, and Colombia, to name just a handful of the more prominent examples for each continent.

RESEARCH APPROACHES

These experiences have stimulated a growing interest among researchers, mostly in think tanks and consultancy firms, but also in conflict research units of universities. They have analyzed the political dynamics that led Western governments and international organizations to adopt such policies; their intended and unintended consequences for the dynamics of ethnic conflicts; and their relative effectiveness in bringing peace, stability, and justice to the victims of such conflict. Much of this applied research was undertaken by scholars who, before 1989, had studied negotiations in the framework of the Cold War, or were specialized in small-scale conflicts such as between local communities and authorities or labor conflicts in the West, or came from the field of applied social psychology and the study of intergroup relations in multicultural societies. After 1989, many "discovered" ethnic conflicts as these gained importance both numerically and in terms of media coverage, and thus contributed greatly to the creation of the image of a "new world disorder" characterized by a multiplicity of civil wars with ethnic overtones (compare Kaldor 1999).

In that process, old concepts were adapted to the new object of study, such as the model of a "security dilemma," originally developed to explain the standoff between NATO and the Soviet Union (Roe 1999), with considerable impact on the way ethnic conflicts were perceived and the kind of questions researchers asked. Some scholars that participated in this debate, it may be noted, have in the meantime moved on to other topics and especially to the recent "war on terror" and its repercussions in the Middle East and elsewhere.

Aside from this field of applied research, we find a larger, more stable and continuous academic research tradition. The ramifications of this literature are manifold and include linkages to the general discussions on nationalism in political science, history, and sociology (Guibernau and Hutchinson 2001); the vast field of ethnicity studies in several social science disciplines (see, among others, Jenkins 1997); the not less extended realms of conflict theories—micro to macro (Miall et al. 2001); the literature on collective action in political science (e.g., Kuran 1998) and intergroup relations in social psychology; and, finally, the literature on political modernization and nation-building (Foster 1991; Alonso 1994). While it is impossible to review even the narrower domain of ethnic conflict research proper, some of the major stages of the development of this tradition should at least be alluded to here.

In the 1950s, studies of the process of tribal fusion and fission, a longstanding and well-established research topic in colonial anthropology, were combined with an emerging interest in "nation-building" in the newly independent states of what now was termed the developing world (Bendix 1964). Both became related to a third tradition that had studied the consequences of cultural pluralism for the political integration and cohesion of colonial societies (Furnivall 1944). These three research strands provided the basis for some important studies of the conflictual nature of postcolonial state building and the politicization of ethnic relations it often brought about (Geertz 1963; Young 1965; M. Smith 1969).

In a second stage during the 1960s and 1970s, a series of conflicts especially on the African continent became the focus of a specializing literature (Kasfir 1976), and were understood as consequences of political underdevelopment (such as in the literature on "tribalism"), or of the manipulation of a new class of leaders (Sklar 1967), or, finally and in contrast to the first view, of the political competition between elites brought about by political integration and social mobilization (Brass 1976; Bates 1974; Milne 1981; Rothschild 1981).

With the 1970s ethnic revival in many peripheral regions of Europe and North America, most notably in the Basque country, Wales and Scotland, Catalonia, Northern Ireland, and Quebec (Hechter and Levi 1979), a new wave of studies mainly in political science and sociology followed. The field broadened considerably, some looking at the link between ethnonationalist revivals and uneven capitalist development (Nairn 1977) or at the process of mobilizing ethnic constituencies by intellectuals and deprived middle classes (Brass 1976; Esman 1977; A. Smith 1984), others being preoccupied with the institutional regulations of such conflicts (Lijphart 1977; Lustick 1979; Horowitz 1985), and still others, in the tradition of the plural-society school mentioned above, examining the various modes in which ethnicity can relate to the institutions of the modern state (Young 1976).

During the 1990s, finally, new approaches to the study of ethnic conflicts mushroomed, specialized conferences were held, new journals such as *Nationalism and Ethnic Politics* and *Nations and Nationalism* were launched, established journals such as the *Journal of Peace Research* or the *Journal of Conflict Resolution* published special issues, and a large number of books and edited volumes appeared. Figure I.2 illustrates this recent wave of books and articles. Interestingly enough, it rises only after the end of the Cold War, in contrast to the number of conflicts themselves, which increased continuously since the middle of the century. Most of the more important lines of this academic debate are represented in this volume and will be introduced in "Authors and Chapters," the final section of this chapter.

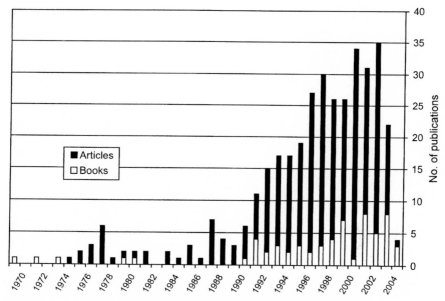

Figure I.2   Trends in Publications on Ethnic Conflicts, 1969–2004

Source: Books with "ethnic conflict" in the title were searched in Amazon.com and the University of California library system; a Social Science Citation Index search produced the number of articles that show "ethnic conflict" in title or abstract, or as a keyword.

A TOWER OF BABEL?

I have identified four major strands of a debate on how to understand ethnic conflict and "what to do about it": public opinion in the West, struggling with an adequate understanding of "new wars," "civilizational clashes," or counterreactions to "globalization"; a mushrooming debate among policymakers about the adequate tools for prevention and intervention; an applied literature of international relations and conflict regulation specialists, intertwined with the policy debate; and, finally, an established academic discourse on ethnic conflicts. There seems to be little systematic communication between these fields. Top journalists, such as the aforementioned Michael Ignatieff, rely on Sigmund Freud to understand the wars in the Balkans—and not on the major works of the specialized academic literature; others ignore scholarly knowledge about the historical and political background and may thus even contribute to an interpretation of a conflict along ethnic lines (see Allen and Seaton 1999). Policymakers stick to ideas about the root causes of conflict, such as the incompatibility of "cultures," which researchers have long since proven to be on shaky ground.[2] Academics discuss proposals, such as supporting groups with a cosmopolitan view of society (cf. Kaldor 1999), that have little chance of being taken into consideration by policymakers because past experience has shown that they are, despite all their merits, not feasible for overcoming violence and war; and the scholars who "discovered" ethnic conflicts in the 1990s usually take little notice of the half-century of scholarly debate that preceded the wars in the Balkans.

On the other hand, we also find intersections between these discursive fields. Most notably, leading academics have been actively involved in the debate about the most appropriate institutional solutions to ethnic conflicts, such as federalism, specific designs for electoral systems, or minority rights regimes (see for example Horowitz 1991). Popularized versions of academic theories—such as the notorious "clash of civilizations"—are circulating among journalists, as noted above, and policymakers alike. Or journalists, policymakers, and academics may independently from each other arrive at the same conclusion, for example attributing the salience of ethnicity to the political manipulations of power-hungry tyrants (Berkeley 2001). Finally, policymakers, journalists, and academics often share an implicit frame of interpretation and normative ideals deriving from a common cultural background and political socialization. Multicultural solutions, to give one example, are dear to most persons, independent of their professional background, that grew up in the United States or the Netherlands. They are less prominent, to say the least, among French policymakers, intellectuals, and academics.

This book is the first, to the editors' knowledge, to bring these various strands of debate together and to represent the state of the art of current thinking about ethnic conflict. More ambitiously, it aims at overcoming the segregation between these strands and to stimulate further discussions across the dividing lines, reinforcing existing overlaps between discursive fields and exploring new ones. This search is motivated, obviously, by the hope that a more integrated knowledge will help bring about better solutions to ethnic conflicts, or at least a policy based on a sounder evaluation of empirical cause and effects as well as new research agendas geared toward policy relevance. To avoid the pitfalls of wishful thinking and technocratic utopia, we should acknowledge that the differences between these fields of discourse are far-reaching (Caplan 1979) and the relations between them mediated by power differences. Thus, bringing representatives from different fields together in one room and their papers in one volume will not automatically help bridge the divides. Building bridges is evidently a long-term goal, and its success depends on contextual factors and institutional constraints (Weiss 1991). However, mapping the different fields and debates is a first step and one that a single book may realistically set as a goal. It allows us to identify the major gaps in communication and differences in approach, but also the common ground on which the various actors stand—perhaps unknowingly—a common ground from which to build a more integrated and more relevant approach in the future. While I will identify such elements of commonality in the conclusion, I will use the remainder of this chapter to introduce authors and their chapters.

AUTHORS AND CHAPTERS

This volume brings together authors from three of the four fields of discourse—from the "old" and "new" research communities as well as from the policy-making world—and from a variety of disciplinary and professional backgrounds: anthropologists, conflict researchers, constitutional lawyers, international relations experts, international lawyers, political scientists, and sociologists; representatives of international organizations such as the Organisation of African Unity, the UN Criminal Tribunal for the Former Yugoslavia, the High Commissioner on National Minorities of the OSCE and the External Relations Directorate General of the European Commission; and experts from NGOs such as the Berghof Research Center for Constructive Conflict Management or consultant firms such as GJW-BSMG Worldwide and Management Systems International (see the notes on authors at the end of this volume).

All authors were asked to represent their version of the state of the art in their respective fields, whenever possible on a cross-regional, general level. Clearly, their views remain shaped by specific experiences, and many chapters have one or more regional foci, some dealing with Africa in general, with the Great Lakes region, with the Chechen conflict, or with Indonesia. Despite diverging regional foci, all chapters center, with varying emphasis, on how to *understand* why ethnic conflicts escalate and what the possibilities are to *prevent* violence, to *intervene* in ongoing conflicts, and to *design institutions* that may guide the dynamics of ethnic politics into nonviolent forms. The book is structured according to this rather straightforward scheme, modeled after the different phases in a conflict cycle. It has three parts, dedicated to understanding, intervening in, and institutionally regulating ethnic conflicts, as well as a final part with two concluding chapters. Each part is divided into two groups of chapters.

In part I, "Understanding Ethnic Conflicts," authors analyze how the ethnic issue arises in the first place and how to best understand the dynamics of escalation that may lead to a spiral of violence difficult to stop and reverse. The first group of chapters analyzes how and why ethnicity becomes politically salient. While Walker Connor argues that ethnicity is a matter of deeply rooted identity and culture and therefore represents a perennial issue of political life, Rogers Brubaker maintains that ethnicity represents only one among many possible schemes of interpretation available to actors on the ground—not a naturally given basis of political solidarity and conflict, but rather the outcome of a specific constellation of circumstances that make it feasible to play the ethnic card. Chris Bakwesegha's chapter situates the rise of ethnic politics within the context of broader historical trends by pointing to the colonial and postcolonial practices of ethnic discrimination as major reasons for the contemporary salience of ethnic politics. The three chapters represent an ethnosymbolic, a constructivist, as well as a political economy approach and thus provide an overview of some of the major trends in contemporary research.

The second set of chapters looks more closely at the political entrepreneurs that mobilize their ethnic constituencies and at the conditions under which they are likely to succeed. René Lemarchand analyzes the complex trans-border connections between the various conflicts in Zaire, Rwanda, Burundi, and Uganda, emphasizing the political and legal discrimination along ethnic lines that provides the fuel for political mobilization. Valery Tishkov describes the politicization of ethnicity in Chechnya, passionately arguing that it relies on political manipulation and misinformation, rather than on deeply rooted identities. Peter Waldmann's chapter dissects the logic of escalation, for example, the security dilemma leading to preventive violence triggering further violence. According to his analysis, there is no similar mechanism leading back to peace—a formidable challenge for domestic and international peace makers.

In part II, "The Politics of Intervention" are under review. The first group of chapters examines the experiences gathered in conflict prevention and peacemaking. Max van der Stoel shows that, when introduced at early stages of the politicization process, minority rights and political representation at the center may lead into a spiral of de-escalation and accommodation. The chapter by Michael Lund offers a comprehensive review of the prospects and problems of preventive action by different actors from international organizations to local NGOs. The two following chapters deal with negotiating a peaceful settlement where armed conflict has erupted. The authors debate various schools of thought on the adequate diplomatic strategies and tactics for negotiating peace, with a special focus on the appropriate moment, political level, actor, and technique of intervention. William Zartman describes the specific problems in negotiating with parties of *ethnic* conflicts, for example the zero-sum situation that arises when the sovereignty of a state is at stake, as is often the case in ethnonational conflicts. Hugh Miall maintains that such negotiations have to be embedded in an encompassing strategy of "conflict transformation" that addresses the structural causes of the conflict.

A second group of chapters is concerned with strategies for overcoming conflicts beyond the negotiation table of diplomats and war leaders— such as mediation between civil society actors or through the judicial system. Norbert Ropers discusses whether mediation projects, which have been integrated into the development and reconstruction programs of many Western governments, indeed keep their promise. Richard Goldstone presents a thoughtful analysis of the circumstances under which truth commissions, criminal courts, or a combination of both provide adequate tools for reconciling conflict-torn societies.

Part III, "Institutional Reform," reflects on how to design institutions, constitutional frameworks, and laws that would channel ethnic conflicts into nonviolent forms or even into other, non-ethnic modes of political competition. Milton Esman's chapter introduces this part by giving a broad overview of the various institutional patterns of dealing with ethnocultural pluralism, including contemporary multiculturalism, an assimilationist model based on the cultural dominance of a *Staatsvolk*, and an ethnicity-blind republicanism *à la française*. Closer to current policy debates, the following four chapters examine the relation between ethnic conflict and democracy. Angel Viñas reminds us that fostering democracy represents a policy goal in itself—independent of democracy's conflict-reducing properties. He reflects about the lessons learned during the past decade of democracy support by the European Union. A less optimistic perspective is presented by Donald Rothchild, who argues that democratization can lead to a reinforcement or even escalation of conflicts if it is not allowed to follow a pace that is in tune with the institutional capacities of conflict absorbtion. The two following chapters scrutinize the potential of various electoral systems to reduce conflict, including first-past-the-post systems of proportional representation and designs enhancing coalition building across ethnic boundaries. Donald Horowitz shows how limited the possibilities of designing electoral systems from the outside are—if we disregard exceptional cases such as Bosnia for a moment—and that local power constellations very strongly influence the approach adopted by reforming governments. In a similar vein, Andrew Ellis reports about his experiences as an electoral systems designer in Indonesia, Sri Lanka, and Guyana and demonstrates that for a proposal from the outside to be adopted, it has to be modestly designed to fit into the political context of an ongoing reform process.

A second group looks at various forms of federalism, autonomy regulations, decentralization, and devolution. Many policymakers and academics considered federalism the "golden road" to sustainable ethnic peace. The three authors of this section take a more differentiated view and discuss the conditions under which federalism does indeed keep this promise and those under which it instead provides a platform for radical positions and spiraling counterreactions. Hurst Hannum gives an overview of the advantages and disadvantages of autonomy regulations and argues for an encompassing institutional approach that includes the option of secession. In Michael Hechter's chapter, a rational choice model combines with statistical evidence to show that federalism can exacerbate as well as mitigate ethnic conflict. Walter Kälin outlines the conditions under which a federalist model reduces rather than heightens the prospects of realizing human rights, especially for members of ethnic minorities.

Part IV offers two concluding chapters. Ulrike Joras and Conrad Schetter take a look at this collection of chapters and show that, despite apparent divergence, policymakers and academics share a number of sometimes implicit understandings about the nature of ethnic conflicts. My own conclusion takes off from there and identifies five common positions that the authors of this volume share—despite the wide variety of disciplinary backgrounds, paradigmatic approaches, and professional experiences. After decades of academic debate and more than a decade of evaluating various policy approaches, we have gained a better understanding of the protracted, deep-seated nature of ethnic conflicts and of the constraints in influencing political reality on the ground when powerful interests drive conflict behavior. This has helped us to develop, as I will argue, a more realistic assessment of how to face ethnic conflicts.

NOTES

The chapters are revised papers given at a conference organized by Ulrike Joras, Conrad Schetter, and Andreas Wimmer at the Center for Development Research of the University of Bonn in mid-December 2000. The conference brought together more than 200 experts from four continents. Of some sixty papers that were delivered at the conference, the editors have chosen the most pertinent to be published in this volume.

The editors would like to thank the German Ministry of Foreign Affairs that provided part of the funding for the conference. Christian Kleidt, Lisa Braukämper, and Nicole Busse edited bibliographies, kept files updated, and performed many other minor and major administrative tasks. My successor as director of the Center in Bonn, Tobias Debiel, upheld my earlier commitment to support the production of this book with resources of the center. We thank all of them.

1. The history of international approaches to ethnic conflicts remains to be written. For an overview of the development of the more general "conflict resolution" school, see Miall et al. (2001), chapter 2. The best summary from an international relations perspective is provided by Krasner and Froats (1998).

2. On the difficulties of having results of civil war research be taken into account by the policy community, see Mack (2002).

REFERENCES

Allen, Tim, and Jean Seaton, eds. 1999. *The Media of Conflict: War Reporting and Representations of Ethnic Violence*. London: Zed Books.

Alonso, Ana María. 1994. The Politics of Space, Time and Substance: State Formation, Nationalism, and Ethnicity. *Annual Review of Anthropology* 23:379–405.

Arendt, Hannah. 1951. *The Origins of Totalitarianism*. New York: Harcourt, Brace.

Bartsch, S. 1995. *Minderheitenschutz in der internationalen Politik. Völkerbund und KSZE/OSZE in neuer Perspektive*. Opladen, Germany: Westdeutscher Verlag.

Bates, Robert. 1974. Ethnic Competition and Modernization in Contemporary Africa. *Comparative Political Studies* 6:457–484.

———. 1999. *Ethnicity, Capital Formation, and Conflict*. Cambridge, MA: Center for International Development, Harvard University.

Beck, Ulrich. 1997. *Was ist Globalisierung?* Frankfurt: Suhrkamp.

Bendix, Reinhard. 1964. *Nation-building and Citizenship: Studies in Our Changing Social Order*. New York: John Wiley.

Bennett, D. Scott, and Christian Davenport. 2003. Minorities at Risk Dataset, MAR-Gene v1.0. Center for International Development and Conflict Management, University of Maryland. Accessed at www.cidcm.umd.edu/inscr/mar/margene.htm.

Berkeley, Bill. 2001. *The Graves Are Not Yet Full: Race, Tribe and Power in the Heart of Africa*. New York: Basic Books.

Bonacich, Edna. 1973. A Theory of Middleman Minorities. *American Sociological Review* 38(3):583–594.

Brass, Paul. 1976. Ethnicity and Nationality Formation. *Ethnicity* 3:225–241.

Brown, Michael E. 1993. Causes and Consequences of Ethnic Conflict. In *Ethnic Conflict and International Security*, ed. Michael E. Brown. Princeton, NJ: Princeton University Press.

Callahan, David. 1998. *Unwinnable Wars: American Power and Ethnic Conflict*. New York: Hill and Wang.

Caplan, Nathan. 1979. The Two Communities Theory and Knowledge Utilization. *American Behavioral Scientist* 22 (3):459–470.

Chiozza, Giacomo. 2002. Is There a Clash of Civilization? Evidence from Patterns of International Conflict Involvement, 1946–97. *Journal of Peace Research* 39 (6):711–734.

Chua, Amy. 2004. *World on Fire: How Exporting Free Market Democracy Breeds Ethnic Hatred and Global Instability*. New York: Anchor Books.

Collier, Paul, and Anke Hoeffler. 2000. *Greed and Grievance in Civil War*. Washington, DC: World Bank Development Research Group.

Ellingsen, Tanja. 2000. Colorful Community or Ethnic Witches' Brew? Multiethnicity and Domestic Conflict During and After the Cold War. *Journal of Conflict Resolution* 44 (2):228–249.

Eriksson, Mikael, Peter Wallensteen, and Margareta Sollenberg. 2003. Armed Conflict, 1989–2002. *Journal of Peace Research* 40 (5):593–607.

Esman, Milton J. 1977. Perspectives on Ethnic Conflict in Industrialized Societies. In *Ethnic Conflict in the Western World*, ed. Milton J. Esman, 371–390. Ithaca, NY: Cornell University Press.

Fearon, James D., and David D. Laitin. 2003. Ethnicity, Insurgency, and Civil War. *American Political Science Review* 97 (1):1–16.

Foster, Robert J. 1991. Making National Cultures in the Global Ecumene. *Annual Review of Anthropology* 20:235–260.

Furnivall, John Sydenham. 1944. *Netherlands India: A Study of a Plural Economy*. Cambridge: Cambridge University Press.

Geertz, Clifford. 1963. The Integrative Revolution: Primordial Sentiments and Civil Politics in the New States. In *Old Societies and New States: The Quest for Modernity in Asia and Africa*, ed. Clifford Geertz, 105–157. New York: The Free Press.

Guibernau, Monserrat, and John Hutchinson. 2001. *Understanding Nationalism*. Cambridge: Polity Press.

Gurr, Ted R. 1994. Peoples against the State: Ethnopolitical Conflict in the Changing World System. *International Studies Quarterly* 38:347–377.

Hechter, Michael, and Margaret Levi. 1979. The Comparative Analysis of Ethnoregional Movements. *Ethnic and Racial Studies* 2 (3):260–274.

Horowitz, Donald. 1985. *Ethnic Groups in Conflict*. Berkeley: University of California Press.

———. 1991. *A Democratic South Africa? Constitutional Engineering in a Divided Society*. Berkeley: University of California Press.

Huntington, Samuel. 1993. The Clash of Civilizations? *Foreign Affairs* 72:22–49.

Ignatieff, Michael. 1997. *The Warrior's Honor: Ethnic War and the Modern Conscience*. New York: Henry Holt.

Jenkins, Richard. 1997. *Rethinking Ethnicity: Arguments and Explorations*. Newbury Park, CA: Sage.

Jentleson, Bruce W. 2001. Preventive Statecraft: A Realist Strategy for the Post-Cold War Era. In *Turbulent Peace: The Challenges of Managing International Conflict*, ed. Chester A Crocker et al., 249–264. Washington, DC: United States Institute of Peace Press.

Kaldor, Mary. 1999. *New and Old Wars: Organized Violence in a Global Era*. Cambridge: Polity Press.

Kaplan, Robert. 1993. *Balkan Ghosts: A Journey through History*. New York: St. Martin's Press.

Kasfir, Nelson. 1976. *The Shrinking Political Arena: Participation and Ethnicity in African Politics with a Case Study of Uganda*. Berkeley: University of California Press.

———. 1979. Explaining Ethnic Political Participation. *World Politics* 31:365–388.

Kovacs, Maria. 2003. Standards of Self-Determination and Standards of Minority-Rights in the Post-Soviet Era: A Historical Perspective. *Nations and Nationalism* 3(3):433–450.

Krasner, Stephen, and Daniel T. Froats. 1998. Minority Rights and the Westphalian Model. In *The International Spread of Ethnic Conflict: Fear, Diffusion, and Escalation*, ed. David A. Lake and Donald Rothchild, 227–250. Princeton, NJ: Princeton University Press.

Kuran, Timur. 1998. Ethnic Norms and Their Transformation through Reputational Cascades. *Journal of Legal Studies* 27:623–659.

Lijphart, Arend. 1977. *Democracy in Plural Societies: A Comparative Exploration*. New Haven, CT: Yale University Press.

Lustick, Ian. 1979. Stability in Deeply Divided Societies: Consociationalism versus Control. *World Politics* 31 (3):325–344.

Mack, Andrew. 2002. Civil War: Academic Research and the Policy Community. *Journal of Peace Research* 39 (5):515–525.

McRae, Kenneth. 1983. *Conflict and Compromise in Multilingual Societies: Switzerland*. Waterloo, Ontario: Wilfrid Laurier University Press.

Miall, Hugh, Oliver Ramsbotham, and Tom Woodhouse. 2001. *Contemporary Conflict Resolution: The Prevention, Management and Transformation of Deadly Conflicts*. Cambridge: Polity Press.

Milne, Robert Stephen. 1981. *Politics in Ethnically Bipolar States*. Vancouver: University of British Columbia Press.

Nairn, Tim. 1977. *The Break-up of Britain: Crisis and Neo-nationalism*. London: New Left Books.

Roe, Paul. 1999. The Intrastate Security Dilemma: Ethnic Conflict as a "Tragedy"? *Journal of Peace Research* 36 (2):183–202.

Rothschild, Joseph. 1981. *Ethnopolitics: A Conceptual Framework*. New York: Columbia University Press.

Russet, Bruce M., John Oneal, and Michaelene Cox. 2000. Clash of Civilization, or Realism and Liberalism Déjà Vu? Some Evidence. *Journal of Peace Research* 37 (5):583–608.

Scherrer, Christian. 1994. *Ethno-Nationalismus als globales Phänomen: Zur Krise der Staaten in der Dritten Welt und der früheren UDSSR*. Duisburg, Germany: Gerhard-Mercator-Universität.

Sklar, Richard L. 1967. Political Science and National Integration: A Radical Approach. *The Journal of Modern African Studies* 5 (1):1–11.

Smith, Anthony D. 1984. *The Ethnic Revival in the Modern World*. Cambridge: Cambridge University Press.

Smith, Michael G. 1969. Institutional and Political Conditions of Pluralism. In *Pluralism in Africa*, ed. Leo Kuper and Michael G. Smith, 27–66. Berkeley: University of California Press.

Vanhanen, T. 1999. Domestic Ethnic Conflict and Ethnic Nepotism: A Comparative Analysis. *Journal of Peace Research* 36:55–73.

Weiss, C. 1991. Policy Research: Data, Ideas or Arguments. In *Social Sciences and Modern States*, ed. P. Wagner et al., 307–332. Cambridge: Cambridge University Press.

Wimmer, Andreas. 1997. Who Owns the State? Understanding Ethnic Conflict in Post-colonial Societies. *Nations and Nationalism* 3 (4):631–665.

———. 2002. *Nationalist Exclusion and Ethnic Conflict: Shadows of Modernity*. Cambridge: Cambridge University Press.

Young, Crawford. 1965. *Politics in the Congo: Decolonization and Independence.* Princeton, NJ: Princeton University Press.

———. 1976. *The Politics of Cultural Pluralism.* Madison: University of Wisconsin Press.

I

UNDERSTANDING ETHNIC CONFLICTS

1

❦

A Few Cautionary Notes on the History and Future of Ethnonational Conflicts

Walker Connor

Long experience has convinced me of the necessity to precede any discussion of ethnicity and nationalism with a few words on terminology. I feel forced to often use the term ethnonationalism. So what is ethnonationalism and how does it differ from just plain nationalism? The answer is that there is no difference if nationalism is used in its proper sense. Unfortunately, this is rarely the case. The comparative study of nationalism has been plagued by improper and inconsistent terminology. Particularly troublesome has been the slipshod use of the two central terms: nations and nationalism.

Although often so used, a nation is *not* a proper synonym for either a state or for the entire population of a state without regard to its ethnic composition. In its pristine sense, a nation refers to a group of people who believe they are ancestrally related. It is the largest group that can be aroused, stimulated to action, by appeals to common ancestors and to a blood-bond. It is, in this sense, the fully extended family. An "American nation," whether used in reference to the United States or to its citizens, is therefore a misnomer.

Nationalism, as properly used, does *not* connote loyalty to the state; that loyalty is properly termed patriotism. Nationalism should connote loyalty to one's nation, one's extended family. One can therefore speak of an English or Welsh nationalism but not of a British one, the latter being a case of patriotism.

This is not a matter of semantic nitpicking, for it is essential that the vital difference between the two loyalties never be blurred. Conflicts involving loyalty to state (patriotism) and loyalty to national group (nationalism) speckle the globe from Tibet to Kashmir to Kurdistan to Chechnya to Transylvania to Kosovo to the Basque country to Shan state to Rwanda to Chiapas to Quebec.

The current vogue among writers on nationalism is to refer to loyalty to the state as civic nationalism and loyalty to the nation as ethnic nationalism. But this only tends to propagate the misconception that we are dealing with two variants of the same phenomenon. If writers prefer to use civic identity or civic loyalty in preference to patriotism—fine. But the fundamental dissimilarities between state loyalty and nationalism should not be glossed over by employing the noun nationalism to refer to two quite different phenomena.

The two loyalties represent two very different orders of things. Loyalty to state is sociopolitical in nature, and is based in large part on rational self-interest. Loyalty to nation is intuitive rather than rational, and is predicated upon a sense of consanguinity. When the two are viewed as being in irreconcilable conflict, loyalty to the nation customarily proves the more powerful.

The term ethnonationalism therefore contains an inner redundancy. If nationalism were consistently employed to refer to the nation or *ethnos* (the Greek equivalent for nation), then ethonationalism would be a one-word tautology (i.e., "national nationalism"). It is used simply to make certain that others are aware that what is being referred to is not loyalty to the state but loyalty to the extended family.

Ethnonational movements, then, are movements conducted in the name of the national group. Their leaders employ familial words and metaphors in their call to arms. The people are quite commonly addressed as "Brothers and Sisters," and common ancestry is stressed. Note, for example, Mao Tse-tung in 1939:

> Fathers, brothers, aunts, and sisters throughout the country: [W]e know that in order to transform this glorious future into a new China, independent, free, and happy, all our fellow countrymen, every single zealous descendent of Huang-ti [the legendary first emperor of China] must determinedly and relentlessly participate in the concerted struggle (Brandt et al. 1952:245).

And here is Ho Chi Minh in 1946:

> Compatriots in the South and Southern part of Central Viet-Nam! The North, Center, and South are part and parcel of Viet-Nam! . . . We have the same ancestors, we are of the same family, we are all brothers and sisters. . . . No one can divide the children of the same family. Likewise, no one can divide Viet-Nam" (Fall 1967:156).

The use of these communist examples is a reminder that leaders of the most diverse ideological inclinations, even ideologies that are ostensibly opposed to nationalism, resort to playing the ethnonational card when trying to mobilize a people.

Examples of such speeches could be multiplied many times over. A more contemporary illustration is offered by Slobodan Milošević, whose 1987 speech to Serbs in Kosovo served as a major catalyst for subsequent Serbian behavior there:

> This is your land. These are your houses. Your meadows and gardens. Your memories. You shouldn't abandon your land just because it's difficult to live, because you are pressured by injustice and degradation. It was never part of the Serbian . . . character to give up in the face of obstacles, to demobilize when it's time to fight. . . . You should stay here for the sake of your ancestors and descendants. Otherwise your ancestors would be defiled and descendants disappointed (Silber and Little 1996:38).

The superabundance of articles, monographs, new journals, and—yes—conferences focused on ethnic conflict that has surfaced in the wake of the collapse of the Soviet Union makes it impossible for anyone to claim total familiarity with the literature. But has this outpouring on balance aided our insight into ethnonational identity and conflict? Rogers Brubaker is among those who feel that the result has been a sharp turn for the worst. Here is how he explains the deterioration:

> [T]his has happened as academic entrepreneurs, in search of windfall profits, have entered the field, unburdened by any but the most minimal acquaintance with the comparative and theoretical literature of the field, to say nothing of the wider theoretical and empirical literature of the social sciences, and hastily converted their intellectual capital from forms suddenly devalued by the end of the Cold War and the collapse of the Soviet regime into newly revalued forms, for example, in the sub-field of "Security studies," from a weapons-oriented understanding of security and insecurity to one centred on ethnic and national conflict (Brubaker 1998:302).

Consonant with the general confusion surrounding the study of nationalism, there is very little agreement concerning the likely impact that ethnic conflict is apt to exert upon tomorrow's political map. Indeed, in a recent issue of the U.S. journal *Foreign Affairs*, Ted Robert Gurr maintains that ethnonational conflict is rapidly becoming a thing of the past (Gurr 2000: 52–64). This is a prognostication shared by others, such as the British historian, Eric Hobsbawm (1990). At the other end of the spectrum are those who contend that ethnic conflict will endure so long as ethnic and political borders fail to coincide. Earlier holders of this viewpoint include the nineteenth-century British philosopher John Stuart Mill ("It is in general a necessary condition of free institutions that the boundaries of government should coincide in the main with those of nationality"; Mill 1873:313) and the early twentieth-century British philosopher Ernest

Barker, who predicted "a worldwide scheme of political organization in which each nation is also a State and each State is also a nation" (Barker 1929:125–126). For those who lean toward the position of Mill and Barker, it is evident that nationalism—far from being on the wane as a force for redrawing political borders—will only be sated when the present political map has been transformed from one divided into 190 countries into one divided into thousands of such units.

Such polar positions often reflect quite different perceptions of the history of ethnic conflict. If ethnic conflict is viewed solely in terms of recent events, then explanations of its wellsprings and proposals for its accommodation are apt to be quite different than if such conflict is viewed over a much longer term. Many explanations of ethnic conflict found in the recent literature are that each rests upon end-of-cold-war elements such as "authoritarian rule preserved through superpower rivalry melting away," "the manipulations of politicians who take advantage of the new political opportunities that have arisen in the wake of 1989," and "a structural and institutional perspective that links the emergence of ethnic strife to post-1989 processes of nation-building and democratization."

Such explanations ignore the lengthy history of ethnic strife. Ethnic groups and ethnic conflicts are at least as old as recorded history. In early history, enemies and potential enemies are quite consistently identified in ethnic terms: Akkadians, Amorites, Aramaens, Canaanites, Chaldeans, Egyptians, Hittites, Hurrians, Kassites, Persians, Lombards, and barbarians in the sense of non-Greek or non-Chinese (i.e., not one of "us"). Ethnic identity was most certainly a prominent fact through ancient Greek eyes. Aristotle boasted about the virtues of what he termed "the Hellenic race" and asserted "if it could be formed into one state, it would be able to rule the world." One fascinating testament to early ethnic identity and dislike of "the other" is offered by stone inscriptions located on barren steppes in central Mongolia. Etched in the early eighth century, and only recently deciphered, they chronicle the sixth and seventh century histories of the Altay Turks. They read in part:

> Above the sons of men stood our ancestors, the khagans [kings] Bumin and Ishtemi. Having become masters of the Turkic people they established and ruled its empire and fixed the law of the country. Many were their enemies in the four corners of the world, but, leading campaigns against them, they subjugated and pacified many nations. [But] Unwise khagans, weak khagans ascended the throne, and their officers were also unwise and weak. And because of the iniquity of the nobility and of the people, because of Chinese guile, because the elder brothers and younger brothers were plotting against each other, because of the quarrel of those who favored the nobles and those who favored the people, the Turkic people brought about the dissolution of the empire that had been its empire, and ruined the khagan who had been its

khagan. The sons of the nobles became the slaves of the Chinese people, their pure daughters became its servants. The noble Turks abandoned their Turkic titles and, assuming Chinese titles, they submitted to the Chinese khagan. But the small people, in its entirety, thus said, "We were a people that had its own empire. Where is now our empire? We were a people that had its own khagan. Where is now our khagan?" And thus speaking they became the enemy of the Chinese.

Ethnic identity and conflict have therefore been around for centuries, which suggests that explanations for today's ethnically predicated conflict should not be sought in terms of post–Cold War factors. To do so risks confusing specific catalysts, exacerbators, human agents (e.g., fomenters), and special conditions to explain a phenomenon that has demonstrated marked disregard for time and place. For example, the phase of ethnic violence between Palestinian Arabs and Israeli Jews, known as the second intifada, was ignited by Ariel Sharon's foray into the Temple Mount, accompanied, according to the *New York Times* (29 September 2000), by a thousand armed policemen and a hovering police helicopter. But the sense of group identity and group resentment thus bared on the part of Christian, as well as Moslem Arabs, clearly antedate this incident.

Similarly, I would suggest that Ted Gurr's vision of a rapidly diminishing role for ethnic conflict—even if his data were uncritically accepted— is predicated upon too abbreviated a period. A longer-range view of history would suggest that a relative lull should not be construed as endless. Ethnic conflict—involving both entire regions and individual peoples— has experienced both troughs and swells. For example, in the immediate post–World War II period, a thoroughly worn-out Western Europe was uncharacteristically lacking in ethnonational conflict. Corsicans, Basques, Bretons, the Irish of Northern Ireland, and other minorities were relatively quiescent, and elites of the dominant nations spoke with confidence of the displacement of ethnonational identities by a single European consciousness. Things changed rather abruptly. In 1975, a Conference on Ethnic Pluralism and Conflict in Contemporary Western Europe and Canada was held at Cornell University under the direction of Milton Esman. Scholars from Western Europe and Canada, as well as United States scholars specializing in Western Europe, were present. The conference had been occasioned by a spate of ethnonationally inspired unrest throughout a number of Western European countries. The clearly predominant view was one of surprise. Time and again, participants raised the question "But why now?" Underlying that query was a view of these ethnonational movements as both historically rootless (and therefore unanticipatable) and as inconsonant with their image of Western Europe. Actually, having greater familiarity with the history of nationalism in Europe might have caused a change in query from "Why now?" to "Why not now?" Far from rootless, most of the ethnic movements were simply making a postwar reappearance.

Parallels with the present are evident. Scholars in the 1970s were surprised because of a lack of historical perspective on ethnonationalism. Similarly, the surprise with which statesmen and academicians have greeted post-1989 ethnonationalism could have been substantively lessened by heeding a small group of scholars who had been tracking the evolution of the national question within the Soviet Union for many years prior to 1989. On the contrary, however, the great number of Soviet specialists accepted the constantly repeated claim of the Soviet authorities that, guided by the legacy of Lenin, the Soviet Union had "solved its national question."

German reunification offers yet another example of a failure to appreciate the enduring power of ethnic identity. The East German authorities had for some time maintained that the different socioeconomic forces within East and West Germany had given rise to a separate national identity on the part of East Germans. It was perhaps not too surprising that many American academics bought this. But so too did the academicians in West Germany. By the mid-1970s, there was a general consensus among German intellectuals that the Germans of West and East Germany had come to develop two totally distinct national identities.[1] There were now two families, so talk of reunification of the family had no relevance. But ethnic identity proved far more durable and powerful than the intellectuals could appreciate. You will recall the events of 1989 when even those who suggested that reunion be carried out by stages proved no match for Helmut Kohl and his seductive banner "Wir sind ein Volk!"[2] On the fifth anniversary of reunification, an editorial in a German newspaper had this to say of those intellectuals who had closed their eyes to a great many indications of the continuing vitality of a single German consciousness:

How . . . was it possible that a large number of . . . luminaries spoke about unity ambivalently or reluctantly? Representatives of intellectual Germany solemnly declared that they had no use for the notion of bringing together Germans in one state. This, they said, was also the feeling of the German people, which (as it turned out) was better than its reputation. After unification, no one in western Germany gave up his/her position or responsibilities on account of such foolishness and lack of character. . . . Should someone who, in freedom and prosperity, turned on his/her own people remain uncensored, indeed stand there blameless? (*Frankfurter Allgemeine Zeitung*, 4 October 1994. Reprinted in *The Week in Germany*, 7 October 1994.)

The writer of this editorial clearly wants revenge on those scholars, fellow ethnics, who failed to appreciate the power of ethnonational identity. As I read it, I could not help but think—consonant with the earlier quoted comments of Rogers Brubaker—that were such draconian measures applied to all of the Soviet and East European specialists throughout Europe and North America who had ignored or misunderstood the significance of ethnonationalism, as well as to all of the authorities in international relations and security studies who did likewise, we would be facing a purge of truly Stalinesque proportions.

Ethnic identity and conflict have, as noted, been a fact throughout history. But this does not mean that present ethnic identities have been around for centuries, that the national awareness of the Dutch, German, French, English, and so on is centuries old. It is, in fact, of very recent vintage. Some two decades ago, Eugen Weber authored a study with the intriguing title, *Peasants into Frenchmen: The Modernization of Rural France, 1870–1914* (Weber 1976). The book's convincingly documented thesis was that most rural and small-town dwellers within France did not conceive of themselves as members of a French nation as recently as 1870 and that many still failed to do so as late as World War I. With the partial exception of regions to the north and east of Paris, the integration of the countryside into the French social and political system was largely fanciful. The typical village was a physical, political, and cultural isolate. The famed road network was in essence a skeleton connecting the major cities to Paris but offering no access roads to the villages. The school system was still inadequate to effect the Jacobin dream of a single and unilingual French nation. To the mass of peasants—and, therefore, to most inhabitants of France—the meaningful world and identity seldom extended beyond the village or valley.

To stress the obvious, Weber's disclosure that a French identity still had not penetrated the rural masses hundreds—in some cases, several hundreds—of years later than scholars had presumed French nationalism to be in full flower holds potentially immense ramifications for the study of nationalism. Is the French experience unique, or has there been a general tendency to assume that national consciousness had rather thoroughly permeated this or that people long before such an assumption was justifiable?

Inspired by Weber's path-breaking scholarship, I have been studying the history of group consciousness among many other peoples. My research indicates that claims of a broadly accepted ethnonational consciousness prior to the late nineteenth century should be treated with healthy skepticism if one is interested in factual history. Mass national consciousness among Germans, Poles, Norwegians, the Dutch, Croats, Serbs, and the like is a relatively recent development. In sum, ethnic groups have been a fixture of history, but today's specific foci of ethnic identity that we call nations are relatively recent creations.

But although contemporary ethnonational identities are modern, members of each group harbor intuitive convictions of their group's ancient

pedigree. How is this to be explained? My references to history thus far
have dwelt with factual/chronological history in order to emphasize that
a proper respect for the history of ethnic conflict protects against treating
this or that outburst as totally explainable in terms of itself rather than as
a manifestation of a phenomenon that has proven remarkably immune to
time and place. But it should be emphasized that convictions concerning
one's ethnic identity are predicated not upon chronological or factual history but upon sentient or felt history. And because its roots lie in the subconscious, rather than in reason, the conviction that one's nation was
somehow created sui generis and remained essentially unadulterated
down to the present is immunized against contrary fact. There is hardly a
nation whom historians have not established to be the offspring of several
ethnic strains. The English, for example, are (at the least) a compound of
Celtic Briton with a heavy overlay of Germanic Angle, Saxon, Jute, Dane,
and Norman. The French are a concoction of Celtic Gaul and Germanic
Frank, Burgundian, Norman, and Visigoth. And scholarship has recently
undermined the Japanese claim of ethnically pure descent (*New York Times*,
6 June 1990). But knowledge of contrary data and even its rational acceptance need not alter the subconscious conviction that one's nation has been
ethnically hermetical. Despite the past infusion of Teutonic blood, an En-
glishman senses no kinship with a German. Contrariwise, no arsenal of
facts concerning their common ancestral background can convince either
the Serbs or the Croats that they share a common national identity.

A potent illustration of a person failing to appreciate the distinction between factual and sentient history and the paramountcy of the latter is offered by Carlos Westendorp, the former top official—the high representative of the UN—charged with carrying out the Bosnian Peace Agreement.
In an interview granted while serving in that role, Westendorp maintained
that the conflict is simply a religious one, noting, "The Bosnians are all the
same people. They are all Slavs" (*New York Times*, 10 April 1998). Well, yes.
But then so are the Poles and the Russians who are not noted for sharing
a sense of common identity. And so too are the Czechs and Slovaks—
now living apart despite both common Slavness and common Catholi-
cism.

Given the imperviousness of subconscious convictions of exclusive descent to contrary fact, it is paradoxical that history should be filled with
attempts to promote or defend the proposition that one's nation is *in fact*
ethnically pure. From at least the time of the ancient Greeks, there have
been recorded attempts to confirm the ethnic purity of one's people. As
noted, even a person with the intellectual stature of Aristotle would write
of the virtues of "the Hellenic race" as contrasted with all others (the *bar-
baroi*). Centuries later, in fifteenth-century France, monks would claim to
have proved the homogeneity of the "French race" by tracing both the

(Celtic) Gauls and the (Teutonic) Franks to the Trojan king, Priam. In sixteenth-century Spain, purity of blood (*limpieza*) was treated as though it were scientifically verifiable; numerous laws were passed that made pure Castilian blood a requirement for public and private office. In the seventeenth century, John Hare insisted that the English had maintained their "so noble an extraction and descent" by not commingling with the indigenous Britons:

> Our Progenitors that transplanted themselves from Germany hither, did not commixe themselves with the ancient inhabitants of the Countrey the Britaines (as other Colonies did with the Natives in those places where they came) but totally expelling them, they took the sole possession of the Land to themselves, thereby preserving their blood, laws, and language incorrupted (quoted in MacDougall 1982:60).

In the early eighteenth century, a French scholar was incarcerated for writing that the Franks were not a distinct German race (and therefore not self-contained and pure) but the descendants of a league of tribes formed in the third century. The nineteenth and early twentieth centuries witnessed a proliferation of writers making invidious comparisons of peoples according to the alleged purity of their pedigree. Armed with the new scientific methodology, they extended the search for evidence of group purity to the frequency of physical characteristics: skin pigmentation, eye and hair color, and, most particularly, the shape of skull were viewed as indexes—proof positive—of "racial" purity. One such late-nineteenth-century survey covered some 15 million schoolchildren throughout Austria, Belgium, Germany, and Switzerland and took more than ten years to complete (Poliakov 1974:265). Fascination with such indexes prevailed into the twentieth century. In 1921, for example, an Institute for Racial Biology was created in Sweden to explore the threat of "racial degeneration" to the Swedish nation, which was described as "the purest" of the Germanic peoples. Measurement of skulls was a central element in its methodology.

Such research ultimately lost favor due in part to a growing awareness that the purported correlations between phenotype and "national characteristics" rested more upon assertion than upon empirical evidence. The point, however, is that members of ethnic groups harbor intuitive convictions of the ancientness and purity of their group's existence. Identity does not draw its sustenance from facts but from perceptions—not, as I said earlier, from chronological/factual history but from sentient/felt history.

Failure to appreciate that national identity is predicated upon sentient history undergirds a current vogue in the literature on national identity to bifurcate contributors in terms of "primordialists" and "modernists." The term primordialist, in particular, is usually used dismissively, so that if you call a very capable scholar such as Clifford Geertz a primordialist, there is no need to contemplate further the rich lode of his ideas. What is missed in all this academic labeling is that, while from the viewpoint of objective history, today's nations are modern creations, subjectively they are primordial. Stathis Gourgouris, professor of comparative literature and Hellenic studies at Princeton, has stated this seeming paradox with remarkable brevity and clarity in a letter to the *New York Times*:

> My long term research into the nature of national formation and the development of nationalism in both Europe and Greece has taught me two insurmountable historical facts: (1) national symbols are always people's inventions, and (2) people often die for them with the satisfaction of serving eternal truth (*New York Times*, 9 May 1994).

This distinction between reality and perceptions of reality is not limited to issues of identity but permeates all aspects of ethnic conflict. Events—past and present—are ethnically filtered. As such, they are often unrecognizable to the other party to the dispute and to outside mediators.

In the fall of 1994, the Atlantic Council sponsored a meeting in Romania that brought together an impressively large number of relatively young members of the business, educational, financial, labor, media, military, and political elites of Western Europe, East Asia, North America, and the former Soviet Union. The purpose was to discuss ethnic and sectarian conflict. Participants were often drawn from bitterly opposed groups. Here is the conclusion from the unpublished final report on the conference:

> Ethnic conflicts cannot be entirely reduced to arguments over resources. . . . Often, ethnic aims are pursued at the expense of other issues because they come from a subjective, emotional commitment the other side finds difficult to understand in objective terms. . . . This theme echoed throughout almost every discussion, leading participants to one of the most simple but profound conclusions of the conference: perceptions are as important or more so than reality when it comes to ethnic issues and must be addressed before discussion can move forward.

In sum, realistic attempts to peacefully resolve ethnic conflicts necessitate an appreciation of the distinction between reality and ethnically filtered reality. Probing these matters requires not a knowledge of "facts" but of commonly held perceptions of facts. Facts perceived through Israeli eyes are remarkedly different than are those same facts when filtered through Palestinian eyes. The same holds true for Russian versus Chechen processed facts; Irish versus Ulsterman processed facts; or Xhosa versus Zulu processed facts. Perhaps this duality helps to explain why fact-finding commissions and mediators whose past experience was limited to non-ethnic disputes find ethnic conflict so perplexing.

NOTES

1. For the review of the works of several West German scholars who were members of the two-nation school, see Verheyen (1991). One of the earliest and more influential works in this genre was originally a Harvard University doctoral dissertation written by a German citizen under the mentorship of a well-known scholar of nationalism, Karl Deutsch, and later published in German within West Germany (Schweigler 1972).

2. The slogan had already become popular in East Germany. As Gerd Knischewski notes:

> In October 1989, the protests against the rigid stance of the government culminated in mass demonstrations which challenged the self-definition of the state as a "people's democracy" with the slogan "We are the people." When after the opening of the Berlin Wall in November 1989 the demonstrations continued, the slogan "We are *one* people" emerged and soon drowned out the earlier version (Knischewski 1996: 142).

Kohl embraced it effectively against the Social Democrats.

REFERENCES

Barker, Ernest. 1929. *National Character and the Factors in Its Formation*. London: Methuen & Co.

Brandt, Conrad, et al. 1952. *A Documentary History of Chinese Communism*. London: Allen & Unwin.

Brubaker, Rogers. 1998. Myths and Misconceptions in the Study of Nationalism. In *The State of the Nation*, ed. John Hall, 272–305. Cambridge: Cambridge University Press.

Fall, Bernard, ed. 1967. *On Revolution: Selected Writings 1920–1966*. New York: Praeger.

Gurr, Ted Robert. 2000. Ethnic Warfare on the Wane. *Foreign Affairs* 79 (3):52–64.

Hobsbawm, Eric. 1990. *Nations and Nationalism since 1780*. Cambridge: Cambridge University Press.

Knischewski, Gerd. 1996. Post-war National Identity in Germany. In *Nation and Identity in Contemporary Europe*, ed. Brian Jenkins, 125–151. London: Routledge.

MacDougall, Hugh. 1982. *Racial Myths in English History*. Montreal: Harvest House.

Mill, John Stuart. 1873. *Considerations on Representative Government*. New York: Harper & Bros.

Poliakov, Leon. 1974. *The Arian Myth*. London: Heinemann.

Schweigler, Gebhard. 1972. *National Consciousness in Divided Germany*. Ph.D. diss., Department of Government, Harvard University, Cambridge, MA.

Silber, Laura, and Alan Little. 1996. *Yugoslavia: Death of a Nation*. New York: TV Books.

Verheyen, Dirk. 1991. *The German Question: A Cultural, Historical, and Geopolitical Exploration*. Boulder, CO: Westview Press.

Weber, Eugen. 1976. *Peasants into Frenchmen: The Modernization of Rural France, 1870–1914*. Stanford, CA: Stanford University Press.

2

❧

Ethnicity without Groups

Rogers Brubaker

COMMONSENSE GROUPISM

Few social science concepts would seem as basic, even indispensable, as that of group. In disciplinary terms, "group" would appear to be a core concept for sociology, political science, anthropology, demography, and social psychology. In substantive terms, it would seem to be fundamental to the study of political mobilization, cultural identity, economic interests, social class, status groups, collective action, kinship, gender, religion, ethnicity, race, multiculturalism, and minorities of every kind.

Yet despite this seeming centrality, the concept "group" has remained curiously unscrutinized in recent years. There is, to be sure, a substantial social psychological literature addressing the concept (Hamilton et al. 1998; McGrath 1984), but this has had little resonance outside that subdiscipline. Elsewhere in the social sciences, the recent literature addressing the concept "group" is sparse, especially by comparison with the immense literature on such concepts as class, identity, gender, ethnicity, or multiculturalism—topics in which the concept "group" is implicated, yet seldom analyzed its own terms.[1] "Group" functions as a seemingly unproblematic, taken-for-granted concept, apparently in no need of particular scrutiny or explication. As a result, we tend to take for granted not only the concept "group" but also "groups"—the putative things-in-the-world to which the concept refers.

My aim in this chapter is not to enter into conceptual or definitional casuistry about the concept of group. It is rather to address one problematic consequence of this tendency to take groups for granted in the study of ethnicity, race, and nationhood, and in the study of ethnic, racial, and national conflict in particular. This is what I will call groupism: the tendency to take discrete, sharply differentiated, internally homogeneous, and externally bounded groups as basic constituents of social life, chief protagonists of social conflicts, and fundamental units of social analysis.[2] In the domain of ethnicity, nationalism, and race, I mean by "groupism" the tendency to treat ethnic groups, nations, and races as substantial entities to which interests and agency can be attributed. I mean the tendency to reify such groups, speaking of Serbs, Croats, Muslims, and Albanians in the former Yugoslavia; of Catholics and Protestants in Northern Ireland; of Jews and Palestinians in Israel and the occupied territories; of Turks and Kurds in Turkey; or of blacks, whites, Asians, Hispanics, and Native Americans in the United States as if they were internally homogeneous, externally bounded groups, even unitary collective actors with common purposes. I mean the tendency to represent the social and cultural world as a multichrome mosaic of monochrome ethnic, racial, or cultural blocs.

From the perspective of broader developments in social theory, the persisting strength of groupism in this sense is surprising. After all, several distinct traditions of social analysis have challenged the treatment of groups as real, substantial things-in-the-world. These include such sharply differing enterprises as ethnomethodology and conversation analysis, social network theory, cognitive theory, feminist theory, and individualist approaches such as rational choice and game theory. More generally, broadly structuralist approaches have yielded to a variety of more "constructivist" theoretical stances, which tend—at the level of rhetoric, at least—to see groups as constructed, contingent, and fluctuating. And a diffuse postmodernist sensibility emphasizes the fragmentary, the ephemeral, and the erosion of fixed forms and clear boundaries. These developments are disparate, even contradictory in analytical style, methodological orientation, and epistemological commitments. Network theory, with its methodological (and sometimes ontological) relationalism (Emirbayer and Goodwin 1994; Wellman 1988) is opposed to rational choice theory, with its methodological (and sometimes ontological) individualism; both are sharply and similarly opposed, in analytical style and epistemological commitments, to postmodernist approaches. Yet these and other developments have converged in problematizing groupness and undermining axioms of stable group being.

Challenges to "groupism," however, have been uneven. They have been striking—to take just one example—in the study of class, especially in the study of the working class, a term that is hard to use today without quotation marks or some other distancing device. Yet ethnic groups continue to be understood as entities and cast as actors. To be sure, constructivist approaches of one kind or another are now dominant in academic discussions of ethnicity. Yet everyday talk, policy analysis, media reports, and even much ostensibly constructivist academic writing routinely frame accounts of ethnic, racial, and national conflict in groupist terms as the struggles "of" ethnic groups, races, and nations.[3] Somehow, when we talk about ethnicity, and even more when we talk about ethnic conflict, we almost automatically find ourselves talking about ethnic groups.

Now it might be asked: "What's wrong with this?" After all, it seems to be mere common sense to treat ethnic struggles as the struggles of ethnic groups, and ethnic conflict as conflict between such groups. I agree that this is the—or at least *a*—commonsense view of the matter. But we cannot rely on common sense here. Ethnic common sense—the tendency to partition the social world into putatively deeply constituted, quasi-natural intrinsic kinds (Hirschfeld 1996)—is a key part of what we want to explain, not what we want to explain things *with*; it belongs to our empirical data, not to our analytical toolkit.[4] Cognitive anthropologists and social psychologists have accumulated a good deal of evidence about commonsense ways of carving up the social world—about what Lawrence Hirschfeld (1996) has called "folk sociologies." The evidence suggests that some commonsense social categories—and notably commonsense ethnic and racial categories—tend to be essentializing and naturalizing (Rothbart and Taylor 1992; Hirschfeld 1996; Gil-White 1999). They are the vehicles of what has been called a "participants' primordialism" (Smith 1998:158) or a "psychological essentialism" (Medin 1989). We obviously cannot ignore such commonsense primordialism. But that does not mean we should simply replicate it in our scholarly analyses or policy assessments. As "analysts *of* naturalizers," we need not be "analytic naturalizers" (Gil-White 1999:803).

Instead, we need to break with vernacular categories and commonsense understandings. We need to break, for example, with the seemingly obvious and uncontroversial point that ethnic conflict involves conflict between ethnic groups. I want to suggest that ethnic conflict—or what might better be called ethnicized or ethnically framed conflict—need not, and should not, be understood as conflict *between ethnic groups*, just as racial or racially framed conflict need not be understood as conflict between *races*, or nationally framed conflict as conflict between *nations*.

Participants, of course, regularly do represent ethnic, racial, and national conflict in such groupist, even primordialist, terms. They often cast ethnic groups, races, or nations as the protagonists—the heroes and martyrs—of such struggles. But this is no warrant for analysts to do so. We must, of course, take vernacular categories and participants' understandings seriously, for they are partly constitutive of our objects of study. But we should not uncritically adopt *categories of ethnopolitical practice* as our *categories of social analysis*. Apart from the general unreliability of ethnic common sense as a guide for social analysis, we should remember that participants' accounts—especially those of specialists in ethnicity such as ethnopolitical entrepreneurs, who, unlike nonspecialists, may live "off" as well as "for" ethnicity—often have what Pierre Bourdieu has called a *performative* character. By invoking groups, they seek to evoke them, summon them, call them into being. Their categories are *for doing*—designed to stir, summon, justify, mobilize, kindle, and energize. By reifying groups, by treating them as substantial things-in-the-world, ethnopolitical entrepreneurs may, as Bourdieu notes, "contribute to producing what they apparently describe or designate" (Bourdieu 1991a:220).[5]

Reification is a social process, not simply an intellectual bad habit. As a social process, it is central to the *practice* of politicized ethnicity. And appropriately so. To criticize ethnopolitical entrepreneurs for reifying ethnic groups would be a kind of category mistake. Reifying groups is precisely what ethnopolitical entrepreneurs are in the business of doing. When they are successful, the political fiction of the unified group can be momentarily yet powerfully realized in practice. As analysts, we should certainly try to *account* for the ways in which—and conditions under which—this practice of reification, this powerful crystallization of group feeling, can work. This may be one of the most important tasks of a theory of ethnic conflict. But we should avoid unintentionally *doubling* or *reinforcing* the reification of ethnic groups in ethnopolitical practice with a reification of such groups in social analysis.

BEYOND GROUPISM

How, then, are we to understand ethnic conflict, if not in commonsense terms as conflict between ethnic groups? And how can we go beyond groupism? Here I sketch eight basic points and then, in the next section, draw out some implications of them.

Rethinking Ethnicity

We need to rethink not only ethnic conflict, but also what we mean by ethnicity itself. This is not a matter of seeking agreement on a definition. The intricate and ever-recommencing definitional casuistry in studies of ethnicity, race, and nationalism has done little to advance the discussion, and indeed can be viewed as a symptom of the noncumulative nature of research in the field. It is rather a matter of critically scrutinizing our conceptual tools. Ethnicity, race, and nation should be conceptualized not as substances or things or entities or organisms or collective individuals— as the imagery of discrete, concrete, tangible, bounded, and enduring "groups" encourages us to do—but rather in relational, processual, dynamic, eventful, and disaggregated terms. This means thinking of ethnicity, race, and nation not in terms of substantial groups or entities but in terms of practical categories, cultural idioms, cognitive schemas, discursive frames, organizational routines, institutional forms, political projects, and contingent events. It means thinking of ethnicization, racialization, and nationalization as political, social, cultural, and psychological processes. And it means taking as a basic analytical category not the "group" as an entity but groupness as a contextually fluctuating conceptual variable. Stated baldly in this fashion, these are of course mere slogans; I will try to fill them out a bit in what follows.

The Reality of Ethnicity

To rethink ethnicity, race, and nationhood along these lines is in no way to dispute their reality, minimize their power, or discount their significance; it is to construe their reality, power, and significance in a different way. Understanding the reality of race, for example, does not require us to posit the existence of races. Racial idioms, ideologies, narratives, categories, and systems of classification, and racialized ways of seeing, thinking, talking, and framing claims, are real and consequential, especially when they are embedded in powerful organizations. But the reality of race—and even its overwhelming coercive power in some settings—does not depend on the existence of "races." Similarly, the reality of ethnicity and nationhood—and the overriding power of ethnic and national identifications in some settings—does not depend on the existence of ethnic groups or nations as substantial groups or entities.

Groupness as Event

Shifting attention from groups to groupness, and treating groupness as variable and contingent rather than fixed and given,[6] allows us to take account of—and, potentially, to account for—phases of extraordinary cohesion, and moments of intensely felt collective solidarity, without implicitly treating high levels of groupness as constant, enduring, or definitionally present. It allows us to treat groupness as an event, as something that "happens," as E. P. Thompson famously said about class. At the same time, it keeps us analytically attuned to the possibility that groupness may not happen, that high levels of groupness may fail to crystallize, despite the group-making efforts of ethnopolitical entrepreneurs, and even in situations of intense elite-level ethnopolitical conflict. Being analytically attuned to "negative" instances in this way enlarges the domain of relevant cases and helps correct for the bias in the literature toward the study of striking instances of high groupness, successful mobilization, or conspicuous violence—a bias that can engender an "overethnicized" view of the social world, a distorted representation of whole world regions as "seething cauldrons" of ethnic tension (Brubaker 1998), and an overestimation of the incidence of ethnic violence (Fearon and Laitin 1996). Sensitivity to such negative instances can also direct potentially fruitful analytical attention toward the problem of explaining failed efforts at ethnopolitical mobilization.

Groups and Categories

Much talk about ethnic, racial, or national groups is obscured by the failure to distinguish between groups and categories. If by "group" we mean a mutually interacting, mutually recognizing, mutually oriented, effectively communicating, bounded collectivity with a sense of solidarity, corporate identity, and capacity for concerted action, or even if we adopt a less exigent understanding of "group," it should be clear that a category is not a group (Sacks 1995:I:41, 401; Handelman 1977; McKay and Lewins 1978; Jenkins 1997:53–55).[7] It is at best a potential basis for group formation or "groupness."[8]

By distinguishing consistently between categories and groups, we can problematize—rather than presume—the relation between them. We can ask about the degree of groupness associated with a particular category in a particular setting, and about the political, social, cultural, and psychological processes through which categories get invested with groupness (Petersen 1987). We can ask how people—and organizations—do things with categories. This includes limiting access to scarce resources or particular domains of activity by excluding categorically distinguished outsiders (Weber 1968 [1922]:43–45, 341–342; Barth 1969; Brubaker 1992; Tilly 1998), but it also includes more mundane actions such as identifying or classifying oneself or others (Levine 1999) or simply "doing being ethnic" in an ethnomethodological sense (Moerman 1968). We can analyze the organizational and discursive careers of categories—the processes through which they become institutionalized and entrenched in administrative routines (Tilly 1998) and embedded in culturally powerful and symbolically resonant myths, memories, and narratives (Armstrong 1982; Smith 1986). We can study the politics of categories, both from above and from below. From above, we can focus on the ways in which categories are proposed, propagated, imposed, institutionalized, discursively articulated, organizationally entrenched, and generally embedded in multifarious forms of "governmentality" (Noiriel 1991; Slezkine 1994; Brubaker 1994; Torpey 2000; Martin 2001). From below, we can study the "micropolitics" of categories, the ways in which the categorized appropriate, internalize, subvert, evade, or transform the categories that are imposed on them (Dominguez 1986). And drawing on advances in cognitive research, ethnomethodology, and conversation analysis,[9] we can study the sociocognitive and interactional processes through which categories are used by individuals to make sense of the social world; linked to stereotypical beliefs and expectations about category members;[10] invested with emotional associations and evaluative judgments; deployed as resources in specific interactional contexts; and activated by situational triggers or cues. A focus on categories, in short, can illuminate the multifarious ways in which ethnicity, race, and nationhood can exist and "work" without the existence of ethnic groups as substantial entities. It can help us envision ethnicity without groups.

Group Making as Project

If we treat groupness as a variable and distinguish between groups and categories, we can attend to the dynamics of group making as a social, cultural, and political project, aimed at transforming categories into groups or increasing levels of groupness (Bourdieu 1991a, 1991b). Sometimes this is done in quite a cynical fashion. Ethnic and other insurgencies, for example, often adopt what is called in French a *politique du pire*, a politics of seeking the worst outcome in the short run so as to bolster their legitimacy or improve their prospects in the longer run. When the small, ill-equipped, ragtag Kosovo Liberation Army stepped up its attacks on Serb police and other targets in early 1998, for example, this was done as a deliberate—and successful—strategy of provoking massive regime reprisals. As in many such situations, the brunt of the reprisals was borne by civilians. The cycle of attacks and counterattacks sharply increased groupness among both Kosovo Albanians and Kosovo Serbs, generated greater support for the Kosovo Liberation Army (KLA) among both Kosovo and diaspora Albanians, and bolstered KLA recruitment and funding. This enabled the KLA to mount a more serious challenge to the regime, which in turn generated more brutal regime reprisals, and so on. In this sense, group crystallization and polarization were the result of violence, not the cause (Brubaker 1999).

Of course, this group-making strategy employed in the late 1990s did not start from scratch. It began already with relatively high levels of groupness, a legacy of earlier phases of conflict. The propitious "raw materials" the KLA had to work with no doubt help explain the success of its strategy. Not all group-making projects succeed, and those that do succeed (more or less) do so in part as a result of the cultural and psychological materials they have to work with. These materials include not only, or especially, "deep," *longue-durée* cultural structures such as the mythomoteurs highlighted by Armstrong (1982) and Smith (1986), but also the moderately durable ways of thinking and feeling that represent "middle-range" legacies of historical experience and political action. Yet while such raw materials—themselves the product and precipitate of past struggles and predicaments—constrain and condition the possibilities for group making in the present, there remains considerable scope for deliberate group-making strategies. Certain dramatic events, in particular, can serve to galvanize and crystallize a potential group or to ratchet up pre-existing levels of groupness. This is why deliberate violence, undertaken as a strategy of provocation, often by a very small number of persons, can sometimes be an exceptionally effective strategy of group making.

Groups and Organizations

Although participants' rhetoric and commonsense accounts treat ethnic groups as the protagonists of ethnic conflict, in fact the chief protagonists of most ethnic conflict—and a fortiori of most ethnic violence—are not ethnic groups as such but various kinds of organizations, broadly understood, and their empowered and authorized incumbents. These include states (or, more broadly, autonomous polities) and their organizational components such as particular ministries, offices, law enforcement agencies, and armed forces units; they include terrorist groups, paramilitary organizations, armed bands, and loosely structured gangs; and they include political parties, ethnic associations, social movement organizations, churches, newspapers, radio and television stations, and so on. Some of these organizations may represent themselves, or may be seen by others, as organizations of and for particular ethnic groups.[11] But even when this is the case, organizations cannot be equated with ethnic groups. It is because and insofar as they are organizations, and possess certain material and organizational resources, that they (or more precisely, their incumbents) are capable of organized action and thereby of acting as more or less coherent protagonists in ethnic conflict.[12] Although common sense and participants' rhetoric attribute discrete existence, boundedness, coherence, identity, interest, and agency to ethnic groups, these attributes are in fact characteristic of organizations. The Irish Republican Army (IRA), KLA, and Kurdish Labour Party (PKK) claim to speak and act in the name of the (Catholic) Irish, the Kosovo Albanians, and the Kurds; but surely analysts must differentiate between such organizations and the putatively homogeneous and bounded groups in whose name they claim to act. The point applies not only to military, paramilitary, and terrorist organizations, of course, but also to all organizations that claim to speak and act in the name of ethnic, racial, or national groups (Heisler 1991).

A fuller and more rounded treatment of this theme, to be sure, would require several qualifications that I can only gesture at here. Conflict and violence vary in the degree to which, as well as the manner in which, organizations are involved. What Donald Horowitz (2001) has called the deadly ethnic riot, for example, differs sharply from organized ethnic insurgencies or terrorist campaigns. Although organizations (sometimes ephemeral ones) may play an important role in preparing, provoking, and permitting such riots, much of the actual violence is committed by broader sets of participants acting in relatively spontaneous fashion and in starkly polarized situations characterized by high levels of groupness. Moreover, even where organizations are the core protagonists, they may depend on a penumbra of ancillary or supportive action on the part of sympathetic nonmembers. The "representativeness" of organizations— the degree to which an organization can justifiably claim to represent the will, express the interests, and enjoy the active or passive support of its constituents—is enormously variable not only between organizations but also over time and across domains. In addition, while organizations are ordinarily the protagonists of conflict and violence, they are not always the objects or targets of conflict and violence. Entire population categories—or putative groups—can be the objects of organized action, much more easily than they can be the subjects or undertakers of such action. Finally, even apart from situations of violence, ethnic conflict may be at least partly amorphous, carried out not by organizations as such but spontaneously by individuals through such everyday actions as shunning, insults, demands for deference or conformity, or withholdings of routine interactional tokens of acknowledgment or respect (Bailey 1997). Still, despite these qualifications, it is clear that organizations, not ethnic groups as such, are the chief protagonists of ethnic conflict and ethnic violence, and that the relationship between organizations and the groups they claim to represent is often deeply ambiguous.

Framing and Coding[13]

If the protagonists of ethnic conflict cannot, in general, be considered ethnic groups, then what makes such conflict count as ethnic conflict? And what makes violence count as ethnic violence? Similar questions can be asked about racial and national conflict and violence. The answer cannot be found in the intrinsic properties of behavior. The "ethnic" quality of "ethnic violence," for example, is not intrinsic to violent conduct itself; it is attributed to instances of violent behavior by perpetrators, victims, politicians, officials, journalists, researchers, relief workers, or others. Such acts of framing and narrative encoding do not simply interpret the violence; they constitute it as ethnic.

Framing may be a key mechanism through which groupness is constructed. The metaphor of framing was popularized by Goffman (1974), drawing on Bateson (1985 [1955]). The notion has been elaborated chiefly in the social movement literature (Snow et al. 1986; Snow and Benford 1988; Gamson and Modigliani 1989; Gamson 1992; for uniting rational choice and framing approaches, see Esser 1999). When ethnic framing is successful, we may "see" conflict and violence not only in ethnic but also in groupist terms. Although such imputed groupness is the product of prevailing interpretive frames, not necessarily a measure of the groupness felt and experienced by the participants in an event, a compelling ex post interpretive framing or encoding may exercise a powerful feedback effect, shaping subsequent experience and increasing levels of groupness. A great deal is at stake, then, in struggles over the interpretive framing and narrative encoding of conflict and violence.

Interpretive framing, of course, is often contested. Violence—and, more generally, conflict—is regularly accompanied by social struggles to label, interpret, and explain it. Such "metaconflicts" or "conflict[s] over the nature of the conflict," as Donald Horowitz has called them (Horowitz 1991:2), do not simply shadow conflicts from the outside, but are integral and consequential parts of the conflicts. To impose a label or prevailing interpretive frame—to cause an event to be seen as a "pogrom" or a "riot" or a "rebellion"—is no mere matter of external interpretation, but a constitutive act of social definition that can have important consequences (Brass 1996a). Social struggles over the proper coding and interpretation of conflict and violence are therefore important subjects of study in their own right (Brass 1996b, 1997; Abelmann and Lie 1995).

Coding and framing practices are heavily influenced by prevailing interpretive frames. Today, ethnic and national frames are accessible and legitimate, suggesting themselves to actors and analysts alike. This generates a "coding bias" in the ethnic direction. And this, in turn, may lead us to overestimate the incidence of ethnic conflict and violence by unjustifiably seeing ethnicity everywhere at work (Bowen 1996). Actors may take advantage of this coding bias, and of the generalized legitimacy of ethnic and national frames, by strategically using ethnic framing to mask the pursuit of clan, clique, or class interests. The point here is not to suggest that clans, cliques, or classes are somehow more real than ethnic groups, but simply to note the existence of structural and cultural incentives for strategic framing.

Ethnicity as Cognition[14]

These observations about the constitutive significance of coding and framing suggest a final point about the cognitive dimension of ethnicity. Ethnicity, race, and nationhood exist only in and through our perceptions, interpretations, representations, categorizations, and identifications. They are not things *in* the world, but perspectives *on* the world.[15] These include ethnicized ways of seeing (and ignoring), of construing (and misconstruing), of inferring (and misinferring), of remembering (and forgetting). They include ethnically oriented frames, schemas, and narratives, and the situational cues that activate them, such as the ubiquitous televised images that have played such an important role in the latest intifada. They include systems of classification, categorization, and identification, formal and informal. And they include the tacit, taken-for-granted background knowledge, embodied in persons and embedded in institutionalized routines and practices, through which people recognize and experience objects, places, persons, actions, or situations as ethnically, racially, or nationally marked or meaningful.

Cognitive perspectives, broadly understood,[16] can help advance constructivist research on ethnicity, race, and nationhood, which has stalled in recent years as it has grown complacent with success. Instead of simply asserting *that* ethnicity, race, and nationhood are constructed, they can help specify *how* they are constructed. They can help specify how—and when—people identify themselves, perceive others, experience the world, and interpret their predicaments in racial, ethnic, or national rather than other terms. They can help specify how "groupness" can "crystallize" in some situations while remaining latent and merely potential in others. And they can help link macro-level outcomes with micro-level processes.

IMPLICATIONS

At this point a critic might interject: "What is the point of all this? Even if we can study 'ethnicity without groups,' why should we? Concepts invariably simplify the world; that the concept of discrete and bounded ethnic groups does so, suggesting something more substantial and clear-cut than really exists, cannot be held against it. The concept of ethnic group may be a blunt instrument, but it's good enough as a first approximation. This talk about groupness and framing and practical categories and cognitive schemas is all well and good, but meanwhile the killing goes on. Does the critique matter in the real world, or—if at all—only in the ivory tower? What practical difference does it make?"

I believe the critique of groupism does have implications, albeit rather general ones, for the ways in which researchers, journalists, policymakers, NGOs, and others come to terms, analytically and practically, with what we ordinarily—though perhaps too readily—call ethnic conflict and ethnic violence. Here I would like to enumerate five of these.

First, sensitivity to framing dynamics, to the generalized coding bias in favor of ethnicity, and to the sometimes strategic or even cynical use of ethnic framing to mask the pursuit of clan, clique, or class interests can alert us to the risk of overethnicized or overly groupist interpretations of (and interventions in) situations of conflict and violence (Bowen 1996). One need not subscribe to a reductionist "elite manipulation" view of politicized ethnicity (Brubaker 1998) to acknowledge that the "spin" put on conflicts by participants may conceal as much as it reveals, and that the representation of conflicts as conflicts between ethnic or national groups may obscure the interests at stake and the dynamics involved. What is represented as ethnic conflict or ethnic war—such as the violence in the former Yugoslavia—may have as much or more to do with thuggery, warlordship, opportunistic looting, and black-market profiteering than with ethnicity (Mueller 2000; cf. Collier 1999).

Second, recognition of the centrality of organizations in ethnic conflict and ethnic violence, of the often equivocal character of their leaders' claims to speak and act in the name of ethnic groups, and of the performative nature of ethnopolitical rhetoric, enlisted in the service of group-making projects, can remind us not to mistake groupist rhetoric for real groupness, the putative groups of ethnopolitical rhetoric for substantial things-in-the-world.

Third, awareness of the interest that ethnic and nationalist leaders may have in living *off* politics, as well as *for* politics, to borrow the classic distinction of Max Weber (1946:84), and awareness of the possible divergence between the interests of leaders and those of their putative constituents, can keep us from accepting at face value leaders' claims about the beliefs, desires, and interests of their constituents.

Fourth, sensitivity to the variable and contingent, waxing and waning nature of groupness, and to the fact that high levels of groupness may be more the result of conflict (especially violent conflict) than its underlying cause, can focus our analytical attention and policy interventions on the processes through which groupness tends to develop and crystallize, and those through which it may subside. Some attention has been given recently to the former, including tipping and cascade mechanisms (Laitin 1995; Kuran 1998) and mechanisms governing the activation and diffusion of schemas and the "epidemiology of representations" (Sperber 1985). But declining curves of groupness have not been studied systematically, although they are just as important, theoretically and practically. Once ratcheted up to a high level, groupness does not remain there out of inertia. If not sustained at high levels through specific social and cognitive mechanisms, it will tend to decline, as everyday interests reassert themselves, through a process of what Weber (in a different but apposite context [Weber 1968 (1922):246–254]) called "routinization" (*Veralltäglichung*, literally "toward everydayness").

Lastly, a disaggregating, nongroupist approach can bring into analytical and policy focus the critical importance of intra-ethnic mechanisms in generating and sustaining putatively interethnic conflict (Brubaker and Laitin 1998:433). These include in-group "policing," monitoring, or sanctioning processes (Laitin 1995); the "ethnic outbidding" through which electoral competition can foster extreme ethnicization (Rothschild 1981; Horowitz 1985); the calculated instigation or provocation of conflict with outsiders by vulnerable incumbents seeking to deflect in-group challenges to their positions; and in-group processes bearing on the dynamics of recruitment into gangs, militias, terrorist groups, or guerrilla armies, including honoring, shaming, and shunning practices; rituals of manhood; intergenerational tensions; and the promising and provision of material and symbolic rewards for martyrs.

CONCLUSION

What are we studying when we study ethnicity and ethnic conflict? This chapter has suggested that we need not frame our analyses in terms of ethnic groups, and that it may be more productive to focus on practical categories, cultural idioms, cognitive schemas, commonsense knowledge, organizational routines and resources, discursive frames, institutionalized forms, political projects, contingent events, and variable groupness. It should be noted in closing, however, that by framing our inquiry in this way, and by bringing to bear a set of analytical perspectives not ordinarily associated with the study of ethnicity—cognitive theory, ethnomethodology, conversation analysis, network analysis, organizational analysis, and institutional theory, for example—we may end up not studying ethnicity at all. It may be that "ethnicity" is simply a convenient—though in certain respects misleading—rubric under which to group highly disparate phenomena that have a great deal in common with other phenomena that are not ordinarily subsumed under the rubric of ethnicity.[17] In other words, by raising questions about the *unit* of analysis—the ethnic group—we may end up questioning the *domain* of analysis—ethnicity itself. But that is an argument for another occasion.

NOTES

This is an abridged version of an article that appeared in *Archives européennes de sociologie* 43, no. 2 (November 2002):163–89. Earlier versions were presented to the conference "Facing Ethnic Conflicts," Center for Development Research,

University of Bonn, December 14, 2000; the Working Group on Ethnicity and Nationalism, UCLA, January 13, 2001; the Anthropology Colloquium, University of Chicago, February 26, 2001; and the Central European University, Budapest, March 20, 2001. Thanks to participants in these events for their comments and criticisms, and to David Laitin, Mara Loveman, Emanuel Schegloff, Peter Stamatov, Peter Waldmann, and the editors of this volume for helpful written comments.

1. Foundational discussions include Cooley (1962 [1909]), chapter 3, and Homans (1950) in sociology; Nadel (1957), chapter 7, in anthropology; and Bentley (1908), chapter 7, and Truman (1951), in political science. More recent discussions include Olson (1965), Tilly (1978), and Hechter (1987).

2. In this very general sense, groupism extends well beyond the domain of ethnicity, race, and nationalism to include accounts of putative groups based on gender, sexuality, age, class, abledness, religion, minority status, and any kind of "culture," as well as putative groups based on combinations of these categorical attributes. Yet while recognizing that it is a wider tendency in social analysis, I limit my discussion here to groupism in the study of ethnicity, race, and nationalism.

3. For useful critical analyses of media representations of ethnic violence, see the collection of essays in Allen and Seaton (1999) as well as Seaton (1999).

4. This is perhaps too sharply put. To the extent that such intrinsic-kind categories are indeed constitutive of commonsense understandings of the social world, to the extent that such categories are used as a resource for participants and are demonstrably deployed or oriented to by participants in interaction, they can also serve as a resource for analysts. But as Emanuel Schegloff notes in another context, with respect to the category "interruption," the fact that this is a vernacular, commonsense category for participants "does not make it a first-order category usable for professional analysis. Rather than being employed *in* professional analysis, it is better treated as a target category *for* professional analysis" (Schegloff 2001:307, italics added). The same might well be said of commonsense ethnic categories.

5. Such performative, group-making practices, of course, are not specific to ethnic entrepreneurs but generic to political mobilization and representation (Bourdieu 1991b:248–251).

6. For accounts (not focused specifically on ethnicity) that treat groupness as variable, see Tilly (1978:62–64), Hechter (1987:8), and Hamilton et al. (1998). These accounts, very different from one another, focus on variability in groupness across cases; my concern is primarily with variability in groupness over time.

7. Fredrik Barth's introductory essay to the collection *Ethnic Groups and Boundaries* (1969) was extraordinarily influential in directing attention to the workings of categories of self- and other-ascription. But Barth does not distinguish sharply or consistently between categories and groups, and his central metaphor of "boundary" carries with it connotations of boundedness, entitativity, and groupness.

8. This point was already made by Max Weber, albeit in somewhat different terms. As Weber argued—in a passage obscured in the English translation—ethnic commonality, based on belief in common descent, is "in itself mere (putative) commonality [(*geglaubte*) *Gemeinsamkeit*], not community [*Gemeinschaft*] . . . but only a factor facilitating communal action [*Vergemeinschaftung*]" (1964:307; cf. 1968:389). Ethnic commonality means more than mere category membership for

Weber. It is—or rather involves—a category that is employed by members themselves. But this shows that even self-categorization does not create a "group."

9. Ethnomethodology and conversation analysis have not focused on the use
of ethnic categories as such, but Sacks, Schegloff, and others have addressed the
problem of situated categorization in general, notably the question of the procedures through which participants in interaction, in deploying categories, choose
among alternative sets of categories (since there is always more than one set of categories in terms of which any person can be correctly described). The import of
this problem has been formulated as follows by Schegloff (2001:309, italics added):

> Given the centrality of . . . categories in organizing vernacular cultural "knowledge,"
> this equivocality can be profoundly consequential, for *which* category is employed will
> carry with it the invocation of commonsense knowledge about *that* category of person
> and bring it to bear on the person referred to on some occasion, rather than bringing to
> bear the knowledge implicated with *another* category, of which the person being re-
> ferred to is equally a member.

(For Sacks on categories, see 1995:I, 40–48, 333–340, 396–403, 578–596; II, 184–187).

10. The language of "stereotypes" is, of course, that of cognitive social psychology (for a review of work in this tradition, see Hamilton and Sherman 1994).
But the general ethnomethodological emphasis on the crucial importance of the
rich though tacit background knowledge that participants bring to interaction,
and—more specifically—Harvey Sacks's discussion of the "inference-rich" categories in terms of which much everyday social knowledge is stored (1995:I, 40–42
et passim; cf. Schegloff 2001:308–309) and of the way in which the knowledge thus
organized is "protected against induction" (Sacks 1995:336–338), suggest a domain of potentially converging concern between cognitive work on the one hand
and ethnomethodological and conversation-analytic work on the other—however
different their analytic stances and methodologies.

11. One should remember, though, that organizations often compete with one
another for the monopolization of the right to represent the same (putative) group.

12. In this respect the resource mobilization perspective on social movements,
eclipsed in recent years by identity-oriented new social movement theory, has
much to offer students of ethnicity. For an integrated statement, see McCarthy and
Zald (1977).

13. These paragraphs draw on Brubaker and Laitin (1998).

14. These paragraphs draw on Brubaker et al. (2004).

15. As Emanuel Schegloff reminded me in a different context, this formulation
is potentially misleading, since perspectives *on* the world—as every Sociology 1
student is taught—are themselves *in* the world, and every bit as "real" and consequential as other sorts of things.

16. Cognitive perspectives, in this broad sense, include not only those developed in cognitive psychology and cognitive anthropology but also those developed in the post- (and anti-) Parsonian "cognitive turn" (DiMaggio and Powell
1991) in sociological and (more broadly) social theory, especially in response to the
influence of phenomenological and ethnomethodological work (Schutz 1962;
Garfinkel 1967; Heritage 1984). Cognitive perspectives are central to the influen-

tial syntheses of Bourdieu and Giddens and—in a very different form—to the enterprise of conversation analysis.

17. As Weber put it nearly a century ago (Weber 1968 [1922]:394–395), a precise and differentiated analysis would "surely throw out the umbrella term 'ethnic' altogether," for it is "entirely unusable" for any "truly rigorous investigation."

REFERENCES

Abelmann, Nancy, and John Lie. 1995. *Blue Dreams: Korean Americans and the Los Angeles Riots*. Cambridge, MA: Harvard University Press.

Allen, Tim, and Jean Seaton, eds. 1999. *The Media of Conflict: War Reporting and Representations of Ethnic Violence*. London: Zed Books.

Armstrong, John A. 1982. *Nations before Nationalism*. Chapel Hill: University of North Carolina Press.

Bailey, Benjamin. 1997. Communication of Respect in Interethnic Service Encounters. *Language in Society* 26:327–356.

Barth, Fredrik. 1969. Introduction. In *Ethnic Groups and Boundaries: The Social Organization of Culture Difference*, ed. Fredrik Barth, 9–38. London: Allen & Unwin.

Bateson, Gregory. 1985 (1955). A Theory of Play and Fantasy. In *Semiotics: An Introductory Anthology*, ed. Robert E. Innis, 131–144. Bloomington: Indiana University Press.

Bentley, Arthur F. 1908. *The Process of Government: A Study of Social Pressures*. Chicago: University of Chicago Press.

Bourdieu, Pierre. 1991a. Identity and Representation: Elements for a Critical Reflection on the Idea of Region. In *Language and Symbolic Power*, ed. Pierre Bourdieu, 220–228. Cambridge, MA: Harvard University Press.

———. 1991b. Social Space and the Genesis of "Classes." In *Language and Symbolic Power*, ed. Pierre Bourdieu, 229–251. Cambridge, MA: Harvard University Press.

Bowen, John R. 1996. The Myth of Global Ethnic Conflict. *Journal of Democracy* 7 (4):3–14.

Brass, Paul R. 1996a. Introduction: Discourse of Ethnicity, Communalism, and Violence. In *Riots and Pogroms*, ed. Paul R. Brass, 1–55. New York: New York University Press.

———, ed. 1996b. *Riots and Pogroms*. New York: New York University Press.

———. 1997. *Theft of an Idol: Text and Context in the Representation of Collective Violence*. Princeton, NJ: Princeton University Press.

Brubaker, Rogers. 1992. *Citizenship and Nationhood in France and Germany*. Cambridge, MA: Harvard University Press.

———. 1994. Nationhood and the National Question in the Soviet Union and Post-Soviet Eurasia. *Theory and Society* 23 (1):47–78.

———. 1998. Myths and Misconceptions in the Study of Nationalism. In *The State of the Nation: Ernest Gellner and the Theory of Nationalism*, ed. John Hall, 272–306. New York: Cambridge University Press.

———. 1999. A Shameful Debacle. *UCLA Magazine* (Summer 1999): 15–16.

Brubaker, Rogers, and David D. Laitin. 1998. Ethnic and Nationalist Violence. *Annual Review of Sociology* 24:423–452.

Brubaker, Rogers, Mara Loveman, and Peter Stamatov. 2004. Ethnicity as Cognition. *Theory and Society* 33 (1):31–64.

Collier, Paul. 1999. Doing Well Out of War. Accessed at www.worldbank.org/research/conflict/paperseconagenda.htm

Cooley, Charles H. 1962 (1909). *Social Organization*. New York: Schocken Books.

DiMaggio, Paul J., and Walter W. Powell. 1991. Introduction. In *The New Institutionalism in Organizational Analysis*, ed. Walter W. Powell and Paul. J. DiMaggio, 1–38. Chicago: University of Chicago Press.

Dominguez, Virginia R. 1986. *White by Definition: Social Classification in Creole Louisiana*. New Brunswick, NJ: Rutgers University Press.

Emirbayer, Mustafa, and Jeff Goodwin. 1994. Network Analysis, Culture, and the Problem of Agency. *American Journal of Sociology* 99 (6):1411–1454.

Esser, Hartmut. 1999. Die Situationslogik ethnischer Konflikte: Auch eine Anmerkung zum Beitrag 'Ethnische Mobilisierung und die Logik von Identitätskämpfen' von Klaus Eder und Oliver Schmidtke. *Zeitschrift für Soziologie* 28 (4):245–262.

Fearon, James, and David D. Laitin. 1996. Explaining Interethnic Cooperation. *American Political Science Review* 90 (4):715–735.

Gamson, William A. 1992. *Talking Politics*. New York: Cambridge University Press.

Gamson, William A., and Andre Modigliani. 1989. Media Discourse and Public Opinion on Nuclear Power: A Constructionist Approach. *American Journal of Sociology* 95:1–37.

Garfinkel, Harold. 1967. *Studies in Ethnomethodology*. Englewood Cliffs, NJ: Prentice-Hall.

Gil-White, Francisco. 1999. How Thick Is Blood? The Plot Thickens. . . : If Ethnic Actors Are Primordialists, What Remains of the Circumstantialist/Primordialist Controversy? *Ethnic and Racial Studies* 22 (5):789–820.

Goffman, Erving. 1974. *Frame Analysis*. San Francisco: Harper Colophon Books.

Hamilton, David L., and Jeffrey W. Sherman. 1994. Stereotypes. In *Handbook of Social Cognition*, 2nd ed., ed. Robert S. Wyer and Thomas K. Srull, 1–68. Hillsdale, NJ: Lawrence Erlbaum.

Hamilton, David L., Steven J. Sherman, and Brian Lickel. 1998. Perceiving Social Groups: The Importance of the Entitativity Continuum. In *Intergroup Cognition and Intergroup Behavior*, ed. Constantine Sedikides, John Schopler, and Chester A. Mahwah Insko, 47–74. Hillsdale, NJ: Lawrence Erlbaum.

Handelman, Don. 1977. The Organization of Ethnicity. *Ethnic Groups* 1:187–200.

Hechter, Michael. 1987. *Principles of Group Solidarity*. Berkeley: University of California Press.

Heisler, Martin. 1991. Ethnicity and Ethnic Relations in the Modern West. In *Conflict and Peacemaking in Multiethnic Societies*, ed. Joseph Montville, 21–52. Lexington, MA: Lexington Books.

Heritage, John. 1984. *Garfinkel and Ethnomethodology*. Cambridge: Polity Press.

Hirschfeld, Lawrence A. 1996. *Race in the Making: Cognition, Culture and the Child's Construction of Human Kinds*. Cambridge, MA: MIT Press.

Homans, George C. 1950. *The Human Group*. New York: Harcourt, Brace & World.

Horowitz, Donald L. 1985. *Ethnic Groups in Conflict*. Berkeley: University of California Press.

———. 1991. *A Democratic South Africa? Constitutional Engineering in a Divided Society*. Berkeley: University of California Press.

———. 2001. *The Deadly Ethnic Riot*. Berkeley: University of California Press.

Jenkins, Richard. 1997. *Rethinking Ethnicity*. London: Sage.

Kuran, Timur. 1998. Ethnic Norms and Their Transformation through Reputational Cascades. *Journal of Legal Studies* 27:623–659.

Laitin, David D. 1995. National Revivals and Violence. *Archives Européenes de Sociologie* 36 (1):3–43.

Levine, Hal B. 1999. Reconstructing Ethnicity. *Journal of the Royal Anthropological Institute* (New Series) 5:165–180.

Martin, Terry. 2001. *The Affirmative Action Empire*. Ithaca, NY: Cornell University Press.

McCarthy, John D., and Mayer N. Zald. 1977. Resource Mobilization and Social Movements: A Partial Theory. *American Journal of Sociology* 82 (6):1212–1241.

McGrath, Joseph E. 1984. *Groups: Interaction and Performance*. Englewood Cliffs, NJ: Prentice-Hall.

McKay, James, and Frank Lewins. 1978. Ethnicity and the Ethnic Group: A Conceptual Analysis and Reformulation. *Ethnic and Racial Studies* 1 (4):412–427.

Medin, Douglas L. 1989. Concepts and Conceptual Structure. *The American Psychologist* 44:1469–1481.

Moerman, Michael. 1968. Being Lue: Uses and Abuses of Ethnic Identification. In *Essays on the Problem of Tribe*, ed. June Helm, 153–169. Seattle: University of Washington Press.

Mueller, John. 2000. The Banality of "Ethnic War." *International Security* 25:42–70.

Nadel, S. F. 1957. *A Theory of Social Structure*. London: Cohen & West.

Noiriel, Gérard. 1991. *La Tyrannie du national: Le droit d'asile en Europe 1793–1993*. Paris: Calmann-Lévy.

Olson, Mancur. 1965. *The Logic of Collective Action: Public Goods and the Theory of Groups*. Cambridge, MA: Harvard University Press.

Petersen, William. 1987. Politics and the Measurement of Ethnicity. In *The Politics of Numbers*, ed. William Alonso and Paul Starr, 187–233. New York: Russell Sage Foundation.

Rothbart, Myron, and Marjorie Taylor. 1992. Category Labels and Social Reality: Do We View Social Categories As Natural Kinds? In *Language, Interaction and Social Cognition*, ed. Gün R. Semin and Klaus Fiedler, 11–36. London: Sage.

Rothschild, Joseph. 1981. *Ethnopolitics: A Conceptual Framework*. New York: Columbia University Press.

Sacks, Harvey. 1995. *Lectures on Conversation*. Oxford: Blackwell.

Schegloff, Emanuel A. 2001. Accounts of Conduct in Interaction: Interruption, Overlap and Turn-Taking. In *Handbook of Sociological Theory*, ed. J. H. Turner, 287–321. New York: Plenum.

Schutz, Alfred. 1962. *Collected Papers I: The Problem of Social Reality*, ed. Maurice Natanson. The Hague: Marinus Nijhoff.

Seaton, Jean. 1999. Why Do We Think the Serbs Do It? The New "Ethnic" Wars and the Media. *Political Quarterly* 70 (3):254–270.

Slezkine, Yuri. 1994. The USSR As a Communal Apartment, or How a Socialist State Promoted Ethnic Particularlism. *Slavic Review* 53 (4):414–452.

Smith, Anthony D. 1986. *The Ethnic Origins of Nations.* Oxford: Basil Blackwell.

———. 1998. *Nationalism and Modernism: A Critical Survey of Recent Theories of Nations and Nationalism.* London: Routledge.

Snow, David A., and Robert D. Benford. 1988. Ideology, Frame Resonance, and Participant Mobilization. *International Social Movement Research* 1:197–217.

Snow, David A., E. B. Rochford, Jr., Steven K. Worden, and Robert D. Benford. 1986. Frame Alignment Processes, Micromobilization, and Movement Participation. *American Sociological Review* 51:464–481.

Sperber, Dan. 1985. Anthropology and Psychology: Towards an Epidemiology of Representations. *Man* 20:73–89.

Tilly, Charles. 1978. *From Mobilization to Revolution.* Reading, MA: Addison-Wesley.

———. 1998. *Durable Inequality.* Berkeley: University of California Press.

Torpey, John. 2000. *The Invention of the Passport: Surveillance, Citizenship and the State.* Cambridge: Cambridge University Press.

Truman, David B. 1951. *The Governmental Process: Political Interests and Public Opinion,* 2nd ed. New York: Alfred A. Knopf.

Weber, Max. 1964 (1922). *Wirtschaft und Gesellschaft.* 4th ed. Cologne: Kiepenheurer and Witsch.

———. 1968 (1922). *Economy and Society,* ed. Guenther Roth and Claus Wittich. Berkeley: University of California Press.

———. 1946. *From Max Weber: Essays in Sociology,* trans., ed., and with an introduction by H. H. Gerth and C. Wright Mills. New York: Oxford University Press.

Wellman, Barry. 1988. Structural Analysis: From Method and Metaphor to Theory and Substance. In *Social Structures: A Network Approach,* ed. Barry Wellman and S. D. Berkowitz, 19–61. Cambridge: Cambridge University Press.

3

Ethnic Conflict and the Colonial Legacy

Christopher J. Bakwesegha

The continent of Africa is currently going through a state of political flux, just like other continents in the world. Every country in the world is currently grappling with the problem of repositioning itself in world affairs, redefining its role, and searching for its own equilibrium in the newly emerging scheme of things. Western Europe is busy trying to adjust itself to a world without the real or perceived fears of the former Soviet Union. Eastern Europe has taken the path of adapting itself to a new type of democracy and maintaining its national unity and sovereignty without the commands of a superpower. The United States has also been adjusting itself to a world without constant worries from the former Soviet Union, and a world in which it has found itself as the only superpower. And Africa is currently searching for a new security regime as a response to the fundamental changes that have been taking place in the world since the end of the East-West rivalry, a security regime that can endure all the pressures from outside the continent, and one that is adequately equipped to defend the interests of the African people, all the people, rather than a security regime that discriminates against people on the basis of race, religion, nationality, or ethnic identity.

For Africa, the security dilemma together with the peaceful settlement of conflict has remained an important issue since the inception of our continental organization, the Organization of African Unity, in 1963. Indeed, in the Preamble of the OAU Charter, the Founding Fathers of the Organization of African Unity were "inspired by a common determination to promote understanding among (their) peoples and cooperation among (their) states in response to the aspirations of (their) peoples for brother-hood and solidarity, in larger unity transcending ethnic and national dif-ferences."

The Founding Fathers of the OAU were fully aware of the degree to which their vision of the continent would be adversely affected by inse-curity, instability, and tension between states. They thus adopted the prin-ciple of "peaceful settlement of disputes by negotiation, mediation, con-ciliation or arbitration," which was later institutionalized through an organ called the Commission of Mediation, Conciliation and Arbitration.

For reasons beyond the scope of the present chapter, the Commission never became operational. Moreover, the Commission, so instituted, was intended only to address interstate conflicts, which, at that time, were the overriding concern of the member states of the OAU. But as is well known, our continent is currently confronted with more intrastate con-flicts than interstate conflicts. And that is why in 1993 the OAU Mecha-nism for preventing, managing, and resolving conflicts was put in place.

In this chapter, I will focus on the issue of ethnic conflicts as it obtains in Africa. However, by so doing I do not want to give the impression that ethnic conflicts are only confined to Africa. Ethnic conflicts are a world-wide phenomenon as the example of Bosnia-Herzegovina reveals. How-ever, there is hardly any country in Africa that has been spared the wrath of ethnic conflicts in terms of loss of lives, destruction of property, as well as human displacement.

A recent report of the United Nations secretary-general indicates that in the last thirty years alone, more than thirty wars have been fought in Africa. In 1996 alone, fourteen of the fifty-three member states of the OAU were affected by armed conflicts accounting for more than half of war-related deaths worldwide and resulting in more than 8 million refugees and displaced persons.[1] Moreover, a good number of these conflicts are not only intrastate in occurrence but also bear an ethnic dimension al-though they may not necessarily and directly be caused by ethnicity.

In this chapter I argue, albeit with some caution, that ethnicity could be a necessary but not always sufficient condition for violent conflict forma-tion. I say this because if, indeed, ethnicity, ipso facto, were to cause vio-lent conflict, then one could also argue that the more ethnic groups you have within a state, the more violent conflicts you will have in that state, and vice versa. But this proposition is false at best. Burundi and Rwanda, which have experienced some of the worst scenarios of conflict in the world, are host to three ethnic groups each. Yet Tanzania, which is host to over 200 ethnic groups, has been enjoying relative peace and stability since independence. At the same time, Somalia, which has always been claimed to be a homogenous society and where ethnic pluralism may not really be an issue, has remained a collapsed state since 1992.

Experience in Africa reveals that states that have been authoritarian, dictatorial, or military in character and have been known to suspend and manipulate constitutions, ignore all democratic institutions and the rule of law, trample down upon all rights of their citizens, and operate with complete impunity end up by fueling or fermenting conflict. Indeed, by their nature, the ordinary people in Africa cherish living in peace and resent the idea of participating in war and violence. It is only when they are, individually and/or collectively, marginalized; excluded from power and from the mainstream of development; and persecuted on ethnic, religious, or racial lines by politicians to achieve their political ambitions that the ordinary people usually rise to their feet to challenge governments by violent means. Ethnicity, therefore, does not automatically lead to violent conflict formation. Rather, it is the way power is exercised, especially in the process of allocating the resources of the state. The so-called ethnic conflicts and wars are merely a reaction to bad governance, arrogance of power, insensitivity and egoism, and total disregard for the rule of law on the part of some leaders and politicians in Africa.

Furthermore, during election times, it is customary for people to vote in blocs and on ethnic lines. The ruling ethnic group would normally mobilize its ethnic comrades in order to remain in power at all costs and continue to enrich themselves at the expense of other ethnic groups. At the same time, those ethnic groups that have been neglected all along usually mobilize themselves for combat against the ruling ethnic clique, which is not expected to win the elections again. The end product is ethnic polarization and tension, which may subsequently give rise to repression, massive violation of human rights, violent conflict, and outright war—all leading to outflows of refugees as well as internal human displacement.

I also wish to argue that what we call ethnic conflicts today are a manifestation of administrative policies and actions of colonialism in Africa, a combination of which has led to ethnic consciousness. In the case of Rwanda, or Burundi for that matter, before colonial intrusion, the Banyarwanda were divided into three major ethnic groups, namely, the Hutus, who were agriculturists and who were the biggest ethnic group in the country; the Tutsis, who were cattle keepers; and the Twas, who were fruit gatherers. These three ethnic entities lived harmoniously and lived a symbiotic life in so far as their economic activities were concerned. There were intermarriages between the three ethnic groups, and people did not regard themselves as enemies of each other.

However, when colonialists burst out on the scene, they started to favor one ethnic group (Tutsis) against the other two ethnic groups, and introduced a card system that bore the ethnic identity of the bearer of the card. They saw Tutsis as people who had been made in the image of the colonizers and proceeded to use them for their colonial administration from which the Hutus and Twas had been excluded with impunity. Hutus and Twas were equally excluded from the educational system that the colonizers had introduced in the country. Later on, when Tutsis began to clamor for independence late in the 1950s, they were damped and replaced by Hutus through a violent and bloody revolution that forced hundred of thousands of Tutsis into exile in neighboring states and beyond.

It took thirty years for the Tutsis to organize themselves and launch a bloody revolution that brought them into power, in 1994, following the genocide in Rwanda that resulted in the killing of over 800,000 people. For us, in the case of Rwanda and Burundi, the rise of the ethnic question and the subsequent cycle of violence and ethnic polarization are more of a function of ethnic favoritism by the colonialists and lack of good governance on the part of the government that immediately succeeded the colonial government, whose era ended at independence in 1960. In both Rwanda and Burundi, ethnicity has always been a means to an end, and that end has been for one ethnic group to monopolize power as well as wealth at the exclusion of other ethnic groups.

When we turn to the Uganda situation, we find basically a similar experience of the administrative policies and actions of colonialism being responsible for the successive conflicts that have been taking place in the country since the departure of the colonizers in 1962. Indeed, prior to colonial intrusion at the turn of the 1880s, Uganda was host to a lot of ethnic groups that were enjoying relative peace and stability; and in Uganda, ethnic and religious considerations were not as pronounced as they came to be in the years that immediately followed independence.

When the colonialists arrived in Uganda, they did not lose any time to team up with ethnic groups whose structure and organization measured up to their taste. Within no time of their stay, the nation was divided along ethnic, religious, and regional lines. The people of the South, who were believed to have greater *brain-power* and to be more organized than those elsewhere in the country, became favored and were used to carry out administrative functions on behalf of the colonialists through a system of "indirect rule." Whatever development endeavors put in place in the country—schools, industries, factories, hospitals, and the like—were all located in the South. The only university of the time was also located in the South.

In terms of socioeconomic development, the remote North was neglected except in terms of labor supply to factories and industries in the South. Another exception, which later turned out to be almost an exclusive domain of the people of the North, was the recruitment of the army and the police force. People in the North were believed to be good for nothing except joining the military and the police force, on the strength of their physique, and supplying labor and services for the favored region of the South, which activities involved north-to-south migratory trends, with all their implications. People in the South, however, were seen as intellectuals and administrators who were too good to be part of the army and the police force. The result was a country divided: The South had the pen and the bible, and the North had the gun and physique. One perception also emerged: The South was seen as a "favored region," while the North was seen as the less favored or neglected region. Some ethnic groups were seen as more intelligent and more civilized than the others; and the development process followed ethnic considerations in general throughout the country with various ethnic groups being governed by different colonial policies. This, in turn, resulted in destructive regional disparities and in ethnic divisions and hate.

When coups d'état became a reality in Africa, people in Northern Uganda who had not benefited much from the colonial education system grabbed power with their gun, in 1971, and started to rule the country with no regard to democratic principles. The result was a spiral of violent conflicts, which subsided only by the people in the South mobilizing themselves and carrying out a revolution that enabled them to assume political power and everything that goes with it. Again in Uganda, we see colonialism sowing seeds of conflict through biased policies and actions, or discriminatory conceptions as well as misconceptions of people's potential, which came to be carried forward by the local people themselves who succeeded the departing colonialists.

Due to space constraints, one cannot go on recounting all cases of the rise of the ethnic question in other African countries; but one would be inclined to believe that in virtually all African countries that were colonized at one time or another, including Nigeria, Ghana, Sierra Leone, Zambia, Kenya, and so on, colonialism had a hand in sowing seeds of what we now erroneously call ethnic conflicts; and the Africans who succeeded the departing colonialists only proceeded to water and nurture the tree of ethnic violence and conflict.

The challenge for the OAU, therefore, is that of creating institutions, or turning our existing institutions around to make them more relevant, to address the ethnic issue and the need to establish a security regime suitable for the African condition. In conclusion, I should like to make the following eight points.

First, the postindependence era of the African continent, especially the period following the end of the Cold War, has been characterized by an increase in intrastate conflicts that constitute a serious drain on the limited resources of African countries, and that have been forcing African states to divert resources from meaningful development endeavors into the prosecution of war. Although often assumed to be caused by ethnic factors, it is my considered opinion that those conflicts are a result of bad governance first caused by the exploitative policies and discriminatory actions of colonialism, and now perpetuated by the African politicians themselves, who inherited discriminatory colonial institutions, structures, and policies without finding the need to turn them around to suit the realities in Africa. In short, ethnic diversity in Africa is not necessarily bad and, in fact, it can be an enrichment of society and not a means to foster division and hate. But it is when this diversity is politicized by those in power to fulfill their personal interests, through discrimination against and official neglect of certain segments of society, coupled with foreign interference for purposes of exploiting mineral resources and promoting arms trade, that ethnic diversity becomes a liability rather than an asset to the people concerned.

Second, the bottom line to ethnic conflict in Africa is not the ethnic factor itself but rather the sharing of power and national resources. The need to provide for equitable distribution of wealth and power and access to economic advancement and full realization of the right to development of all groups of the society will help in the prevention of conflict and should be part of national constitutions.

Third, for purposes of averting the growing cases of xenophobia and violence against refugees and aliens as well as humanitarian workers including peacekeepers, states that have not yet done so should consider ratifying the relevant international instruments on these issues, including the 1951 UN convention on refugees together with the 1967 Protocol relating thereto, the 1969 OAU Convention Governing Specific Aspects of Refugee Problems in Africa, as well as the African Charter on Human and Peoples' Rights of 1982. Furthermore, the adherence to and implementation of these instruments should entail training all state organs such as the police, the security and prison personnel, the media, the judges and lawyers, as well as the army and immigration officers of the provisions of those instruments.

Fourth, there is no doubt that wealth is a blessing, but it can also be a curse. My experience with conflict situations in Africa reveals that most conflicts are taking place in countries that have considerable potential wealth such as Angola, the Democratic Republic of the Congo, Sierra Leone, Congo-Brazzaville, the Sudan, and Liberia. The wars and conflicts in all those countries are claiming a lion's share of the wealth of these countries. Indeed, to finance such wars, states and rebel groups either have to finance their efforts by mortgaging the resources of the country, or by engaging in smuggling out of the state concerned raw materials such as diamonds (e.g., by UNITA and RUF). There are also cases where external agents enter a theatre of conflict partly for purpose of looting the wealth of the country concerned. In the case of the Democratic Republic of the Congo, all parties to the conflict are sustaining their war efforts by exploiting the resources of that country. What is worse, the rewards from those cases of exploitation are not to promote socioeconomic endeavors or enduring peace in countries where those external agents come from. Those rewards end up in the pockets of individuals, who then proceed to finance yet another chain of ethnic wars in their own countries through political mobilization.

Fifth, the protection of minorities in Africa is something that our governments should take seriously and even incorporate in national constitutions. But caution should be exercised not to turn minorities into centers of privilege, if only to avoid political backlash.

Sixth, there is a need to recognize women as agents of change and promoters of peace and reconciliation through domestic peace education. Therefore, women should be given an opportunity to play that role and to participate equally and at all levels of decision making in the activities that affect their lives. Furthermore, human rights education should be part of the school curricula starting at the elementary school level, and women should be trained to train additional trainers. Moreover, human rights education programs should be focused on the promotion of tolerance, reconciliation, friendship, and comradeship and the value of life among peoples of different racial, cultural, ethnic, and religious backgrounds.

Seventh, a high correlation exists between violations of human rights, including economic, social, and cultural rights, on the one hand and what we call ethnic conflicts in Africa on the other hand. In situations where ethnic groups inhabiting areas with minerals and natural resources have been forced to participate in violence and conflict, you often find that foreign agents in collaboration with local politicians have been exploiting the wealth of those mineral-rich areas without any development endeavors ploughed back into those areas. In such instances, it is capital flight or exploitation that provokes violent acts and not necessarily ethnicity. Full participation in political life for all, nondiscriminatory treatment of all regions and ethnic groups within the country of concern, respect for the rights of minorities, as well as accountability, transparency, and respect for the rule of law, therefore, constitute an essential element for any conflict prevention strategy.

Finally, the international media, especially the Western media, should desist from inflaming situations of protest and differences in Africa by reducing them to the level of ethnicity in origin and without making honest and in-depth searches as to their real causes. You cannot prevent a conflict whose causes you do not understand. The time has, therefore, come for us to stop looking at the complexities of our societies through the prism of foreign or traditional anthropology. Africa should aim at training its own people to be capable of understanding the dynamics and complexities of

African society. African governments should also strengthen their democratization programs for the full enjoyment of human rights and fundamental freedoms by all their people regardless of their religion, ethnic background, political opinion, or gender. Most fundamentally, in the name of common humanity, international cooperation, and solidarity, our external friends in the North should consider helping the OAU Mechanism for Conflict Prevention, Management and Resolutions with the necessary resources to enable the Organization to implement its program for securing durable peace, security, stability, and development.

NOTES

The views expressed in this chapter are those of the author and not necessarily those of the Organization of African Unity.

1. See *Report of the UN Secretary General on the Causes of Conflicts and the Promotion of Durable Peace and Sustainable Development in Africa*, 1998, accessed at www.un.org/ecosocdev/geninfo/afrec/sgreport/index.html.

4

♨

Exclusion, Marginalization, and Political Mobilization: The Road to Hell in the Great Lakes

René Lemarchand

If the fate of the African continent evokes hopelessness, nowhere is this sense of despair more evident than in former Belgian Africa. No other region has experienced a more deadly combination of external aggression, foreign-linked factionalism, interstate violence, factional strife, and ethnic rivalries. Nowhere else in Africa has genocide exacted a more horrendous price in human lives lost, economic and financial resources squandered, and developmental opportunities wasted. The scale of the disaster is in sharp contrast with the polite indifference of the international community in the face of this unprecedented human tragedy. What has been called Africa's first world war has yet to attract the world's attention.

The marginal ranking of Africa in the scale of international priorities is one obvious explanation for this generalized lack of interest in the Great Lakes crisis. Another is the sheer complexity of the forces involved. When one considers the multiplicity of political actors, domestic and foreign; the fluidity of factional alliances; the spillover of ethnic violence across boundaries; and the extreme fragmentation of political arenas, it is easy to see why the international community should have second thoughts about the wisdom of a concerted peace initiative. No other crisis in the continent seems more resistant to conflict resolution.

Adding to the confusion is the plethora of competing explanatory models that come to mind. How much credence should one give to Paul Collier's recent thesis that "it is the feasibility of predation which determines the risk of conflict" (Collier 2000:4)? Is the crisis in the Great Lakes an extreme example of the "criminalization of the state" (Bayart et al. 1997)? Or should one turn instead to Jeffrey Herbst's demographic argument and look for evidence of low population density, combined with the weakness of state boundaries, as an explanation for Kabila's inability to effectively broadcast the power of the Congo state (Herbst 2000)? If Samuel Huntington's "clash of civilizations" model hardly applies, what of his contention that the "kin-country syndrome" is the key to an understanding of regional instability (Huntington 1996:272–274)? To these questions we shall return.

This chapter offers a different prism to view the roots of the crisis. The key concept around which much of this discussion revolves is that of exclusion. Political, economic, and social exclusion are seen as the principal dimensions that need to be explored if we are to grasp the dynamics of domestic and interstate violence in the Great Lakes. This is not meant to minimize the significance of external aggression. The capacity of Rwanda and Uganda to effectively project their military force into eastern Congo, albeit with mixed results for both, is unquestionably a major contributory factor to regional instability. External intervention, however, must be seen in the broader historical context of the forces that have shaped the tragic destinies of former Belgian Africa. Briefly stated, the central pattern that recurs time and again is one in which ethnic polarization paves the way for political exclusion, exclusion eventually leading to insurrection, insurrection to repression, and repression to massive flows of refugees and internally displaced persons, which in turn become the vectors of further instability. The involvement of external actors, as we shall see, is inseparable from the perceived threats posed by mobilized refugee diasporas to their countries of origin as well as to specific communities within the host country.

HISTORICAL BACKDROP

Let us begin with a brief reminder of basic historical facts.

Ranked Societies, Exclusion, and Insurrection

In the context of ranked societies like Rwanda and Burundi, where a two-tier structure of ethnic domination tended to vest power and privilege in the hands of the Tutsi minority, political exclusion was the rule for roughly 80 percent of the population, consisting essentially of Hutu peasants. In Rwanda the Hutu revolution of 1959–1962—powerfully assisted if not engineered by the Belgian authorities—brought to a close the era of Tutsi hegemony (Lemarchand 1970). While opening the way for the enthronement of the representatives of the Hutu, an estimated 200,000 Tutsi were forced into exile in neighboring and other countries between 1959 and 1963—approximately 70,000 to Uganda, 25,000 to the Congo, and 50,000 to Burundi (Guichaoua 1992:17).

In Burundi, by contrast, where the "premise of inequality" was far less institutionalized and social relations were more complex, ethnic polarization proceeded at a slower pace, allowing the Tutsi elites to consolidate their grip on the government and the army long before they faced the challenge of a servile insurrection. Every attempt made by Hutu leaders to overthrow the government—in 1965, 1969, and 1972—ended up in dismal failure, each time resulting in extremely brutal repression, culminating in 1972 with the genocidal massacre of anywhere from 100,000 to 200,000 Hutu (Lemarchand 1995). Not until 1993, with the election of a Hutu, Melchior Ndadaye, to the presidency, were the Hutu given to believe that they would soon control their political destinies, only to be robbed of this opportunity on October 21, when a radical faction within the all-Tutsi army killed the newly elected president, the speaker, and the deputy speaker of the National Assembly and overthrew the government. Six months later, after three and a half years of bitter civil war, opposing the predominantly Tutsi troops of the Rwanda Patriotic Front (RPF) against the Forces Armées Rwandaises (FAR), Rwanda became the scene of one of the biggest genocides of the last century: Between 600,000 and 800,000 people, mostly Tutsi, were sent to their graves by Hutu militias (*Interahamwe*) and army men (Prunier 1997).

The "Banyarwanda" of Eastern Congo

Until then, the principal victims of political exclusion were the Tutsi of Rwanda and the Hutu of Burundi. Their closest analogues in eastern Congo were the "Banyarwanda," a label that belies the diversity of their ethnic and regional origins (Willame 1997). Included under that rubric were three distinctive communities: (1) Hutu and Tutsi who had settled in the Kivu region long before the advent of colonial rule, including a group of ethnic Tutsi indigenous to south Kivu (located in the Mulenge region) known as Banyamulenge; (2) descendants of migrant workers, mostly Hutu, brought in from Rwanda in the 1930s and 1940s under the auspices of the colonial state; and (3) tens of thousands of Tutsi refugees who fled Rwanda in the wake of the 1959 Hutu revolution, and hence referred to as "fifty-niners." By 1981, following the promulgation of a retroactive nationality law, the Banyarwanda were for all intents and purposes denied citizenship since none could possibly meet the legal requirement of proof of ancestral residence before October 18, 1908, when the Congo Free State formally became a Belgian colony. By 1990, at the time of the RPF invasion of Rwanda, Banyarwanda resentment of Mobutu's exclusionary policies were matched by their growing sympathy for the cause of the RPF. Many did in fact join the ranks of the RPF and fought alongside their Ugandan kinsmen. By then, both groups shared the deepest anxieties about their future in their respective countries of asylum. They would soon become critically important actors in the regional political equation (Reyntjens 1999).

The devastating ripple effects of the Rwanda cataclysm were felt immediately in eastern Congo. The sudden influx of over a million Hutu refugees across the border, accompanied by the fleeing remnants of the FAR and *Interahamwe*, brought a major environmental and human disaster to the region, while at the same time triggering a drastic reordering of ethnic loyalties. Almost overnight the Banyarwanda community split into warring factions, pitting Hutu against Tutsi (Lemarchand 1997; Reyntjens 1999). Meanwhile, in the interstices of the Hutu-Tutsi tug-of-war emerged a shadowy constellation of armed factions, the Mai-Mai. Drawn from ethnic groups indigenous to the region—Hunde, Nande, Nyanga, Bashi, and so on—to this day the Mai-Mai are notorious for the fickleness of their political options, the fluidity of their political alignments, and their addiction to violence. Swiftly responding to changing circumstances, they first turned against Hutu elements, then against local Tutsi, and ultimately against the Rwandan invaders and their Congolese allies.

1996: The Turning of the Tide

The destruction of the refugee camps by units of the Rwandan Patriotic Army (RPA) in October 1996 marks a turning point in the tortured history of the region. It signals the meteoric rise to power of Laurent-Desiré Kabila as the deus ex machina imposed by Museveni upon Kagame to lead the anti-Mobutist crusade under the banner of the Alliance des Forces Démocratiques pour la Libération du Congo (AFDL). While the AFDL and its Rwandan allies fought their way to Kinshasa, forcing Mobutu to throw in the sponge in May 1997, the shooting up of the camps released a huge flow of refugees across the Congo, fleeing the RPA's search-and-destroy operations. The attack on the camps also marks the entry of new international actors in the Congolese arena, most notably Rwanda and Uganda. For a brief moment, the surge of popular enthusiasm caused by the overthrow of the Mobutist dictatorship seemed to submerge factional and ethnic divisions—but only for a while. With a substantial presence of Rwandans on the ground acting in military and administrative capacities, anti-Tutsi feelings rapidly spread among a broad spectrum of the Congolese population in North and South Kivu, in the Katanga as well as in the capital city. Unable or unwilling to discriminate between Rwandan Tutsi, on the one hand, and Banyamulenge and fifty-niners on the other, for the self-styled "Congolais authentiques" anyone with the looks of a Tutsi would be fair game when push came to shove in July 1998.

1998: The Turning of the Tables

The next and most critical stage in the Great Lakes saga came in August 1998 when, sensing the liabilities involved in his dependency on Tutsi "advisers," the new king of the Congo took the fateful step of turning against the kingmakers, thus paving the way for a replay of 1996. Yet the state of the play on the ground was now very different from the quasi-unanimous crusade of 1996. As 1998 drew to a close, no fewer than six African armies were involved, albeit to a greater or lesser extent, on the side of Kabila (Angola, Namibia, Zimbabwe, Chad, Congo-Brazzaville, and the Sudan); against this formidable coalition stood the fragile alliance of Rwanda and Uganda and their Congolese client faction, the Congolese Rally for Democracy (CRD), soon to break into two rival groups; while a third rebel faction emerged in northern Congo, Jean-Pierre Bemba's Movement for the Liberation of the Congo (MLC).

The 1998 crisis brought to light an immediate hardening of anti-Tutsi sentiment throughout the Congo, and particularly in North and South Kivu, where it was now the turn of the Congolese "autochthons" (i.e., non-Banyarwanda) to pay the price of exclusion. Denied all possibility of political participation, economically exploited by Rwandan interlopers, trampled underfoot by foreign occupying forces, their most salient common characteristic is their visceral hatred of all Tutsi, whether of Rwandan or Congolese origins. Little wonder if today the Mai-Mai are increasingly training their gun sights on RPA units operating in the Kivu—and in the process unleashing a terrible retribution upon civilian populations—as well as on the Banyamulenge, even though the latter fully qualify as autochthons. Evidently, their deep historic roots in South Kivu do not exonerate them of the suspicion of being in league with the Kagame government. The truth is that the Banyamulenge and ethnic Tutsi in general are anything but united in their attitude toward Kigali. Many Banyamulenge resent the fact that they have been instrumentalized by Kagame, that they have become mere pawns in the regional poker game. Most of them, however, privately admit that Rwanda's military presence in eastern Congo is their sole protection against another genocidal carnage.

To sum up: Exclusion does not just suddenly materialize out of the primeval fissures of the plural society; its roots are traceable to the rapid mobilization of ethnic identities unleashed by the democratization of societies built on the "premise of inequality" and to the profoundly discriminatory implications of public policies directed against specific ethnic communities. In all three states, however, refugee flows were the crucial factor behind the rapid polarization of ethnic feelings in the host countries. Everywhere, refugee-generating violence has produced violence-generating refugee flows.

DIMENSIONS OF EXCLUSION

In the context of this discussion, political exclusion means the denial of political rights to specific ethnic or ethnoregional communities, most notably the right to vote, organize political parties, freely contest elections, and thus become full participants in the political life of their country. Obvious cases are the Tutsi in postrevolutionary Rwanda and the Hutu in Burundi until the 1993 aborted transition to multiparty democracy (some might argue that relatively little changed since then), to which must be added the Banyarwanda of eastern Congo, after being disenfranchised by the 1981 nationality law, as well as the Tutsi refugee diaspora of Uganda, for whom naturalization was never envisaged. Admittedly, political exclusion is a relative concept both in terms of the range of disabilities suffered by the excluded communities and the context in which it occurs. It is easy to see why, for example, in the context of Mobutu's dictatorship, the withdrawal of citizenship rights from the Banyarwanda did not produce the same violent reaction as the refusal of the Burundi authority to recognize the victory of the Hutu at the polls in 1965. Again, it is one thing for a minority to be politically excluded and quite another for a group representing 80 percent of the population to be reduced to a silent majority, as is clearly the case today for the Hutu of Rwanda and, to a lesser extent, in Burundi.

Economic exclusion, on the other hand, refers first and foremost to the denial of traditional rights to land. Given that land is the principal economic resource of peasant communities, denial of access to land use inevitably implies economic impoverishment or worse. Here, again, contextual factors are important. Although rising population densities and environmental degradation are everywhere a fundamental aspect of the land problem, nowhere is the problem more acute than where land has been redistributed to meet the needs of machine politics (as in pre-genocide Rwanda) or reallocated to new claimants (as happened in North Kivu in the 1970s when tens of thousands of acres of land were bought off by Tutsi fifty-niners), or where rural insecurity becomes a pretext for massive population transfers in regroupment camps (as in Burundi and northern Rwanda).

Social exclusion goes hand in hand with the erosion of traditional social networks and the collapse of the safety nets that once supported the traditional social order of peasant communities. The result is a growing marginalization of rural youth. Deprived of the minimal economic security and coping mechanisms built into the customary social nets, yet denied the opportunity to make their mark in life through alternative channels, their life chances are almost nil.

To be sure, political exclusion does not always imply economic exclusion. If there is little doubt that the 1959 Hutu revolution in Rwanda received its impetus from the political exclusion of Western-educated Hutu elites, it is equally clear that economic exclusion had relatively little to do with the Hutu-Tutsi conflict. One might even argue that in some instances withdrawal of political rights translates into rising levels of economic achievement for the excluded community, as shown by the large number of relatively well-to-do Tutsi entrepreneurs in pre-genocide Rwanda. Nonetheless, processes of political, economic, and social exclusion are closely interconnected: Just as refugee diasporas have exacerbated the problem of natural resource scarcities in the host countries, most conspicuously in eastern Congo and to a lesser extent in Uganda, the resultant shrinkage of cultivable land, along with the dislocation of traditional social networks, must be seen as major contributory factors to the marginalization of youth and the rise of armed militias. The cumulative effect of these phenomena is nowhere more potentially disruptive than where specific ethnic communities bear the full brunt of economic and social exclusion.

Refugee flows provide the conceptual link among all three forms of exclusion. Not that refugees are always on the losing side, economically, although in most cases they are. The more important point is that the side effects of large numbers of refugees moving into any given country of asylum translate into severe economic and social hardships for the host society. Rising commodity prices, the rapid depletion of environmental resources, and the frequency of petty crimes within and outside the camps, not to mention the systematic raiding of cattle, crops, and vehicles (as happened in eastern Congo in 1994), are all part of the catalogue of deprivations inflicted on the host communities. In such circumstances, refugees become an easy target for politicians eager to translate diffuse grievances into political capital. In different circumstances, however, they can also be mobilized by opposition groups to strengthen their hand against domestic foes, as indeed happened in Uganda in the 1980s and in Burundi in the 1960s. Refugee populations, in short, have served as a major political resource, either as foil or as a source of support.

THE POLITICS OF MOBILIZED DIASPORAS

Since 1959 the multiplicity of crises experienced by Rwanda and Burundi have generated four major refugee flows: (1) Between 1959 and 1963, an estimated 150,000 Tutsis fled Rwanda in the wake of the Hutu revolution, the majority seeking asylum in Uganda, Burundi, and eastern Congo; (2) the second major exodus involved approximately 300,000 Hutu from Burundi fleeing the 1972 genocidal massacres of Hutu by the Tutsi-dominated army, most of them headed for Tanzania and Rwanda; (3) the next wave of

Hutu refugees from Burundi, numbering perhaps as many as 400,000, of whom more than half ended up in Rwanda, followed the reciprocal massacres of Tutsi and Hutu triggered by the assassination of President-Elect Melchior Ndadaye on October 21, 1993, adding tens of thousands to the refugee camps in Tanzania, Rwanda, and South Kivu; and (4) the fourth and largest outpouring of refugees, in 1994, involved approximately 2 million Hutu from Rwanda fleeing the avenging arm of the FPR. Over a million settled in eastern Congo, the rest in Tanzania.

All of the above qualify as mobilized diasporas, in that they shared specific political objectives, were politically organized, and made a sustained effort to consolidate their grip on the refugee population. This is still the case for the Hutu diaspora from Burundi, and what little is left of its counterpart from Rwanda. Ultimately their overriding goal was to return to their homeland as citizens, by force if necessary. So far only the Tutsi refugees, under the banner of the FPR, after thirty-five years of exile, were able to do so.

But if the saga of the Tutsi diaspora is a success story of sorts—but at what price!—its early history is a tale of consistent failure, political and military, causing enormous bloodshed inside Rwanda, a situation for which there are tragic recent parallels among the Hutu diasporas from Burundi and Rwanda.

Refugees are first and foremost an object of humanitarian concern; only at a later stage, after metamorphosing into a mobilized diaspora, do they emerge as a source of political concern for domestic, regional, and international actors. The obstacles in the way of effective political mobilization cover a wide gamut: the material and emotional costs of uprootedness, the geographical dispersal of the camps, the inadequacy of communication facilities, the factional rivalries, the constraints on political activities imposed by the host country—such are the usual handicaps faced by refugee diasporas. These disabilities vary enormously over time, however, and from one setting to another. The single most important conditioning factor, however, lies in the receptivity of the host country to the political goals and organizational efforts of refugee communities.

The Fifty-Niners in Eastern Congo: Inyenzi and Mulelistes

A brief comparative glance at the record of the first Tutsi diaspora in the early 1960s (the fifty-niners) with that of the second generation of refugee warriors in the 1990s is instructive in this regard (Reyntjens 1992). Even more revealing is the comparison with the Hutu diasporas.

Organizational strength, internal cohesion, leadership skills, the ability to draw maximum tactical advantage from the domestic politics of the host country: These are the key ingredients that spell the difference between success and failure. On each count, the record of the Tutsi fifty-niners can only be described as dismal. Though formally affiliated to the monarchist Union Nationale Rwandaise (Unar), the party virtually disintegrated after its leadership was forced into exile. While some Unaristes joined hands with the Muleliste rebellion in eastern Congo in 1964–1965, a small group went to communist China for military training; others, labeled *inyenzi* ("cockroaches") by the new Rwanda government, opted for a "direct action" strategy and proceeded to launch armed raids from Burundi, the Congo, and Uganda, only to be repulsed—at great cost to themselves and Tutsi civilians inside Rwanda—by the Rwandan National Guard and their Belgian advisers (Reyntjens 1992). Despite substantial support from a group of radical Tutsi politicians in Bujumbura (but not from the Crown), they never were able to translate this informal alliance into an effective military posture. In eastern Congo, their tactical alliance with the Banyamulenge of South Kivu proved short-lived; the Banyamulenge rapidly switched sides after the setbacks inflicted to the Mulelistes by the ANC. Even more damaging to their ultimate goals was their international image as crypto-communists in league with communist China.

The Second-Generation Tutsi Diaspora: Uganda

The second generation of Tutsi exiles drew important lessons from their elders' inability to get their act together. None were more aware of the necessity to clean up their act than the Ugandan exiles who provided the spearhead of the military crusade that ultimately led to the capture of power in Kigali in July 1994. Though space limitations do not permit a full discussion of their troubled history, most observers would agree that the key to their success lies as much in their organizational skills as in their ability to make the most of the opportunities offered by the rise in 1981 of the anti-Obote guerilla movement headed by Yoweri Museveni, the National Resistance Army (NRA). Already in the 1970s, the Rwandan Alliance for National Unity (RANU) provided a coherent organizational frame for mobilizing support within and outside Uganda, collecting funds, coordinating cultural activities, reaching out to the international community, and lobbying for their right to return to Rwanda. Between 1981 and 1986, when the NRA seized power in Kampala, a solid phalanx of second-generation fifty-niners joined Museveni's movement, fought pitched battles in the Luwero triangle at a cost of 60,000 killed in action, and ultimately gained strategic access to Museveni's security apparatus when two of their officers, Fred Rwigema and Paul Kagame, rose respectively to the positions of deputy minister of defence and deputy chief of military intelligence. Meanwhile, a series of initiatives from Tutsi exiles in Uganda and the United States led to the birth, in 1987, of the Rwanda Patriotic Front

(RPF), and the tacit endorsement by many of its leaders of the military option of a return by force. On the eve of the October 1, 1990, attack on Rwanda, the RPF had grown into a powerful politico-military organization, combining political mobilization and military training with wide-ranging lobbying activities in the United States and Europe. By then, its recruitment net extended to Tutsi exile communities in Burundi, Kenya, Tanzania, and eastern Congo, infusing further strength into its ranks. Only after its capture of power on July 4, 1994, did the Rwandan Patriotic Army (RPA) develop into a formidable military machine, capable effectively of projecting its muscle into eastern Congo and beyond.

The Hutu Diasporas

If the destinies of the RPF were served by an exceptionally good fortune, the same cannot be said of the Burundi Hutu diasporas. Although the 1972 diaspora gave birth to the Parti de la Libération du Peuple Hutu (Palipehutu) in the Mishamo refugee camp in Tanzania, at no time was the party able to aggregate a range of political and military resources comparable to those of the RPF; its leadership never was able to match the organizational and strategic talent of a Rwigema or a Paul Kagame, let alone the latter's diplomatic skill in reaching out to external actors. At no time was the party able to capitalize on anything like the extraordinary good luck of the FPR in Uganda in the early 1980s. Burundi exiles are notorious for their lack of internal cohesion (Turner 1998). Their history is one of incessant splits, whether in Europe, in Rwanda, or in Tanzania. Their fissiparous characteristics became even more evident after the 1993 exodus and the emergence of several military wings of rival parties, the Front de Libération National (Frolina), the Forces pour la Défense de la Démocratie (FDD), and the division of the Palipehutu into three separate factions. Though some are said to draw benefits from the smuggling networks in Kigoma, and more recently from the shipment of arms from Zimbabwe and Kinshasa (International Crisis Group 1999:20), their resource base is hopelessly inadequate for the task at hand: "All of the rebel groups (in Tanzania) complain of the lack of funding, arms and other resources necessary to carry out a sustained military campaign in Burundi" (International Crisis Group 1999:20). Again, compared to the RPF's ability to draw international support (most notably from the U.S. Committee for Refugees in Washington) and visibility, the performance of the refugee factions on that score is less than impressive. "The main complaint of the rebels," notes a recent International Crisis Group report, "is the lack of international support. As one rebel leader said: 'we don't have anyone to support us the way the Banyamulenge are supported by Rwanda and Uganda' (International Crisis Group 1999:20).

The case of the 1994 refugees from Rwanda is unlike any other in terms of the magnitude of the human flow, the volume of weaponry transferred, the tightness of the political and military encadrement, the extensive support it received from the Mobutist state, its devastating impact on the natural environment, its catalytic effect on ethnic loyalties, the questions it raises about the political implications of humanitarian aid, and, last but not least, the ultimate tragedy of its "final solution." To review each of these dimensions would take us too far afield. Suffice to note that the seriousness of the threats posed to the new Rwandan state was without parallel in the history of mobilized diasporas. Exceptional circumstances called for exceptional measures. The destruction of the camps in October 1996 by the RPA was part of a wider underlying design, however, in other words not just to "secure" Rwanda's western border, but (1) to extend the search-and-destroy operations to the campsites in South Kivu and in so doing deal a crippling blow to the Burundi refugees mobilized under the banner of the FDD, (2) to deny Uganda's armed opposition movements (notably Tabliq and the West Nile Liberation Front) access to safe havens in the Congo, and (3) to pave the way for Kabila's "second coming" (Lemarchand 1997). On each count the Kagame strategy succeeded beyond all expectations, at least in the short run. From a wider perspective, and with the benefit of hindsight, it is clear that the ultimate goal of the operation—making the Congo safe for Rwanda—has fallen somewhat short of the master planners' expectations.

The Tools of Political Mobilization

As this discussion makes clear, contextual variables are of critical importance in explaining the success or failure of mobilized diasporas. Nonetheless, agency also matters. Context alone is not enough to explain the different tools and techniques that enter into processes of mobilization, ranging from coercion to ideological manipulation, from rumormongering to arms smuggling, from practices and attitudes borrowed from the world of the invisible to the use and misuse of information designed to raise the political awareness of the rank and file. Not all of these are productive of success. Coercive mobilization by some factions of the Hutu diaspora has often had the opposite effect of what was intended, causing tremendous disaffection among civilians and bitter rivalries among exile factions. What some factions view as legitimate means of ideological mobilization—such as the diffusion of historical narratives designed to demonize the Tutsi enemy, a favorite Palipehutiste technique (Lemarchand 1995)—others tend to reject. Recourse to magic looms large in the arsenal of Congolese factions, notably among the Mai-Mai and the Congolese Rally for Democracy (CRD), sometimes with disastrous consequences for the families and communities to whom, wrongly or rightly, magic powers have been attributed. Next to the availability of funding and weapons, information (or misinformation) is of critical importance. On that score, the performance of the Tutsi diaspora in Uganda ranks far above its Hutu counterparts. Quite aside from its efficiency in collecting funds from exile Tutsi communities and gaining a privileged access to NRA equipment, compared to Hutu refugee movements the Uganda exiles have been remarkably adept at mobilizing support through their skilful manipulation of information. This fact goes far in explaining its capacity to sway international public opinion long after the diaspora had become a nation.

ANOTHER LOOK AT THEORY

What new light do the theories mentioned earlier shed on the dynamics of ethnoregional conflict in the Great Lakes? The answer, in part, depends on how they "fit" into any particular aspect of the crisis.

Let us begin with Huntington. The whole drift of our argument, centered on the concept of exclusion, can be read as a refutation of the "clash of civilization" thesis (Huntington 1996); by the same token, his discussion of the "kin-country syndrome" is of direct relevance to an understanding of the patterns of ethnic mobilization unleashed by refugee diasporas. As our previous discussion makes clear, where ethnic fault lines cut across national boundaries, conflict tends to spill over from one national arena to the next, transforming kin solidarities into a powerful vector of transnational violence. An action-reaction pattern sets in whereby victims in one setting become instigators of violence in the other. Largely missing from Huntington's discussion, however, is sustained attention to mobilization strategies, including the kinds of resources employed to mobilize support.

This is where Collier's article offers some challenging insights. I refer specifically to his analysis of the role of diasporas and access to financial resources as crucial factors in explaining the risk of civil war. On the other hand, serious questions arise as to whether the financial viability of rebel factions, including refugee diasporas, is entirely reducible to the opportunities offered by commodity export economies. If this were the case, the whole of the continent would be tottering on the brink of insurrection. Not just any export commodity but gold and diamonds are the rebels' best friends.

Whether through gem trading or any other source of profits, financial viability matters. There is no denying the cardinal importance of the looting of gold and diamond resources in eastern Congo in the funding of war effort by Kigali and Kampala, and of the deadly rivalries over the loot in pitting Rwanda against Uganda in Kisangani. Nonetheless, "financial viability" only tells part of the story. Crucial as they are in explaining the failure or success of mobilized diasporas, contextual opportunities are not limited to financial viability; equally important is the political viability of rebel and refugee movements, most notably their ability to negotiate political and military support. This is true not only of the CRD factions today, but also was certainly the case for the second-generation Tutsi refugees in Uganda in the 1980s.

Where the Collier thesis seems most vulnerable is in the rejection of objective socioeconomic indicators as a source of civil violence: "Objective measures of social grievance, such as inequality, a lack of democracy, and ethnic and religious divisions, have no systematic effect on risk . . . because civil wars occur when rebel organizations are financially viable" (Collier 2000:1). Quite aside from the fact that the argument simply doesn't hold up in the face of the overwhelming evidence to the contrary—a fact that Collier might conceivably explain away by relegating Rwanda, Burundi, and eastern Congo to deviant cases—one wonders why one set of independent variables (objective measures of social grievance) should exclude the other (financial viability).

Categorically dismissing rebellion as "protest motivated by genuine and extreme grievance," Collier offers a striking analogy: "For a few moments suspend disbelief," he writes, "and suppose that most rebel movements are pretty close to being large-scale variants of organized crime. The discourse would be exactly the same as if they were protest movements" (Collier 2000:3). Nowhere, however, does he consider the alternative proposition that the state might qualify as the criminal and the rebels as victims of state crimes. This is, of course, the central argument set forth by Bayart et al. in their recent work on the criminalization of the state (Bayart et al. 1997). This is not meant to deny the propensity of rebel and refugees, and refugees turned rebels, to engage in criminal activities, yet it is important to note that the phrase covers a wide spectrum of illegal activities, and that such criminal activities often pale in comparison with those carried out by the state. Rwanda under Habyalimana, Zaire under Mobutu, and the Burundi armed forces under Buyoya all exhibit, to some degree or another, at one point or another, what can only be described as criminal behavior of the worst kind, including political assassination, theft, and corruption on a grand scale. It is difficult to avoid the conclusion that the result has been to promote huge social and economic inequalities, along with corresponding "genuine and extreme grievances," and thus pave the way for the exclusionary policies that lie at the heart of ethnic violence in the Great Lakes.

The Herbst thesis has the merit of looking at a range of variables seldom taken into account by political scientists: the combined effect on state failure of low population densities, weak and artificial boundaries, and the resultant inability of the state to control its hinterland; this, he adds, is in striking contrast with the historical record of European states, all of which have experienced "the brutality of interstate war" as a major ingredient of state consolidation (Herbst 2000:272). On each of these counts, however, the recent history of the Great Lakes offers massive counterfactual evidence. The region claims the highest population density in the continent; the precolonial boundaries of the interlacustrine kingdoms of Rwanda and Burundi were fairly well delineated, at least by comparison with the rest of Africa; control of these states over the hinterland was relatively well established; and the "brutality of interstate war" was a major feature of their precolonial histories, though by no means comparable to the devastation caused by the internal and interstate wars currently ravaging the region. What Herbst leaves out of the picture is the impact of colonial and postcolonial history. It leaves out what Crawford Young (1965) has so ably brought into view—the enduring disabilities arising from the impact of the colonial state on African societies. Predictably, it makes no reference to the multifaceted crises of exclusion and social marginalization around which much of this discussion revolves, and for which there are many parallels in the continent. Only by confusing optimism with fantasy, and reality with illusion, can one take comfort in the view, implicit in the Herbst thesis, that the violent confrontations in former Belgian Africa will ultimately bring to the region the benefits of state consolidation along a blood-stained path similar to the one historically taken by European states.

POLICY IMPLICATIONS

By postulating exclusion as a crucial dimension of the Great Lakes crisis, I do not mean to suggest that its conceptual opposite is the only solution to the region's woes. Inclusion is a theme that admits of many variations. It can easily mask a policy of co-optation and serve as a substitute for a genuine sharing of power; carried to an extreme, with little or no attention paid to contextual realities, the result may be chronic instability, as happened in Burundi in 1995, following the so-called Convention of Government of 1994. The diffusion of ethnic violence across national boundaries, sustained by external forces, imposes severe limitations on the benefits of power sharing.

The case of Burundi is instructive in this respect. A key provision of the precarious peace deal worked out in Arusha, Tanzania, in July 2000, through Nelson Mandela's painstaking facilitating efforts, involves a broadly based three-year transitional government incorporating the representatives of fifteen parties, almost evenly distributed between predominantly Tutsi and Hutu parties. For the next eighteen months a Tutsi, Pierre Buyoya, will serve as president and a Hutu, Domitien Ndaziye, as vice president; during the following eighteen-month period, the roles will be reversed. This power-sharing arrangement is bolstered by more fundamental concessions to the Hutu majority, such as a commitment to restructuring the all-Tutsi army on the basis of ethnic parity. Demands that until recently were nonnegotiable have now been met, such as the presence of a 1,400-strong South African peacekeeping force; others will be negotiated in months ahead, such as the restructuring of the army, the dismantling of regroupment camps, and the appointment of an international judicial commission to address issues of justice and impunity. Incentives to cooperate go beyond the allocation of portfolios to a wide array of coalition partners. To the extent that the Burundi state is becoming less hegemonic and more open to the demands of the Hutu majority, it has gone a long way toward promoting a climate of trust. Nor has the international community faltered in its efforts to reward cooperative behavior, as shown by the promise of a generous aid package from the European community ($440 million).

Despite efforts to widen the scope of Hutu-Tutsi cooperation, the Arusha framework faces an uncertain future. Inclusionary strategies have failed so far to convince the leaders of two extremist Hutu rebel groups, the Forces pour la Défense de la Démocratie (FDD) and the Palipehutu-FLN (Forces Nationales de Libération), to lay down their arms. That their obduracy is in part motivated by the financial and military support they have come to expect from external actors—whether from Zimbabwe or Congo-Kinshasa, or from their ethnic kinsmen in the Congo or Tanzania—is reasonably clear. Equally plain is that Hutu extremism is bound to generate a response in kind from Tutsi hard-liners. Expectations of strategic assistance from external actors are not limited to any one group. They constitute major incentives for extremists at both ends of the ethnic spectrum not to cooperate in power-sharing arrangements.

If so, there are compelling reasons for encouraging the full implementation of the Lusaka accords (1998), especially as regards the withdrawal of foreign armed forces, the disarming of the so-called negative forces (the *Interahamwe* militias and Mai-Mai factions), and the resumption of an inter-Congolese dialogue. The success of the Arusha accords is intimately linked to a global settlement in the Congo. Only if the rebel factions in Burundi are deprived of the support of participants (i.e., Zimbabwe or Congo-Kinshasa) will they join in the peace process or at least desist from violence. The same is true of the rebel RCD factions in the Congo, currently supported by Uganda and Rwanda.

Given the considerable economic stakes they have in the conflict, neither Rwanda nor Uganda are likely to envisage a withdrawal of their armies unless faced with vigorous pressures from the international community. Though providing convenient justification for their presence in eastern Congo, security concerns are of secondary importance for Presidents Kagame and Museveni; far more significant as a policy imperative are the enormous profits derived from the wholesale plunder of the Congo's mineral wealth. This is where a major reappraisal of strategic priorities is needed from donors, specifically from the World Bank, the United States, and Great Britain. By turning a blind eye to the "imperial" designs of Rwanda and Uganda in eastern Congo while at the same time rewarding their economic performance, donors are in effect subsidizing their war effort. The time has come to recognize the fundamental contradiction involved in the pro forma support of the Lusaka accords and assistance policies designed to undermine their full implementation.

A more fundamental contradiction exists between the ethos of participatory politics and the exclusionary implications of the foreign-linked clientelism operating in much of the Great Lakes region. Reinforcing the neopatrimonial features of their domestic politics, Rwanda and Uganda have developed multiple linkages—economic, military, and political—with their respective client factions, but these linkages extend far beyond the boundaries of the Great Lakes. Corporate interests in the West and elsewhere in the world also have stakes in the rents generated through the illicit exploitation of the Congo's resources. The unpalatable truth is that the multiplicity of interests in support of the regional status quo far exceeds the pressures of the UN for implementing the Lusaka accords. Nonetheless, no matter how daunting the obstacles ahead, Lusaka is the only road map for charting a new course toward peace. From all the evidence, this basic truth has yet to sink in among certain key members of the international community.

REFERENCES

Bayart, Jean-François, Stephen Ellis, and Beatrice Hibou. 1997. *La Criminalisation de l'Etat en Afrique*. Paris: Editions Complexe.

Collier, Paul. 2000. *Economic Causes of Civil Conflict and Their Implications for Policy*. Washington, DC: World Bank.

Guichaoua, André. 1992. *Le problème des réfugiés Rwandais et des populations Banyarwanda dans la région des Grands Lacs*. Geneva: UN High Commissioner for Refugees.

Herbst, Jeffrey. 2000. *States and Power in Africa: Comparative Lessons in Authority and Control*. Princeton, NJ: Princeton University Press.

Huntington, Samuel. 1996. *The Clash of Civilizations and the Remaking of World Order*. New York: Simon & Schuster.

International Crisis Group. 1999. *Burundian Refugees in Tanzania: The Key Factor to the Burundi Peace Process.* Brussels: International Crisis Group.

Lemarchand, René. 1970. *Rwanda and Burundi.* London: Pall Mall Press.

———. 1995. *Burundi: Ethnic Conflict and Genocide.* New York: Wilson Center Press; Cambridge University Press.

———. 1997. Patterns of State Collapse and Reconstruction in Central Africa: Reflections on the Crisis in the Great Lakes Region. *Afrika Spectrum* 32:173–193.

Prunier, Gérard. 1997. *The Rwanda Crisis: History of a Genocide.* London: Hurst & Company.

Reyntjens, Filip. 1992. Les mouvements armés de réfugiés Rwandais: Rupture ou continuité? In *Mélanges Pierre Salmon,* ed. G. Thoveron and H. Legros, 170–182. Civilisations, vol. 40, no. 2. Brussels: Institut de Sociologie de l'Université Libre de Bruxelles.

———. 1999. *La Guerre des Grands Lacs.* Paris: L'Harmattan.

Turner, Simon. 1998. Representing the Past in Exile: The Politics of National History among Burundian Refugees. *Refuge* 17 (6):22–28.

Willame, Jean Claude. 1997. *Banyarwanda et Banyamulenge.* Paris: L'Harmattan.

Young, Crawford. 1965. *Politics in the Congo: Decolonization and Independence.* Princeton, NJ: Princeton University Press.

5

❦

Conflicts Start with Words: Fighting Categories in the Chechen Conflict

Valery A. Tishkov

The protagonists, both the leaders and the rank-and-file participants, of today's violent conflicts are often mobilized on the basis of the doctrine and political practice of ethnic nationalism. It maintains that each people—understood not as a territorial entity (*demos*) but as an ethnic community (*ethnos*) or ethnonation—has the right to self-determination, to "its own" state. Even though this doctrine fails to correspond to international legal norms and contradicts national legislation of all the states in the world, and despite its practical impossibility, this is a doctrine with many supporters in today's world. Contemporary "wars of independence" or ethnonationalist conflicts are the most widespread form of violent conflict (Smith 1997), and they are the main challenge to international security. They are also a tool of global and regional rivalries as well as a strategy of local actors to acquire resources, status, and power. Territories of secessionist conflicts often become a hub for international terrorist networks, including those led by radical Islamists.

The Chechen war belongs to this category of violent ethnic conflicts. This characterization as an "ethnic" conflict is not challenged by the fact that non-Chechen nationals are among the leaders and rank-and-file participants on Chechnya's side, nor by the fact that on the opposite side there is a state with a "non-ethnic" military machine. The blurring of ethnic and non-ethnic aspects is the rule rather than the exception in most conflicts. Cases of ethnic conflicts in their "pure form"—with one group acting against another because of some "natural" hostility—are rarely encountered. However, as violence escalates, ethnic or religious affiliation can emerge as the sole principle for the choice of victims, thus completing a process of "ethnicization" of a conflict.

The road to violence in Chechnya and the story of the "small victorious war" of 1994–1996 has already been the subject of historical and political science analysis as well as of enlightening narrations by journalists (Dunlop 1998; Gakayev 1999; Gall and de Waal 1998; Furman 1999; Lieven 1998; Tishkov 1997a, 1997b). My most recent research has disclosed the cultural dynamics of the Chechen war from an anthropological perspective and showed what it means to *live* in a war-torn society (Tishkov 2001, 2004). In spite of an abundance of facts, many aspects are still poorly understood and inadequately interpreted, especially the role of political rhetoric and intellectual mythopoetics in mobilizing protagonists of violence as well as their significance for the process of postconflict reconstruction.

After a decade of fighting and after numerous academic studies and political analysis, it is becoming more and more clear that Chechnya and the Chechens should be considered not only as actors, but also as *a stage and as a role model* in a much wider sociocultural and political context. The phenomenon of violent conflict manifested itself in that society falling victim, or hostage (or, more exactly, surrendering), to a small but powerful group of protagonists of violence, participants in a new geopolitical strategy aiming at global "decommunization," "decolonization," and "islamization."

Chechnya became a victim of this "liberation project." Many representatives of the intellectual and political elite of Russia have stimulated and supported the "Chechen revolution" since the autumn of 1991. In a doctrinal and political sense, Chechnya's "national self-determination" was initiated and legitimated precisely by the Russian (Soviet) ideology and political practice of those years when it seemed to many that along with improving government there was a simpler, more natural way to realize democratic transformations: to create sovereign polities on an ethnic basis and to destroy the "multinational empires" doomed to vanish by the logic of historical law (Starovoitova 1997).

Not even the end of the war in 1996 released Chechnya from the imposed role of a vanguard in fighting against "the last empire." Besides receiving worldwide sympathies as the builders of "the tombstone of Russian power," Chechnya has also been influenced by the import of the most extremist ideologies and of the material resources necessary for continued warfare. Warlordism, Islamic radicalism, and anarchy reigned in Chechnya for about three years. It also seriously affected federal politics and the entire Russian society, especially after a series of terrorist acts in Moscow and other cities. In 1999, with the goal of widening the arena of armed separatism in the name of "true Islam," Chechen rebels launched attacks on western Dagestan, a neighboring republic that is a part of the Russian Federation. In other words, the "freedom" struggle became also an "Islamic" war.

This led to a new cycle of conflict. In August 1999, the Russian federal government started a military campaign to stop the spread of armed separatism and terrorism in the North Caucasus. After the federal army and local loyal militia had regained control of most of Chechnya, the Chechen rebels turned to guerrilla war tactics, aided by a number of foreign mercenaries, committing ambush attacks and terrorist acts against the federal army and local Chechens collaborating with the Russian authorities. As in the first Chechen war, outside financial and other support came mainly from Islamist networks.

Tragically, however, the federal troops committed atrocities and violated the rights of the civilian population during what was officially categorized as an antiterrorist campaign. At the same time, the Russian government and the Chechen provisional administration put a great deal of effort and material resources into restoring basic order and subsistence-level living standards. In March 2003, in a referendum on a new constitution in Chechnya, 90 percent of the votes were in favor of a federation with Russia. Mufti Akhmad Kadyrov was elected president in elections held in October 2003. With limited results, the new authorities in Chechnya are trying to consolidate local anti-separatist forces and to move ahead on the rocky road of postconflict reconstruction.

FIGHTING CATEGORIES

Conflicts start with words and words can kill no less than bullets. In order to fight effectively, one should not only be trained on how to master Kalashnikovs and grenade launchers but also be able to explain why it is necessary to fight, who is the enemy, and why it is the warrior's honor to die for a nation. Without these arguments, people are poor fighters, and for sure this is not the case with Chechens. Those who fought in Chechnya did it in an effective way, so much so that it made some analysts search for fantastic analogies with ancient mythological heroes, like "Aeneas with grenade launcher" in Anatol Lieven's words (Lieven 1998: 327). Moral/ideological justifications are needed not only for those who are in the battlefields but also for those who issue orders, rule frontline communities, organize political rallies, produce illegal gasoline, take hostages for sale, and kill.

These "fighting categories" have their own historical trajectories and are carried by specific propagators. They express vested emotions and interests, they live their own lives amidst elite and mass mentalities, and they can be dismantled only through purposeful efforts to display their destructive natures and their political decrepitude. Some of these categories are a part of sophisticated academic constructions; some are a reflection of an everyday language that embodies and naturalizes a political conflict. Here are some of these "mental killers" that should be disclosed and detained in a framework of postconflict reconstruction.

Neither the cultural nor the geographic/political names are neutral with respect to the Chechen war. It is "Russia," "Moscow," and "Russians" that are chiefly projected as one of the conflicting sides and blamed for the recent tragedy. These names (labels) represent to many people, including Chechens, a quasi-explanatory model of the war, of its reasons and culprits. I noticed that the collective image of Russia, Moscow, and Russians as the culprit is widespread among the Chechens who live in Chechnya.

However, the blame is laid on the direct perpetrators of violence, such as the Russian army; the rest of Russians are merely seen as "passive culprits." In the words of my Chechen informant, Rustam Kaliev, their guilt lies in the fact that "Russians did not protest actively enough and so failed to prevent the war." A Chechen researcher, Zalpa Bersanova, did a serious sociological work during the war and asked in 1995 the following survey question: "Do you regard the Russian people to be guilty of a tragedy that happened to the Chechens?" She received the following results: Among elder people (60–80 years), 15 percent said "Yes" and 67 percent said "No" (18 percent could not answer); among young people (17–30 years) 32 percent said "Yes" and 46 percent said "No" (22 percent could not answer). As Bersanova concluded,

> The Chechens differentiate clearly *Rossiya* (more precise transliteration of the state's title), its authorities, and Russians (*Russkie* as a ethnic entity); and the very fact that, in spite of all sufferings, the Chechen majority does not blame the Russian people speaks for a potential of tolerance on the part of the Chechen (Bersanova 1999:223–249).

The world public is not familiar with this important semantic difference and maintains a simplistic "Russia-Chechnya" dichotomy. Partly, this dichotomy repeats everyday language used in Russia itself, where they are used as synonyms for "center" and "periphery." The problem is that Russia (precisely *Rossiya*) means for many people not more than Moscow and "the Kremlin" as a kind of symbolic center, which does not imply a denial of belonging to one country and of sharing a common citizenship. Chechens are not Russians in ethnic terms but they are *Rossians* in terms of civic and political identities. Cultural/ethnic and civic identities are not mutually exclusive. As Movladi Movsayev, one of the field commanders in Chechnya, told me: "I am a Chechen, but I am a *Rossiaynin* also." It is this predominant feeling of double, nonexclusive identity among Chechens that is deliberately ignored or despised by mentalities and language produced by the conflict.

No doubt, the war drew a more rigid line between the Chechens and others and heightened their sense of distinction not only on the level of group identity. But I cannot accept the premise that my Chechen research collaborators and interviewees are people of another civilization. My materials do not substantiate such a claim. There are certainly marked differences in life situations, also some important distinctive cultural characteristics. Still, I find more in common between a Russian professor in Moscow and a Chechen professor from Grozny than between the latter and a Chechen combatant from a mountain village, even if the professor originates from that same place. The cultural watershed *results* from the conflict, and it divides members of the war-torn society from outsiders and those who are on the fringes of the conflict. In a certain sense, *it is the conflict that constructed Chechens, not vice versa.*

There are many other conflict-generating and conflict-generated metaphors. One of the most mobilizing ones is coined by the Chechen émigré political scientist, Abdurakhman Avtorkhanov, who wrote a book on "nation killing," one of the first painful accounts of the Chechen-Ingush deportation. By scholarly standards, it was a poor book, but after being translated into Russian (Avtorkhanov 1991) and widely circulated in the country in the early 1990s, it became a powerful argument against the state that had permitted and executed *narodoubiistvo* (nation killing) against the Chechens. It has been a form of revenge of the old generation who suffered from Stalin and who wanted to pass this experience down to their fighting grandsons. It resulted in a tragedy for the living generation and for their future, which became hostages of the past traumas. Postconflict reconstruction should learn this lesson of "the burden of the past" and include measures preventing the misuse of history for sponsoring pain, hate, and discontent.

By tracing the language of the conflict, we discovered the conflict-generating logic of transforming a recently invented, politically motivated category of *fighting for freedom* into a category of rigid prescription with considerable moral weight, i.e., into the category of *freedom fighters*. Some of my Chechen informants, who were fighters (*boeviks*), told me how local village mullahs explained to young people what it means to be a *shakhid* (those who fight and die for Islam) first, and then "they selected from each village two most clean and brave young men to serve in Dudayev's national guard" (Akhyad D.). *Freedom fighters* became a common denomination for Chechen combatants among the Western mass media and public. Blatant terrorist acts committed before and during the war were portrayed as being committed by "hostage takers," not terrorists. Thanks to this mild and sympathetic description, the door for potential executors of violence has been left open because outside understanding and even support has been promised.

Some conflict-generating categories are a great predicament for negotiating peace and reconciliation. Among them is the *Chechen independence* as a nonnegotiable category in Dudayev's, Maskhadov's, and other leaders' discourse. Out of this independentist rhetoric came other problematic notions, for example being a "subject of international law," which post-Soviet radicals read unanimously as being recognized as a separate state entity. On the federal side as well, policymakers fight for (or against) words with little substantive meaning. "I do not care what you are negotiating there. In all cases, there should be words that 'Chechnya is a subject of the Federation,'" cried Nikolai Yegorov, the acting minister of nationalities and Yeltsin's special envoy to Chechnya, by phone from a Russian military base, Mozdok. Leaders of the Russian delegation at the negotiations in Vladikavkaz in December 1994 (the days the war in Chechnya started) had tried to convince their superior to accept a milder formula that would have avoided definition of status and would have demanded the simultaneous withdrawal of the federal troops and the disarmament of the Chechen military formations. A rare chance of stopping the war in its infant stage has been lost partly because of verbal cages and verbal instructions limiting the search for innovative peace strategies.

Thus, before starting reconstruction programs, something should be done to bring to public attention the attitudes that clean the road of the conflict and allow Chechens to maintain and rediscover multiple identities as citizens of Russia and as members of the Chechen ethnic group. Otherwise, Chechens are excluded from the country's populace, justifying not only atrocities on the part of the military but also of caging representatives of the whole group into a category of "no-citizens" or "enemy citizens" without rights and privileges.

THE ILLUSION OF "A GREAT VICTORY"

The war did not really end for Chechnya in August 1996. The war went on in the minds and actions of many people, particularly the armed "veterans," the neophyte politicians, and the "warriors of the intellectual front" (poets, journalists, historians, and others). The war was replayed in the daily propaganda of the "great victory," in extolling the Chechen military gallantry, in asserting Chechen superiority over the rest of the world, in cultivating the image of the enemy—Russia and the Russians—and in ideological messianism, particularly in the form of the Caucasian liberation project. The war was also fanned by many outsiders—the inveterate supporters of Chechnya's independence from Russia. Together they generated an exalted, romantic (mytho-poetic) account of history that inspired part of the local society to follow the path of uncompromising secession and further social disruption demanding an independent "national state."

In 1999, Dmitri Furman, editor of the book *Chechnya and Russia: Societies and States*, wrote in the preface,

> The Chechens' resistance and victory were a kind of miracle, which were made possible by the same reasons that had led to the war. If the Chechens had a different system of values and a different historic memory, if they had been led not by ignorant (semiliterate) field commanders, many of them with a criminal past, but by usual ("normal") post-Soviet communist party officials turned nationalists—in a word, if the Chechens were more rational, "modern" people, they would have never risked such a resistance and, still less, would have won. For such a war and a victory they needed complete unwillingness and inability to "bow (subdue) to reality"—only that helps to reverse and overcome this very reality. The Chechen resistance was led by two factors: the desperate resolve by a (the) people that had been subjected to genocide to never let that happen again (similar to the Jews whose tiny state defeated huge Arab armies) and a revolutionary popular upsurge, similar to the victorious French revolutionary wars or the Bolshevik army defeating the flower of old Russia's officers and generals supported by nearly all [the] outside world (Furman 1999:14).

In view of the rise of extreme anti-Semitism in the postwar Chechnya, one may suppose the comparison with the Jews is not exactly flattering to the "Frenchmen of the Caucasus," but the parallels with the French Revolution and the Bolsheviks are quite inspiring to local radicals for they had been nurtured for decades on those heroic images. "The people" (in Furman's terms) developed even further, reaching heroic fantasies and more grandiose projects: "If the Chechens made war with all the available forces, they might go as far as La Manche," declared Aslan Maskhadov soon after his inauguration as the president of Chechnya.

During these three years, Chechnya was moving toward a new war, as if following the advice given by the well-known ultra-radical activist Valeria Novodvorskaya in an interview with Chechen television:

> A peace treaty is a good thing, of course. But knowing how unpredictable Russia is, I would advise the Chechens to trust Allah, but to keep the camel tied up. As long as the Chechens have arms, the peace will be observed. So, they should not lay arms down. Russia is a godless country where Patriarch Alexis II is a KGB man who gives a blessing to Russian soldiers going to war with Chechnya, as if killing civilians was charity, or opposes taking Lenin's mummy out of the Mausoleum. Therefore, the Chechens should by no means lay down arms if they want peace (*Put Dzhokhara*, no. 9, 28 July–3 August, 1997:4).

After the Khasavyurt agreements of August 1996 and the treaty signed by Yeltsin and Maskhadov in May 1997, most of the external world took

the question of Chechnya's independence as decided de facto. The circle
of those who wished that the Chechens continued to fight after August
1996 was no less influential than during the war. The script of Russia's
disintegration—first losing Chechnya, then other Muslim regions—
seemed more and more plausible. In the meantime, Western sympathies
toward Chechnya, as well as toward its imagined independence, suffered
a most tangible blow from the Chechen leaders transferring their allegiance from the West to the Islamic world. This shift was due both to
changes in the political positions of the leading Western countries (limiting their attention and moral support for Chechnya) and to Chechnya's
growing reliance on the ideological and military resources of Muslim
Arab allies. The Chechens' ideas of the external world was radically altered: The West began to be seen as a traitor, Israel and Russia as arch-
enemies, the Muslim world as the only friend besides Azerbaijan and the
Baltic countries.

In February 1998, the Chechen military newspaper *Zashchitnik Otechestva* (no. 1, February 1998:1) reported on the visit by Chechnya's Defense
Minister Khamzat Gelayev to Pakistan on the occasion of the "World
Muslim congress" (in his words, "with delegates from 170 countries with
a total population of four billion, lasting for 40 days"). Here is an excerpt
from Gelayev's impressions of that visit:

> In Pakistan there lives an elderly emir, head of the Muslim society. I had a
> long talk with him. I asked him to say a prayer for alleviating the suffering
> of Chechnya. After some time I met him again. He said that he and his fol-
> lowers had said (read) 125,000 prayers for peace in Chechnya—more than
> they ever said in 70 years of his preaching Islam. They said Allah had blessed
> the Chechens who, though small in numbers, have chosen the way of Gaza-
> vat. So, the Almighty sent them victory and all the Muslim world loves them.
>
> Our delegation was given a top-level reception. For the opening of the
> Muslim congress they had built a shrine modelled on the Kaaba. After a long
> deliberation the holy (Shura) council decided that the new shrine (ziayrat)
> should be consecrated by the Chechen clergy. That surprised the Arab guests,
> descendants of the Prophet Mohammed (may Allah bless and greet him) in
> whose language the Koran was written. Pakistan also has famous Alims who
> work hard for the good of Islam. They have 20 million followers who know
> the Koran by heart. They were also surprised by the preference given to the
> Chechen delegation.

Many similar reports on the outside world (or, rather, on the Chechen
imagined version of it) were absorbed by the Chechen public, or at least
by the readers of the newspaper *Zashchitnik Otechestva*, which was popular among the armed part of the population. Thus, the idea of Chechnya's
independence was gradually internalized as part of individual as well as

collective identities. The media were no less important in this process than individual experience and the learned postulates of local intellectuals. As a result, Chechnya was involved in a new war that proved to be just as senseless and destructive as the first one.

CONFLICT USURPED BY "INTERVENTIONISTS"

In the period between the first and the second Chechen wars, yet another factor surfaced: the inertia of pro-Chechen sympathies that had formed at the beginning of the first war and even earlier, also as an element of the anti-Russian stance that, in turn, was a remnant of Cold War mentality. The West couldn't part with the image of the "big" enemy that had for so long kept its ranks together, and it had nothing equal to substitute for it: neither the Islamic threat, nor communist China, nor North Korea could take the place of the great hostile state armed with nuclear missiles. The inertia of fear as a tool to hold the Western community together was complemented by new geopolitical rivalries. The great Western powers and other major states (Turkey and Saudi Arabia) hastened to assert their influence on the suddenly emerged *terra nullis*—the new independent states formed on the periphery of the former USSR. Lurking behind those rivalries was global business—particularly oil and gas and military-industrial complexes.

Ousting Russia from its own backyard seemed such an enticing prospect that the radical ethnonationalisms in the Northern Caucasus, better still the armed secession of Chechnya, looked like a good opportunity for having look Russia like a "staggering state." Then, all the support for Dudayev's regime and the Chechen resistance invested in the first war, which ended, as it seemed to the external actors, in complete triumph for Chechnya (the title of Anatol Lieven's book is *Chechnya: The Tombstone of the Russian Power*; see Lieven 1998), made it hard to accept Russia's subsequent retaliation and crunch of the separatist project. As to the foreign Islamic radicals, they openly chose to give Chechnya direct support in its armed struggle with Russia including arms supplies, money, and mercenaries prepared to fight in a jihad.

The intellectual antiwar movement was led not by journalists, but by novelists, philosophers, and other cultural figures of our time. The international Pen Club held its 67th congress in Moscow, in May 2000, and passed a resolution on "the last mass crime of the XXth century." The document contained the entire ideological menu needed for mobilizing the armed formations in Chechnya to go on with the war: the rigid definition of the warring sides ("Russia is waging an undeclared war on the territory of the independent republic of Chechnya"); the extreme dramatization of "the tragedy acted out before the whole world"; condemnation of "the second attempt by the Russian authorities to resolve the tragic situation by military means"; recognition of "the legitimate government of Maskhadov being ready for a peace settlement"; demand that Russia should end the war immediately and start negotiations; and reference to "the Chechen ethnos" (learning the jargon of Soviet ethnography) whose "normal development is impossible without the lost cultural values and institutions." All that is coached in the moral tones of humanism and democracy strongly upheld by the Pen Club and its Russian Center. The undoubtedly sincere concern of the writers was tainted by their inability to see the other side of the coin.

Such liberal interventionists reject war and violence as totally evil and, in the spirit of the Western antimilitary tradition, they point to the state as the main agent of violence and the source of war. They dehumanize the state by failing to see the people who constitute it and treating it as an impersonal power. On the other hand, they ascribe all human values to the "ethnos," failing to see bandits or extremist leaders in its midst who might have chosen a tragically fallacious path in the name of that ethnos. I agree with Michael Ignatieff when he writes: "However paradoxical it may sound, the police and armies of the nation-states remain the only available institutions we have ever developed with capacity to control and channel large-scale violence" (Ignatieff 1999: 176).

In that light we may ask the questions: To what extent do people who remain in the zones of relative security help those who find themselves in a zone of violence to recreate those viable and effective institutions of the state? And to what extent may our external interference further exacerbate the situation if we supply the conflicting sides with more weapons encouraging them to continue the conflict? One of the more prudent answers to this question is the following:

> Sometimes, hard as it is, the best thing to do is to do nothing: to let a victor emerge and then to assist him to establish and sustain the monopoly on violence upon which order depends. In the other case, where the adversaries are too evenly balanced to allow a decisive outcome, we may have to intervene on the side that appears to be most in the right and assist it to consolidate its power. This means, of course, accepting that war may be an unavoidable solution to ethnic conflict. It means accepting a moral pact with the devil of war, seeking to use its flames to burn a path to peace (Ignatieff 1999:176).

This explicit advice is not meant for social scientists but for policymakers. But with certain reservations, it can also be applied to intellectuals who often interfere with local societies and conflicts in a partial way—with research designs favoring one side of the conflict or by public statements and appeals.

I think that one of the principles of the anthropologist's professional code—not to disturb the integrity and social balance of the society one is studying and writing about—was badly violated in Chechnya. I blame those who, having previously never even heard the name of Chechnya, let alone acquired any deeper knowledge of its society, assumed a right of interference and judgment. Their pro-separatist bias was linked either to a tenacious and chronic anti-Russian syndrome or to the liberal utopia of ethnic "self-determination of the oppressed minorities." Strangely enough, I don't observe similar sympathies in favor of the armed separatism of the Turkish Kurds (though there are some in favor of the Iraqi Kurds) or the armed separatists in the Basque country or in Northern Ireland. The label of a democratic country, or of NATO and EU membership, evidently makes the use of force by the state justified in those cases. But the same liberal interventionist club caused destabilization in Tibet by supporting the actions of the local Buddhist monks against the Chinese state as early as the 1950s. The latest victims of that "international concern" were the Kosovo Albanians who were given arms, training, and political support from outside in order to complete the process of destruction ("self-determination") of the new Yugoslavia. Talking of double standards is not just empty rhetoric: This is the sad reality of external forces manipulating actors in local arenas chosen as playing fields for geopolitical rivalries and the pursuit of utopian projects. Chechnya has become one of such scenes on which external actors stage their performances.

Where, when, and why is this or that spot on the globe chosen as a scene for yet another violent conflict or destructive war? It would be wrong and naïve to think that the choice could be made without appropriate internal conditions and enthusiastic participation from local activists. However, the world abounds in situations that can be summarily described by the formula "minorities at risk." The risk factors may consist in the local state being unable to maintain tolerable living standards for its people, or being unwilling to permit some part of the population to preserve its cultural and group identity, or the state failing to provide security for local communities and individuals. All such factors may indeed breed fear and concern, even a desire to withdraw from the common political space. But most often, those feelings and demands are learned and articulated by the activists of such groups, by radicals who create an irreconcilable, militant opposition.

To what extent such irreconcilable radicals express the "will of the people" is usually questionable at least, and the answer to that question informs the opinion on how "just" or "unjust" their struggle is. This just-unjust dichotomy has become the curse of our modern world, including the former USSR. True enough, it was the USSR that adhered to the moral principle of distinguishing between "just and unjust wars" as one of the basic points of the Marxist ideology of world revolution. In actual fact, the conception of just and unjust wars has far deeper roots than the USSR and

Marxist theory. This notion has a long history and is still being used both in social anthropology and in real politics; it is also popular in the jargon of political writers. Even such a thorough thinker as Michael Ignatieff did not avoid a bow to that dubious dichotomy in writing, "In Afghanistan and Chechnya wars that began as genuine national uprisings against foreign occupation have degenerated into vicious fights for territory, resources, drugs, and arms among militias who are often no different from criminal gangs" (Ignatieff 1999: 176).

Why then is Chechnya listed together with Afghanistan and not with Tibet, Sri Lanka's Tamils, and Iraqi and Turkish Kurds? Aren't the slogans of the nationalist radicals quite similar in all those cases? Maybe because only in those two places, the "foreign occupation" was by the USSR-Russia, which is still treated as the archenemy? China has not yet graduated to that important role, Sri Lanka is on the periphery of world politics, Iraq has been punished and its Kurds have benefited from U.S. air protection, and Turkey is NATO's outpost in Asia—so who would worry about Abdullah Öcalan's death sentence?

In most cases, the national states cope adequately with their ethnocultural and ethnopolitical problems through bettering governance, introducing affirmative action, making political concessions, and introducing minority rights schemes or, if necessary, using armed force. Ethnic radicalism and ethnic wars arise not where they are caused by group fear but where the state itself encourages ethnic divisions through its system of governance (as it was in the USSR and still is in the post-Soviet states) or where the state is no longer able to guarantee law and order, loses its control over the arms arsenals, and permits the rise of irregular armed groups led by ethnic impostors and irresponsible adventurers. These areas then provide the weak spot and the opportune moment for external forces to construct the image of an "enslaved people" struggling for its freedom and independence.

To create an ethnic group radically different from the rest of the country's population, such actors make use of naively romantic ethnography and mythologized history, depicting the group in question as a "Muslim nation" or noble savage, warriors like the ancient Aeneas armed with grenade throwers. Thus, the chosen "people" then have to play a prescribed role. What role was assigned to the Chechens by internal and external scriptwriters, many of whom will never agree, never even suspect that they belong to the stage managers of the war drama?

FORGING CHECHENS FROM ETHNOGRAPHIC CRUMBS

Paradoxical as it may seem, it wasn't so much "the Chechen people" who generated a deep conflict in the country (surely, with the participation of the Russian state and its army), an idea created by the war, but the idea of such a people presented to an outside world that had earlier never heard of their existence. Just as the Serbs and Croats before the war in Yugoslavia had identified themselves less with their ethnic brethren, but more with certain civic networks or local communities, so the Chechens before 1991 had defined themselves first and foremost as Soviet citizens, some of them as members of the Communist Party and local administrative bureaucracies, as Muslims or atheists, and as members of various professions, age groups, and family circles. Even their secret identity as "formerly deported" was not ethnically exclusive because there were millions of other people of all nationalities who had been deported, exiled, dispossessed, limited in their rights, released after serving long terms in the prison camps, and the like. That was the legacy of the Stalinist period borne by several generations including that of myself as well as of Khasbulatov, Dudayev, and Maskhadov.

The evidence that my research partners and I have collected shows that for the prewar (the 1990s) generation of Chechens, neither their ethnic identity nor the fact of deportation constituted their main social status or identity. As to the tribal (*teip*) affiliation, very few of them made any references to it. They were concerned with their earnings and living, their chances of getting a good education, advancing their professional careers in the army and other state services, and so on, just as the rest of the population of the Soviet Union. In the hierarchy of their personal social identification, ethnicity was not in the frontline, and Chechens were no different from any other ethnic group, least of all from the other Northern Caucasian nationalities (Ingush, Dagestani, Kabardins, Balkars, and others).

Chechenness was reified as a result of the conflicts and deep social transformations of the Gorbachev-Yeltsin era. The idea of a Chechen nation was constructed from the available historic and ethnographic material (most of it fictitious), from literary and pseudo-scientific accounts, also from deliberate political inventions. All of it served to impose on the Chechens a kind of primordial and premodern identity and the idea of a special historic mission based on a mixture of nationalistic narcissism, victimization complex, and messianic ideas of being "grave-diggers of the empire," "liberators of the Caucasus," and "the vanguard of Islam."

Pain and fear are often presented as the cornerstones of Chechen identity, of the Chechen internal world, and *self-defense* as the motive for fighting. Frankly speaking, I have a problem to judge about the adequateness of this description. Probably it would need more research, or maybe Chechen identity represents an impenetrable fabric for an outsider. For the time being, I assume that my own explanatory capacities are not weaker than that of journalists or of those social scientists obsessed with providing historic-ethnographic references as a proof of a high standard analysis. I limit myself here to give some examples of scholarly misinterpretation of history and ethnography and how they travel from one text to another and from one level of discourse to another. These constructions of a mytho-poetic Chechen past then forge the image of living Chechens and prescribe their present-day role. As part of this forging procedure, other aspects of reality, including everyday practices and concerns that do not correspond to the constructed image, are hidden from sight. This creates beliefs and expectations that reduce the mental and behavioral space.

Much of what looks like a manifestation of "hard reality" has its roots in academic texts. Journalists and policymakers later borrow these references to history and ethnographic data. Then it becomes a part of everyday talk and is represented as an objective reality. Articles published by a member of my institute, Dr. Yan Chesnov, are most often a source of references for Chechen ethnography, and some authors regard them as "irreplaceable work on the structures of Chechen traditional society" (Lieven 1998:335).

My colleague made undoubtedly a decisive contribution to forging myths of a unique Chechen civilization and of 400 years of fighting between Chechens and Russians—one of the main sources of nationalistic narcissism—later parroted by Yeltsin and Maskhadov. The following excerpt is characteristic of his romanticizing account:

> Russian totalitarianism always attempts to suppress the mountain democracy of the nationalities of the Caucasus, and first and foremost that of the Vainakhs, in the most barbaric fashion. It has already been 400 years since the Vainakh civilization liquidated the institutions of a feudal aristocracy and of a natural, inherited inequality among people. The individual's natural freedom is the essence of the Vainakh democracy. This freedom found powerful support in the institutions of the Islamic religion. For totalitarian, imperial regimes, a free nationality within the composition of Russia is not simply a thorn in the side, but by its example is dangerous for the enslaved fellow-citizens of the entire country. . . . [We should recognize] that the ancestors of these peoples once lived on the shores of the Tigris and the Euphrates, where the great beginnings of the spiritual life of humanity were born. These nationalities are the creators of the unique Vainakh civilization, about which we know that it maintains the freedom of the individual as the most important value. Among the Chechens, this concept is so highly developed that I had the opportunity to record the following assertion: "One cannot be a slave—even to circumstances" (Chesnov 1995–1996:30–32).

Sergei Arutiunov, an outstanding Russian anthropologist, also tends to focus on the traditional Vainakh military democracy and historical memory in explaining the high degree of mobilization of the Chechens in the conflict:

> Chechnya was and is a society of military democracy. Chechnya never had any kings, emirs, princes, or barons. Unlike other Caucasian nations, there was never feudalism in Chechnya. Traditionally, it was governed by a council of elders on the basis of consensus, but like all military democracies—like the Iroquois in America or Zulu in southern Africa—Chechens retain the institution of military chief. In peacetime, they recognize no sovereign authority and may be fragmented into a hundred rival clans. However, in time of danger, when faced with aggression, the rival clans unite and elect a military leader. This leader may be known to everyone as an unpleasant personality, but is elected nonetheless for being a good general. While the war is on, this leader is obeyed (Arutiunov 1995:17).

These two Russian authorities on Chechnya serve as a basis for many other texts whose authors repeat or elaborate further these postulates, as the following example shows:

> They are a nationality with no identification with the state and the society in which they live, and no motivation whatsoever to conform with its laws; equipped with ancient traditions which are in contradiction to those of "enlightened," "pluralist" and "progressive" liberalism; with social forms which make them opaque to outside investigation; internally cohesive, and remarkably efficient and ruthless in pursuit of their aims; and in a country in which a mixture of poorly institutionalised "democracy," social disintegration, state weakness and state corruption have opened up the most enormous opportunities and spaces for organized criminal activity. One might almost say, to adapt a phrase of Robert Musil's, that if the modern Western bourgeoisie could dream, it would dream Chechens (Lieven 1998:354).

Anatol Lieven calls "the Russian intervention" "an error of colonial ethnography," meaning that there were fundamental misconceptions among the Russian KGB and military experts regarding the nature of the Chechen clan system and their society, which they had described as "traditional, irrational, divided, static and inflexible" (Lieven 1998:335–339). We confront here a more serious phenomenon of anthropological reductionism when, for a variety of reasons, a culturally distinctive but modern people is portrayed as an "ancient tribal ethnos" or "premodern nation." This leads to the conclusion that because of radical differences from the rest of society, a group deserves unquestionable sympathy, patronage, support, and protection. By citing poorly documented or even fictitious data on fundamental cultural differences and by rejecting commonalities across ethnic boundaries, this kind of anthropology pretends to follow high disciplinary standards and to place itself on the "correct" side of the political divide. Putting modern Chechens into iron ethnographic cages and granting them a carte blanche for despising law, committing crime, and ruthlessly fighting, this approach only provides lip service to the true interests of the people.

WHY DOES A PRESCRIBED PROJECT FAIL?

The Chechen independence project has proven to be unrealizable for several reasons. Among them, Robert Ware has noted Russian opposition to independence, the impact of Chechen lawlessness upon its neighbors (such as cross-border incursions, hostage taking, and other forms of criminal activity), and deficits in Chechnya's economic, social, and political development.

> Chechnya lacks capital, infrastructure, non-military investment, and viable trade routes through non-Russian territory. It has essentially no civil society and hardships imposed by its lawlessness are even greater for ordinary Chechens than for citizens in the neighbouring territories. It has developed no authoritative political order and it has inspired little confidence abroad. Some of these problems can be traced to traditional Chechen social structure (Kisriev and Ware 2000:36).

During the war, Chechens were not united in their struggle with Moscow, while Russian society was deeply divided in its views of that disastrous war. During the three years after the war, Chechen society disintegrated even more due to rivalries between different political/military factions. Power has been divided between the regime that was relatively conciliatory in its approach to Moscow and an opposition that turned toward a militant expansionist stance and political Islam in an effort to acquire legitimacy. This polarity has been confined mainly to the armed factions of society. More and more people who did not fight were alienated from both warring sects that were held responsible for deep economic and political chaos and personal insecurity. However, this majority lacking Kalashnikovs could not raise its voice without immediate punishment. The Chechen society did not fail to build its own nation state because of the absence of a tradition of a unifying political organization. There were several other more "contemporary" factors that have inhibited the building of a functioning polity out of the chaos of Chechnya's war-torn society. First, many Chechens found comfort in the nationalist mythology enriched by the postwar discourse of a "great victory." Heroic mythology served well as an inspiration in a time of fighting, but it turned out to be an obstacle for reconstruction and negotiating peace with the warring parties. In Ware's words, "This warrior mythology is self-destructive particularly because it is self-perpetuating" (Kisriev and Ware 2000:36).

Second, the Chechen self-conception, as it had emerged during the conflict, included Islam as a recipe to address the deficiencies of their political situation. But traditional Sufi brotherhoods reemerged among a population poorly educated in religious terms and deeply influenced by the secular Soviet legacy. The expected pacifying role of *tariqatist* Islam did not materialize. It was hampered by warrior mythology and ethnic/regional cleavages that opposed the idea of united Islamic *umma*. It was also hampered by the ideological radicalization that occurred during the last three years as competing clan and military sect leaders appealed to Islam in order to acquire political legitimacy and supremacy. The return of Islamism into Chechen society had disastrous consequences when it took the form of Wahhabite Islamic fundamentalism, which spread through the most militant factions fighting against *muftiat* and the Maskhadov's government (Akaev 1999). These factions were supported both morally and materially by political groups from the Persian Gulf, Pakistan, and Afghanistan.

Finally, I should like to mention the no less important, but often ignored, fact that the Chechen revolution implies a double negation both of the destroyed Soviet system of rule and of its ideology. To fill the vacuum, its leaders indulged in the unrealistic project of restoring an imagined order (based on clan structure or on religion) that has never existed in the past, at least since the time of incorporating Chechnya into the Russian state. The most feasible option would be to restore the pre-1991 order. But this model has vanished in the rest of the post-Soviet space and has been completely delegitimized by internal and external forces. The war-torn society of Chechnya finds itself thrown into a dramatic situation: to build a future on the basis of invented images of the past or according to imported recipes alien to the Chechen society.

REFERENCES

Akaev, Vakhid. 1999. *Sifism i vakhabism na Severnov Kavkaze* [Sufism and Wahhabism in the North Caucasus]. Working Papers in Urgent and Applied Ethnology 127. Moscow: Institute of Ethnology and Anthropology.

Arutiunov, Sergei. 1995. Ethnicity and Conflict in the Caucasus. In *Ethnic Conflict and Russian Intervention in the Caucasus*, ed. Fred Wehling, 15–18. Policy Paper 16 (August). Institute on Global Conflict and Cooperation. San Diego: University of California, San Diego.

Avtorkhanov, Abdurakhman. 1991. *Ubiistvo checheno-ingushskogo naroda: Narodoubiistvo v SSSR* [The Killing of Chechen-Ingush People: Genocide in the USSR]. Moscow: Vsya Moskva.

Bersanova, Zalpa. 1999. *Systema zennostei sovremennykh chechentsev (po materialam oprosov)* [The Values System of Contemporary Chechens (Results of Sociological Surveys)]. In *Chechnya i Rossiya: Obschestvo i gosudarstvo* [Chechnya and Russia: State and Society], ed. Dmitri Furman, 223–249. Moscow: Izdat. Polinform-Talburi.

Chesnov, Yan. 1995–1996. Civilization and the Chechen. *Anthropology & Archeology of Eurasia* 34 (3):28–40.

Dunlop, John B. 1998. *Russia Confronts Chechnya: Roots of a Separatist Conflict.* Cambridge: Cambridge University Press.

Furman, Dmitri, ed. 1999. *Chechnya i Rossiya: Obschestvo i gosudarstvo* [Chechnya and Russia: State and Society]. Moscow: Izdat. Polinform-Talburi.

Gakayev, Dzhabrail D. 1997. *Ocherki politicheskoi istorii Chechni (XX vek)* [Essays on Political History of Chechnya]. Moscow: Chechen Cultural Center.

———. 1999. *Chechenskii krisis: Istoki, itogi, perspektivy (Politicheskii aspekt)* [Chechen Crisis: Roots, Results, and Perspectives (Political Aspect)]. Moscow: Chechen Cultural Center.

Gall, Carlotta, and Thomas de Waal. 1998. *Chechnya: Calamity in the Caucasus.* New York: New York University Press.

Ignatieff, Michael. 1999. *The Warrior's Honor: Ethnic War and the Modern Conscience.* London: Vintage.

Kisriev, Enver, and Robert Ware. 2000. Social Tradition and Political Stability in Dagestan and Chechnya: Developments since September 1999. Unpublished manuscript.

Lieven, Anatol. 1998. *Chechnya: Tombstone of Russian Power.* New Haven, CT: Yale University Press.

Smith, Dan. 1997. *The State of War and Peace.* London: Penguin.

Starovoitova, Galina. 1997. *National Self-Determination: Approaches and Case Studies.* Thomas J. Watson Jr. Institute for International Studies, Occasional Paper 27. Providence, RI: Brown University.

Tishkov, Valery. 1997a. *Ethnicity, Nationalism, and Conflict in and After the Soviet Union: The Mind Aflame.* London: Sage.

———. 1997b. The Political Anthropology of the Chechen War. *Security Dialogue* 28 (4):425–437.

———. 1999. Ethnic Conflicts in the Former USSR: The Use and Misuse of Typologies and Data. *Journal of Peace Research* 36 (5):571–592.

———. 2001. *Obschestvo v vooruzhennom konflikte. Etnografia chechenskoi voiny* [The War-Torn Society. The Ethnography of the Chechen War]. Moscow: Nauka.

———. 2004. *Chechnya: Life in a War-Torn Society.* Berkeley: University of California Press.

6

❦

The Asymmetry between the Dynamics of Violence and the Dynamics of Peace: The Case of Civil Wars

Peter Waldmann

While the period prior to World War II was strongly marked by interstate conflicts, intrastate armed disputes gained increasing importance during the postwar decades. The global statistic of wars for the years between 1945 and 1993 shows a total of 164 wars, of which 126 (77 percent) represent civil wars and the rest (23 percent) represent wars between different states (Holsti 1996:22). When defining "war" as only armed conflicts of considerable dimensions, accompanied by a considerable contingent of troops or other armed units, and claiming at least 1,000 victims (Small and Singer 1982:55), the statistics show only a rough tendency. If we include smaller conflicts in our deliberations, it becomes clear that, worldwide, states are challenged more by inner ruptures and armed riots than by external threats of war.

The outstanding characteristics of armed conflicts within a state are their longevity and the cruelty and tenacity with which they are fought (Licklider 1993:8). In this respect, too, the statistics of war give us some interesting information. More than half of the civil wars fought between 1945 and 1993 lasted a maximum of five years, but 20 percent lasted ten or more years. Although 55 percent of the wars between states during this period were solved by negotiations, this was possible for only one-fourth of the civil wars, three-quarters being decided by military measures. Curiously, in civil wars, a victory imposed by a military defeat showed a greater stability than an agreement based on negotiations: In 50 percent of civil wars in which peace was achieved by negotiation, conflict resumed, yet this was the case for only 15 percent of those ended by military defeat

(Licklider 1995:681; David 1997:568–560). All this underscores the extreme obstinacy with which civil wars or similar conflicts are fought.

There are several explanations for this that are beyond the scope of this chapter (but see Waldmann 1998b:18–20). Here, I am primarily interested in civil wars as typical cases to illustrate and prove the thesis put forward in the chapter title of the superior dynamics of violent processes versus processes of peace.[1] For this purpose, I shall not take as a basis too narrow a concept of civil war. My deliberations refer to wars in the strictest sense of the word as well as to cases of "low-intensity wars," in which far fewer than 1,000 people per year lose their lives. I shall use material from Europe as well as from the Middle East, and also from India and Latin America. Most of the material refers to ethnic and religious conflicts.

I split the general thesis of the asymmetry between violent processes and peace processes in three partial theses: the problem of generalization, the problem of temporal perpetuation, and the problem of social penetration and diffusion.

THE DILEMMA OF GENERALIZATION

Just as there is an asymmetrical relation between trust and mistrust, there is an asymmetrical relationship between the intention to achieve peace and the disposition to violence. One who trusts an untrustworthy business companion risks being swindled (Dasgupta 1988). If, within a group, only a few people or even only one person declares violence to be the key to the distribution of power, it is of little use to the others to protest in favor of a peaceful solution. They can only fend off the claim of power of those who use violence if they confront them with the same violent means. In order to guarantee the proper functioning of an order based on consensus, all participants must agree. To impose the principle of the mightier, however, it takes only the initiative of a few individuals.

This asymmetry of the chances of diffusion of violent and peaceful processes can be examined on several levels. Its disastrous implications are most notable in situations generally described as "security dilemmas." Originally developed especially for the relationship between states that is characterized as anarchic (i.e., lacking any form of superior power), it is nowadays increasingly applied to conflicts within states. The dilemma is that, in view of the menace from its rivals, no group or party can afford to desist all means of self-defense. Yet measures to defend itself have exactly the opposite effect of what they are intended to do: They don't actually secure peace, but rather favor the escalation of conflict.

Let us suppose that a state in Africa, with a government preoccupied with providing a just equilibrium among its different ethnic groups, suddenly collapses: To which extent can these groups be certain that the other groups are willing to maintain the status quo of the distribution of power? Would it not be reasonable to assume that one of them, taking advantage of the new situation, would suddenly assault and annihilate the others, or take possession of the remnants of the state bureaucracy and establish a permanent hegemony? Since the risk to be overwhelmed and decimated is too great if a group attempts to take a trusting attitude, each group has no other choice but to secure a minimum capacity of defense. But, tragically, by its defensive measures a group necessarily calls forth the distrust and suspicion of the others. The result is an atmosphere of mistrust and secret arming that, at the slightest provocation, can turn into an open conflict.

Basically, what we are confronted with is an example of the prisoner's dilemma (Williams 1988; Axelrod 1984). All parties involved choose a procedure second to best, since they cannot afford the risk involved in the best solution (here, the continuation of the status quo). Such patterns of conduct dictated by the tough logic of the prisoner's dilemma are to be found wherever central power is nonexistent or widely weakened. They were nonexistent, for example, in tribal societies still found in the Amazon basin or in Polynesia. As Helbling proved in the case of the Yanomami living in the Amazon basin, wars of extinction are best interpreted as a consequence of the security dilemma (Helbling 1999b). They do not result from the battle for scarce resources, nor from an exaggerated sense of honor combined with a compulsion of revenge, but go back to an impulse of survival: the attempt to annihilate a rival tribe in order to secure one's survival. This image of a battle of all against all is further confirmed when Helbling shows, at another place, that among the tribes lacking a political central power, the belligerent are far more numerous than the peaceful ones (the relation being 130:5, or 30:4 according to another investigation). The latter consist mainly of simple collectors and hunters that, contrary to the farmers, have nothing to lose and therefore can escape an armed conflict without any consecutive costs (Helbling 1999a).

Currently throughout the world, we see a lot of underdeveloped countries with weak or highly unstable structures of state. Barbara Walter analyzed forty civil wars that took place after World War II, mainly in Asia, Africa, and Latin America. She came to very similar conclusions as Helbling: Under anarchic or anarchy-like conditions, none of the rival groups or parties were interested in giving in and trying to achieve peace. The main reason for this attitude is the fact that, in absence of a superior power able to guarantee by its sanctions the fulfilment of agreements, any party must fear that the opposite side might abuse its confidence, inflicting an irreparable loss (Walter 1997).

As shown by Walter's argument, the dilemma of security is not only responsible for the outbreak of civil wars, but it also obstructs their appeasement by peaceful means. The ongoing Northern Irish peace process is a good example of this, in which the IRA consented to an inspection of its arsenal of arms by an independent side, yet in turn obstinately refuses to destroy its weapons. This was not without reason: The outbreak of the "troubles" in the years of 1969–1970, in which Catholics were exposed, unprotected, to a Protestant mob who ignited complete rows of houses and obliged the residents to flee, is still vividly present in the minds of IRA fighters (Waldmann 1989:86–87; Richardson 2000:167). The IRA is trying to avoid a similar situation at all costs.[2]

The security dilemma is the sharpest expression of the unequal chances of the success of processes of violence and of peace, since in these cases what is at stake is the very existence of the social collectivities in question, be they tribes of farmers in the past or ethnic groups of the present. Also, in less exposed situations in which both sides need not fear for their survival, the dynamic of violent processes might favor a dangerous escalation of the conflict. This is mostly the case when "entrepreneurs of violence" appear on the scene.[3]

According to Julia Eckert, this kind of situation arose in Bombay at the beginning of the 1990s. Hindus and Muslims, after having lived together relatively peacefully for a long time, gradually changed to a route of confrontation—initiated mainly by a Hindu party (Eckert 2001). Slander and agitating campaigns led to violent riots and acts of revenge. As Eckert rightfully observed, the media's attempts to enlighten the public and other initiatives of reconciliation eventually showed little results, since each group accused the opposite side of the worst of intentions. A similar spiral of mistrust can be observed currently in Israel. Independent of the basic disposition of most Israelis and Palestinians to reach a peaceful agreement, small radical minorities on both sides manage to impose a continuation of violent disputes.

At a comparable yet much more harmless level, an episode in Germany demonstrated the helplessness of a majority defending tolerance and understanding that is faced with splinter groups determined to apply violence. I refer here to the parade of "die Anständigen" ("the correct ones") in the center of Berlin on November 2000 against hatred, racism, and torture of aliens, respectively of people of different faith. After the mass demonstration, a well-known Swiss newspaper ironically asked if demonstrations of this kind had more than a mere placebo effect (*Neue Zürcher Zeitung*, 23 November, 2000:5), since a similar march had taken place a couple of years before, yet in spite of it the number of violent acts from the extreme right in Germany had not notably decreased.

In brief, violence is contagious and disseminates itself, even against the intention of the actors involved, while peace requires a broad basis of trust and conviction that first needs to be established yet can be questioned at any time.

THE DILEMMA OF PERPETUATION

The dilemma of perpetuation deals with the time factor in the problematic relationship of peace and violence. Scholars very often emphasize the auto-dynamics of violence without explaining, however, what is to be understood by "auto-dynamics." Following the exposition from Mayntz and Nedelmann about auto-dynamic social processes, I would like to distinguish here between the characteristics of the process itself, which are able to start an auto-dynamic development of violence, respectively of peace; and emerging characteristics or institutions that reinforce these auto-dynamics (Mayntz and Nedelmann 1987:656–658).

Regarding the characteristics of the process, it should be mentioned that one of the typical traces of violence is a compulsory reaction of the same kind. Violent actions most probably lead to violent reactions, except when applied against a far inferior opponent. This produces a chain of successive violent actions, in which every action (except the first) is at the same time provocation and reaction, cause and effect (Neidhardt 1981:251–252).

As far the political arena is concerned, this compulsory connection is reflected in two specific strategies and patterns of argumentation, depending on if it refers to an attack on the superior state or to armed disputes between rival groups (very often after the dissolution of the state). The recipe for success by which violent inferior groups manage to involve the state in a costly conflict was clearly demonstrated by the Basque ETA in the 1960s. The ETA called its strategic concept "the spiral of action and repression" (Waldmann 1989:119–121): Police stations and institutions of great symbolic significance were attacked, hurting the Spanish state's sovereignty and forcing it to take drastic measures against it. Since these measures inevitably also cause innocent victims, they create an atmosphere of unrest and discontent, from which the rebels draw strength and support to carry out the next attack. This process of escalation is not deterministic. It is imaginable that a prudent government might avoid overreacting, that the population refuses to support the rebel group, or that the rebels are destroyed by the security forces. Yet, in reality, states have great difficulty extinguishing the flames of resistance on their territory once they are ignited.

The function of the "spiral of action and repression" in a vertical battle for power has its equivalent in the principle of retaliation and vengeance in the disputes among more or less equal opponents (Waldmann 2000). It can become effective spontaneously or be embedded in a long-time strategy. As citizens of a Western European state that was finally able to impose a monopoly of legitimate violence on society, we have become accustomed to consider armed self-defense detestable and acts of vengeance pathological. If we take a closer look at violent conflicts, however, we recurrently find the strong motivating force of "eye for an eye, a tooth for a tooth." Albania represents a classical example of the violence-generating effect of the principle of retaliation. Once limited mainly to northern Albania, it has meanwhile developed a force of its own and serves to justify the arbitrary application of violence throughout the entire country (Schwandner-Sievers 1998). In Colombia also, increasing violence is strongly dominated by revenge and is used for settling open accounts (Waldmann 1997:147). Depending on tradition and ideology, retaliation can be legitimated by a specific code of honor, or be based on certain ideas of compromise or sacrifice. In the last resort, its persistency might be explained by the fact that it is a specific expression of a more generalized and comprehensive pattern of thought and conduct, that is, the principle of reciprocity (Rehfeldt 1951:13–14).

The escalation of acts of revenge, as well as the escalation of violence according to the principle of "action and reaction," can be slowed down or interrupted. Its control, however, becomes more difficult as soon as the limit to the emergence of new qualities and institutional arrangements that incite these processes retroactively and support them is trespassed. Already, the ritualization and formalization of the exchange of violent acts represent a first step toward violence, since any aggression is almost automatically met by a revenge of equal dimensions (Mayntz and Nedelmann 1987:661). Here we are, however, considering two other structural arrangements that give violence considerable additional propulsion: the creation of an organization specially focused on it and closely connected to it, and the emergence of one's tradition of violence (see Waldmann 1995:354–355).

The founding of an organization marks a decisive step in the consolidation of violence. The continuation of the chain of violence thereby becomes independent from the initiative of a single individual or a small group, adopting predictable characteristics. Organization means the systematic recruitment, selection, and training of members. Furthermore, organization means the functional and hierarchic differentiation of group structures in order to use each member in the best possible manner according to his or her talents and capabilities. Parallel to the building of an organization, there is also a stronger need of justification and planning for violent actors. A circle of intellectuals, often unsuited for participating directly in the execution of violence acts, takes over these tasks, producing strategies, programs, and propaganda material. Since an organization without a minimal infrastructure is unable to survive, the number of violent acts increases considerably. These, however, do not have to exclusively or primarily fulfil political or ideological functions, but can serve also for the acquisition of money to cover the financial needs of the organization.

The increase of violence creates an increase in the number of deaths and injuries committed by and against the organization. Here lies the connection to the second emerging trace: the creation of a tradition. The dead become victims who gave their life for a "just cause." The fact that old rebel organizations like the IRA have produced a carefully elaborated and glorified history of their defensive battle against the hegemonic British state is not surprising. Yet it is surprising to see how in a relatively short time, relatively new cells and groups of rebels create a tradition of "heroes" or tragically killed "martyrs."[4] The reference to sacrifices paid in the past, moreover, helps the organization to justify its violent course, creating at the same time loyalty and a sense of commitment among its young members. It leads to a moral obligation to remain faithful to the cause consecrated by the bloodshed and to follow the steps of the venerated idols, to continue the struggle.

I must warn once more not to overestimate the logic of the auto-dynamic of violence in its stringency as pointed out here. In the collective memory of entire societies and of limited groups, not only their war heroes and martyrs but also their peacemakers and peacekeepers remain vivid. The principle of paying back the opponent with revenge not only legitimizes the application of violence but also limits it at the same time. Generally, it is wrong to assume that people in countries in which a civil war is being fought would lose all normative measures in the judgment of violence and would accept any kind of bloodshed. Societies with a long tradition of violence, like the Lebanese or the Northern Irish, on the contrary, supply evidence that even continuous armed disputes do not necessarily erase the idea of which kind of violence is still considered legitimate and which clearly surpasses tolerable limits (Darby 1994; Hanf 1990:755–756).

Another question is, however, how relevant these ideas are for the peace process and if they can help to stop the violence. Here, I must stress once more that there is no auto-dynamic of processes of peace that can be compared to the auto-dynamic of violence. Peace proposals and peace negotiations do not generate an obligation to continue. They can collapse or be interrupted at any given time if one of the negotiating parties leaves the table and resumes animosities.[5] William Zartman introduced the concept of the "mature moment," which suggests that from a certain level on, peace talks continue more easily (Zartman 1985). But others have convincingly objected that the adjective "mature" disguises the simple fact that out of rational choice, the decisive parties of the conflict prefer the continuation of negotiations instead of war (Krumwiede 1998:42–44). Innumerable examples demonstrate how little can be achieved by peace demonstrations, peace marches, and peace initiatives as long as the contesting parties are not convinced of the adequacy of peace negotiations. The population might be worn out by war, and third parties and the national and international press might insist on a successful outcome of peace negotiations. No matter how important this might be, it does not, however, generate the auto-dynamics of peace.

If a peace treaty is achieved, an institutional framework arises simultaneously that could function as an equivalent to the violent organizations discussed above. Yet one misses the capability of imposition and survival characteristic of the terror organizations. At the beginning, I remarked that only about half of the peace treaties are of permanent duration; often they are broken after a short time. But even if they remain untouched because they are backed up by a superpower, as for example the Dayton Agreement of 1995 between Muslims, Serbs, and Croatians, this does not prevent them from being permanently undermined and disobeyed at the local level.

Summing up, it can be said that, contrary to violence, which perpetuates itself almost automatically, peace lives from the engagement and the conscious consensus of the participants. It is a precarious construct that can be disrupted at any time if one of the actors abandons the consensus.

THE DILEMMA OF PENETRATION

Observers are amazed by how quickly and directly violence penetrates the different levels of a society in which a civil war has broken out. In vain we look for a similar dynamic for processes of peace. It seems that only the ones that have committed themselves feel bound by it, yet even then by no means permanently. At the beginning of an intrastate conflict, in many cases spontaneous militia arise: groups of young men who, recruited by dubious leaders, cannot wait to fight and measure up to opponent groups. But who ever heard of groups and circles that arise spontaneously at the beginning of peace talks, from within the enemy parties, to demonstrate that tolerance and peaceful coexistence between them is possible on a small scale?

This is a third partial dimension of the asymmetry of peace and violence: the different chances of diffusion of both competing processes within sectors of society still untouched by the conflict. The nature of the process in question is not free of a certain ambiguity. It can be interpreted

as the penetration of society by peace or violence and its following transformation, or it can be interpreted as a kind of mutual assimilation. But,
indifferent from which aspect one judges it, there is hardly any doubt that
the capacity of imposition of violent processes by far surpasses that of the
processes of peace.

A few exemplary hints will illustrate this. I have already mentioned the
superior and generally longer-lasting mobilizing capacity of violent organizations compared to peace initiatives. A certain category of young
men is specially attracted by the possibility to prove their bravery and
their capabilities in a dangerous situation (Creveld 1998:238–240). Coser
underlined the fact that conflicts with third parties tend to have a considerable integrating effect on groups (Coser 1972:101–103). Wherein, on the
other hand, lies the effect of peace movements and peace initiatives in
generating collective identity and permanent ties?

The press and, above all, the mass media give us a further example. It
is well known that negative news received greater attention than positive
news. Terrorist groups all around the globe have managed to develop a
strategy in rising worldwide attention by committing shocking acts of terror. But also armed conflicts, which do not necessarily cause general in-
dignation, can count on regularly finding a certain echo in the mass media (Waldmann 1998a:12–13). This can hardly be said of the peace
initiatives, which take place simultaneously in most of the conflict areas.

The third example is the economy. There are numerous testimonies that
prove that violence void of political control primarily serves for the purpose of material gain. In Colombia, there are regular "death offices" in
which one can order killings, the cost of which vary according to the pro-
tective measures of the targets (Waldmann 1997:148). Elwert developed
for sub-Saharan Africa and for Asia the concept of the "markets of violence," a specific combination of trade and violence for the purpose of material gain (Elwert 1999). Rufin elaborates the main features of an economy of civil wars and shows how international aid retained by the
conflicting parties helps continue rather than end the war (Rufin 1999).
According to newspapers and scientific reports, one can observe the renaissance of the "warlord," a figure first documented in China during the
decade of the 1920s, who lived from and for the war (Waldmann
1998b:30–31). Where do we find the counterfigure, the peace lord, who
draws profit in a similarly immediate way from peace efforts?

This list of examples could be extended. In a similar way, one could
show the symbiosis of space, respectively territory, and violence; of law
and violence; and of religion and violence. Yet there is no need to exagger-
ate the corresponding affinity. Asymmetry does not mean one-sidedness.
The close connection of numerous functional areas with violence often has
its counterpart in a parallel, however weaker, tie to the opposite pole of

peace. Fundamentalist religious movements, for example, are considered important stimulants for violent actions from Islamic terrorism to massive violent disputes with a religious background, which could recently be observed in the Balkans, the Middle East, or in India. Yet if analyzed more thoroughly, the key function of religious convictions becomes relative as these convictions are combined with other conflict-generating factors (Scheffler 1999). Furthermore, the religious parties in question also regularly produce nonconformist priests, who plead for peace and understanding between enemy groups.

These conciliatory elements, however, are the exception, which does not necessarily contradict the thesis of affinity between religious convictions and the application of violence, but only weakens it. Something similar is also valid for many other structural and functional areas.[6] The most impressive (and depressing) proof for the great capacity of penetration of violence compared to the efforts to achieve peace is given by societies in which the combatants have reached a temporary armistice or even signed a peace agreement. In the case of Northern Ireland, it became evident that in phases of armistice, the level of violence hardly receded, but rather shifted from the conflict between different religious groups to rivalries between different sectors within the groups (Richardson 2000:169). A further example is offered by El Salvador, where peace was established toward the end of the 1980s after a long and bloody struggle and equally tough yearlong negotiations. El Salvador was for a long time considered an outstanding example of the fact that bloody civil wars can be ended by peaceful means and without bloodshed through a compromise reached by negotiations (Krumwiede 1995). But although such a compromise put an end to the political disputes, it did not stop the spiral of violence. The result is that today more people die by criminal violence than were killed for political reasons during the worst phase of the civil war, even more than in Colombia, a country that until recently held the sad record of homicides among Latin America countries.

If we ask for the reasons of the great force of penetration of violence throughout society, we encounter a paradox. Violence and those who apply it more or less professionally as a medium of power hardly ever play or claim a dominant role. Instead, they pretend to be a tool, a functional means in order to reach certain goals or to solve difficult problems more effectively and quicker. After having settled down and established themselves in this apparently instrumental function, the auto-dynamic becomes effective. They begin to transform and control a corresponding segment of society according to their own logic of violence. In other words, violence as a resource of power seems to be easily convertible into other attractive resources of power like high political posts, economic influence, personal prestige, territorial gains, and the imposition of secular and religious ideas.

Yet, once admitted, it quickly becomes the key resource, relegating all other resources to a secondary rank.

Peace has no similar force of attraction. Of course, it is a precondition for several public goods, like general well-being, law and order, and religious tolerance, yet it is not a medium to create or "generate" them. Being at best indirectly connected with other values and goals, it must be pursued for its own sake. Just the fact that it represents a desirable goal in itself often makes it unattractive. Where people are accustomed to peaceful conditions and these are taken for granted, they tend to lack the necessary appreciation for it and often get tired of it. In societies that have suffered for a long time under warlike conditions, on the other hand, the proper value of peace is recognized and estimated.

CHANCES FOR PEACE

What, then, can be deduced from the thesis of the structural superiority of violent processes compared to processes of peace? As far as we can see, it leads to three conclusions. The first one is already an old one: Considering the auto-dynamics of violence, the most effective remedy to stop it is extreme counterviolence (the state or another powerful instance) or at least equal counterviolence. Civil wars give us more than enough evidence to assume that violence is best controlled by violence: for example, the observation that a proliferation of violence is best hampered or stopped when the conflicting parties are organized hierarchically and its members are subject to a strict discipline secured by force. Decisive for the successful outcome of peace negotiations, more than the goodwill of the participants ready to compromise, is the comprehension of the "hardliners" that they cannot win the battle by military means (Krumwiede 1998:40–42). Finally, the more intensively a peace treaty is supported by warrants of a superior power, the longer it will last.

My thesis does not question the sense of peace initiatives and peace negotiations. It does, however—and this is the second conclusion—draw attention to the fact that their success depends on specific conditions. There is no such thing as a causality of peace or a dynamic of peace, as a normative rhetoric of peace at times likes to make us believe. A positive outcome of negotiations depends essentially on the readiness to compromise—the understanding and the goodwill of the conflicting parties. This can be influenced, for example, by making sure that the rebel leaders must not fear losing their positions of power once the civil war is ended, that the loss of advantages resulting from the end of the war are compensated adequately, and that the eventual security risks resulting from a peace treaty remain limited. The saying "Making moderation pay" alone will certainly not guarantee progress toward peace, yet it clearly shows how much its successful outcome depends on the perspective, attitude, and interests of the participants in the conflict.

Finally, as far as the guidelines of a peace treaty are concerned, the above deliberations implicitly include the petition to erect them on a basis of "institutionalized mistrust" rather than on a basis of trust, at least temporarily. This means that the increasing segregation of the population in more or less closed confessionals of ethnic groups is to be accepted (Kaufmann 1999). Experience shows spatial separation to be one of the most important preventive measures to limit conflicts and tensions between enemy social groups (Helbling 1999a:10f.). Individuals or families who, trusting the peace treaty, establish their habitat on the territory of the opposite group or even marry a partner of the other group risk becoming the first victims in case the animosities reemerge.

Another political consequence of the principle of mistrust is the division of power. If all relevant ethnic and religious groups within a state dispose of a fair share of power, an abuse of power by the majority is prevented and the arrangement offers minority groups a chance to voice their claims in the political arena. This eliminates the need to use violence. The model of consociational democracy developed specially by Lijphart in the 1970s prescribes in this context, among others, a federal structure, a pluralism of parties, and a division of power, not only within the executive level but eventually also on the level of the security forces (Lijphart 1977).

NOTES

1. One could pose the question of whether it makes sense to compare violence to peace, since the first one is a resource of power, a medium, and the latter is a desirable condition. But, as can be seen in the sections "The Dilemma of Perpetuation" and "The Dilemma of Penetration," the difference between medium and goal is considerably put into perspective, as violence can become a self-fulfilment.

2. Walter consequently sees little chances of influencing civil wars from the outside through international organizations or interested third states. They cannot force the conflicting parties to negotiate if they insist either on victory or defeat, but they can see to it that the eventually reached agreements are respected by all sides (see Walter 1997:340).

3. Georg Elwert and his working team call them "war instigators" who, in order to profit from the escalation of conflicts, spread bad rumors about the opposite side that stir the emotions and feelings of imminent mutual threat.

4. Among others, we have in mind the German RAF, in which after only a few years a myth grew around its key founders, Baader and Meinhoff; these myths almost inevitably captivated later members of the organization. Presumably this

characteristic is connected to the accelerated change of successive generations of members under the pressure of persecution and sentence.

5. It is sensible to distinguish between serious peace talks and talks about peace. The latter can possibly develop a certain auto-dynamic, as is shown in the case of Colombia: The endless conferences, forums, and proclamations about the necessity of peace in Colombia go on without the least effect on the violent processes as such.

6. Some scholars who read the text critically commented that it does not give due importance to peace movements and peace lords coming up spontaneously in civil war–ridden societies. I do not deny the existence of these movements and roles, but I doubt whether they can compete with the forces driving in the opposite direction of stimulating violence.

REFERENCES

Axelrod, R. 1984. *The Evolution of Cooperation*. New York: Basic Books.

Coser, Lewis A. 1972. *Theorie sozialer Konflikte*. Neuwied/Berlin: Luchterhand.

Creveld, Martin v. 1998. *Die Zukunft des Krieges*. Munich: Gerling-Verlag.

Darby, John. 1994. Legitimate Targets: A Control on Violence. In *New Perspectives on the Northern Ireland Conflict*, ed. Adrian Guelfe, 46–64. Aldershot, UK: Avebury.

Dasgupta, Partha. 1988. Trust as a commodity. In *Trust. Making and Breaking Cooperative Relations*, ed. Diego Gambetta, 49–72. Oxford: Basil Blackwell.

David, Steven R. 1997. Internal War: Causes and Cures. *World Politics* 49 (4):552–576.

Eckert, Julia. 2001. Reconciling the Mohalla: Politics of Violence and the Strength and Limits of Mediation. In *Religion between Violence and Reconciliation*, ed. Thomas Scheffler, 365–389. Beiruter Texte und Studien 76. Beirut, Lebanon: Steiner.

Elwert, Georg. 1999. Markets of Violence. In *Dynamics of Violence: Processes of Escalation and De-escalation of Violent Group Conflicts*, ed. Georg Elwert, Dieter Neubert, and Stephan Feuchtwang, 85–102. Berlin: Duncker & Humblot.

Hanf, Theodor. 1990. *Koexistenz im Krieg. Staatszerfall und Entstehen einer Nation im Libanon*. Baden-Baden, Germany: Nomos.

Helbling, Jürg. 1999a. Krieg und Frieden in Gesellschaften ohne Zentralgewalt: Theorien und Perspektiven. *Tsantsa* 4:11–25.

———. 1999b. The Dynamics of War and Alliance among the Yanomami. In *Dynamics of Violence: Processes of Escalation and De-escalation of Violent Group Conflicts*, ed. Georg Elwert, Dieter Neubert, and Stephan Feuchtwang, 103–116. Berlin: Duncker & Humblot.

Holsti, Kalevi J. 1996. *The State, War and the State of War*. Cambridge: Cambridge University Press.

Kaufmann, Chaim D. 1999. When All Else Fails: Evaluating Population Transfer and Partition as Solution to Ethnic Conflict. In *Civil Wars, Insecurity and Intervention*, ed. Barbara F. Walter and Jack Snyder, 222–260. New York: Columbia University Press.

Krumwiede, Heinrich W. 1995. El Salvador: Erfolgreiche Konfliktregulierung. In *Rüstung statt Entwicklung? Sicherheitspolitik, Militärausgaben und Rüstungskontrolle in der Dritten Welt*, ed. Veronika Büttner and Joachim Krause, 476–506. Baden-Baden, Germany: Nomos.

———. 1998. Regulierungsmöglichkeiten von Bürgerkriegen: Fragen und Hypothesen. In *Bürgerkriege: Folgen und Regulierungsmöglichkeiten*, ed. Heinrich W. Krumwiede and Peter Waldmann, 37–60. Baden-Baden, Germany: Nomos.

Licklider, Roy. 1995. The Consequences of Negotiated Settlement in Civil Wars, 1945–1993. *American Political Science Review* 89 (3):681–690.

———, ed. 1993. *Stopping the Killing: How Civil Wars End*. New York: New York University Press.

Lijphart, Arend. 1977. *Democracy in Plural Societies: A Comparative Exploration*. New Haven, CT: Yale University Press.

Mayntz, Renate, and Birgitta Nedelmann. 1987. Eigendynamische Prozesse: Anmerkungen zu einem analytischen Paradigma. *Kölner Zeitschrift für Soziologie und Sozialpsychologie* 39:648–667.

Neidhardt, Friedhelm. 1981. Über Zufall, Eigendynamik und die Institutionalisierbarkeit absurder Prozesse: Notizen am Beispiel einer terroristischen Gruppe. In *Festschrift für René König zum 75 Geburtstag*, ed. H. von Alemann and P. Thurn, 243–257. Opladen, Germany: Westdeutscher Verlag.

Neue Zürcher Zeitung. 2000, November 23. 5.

Rehfeldt, Bernhard. 1951. *Die Wurzeln des Rechts*. Berlin: Duncker & Humblot.

Richardson, Louise. 2000. A Spiral of Peace? Bringing an End to Ethnic Conflict in Northern Ireland. In *Civil Wars: Consequences and Possibilities of Regulation*, ed. Heinrich W. Krumwiede and Peter Waldmann, 166–184. New York: Nomos.

Rufin, Jean-Christophe. 1999. Kriegswirtschaft in internen Konflikten. In *Ökonomie der Bürgerkriege*, ed. Jean François and Jean-Christophe Rufin, 15–46. Hamburg, Germany: Hamburger Edition.

Scheffler, Thomas. 1999. Religion, Violence and the Civilizing Process: The Case of Lebanon. In *Guerres civiles: Economies de la violence, dimension de la civilité*, ed. Jean Hannoyer, 163–185. Paris: Karthala et Cermoc.

Schwandner-Sievers, Stephanie. 1998. Wer besitzt die Lizenz zum Töten in Albanien? oder Fragen zur Gruppensolidarität und Gewaltlegitimation in einer „anderen Modernisierung." In *Anthropologie der Gewalt*, ed. Jan Köhler and Sonja Heyer, 71–88. Berlin: Verlag für Wissenschaft und Forschung.

Small, Melvin, and David Singer. 1982. *Resort to Arms: International and Civil Wars, 1876–1980*. Beverly Hills, CA: Sage.

Waldmann, Peter. 1989. *Ethnischer Radikalismus: Ursachen und Folgen gewaltsamer Minderheitenkonflikte am Beispiel des Baskenlandes, Nordirlands und Quebecs*. Opladen, Germany: Westdeutscher Verlag.

———. 1995. Gesellschaften im Bürgerkrieg. Zur Eigendynamik entfesselter Gewalt. *Zeitschrift für Politik* 42 (4):343–348.

———. 1997. Veralltäglichung der Gewalt: Das Beispiel Kolumbien. In *Soziologie der Gewalt*, ed. Trutz v. Trotha, 141–161. Opladen, Germany: Westdeutscher Verlag.

———. 1998a. *Terrorismus: Provokation der Macht*. Munich: Gerling-Verlag.

———. 1998b. Bürgerkrieg—Annäherung an einen schwer faßbaren Begriff. In

Bürgerkriege: Folgen und Regulierungsmöglichkeiten, ed. Heinrich W. Krumwiede and Peter Waldmann, 15–36. Baden-Baden, Germany: Nomos.

——. 2000. Rache ohne Regeln: Zur Renaissance eines archaischen Gewaltmotivs. *Mittelweg* 9 (36):4–25.

Walter, Barbara F. 1997. The Critical Barrier to Civil War Settlement. *International Organization* 51 (3):335–364.

Williams, Bernard. 1988. Formal Structures and Social Reality. In *Trust. Making and Breaking Cooperative Relations*, ed. Diego Gambetta, 3–13. Oxford: Basil Blackwell.

Zartman, William. 1985. *Ripe for Solution: Conflict and Intervention in Africa*. New York: Oxford University Press.

II

THE POLITICS OF INTERVENTION

7

❦

Looking Back,
Looking Forward:
Reflections on Preventing
Inter-ethnic Conflict

Max van der Stoel

Nationalism is alive and well. Although I hope Ted Gurr is right when he says that ethnic warfare's heyday may belong to the last century (Gurr 2000:52), we are by no means out of the woods yet. Just when we think someone like Milošević is moving into the shadows, someone like Vadim Tudor steals the spotlight. While the media focus on one conflict, another one brews below the surface. A century marred by inter-ethnic conflict and excessive nationalism is only just behind us, but its legacy lingers on. What lessons can we take from the past, and what are the prospects for facing ethnic conflicts in the future? Based on my experience as the Organization for Security and Cooperation in Europe (OSCE) high commissioner on national minorities between 1993 and 2001, I would like to make some observations on preventing inter-ethnic conflict (van der Stoel 2001; Kemp 2001).

ETHNIC CONFLICT: PAST AND PRESENT

Although our world is changing rapidly, some of the fundamental issues that we are facing today are those that theorists and practitioners have been struggling with over the past 150 years. These include protecting and promoting minority rights and identities within multi-ethnic states, and reconciling claims for self-determination with the interest in preserving the territorial integrity of states. These issues plagued the Austro-Hungarian and Ottoman empires. Indeed, one could argue that the collapse of those empires was due in part to their failure to reconcile

113

competing national and state interests. During the interwar period, the great powers and later the League of Nations tried to satisfy the desire of some nations for self-determination and to protect minorities that lived in multi-ethnic states. However, there were few international standards to meet these challenges, and those that existed were often undermined by power politics. Minority rights and self-determination were therefore open to abuse, as demonstrated by Hitler's justification for his expansionist plans.

Communist countries also had difficulties coping with so-called nationalities problems. Indeed, nationalism was a contributing factor to the breakup of the Soviet Union and the Socialist Federal Republic of Yugoslavia.

The immediate postcommunist period was characterized by an explosion of nationalism. While euphoria welcomed the birth or rebirth of states, the accentuation and revival of national identity were often accompanied by a complete disrespect for the rights of others. Violent conflicts raged in a number of former communist bloc countries, and inter-ethnic tensions threatened to erupt in others.

In short, one of the defining characteristics of the twentieth century was the impact of excessive nationalism and the clash between the principles of sovereignty and self-determination. Wars were fought in defense of these principles, states have been created and broken up in their name, ideologies have been driven by them, and millions of people have been expelled or killed either fighting for, or being victimized by, nationalistic or ethnically based ideals. As a result, one legacy of the twentieth century is that we almost automatically associate the word "ethnic" with conflict.

PREVENTING CONFLICT, INTEGRATING DIVERSITY

What can we do to reverse this trend? How can we face, or better still prevent, violent ethnic conflict? I believe that there are three main considerations. The first is the need for a strong legal basis for minority rights protection. The second requires finding imaginative solutions for integrating multi-ethnic diversity. And the third is to improve our techniques for assisting all groups in society to work toward these ends. Related to this latter point is the need to put greater emphasis on conflict prevention.

The protection of minorities is centered on the protection and promotion of the human rights of persons belonging to minorities. If these rights are respected in a democratic political framework based on the rule of law, then all persons, regardless of ethnicity, language, or religion, will have the opportunity and the equal right to freely express and pursue their legitimate interests and aspirations.

In addition to established human rights standards, minority rights protection has been strengthened in recent years by the OSCE's Copenhagen Document and the Council of Europe's Framework Convention for the Protection of National Minorities. These standards have not been developed abstractly. They reflect the common views and wisdom of experts and practitioners and, above all, governments who have sought reasonable and fair ways of accommodating different identities and cultures while protecting the rights of individuals.

To be effective, these standards have to be applied. I think that many OSCE states are heading in the right direction. The fact that the respect for human rights, including the rights of persons belonging to national minorities, is part of the European Union's criteria for admission of new members has made an important impact on applicant states.

But applying these standards is not a matter of scraping over the bar for the sake of appeasing the international community. The message that I try to convey to governments is that they should implement their commitments not because they have to, but because it makes sense. Minorities are not going to go away. Marginalizing or ignoring minorities risks isolating them from mainstream society. If minorities do not feel like active and equal members of the state, they will not act like active and equal members of the state. They might seek to create their own parallel institutions and may tend to keep to themselves. This strengthens their sense of uniqueness or separateness and, by extension, the sense of difference between themselves and the majority. There is a danger that this divisiveness can sow the seeds of distrust, suspicion, and misunderstanding—the worst-case outcomes of which we know all too well.

Conversely, if minorities are given the opportunity to be full and equal members of society and do not feel that their identities are threatened, then the chances of inter-ethnic tension will be greatly reduced. If ethnicity is depoliticized and politics is de-ethnicized, then one's ethnic identity will not be an issue. Instead, people from all communities will concentrate on common interests and common concerns. Involving minorities in society and protecting their rights and identities are therefore good governance.

Because few modern states are ethnically homogeneous, legal and political frameworks should be devised to reflect the multi-ethnic reality rather than the nation-state myth. This is especially the case where there are sizeable and concentrated minority populations. For example, legislation, including a country's constitution, should be inclusive and stress civic rather than ethnic attributes. States should ensure that opportunities exist for minorities to have an effective voice in government. Minorities should have opportunities to give input to decisions that affect them. There should be mechanisms through which they can discuss their points of view and opportunities for dialogue with government representatives.

Because dialogue between the government and minorities is seldom limited to a single issue, it is important that these channels are established for the long term. A number of countries in the OSCE area have created government departments for minority issues, and have appointed ombudsmen or commissioners on ethnic and human rights issues. Several have also established minority consultative or advisory councils, either connected to legislative bodies or freestanding. Still, more needs to be done to have minorities adequately represented in the civil service, for example police and local officials.

These ideas should not be seen as a means of pandering to minority interests. Nor should they be implemented in a superficial way that amounts to little more than tokenism. Rather, the key is to strike a balance between minority and majority interests that allows for all sides to enjoy their individual identities while realizing and valuing shared interests.

For example, an effective language policy is one that concentrates on protecting the state language without limiting opportunities for use of minority languages. This is especially the case in education. On the one hand, the right of persons belonging to national minorities to maintain their identity can only be fully realized if they acquire a proper knowledge of their mother tongue during the educational process. At the same time, persons belonging to national minorities have a responsibility to integrate into the wider national society through the acquisition of a proper knowledge of the state language. This knowledge improves their economic prospects and their possibilities to exercise civic and political rights. Minority and majority interests can therefore be seen as complementary rather than mutually exclusive.

The same goes for culture. Persons belonging to national minorities have the right to express, preserve, and develop their cultural identity free of any attempts at assimilation against their will. Of course, with equal rights come equal obligations. Minorities must be good citizens and not pursue their interests to the detriment of the human and civic rights of others.

Integrating diversity may, in some cases, be well served by allowing for a certain amount of self-government. There is a vastly unexplored range of possibilities between assimilation on one hand and secession on the other that has yet to be fully appreciated. More attention needs to be focused on so-called internal self-determination whereby self-government is arranged in such a way as to respond to the desire by a significant minority group to have a considerable amount of control over its own administration, without challenging the sovereignty and integrity of the state. These ideas are fleshed out in the *Lund Recommendations on the Effective Participation of Minorities in Public Life*, which were prepared, under my guidance, by international experts in 1999.

Accepting that integrating diversity is both desirable and possible, what can be done to assist this process?

EARLY WARNING AND EARLY ACTION

The onus is on governments. They have the main responsibility to devise legislation and political frameworks to protect and integrate minorities. An overall integration strategy can be helpful in this respect. In this process, it is important for the government to send the right political signals and to involve minorities in decisions that affect them. Furthermore, promises that are given should be kept. Statements of good intention that are not fulfilled will erode the minority's confidence in the government. This can lead to disillusionment and an unwillingness to compromise in the future. Of course, this works both ways. Minorities must make full use of the opportunities available to them and demonstrate that they are responsible partners.

The international community can also play a role. Multilateral monitoring of the compliance of states to their international commitments increases transparency. Support for specific projects can help to reduce tensions and build long-term stability. I think we sometimes underestimate the impact that targeted resources can have on preventing conflict. Resources are often dedicated to people in need, either during or after a crisis. But we have to do more to prevent crises from getting to that stage at all. That requires political will, but also investment. It is hard to quantify successful preventive diplomacy because if it works, nothing happens. But it is certainly easy to spot failure. Therefore, although investment in conflict prevention may not be glamorous and may take years to pay dividends, it is money very well spent.

Of course, integration is a long-term process and there may be setbacks along the way. We must therefore be vigilant and committed to preventing any tensions involving national minority issues that have the potential to develop into conflict situations. My philosophy over the past eight years has been that the sooner we head off smoldering disputes, the better the chance that we will prevent them from igniting into full-scale conflicts later on. The longer the fuse burns, the more entrenched positions become and the harder it is to undo the damage.

Early information and careful analysis provide the background for early warning. Depending on the level of threat to security, early warning should be followed by early action. This action does not have to be dramatic. But it has to be timely and it should get to the heart of the issues. My experience is that this is best done quietly and cooperatively. Furthermore, one should take a step-by-step approach that creates a momentum for change.

While being sensitive to questions of culture, history, and symbolism, I try to get the parties to concentrate on questions of substance. Nationalism feeds off stereotypes and vague generalizations. If one can put these aside and look at the specific underlying considerations, one can begin to pragmatically tackle concrete issues in dispute. In the process, the parties might even discover that their respective positions are not as far removed from each other as they may have thought. And if they are, they often welcome outside assistance in finding common ground and building consensus.

This is not the case when parties or individuals have no interest in compromise. Extreme nationalists often stick to their guns (sometimes literally) because compromise would undermine vested interests that often have nothing to do with ethnicity. National or ethnic arguments often mask interests of power, prestige, and resources. In such cases, we have to be careful to make a distinction between populists, demagogues, extremists, and their followers on one hand and the silent majority on the other. Efforts to condemn all members of an ethnic or religious group because of the actions of a few may not only infringe on their rights, but may also create the very conditions that extremists thrive on.

Bearing that in mind, my goal has been to find common ground among the parties. I try to get governments to stretch the bounds of the politically possible while reminding minorities to keep their demands within the realm of the probable. During my visits and in my recommendations, I try to indicate possible compromise formulae and explain that protecting the interests of one group does not have to come at the expense of another.

Looking back, I hope that it can be said that my office has been able to play a useful role in taking early action on issues that could have exacerbated inter-ethnic tensions. Of course, the successful outcome of my intervention depends on the willingness of the parties to take to heart and implement the advice that I give. I see my role as that of a conciliator and catalyst. I think that the flexibility of my mandate has allowed me to be inventive in my approach. The intrusiveness of my mandate has allowed me to play an active and legitimate role in the internal affairs of states. Constructive, long-term engagement has helped to ensure that states stick to and implement their commitments.

But I must admit that it is a bit discouraging to think that my workload has not decreased in the last few years. That is why I would caution against any complacency about the reduced threat of ethnic conflict. There is a certain wishful linear logic that we are all progressing in the same direction according to the good intentions of high-level international documents. That certainly is the goal, but reality sometimes has a nasty way of interfering. There is no guarantee that we will continue moving in the right direction. We must therefore keep an eye on any backsliding on minority rights protection and continue to assist and monitor the process of implementing legal and political reform. We must also follow up on early warning with early action. We cannot simply hope that when there are clouds on the horizon, they will disperse. I do not want to sound like a Cassandra, but I want to warn against the view that excessive nationalism is a by-product of postcommunist transition and as we move out of that phase, nationalism will fade away. If that is true, how does one explain recent election results in Bosnia and Romania? Or the evident rise of xenophobia and racism in many European countries? Or persistent separatist movements in some countries? Or the assertive tendency of some countries to defend the interests of their kin abroad while neglecting the role that international organizations can play in this regard? Or the continued suspicion among certain ethnic communities that their neighbors cannot be trusted? There is no end of nationalism as there is no end of history. We will be facing ethnic conflict for some time to come.

My intention is not to prophesize doom and gloom. Rather, it is to underline the importance of facing ethnic conflicts with a new realism.

Over the past few years, thanks in large part to many of the experts who have contributed to this book, we have learned a great deal about the symptoms of crisis situations, characteristics of nationalism, techniques for conflict management, and priorities for postconflict rehabilitation. My hope is that in the years ahead, issues of ethnicity and nationalism will not only be better understood, but also more effectively addressed. They will become part of the normal discourse rather than sources of conflict. This will not only require a greater emphasis on conflict prevention, but also a change in thinking about the traditional paradigm of the nation-state and the meaning of sovereignty. We will never do away with national identity, nor should we aspire to it. But we can reduce the likelihood of violent inter-ethnic conflict.

REFERENCES

Gurr, Ted Robert. 2000. Ethnic Warfare on the Wane. *Foreign Affairs* 79 (3):52–65.
Kemp, Walter, ed. 2001. *Quiet Diplomacy in Action: The OSCE High Commissioner on National Minorities*. The Hague: Kluwer International Law.
van der Stoel, Max. 2001. *Peace and Stability through Human and Minority Rights: Speeches by the OSCE High Commissioner on National Minorities*, ed. Wolfgang Zellner and Falk Lange. Baden-Baden, Germany: Nomos.

8

⚜

Operationalizing the Lessons from Recent Experience in Field-Level Conflict Prevention Strategies

Michael S. Lund

THE STATE OF THE ART—CONFLICT
PREVENTION REACHES ADOLESCENCE

Since the early 1990s, a series of new intrastate conflicts, and the human suffering and diplomatic and peacekeeping travails that they cause, have swayed more and more leaders and organizations to the argument that it might be more humane and cost-effective to try to keep these horrible and costly wars from erupting in the first place. In 2004, this idea is no longer novel, at least in certain circles. But since the vast bulk of discourse and study concerning international conflicts still focuses on full-blown wars and crises, it is useful to describe some of the recent developments and research concerning preventing wars from starting in the first place. Numerous intergovernmental and NGO international conferences in Europe, North America, Africa, and Asia have taken up this subject. Although not a household word, conflict *prevention* is now frequently urged in the policy statements of major governments, the UN, the EU, and many regional bodies. As a priority urged in July 2000 by the G-8 Okinawa Summit, and the focus of a report of the UN secretary-general in June 2001 that was endorsed by the Security Council, conflict prevention has never been higher on the international policy agenda. The events of September 11 have also begun to spark discussions about the need to address the socioeconomic roots of extremism in corrupt states that support terrorists and marginalized or failed states that harbor them.

This recent interest in the prevention of violent conflicts has also gone considerably beyond exhortation and talk. It is being practiced more and more through a variety of concrete efforts—usually little publicized and not always explicitly referred to as such—in Eastern Europe, Africa, Latin America, and Asia. In addition, the UN Secretariat, the European Commission, regional intergovernmental bodies (e.g., Organization for Security and Cooperation in Europe [OSCE], Organisation of African Unity [OAU], and Organization of American States [OAS]), and subregional bodies (e.g., Southern Africa Development Community [SADC], Intergovernmental Authority on Development [IGAD], and Economic Community of West African States [ECOWAS]) have created mechanisms that assign staff to look for early warning signs and to consider preventive responses. Such mechanisms have been used to respond to threatening situations arising in countries such as Congo-Brazzaville, Guatemala, Peru, and Venezuela. New NGOs have sprouted up that are dedicated to advocacy, analysis, and action in conflict prevention (e.g., Forum for Early Warning and Early Response [FEWER] and International Crisis Group), and they are forwarding country situation reports to governmental bodies, accompanied by policy recommendations.[1] Also noteworthy is the recognition in recent postconflict peace operations that international programs must address basic causes of conflict through fundamental peace-building activities—indeed, nation-building—in order to prevent the reemergence of violence.

Furthermore, the procedures entailed in doing early warning and identifying and implementing appropriate preventive responses are beginning to be "mainstreamed" in the regular ongoing operations at the country-mission and program level of the European Commission, the UN, and most major bilateral donor agencies through the development of conflict assessments and other practical analytical and planning tools. This flows from the idea that conflict prevention is not a specific policy sector in itself. It is an orientation, a potential policy and bureaucratic "culture of prevention," which ideally cuts across and pervades to some degree all the major policy sectors and organizations that are involved. It thus potentially entails not just diplomacy and conflict resolution, but also development, democracy building, human rights, military affairs, environment, small enterprise development, education, health, agriculture, and so on, as well as international economic activity such as international trade, finance, and natural resource development. It must also involve actors within the affected countries themselves.

In sum, the policy "toolbox" on which prevention can draw is extensive. In the "culture of prevention," the various sectoral policies are not necessarily carried out in the usual ways, however. The difference is that these activities are seen through a "conflict lens" and modified to make them sensitive to their positive and negative impacts on conflict and peace.

Actually, the trendiness of conflict prevention is such that, as it is discovered more and more widely, many program activities that were once described as "conflict resolution" or "conflict management" have now been relabeled "conflict prevention" or its synonyms, in a bandwagon process. Conflict prevention now seems to be the term of choice, fast displacing the previously ubiquitous conflict resolution. This ascendancy may reflect genuine diffusion of the essential idea of prevention. But with so much varied activity now being lumped under conflict prevention, there is also a risk it will lose its distinctive meaning.

In particular, the popularization of prevention discourse seems to have led to the remuddling of a vital conceptual distinction—that between *proactive efforts that respond before significant violence has arisen at all* and *reactive efforts taken after armed conflict has ensued*. To keep things straight, a core definition of conflict prevention would read as follows: any structural or intercessory means to keep intrastate or interstate tensions and disputes from escalating into significant violence and the use of armed force, to strengthen the capabilities of potential parties to violent conflicts for resolving disputes peacefully, and to progressively reduce the underlying problems that produce those tensions and disputes.[2] To ignore the emphasis on preempting the eruption of violence and instead to define prevention loosely as applying also to postescalation levels of hostility ignores the original practical reason why this idea was raised in the early 1990s. Namely, social tensions and political disputes should be addressed before they spiral into destructive violence, not after. Behind that belief is considerable empirical evidence that the initial, largely nonviolent, stage of a potentially emerging violent conflict is more amenable to influence than are more escalated or militarized stages, and also the postconflict stage when war-ravaged societies have to be put back together.[3]

Despite the remaining conceptual confusion, however, the international climate in which conflicts are now perceived and discussed seems to be accepting the imperative at the normative level, albeit slowly and tacitly, of engaging early to keep wars from breaking out. As each successive bloody crisis has hit the headlines, there is less heard about how they are inevitable tragedies resulting from age-old animosities. Instead, more doubts seem to be publicly voiced that perhaps the calamity could have been avoided, and questions are asked about what went wrong and who is responsible. Both UN Secretary-General Kofi Annan and U.S. President Bill Clinton publicly acknowledged in 1998 that their bureaucracies could have acted earlier to prevent the Rwanda genocide in 1994. Parliamentary official public inquiries were made in France and Belgium into the roles that their governments may have played in neglecting or worsening that horrendous human calamity. A legal suit has even been brought by some families of victims of the Rwandan genocide against the UN secretary-general for failing to prevent it! Evidently, the moral and legal stakes are being raised a bit for well-positioned international actors, who now may be held more accountable for purported lapses of duty on their presumed conflict prevention watch. Despite some dramatic failures of prevention, or perhaps because of them, a new international norm may be receiving gradual acceptance: If violent conflicts are not inevitable and can be prevented with reasonable effort, international actors are morally bound to act to do what is possible wherever situations could very likely lead to massive violence.

In sum, conflict prevention, while clearly not mature, is no longer in its infancy. It has reached adolescence. It is twelve years since *Agenda for Peace* called for "preventive diplomacy" toward conflicts such as in Yugoslavia, and it is ten years since the genocide in Rwanda. It could be debated whether the amount of attention that conflict prevention is getting today is remarkable progress or woefully overdue. But it is clear that the idea and practice of conflict prevention have achieved wide acceptance.

In order to advance further, however, this field must continue to deal with certain basic questions. These concerns are:

1. *Causation*: What are the various underlying and more immediate sources of violent, destructive conflict, and what useful warning signs reflect these factors?
2. *"Political will"*: How can concerned people obtain sufficient political support and resources from publics, governments, and bureaucracies to undertake timely preventive action when and where it is needed?
3. *Effectiveness*: What methods of preventive action actually work in various contexts?
4. *Institutionalization*: How can procedures and policies for anticipating and responding to possible conflicts be operationalized in the regular functioning of international and national governmental and nongovernmental organizations, and how can their separate actions be carried out in a more concerted way?

A disproportionate amount of time and timber has been used up on questions 1 and 2. The field is very long on the diagnosis and analysis of the nature and incidence of intrastate conflicts, and a great deal of hand-wringing is done about the lack of political will (almost to the exclusion of the other issues). But relatively more urgent and less examined are questions 3 and 4. The field is very short on the identification and organization of effective preventive policy prescriptions. To help rectify this imbalance, the remainder of this chapter makes only a few observations on the issues of conflict causes and political will, respectively. It then takes up more extensively the questions of:

- effectiveness, by identifying several important decision-making levels in the international system at which prevention policy is now operating, and then summarizing some lessons about what is effective at one such level; and
- institutionalization, by suggesting how to link the lessons being learned to routine country-specific decision-making and implementation processes in development agencies, foreign ministries, and multilateral organizations.

CONTEMPORARY CONFLICTS:
THE LIBERAL SOLUTION AS PROBLEM

An important starting point for understanding the sources of recent conflicts is to put them in the perspective of the fundamental global-historical forces that are shaping the post–Cold War phase of state and nation-building. The intensified globalization following the end of the two blocs' ideological competition and confrontation during the Cold War has brought strong pressures—some from within and some from outside—to remake many developing societies' economies and polities. The ascendant values are more open markets to achieve economic growth, enlarge political pluralism and participation, improve governance, redress existing social hierarchies, as well as express more toleration for unconventional styles of life and belief. The current "liberal consensus" that prevails on these values, especially among the major Western powers, is now also deeply ensconced in their donor agencies as well as in the UN system, especially the World Bank and IMF. These bodies are widely and vigorously promoting economic reform, democratization, human rights, rule of law, civil society, and good governance in developing countries.

While much of this activity is beneficial, it presents a largely ignored policy dilemma for conflict prevention policy. At present, most officials and professionals within these organizations tend to assume that any and all of these liberal values advance peace and prevent conflict ipso facto—in any context, form, and increment in which they are applied. It is perhaps true, that in the long run, the basic liberal model for national and international order, once achieved, is the best preventer of interstate and intrastate violent conflict. But in the short run, the shift toward more political and economic openness that liberalism seeks can, and often has, contributed to the intrastate instabilities in which violent conflicts have erupted.

Most developing countries are now in one status or other of evolving from a relatively centralized political order (e.g., autocratic or authoritarian regimes, communist or other one-party states, military governments, and executive-dominated clientelist and oligarchical political systems) to some other uncertain political order in which power and privilege are more devolved and fragmented. Indeed, much of the world may be said to be engaged in a clash of values—not so much among civilizations as within societies. This "World War III" is a global competition between the governing principles of liberalism on the one hand, and political, economic, and ideological centralism or patrimonialism on the other. In some instances, this movement has seen the assertion of desires for more self-determination through autonomy or full independence vis-à-vis existing states. In others, it has seen power struggles over control of the existing state. One country that is currently illustrating this war between differing systems of rule in an especially vivid way is Zimbabwe. But it is emerging also in places like Uzbekistan.

Many countries experiencing this transition have handled the recent pressures to devolve power more or less peacefully, such as Poland, the USSR, Macedonia, the Baltics, Slovakia, Ukraine, and South Africa. But others, apparently with newer and weaker states and political systems, have fallen into violent, destructive conflicts, such as parts of the former Yugoslavia (Croatia, Bosnia, and Kosovo), Rwanda, Burundi, the DRC, Afghanistan, Tajikistan, East Timor, and others. Because most societies with re-aroused ethnicity have remained peaceful during this period, it is not ethnic identities, or even their mobilization in nationalist causes per se, that should be the utmost concern. It is their *violent* expression. Thus, the fundamental problem is the inability of some political systems to regulate through peaceful processes the clashes between possible winners and losers that are to be expected over the redistribution of political and economic power and the dispersion or dissolution of state authority that is occurring. In this sense, all post–Cold War conflicts, peaceful or otherwise, are not simply "ethnic" or "self-determination" conflicts or "genocide." They are most fundamentally *liberalization conflicts*.

This unfolding liberal revolution presents a dilemma for conflict prevention policymakers. International aid and foreign policies that provide unqualified support for such values as democracy, economic restructuring, and respect for human rights and minority rights *alone*, whatever the political and economic context—even at the expense of creating serious political and economic uncertainty—can sometimes contribute to the breakdown of a state and help to precipitate violent conflicts. This has occurred in Croatia, Bosnia, and Burundi.[4] However oppressive of minorities or oppositions that the existing preliberal orders have been under many noxious regimes, they represented a certain power equilibrium, social modus vivendi, and even perhaps perception of justice. They provided in some instances a measure of physical and economic security for large numbers of people. If a rapid or radical shift from these arrangements to a new and highly uncertain order then brings widespread violence, destruction, and human suffering, the overall price that has been paid in the pursuit of reform, assuming that it actually follows (which is often dubious), has been exceedingly high.

One policy implication here is that, rather than a "one-size-fits-all" approach in diplomacy and aid strategies that presses for the same liberal reforms everywhere, individual countries need to be differentiated according to their capacity to absorb disruptive shifts in unregulated power and economic assets, and the consequent instability, without breaking out into violent conflict. Rather than a moralistic approach, a more politically astute, balanced, holistic, and contextualized approach needs to be taken for fostering manageable change. Moves toward democratization and other liberal reforms, such as a multiparty truly competitive election, may in specific settings be among the adaptive mechanisms that help ensure a peaceful transition in this place or that. But the overriding policy goal should not be simply such mechanisms or even simply democracy or human rights or markets or the like at any cost. It should rather be *peaceful transition* toward ultimately more democratic, or at least legitimate and effective, governments and, above all, increasingly more productive economies and humane societies. Tailored policy strategies are needed that are country specific, but their overall aims should be (1) at a minimum, to "do no harm" by taking care in changing vulnerable societies not to inadvertently increase the risks of destructive conflict; and (2) if possible, to "do some good" by more deliberately and sensitively avoiding violent destructive expression of the clashes between interests and by fostering peaceful and constructive political conflict during a tumultuous period. How more contextualized prevention policies can be formulated is addressed in a later section of this chapter, "Linking Lessons Learned to Standard Operating Procedures."

LACK OF WILL, OR LACK OF THE WAY?

The problem of the lack of political will in conflict prevention, and the corollary problem of the lack of resources devoted to it, have been much discussed. Its ubiquity, however, may be based largely on the few highly dramatic and publicized instances such as Rwanda and Kosovo, when conflicts had reached a point when violence was imminent or had already broken out, and the international community failed to take the extraordinary measures that are required at such moments to deter or stem the escalation into higher levels of violence. Because some kind of forceful and intrusive action is usually needed at that stage of hostilities, international actors find it much more difficult politically to take the required robust diplomatic and/or military action. Among other things, security risks are higher, the use of coercion is controversial, and familiar arguments can be raised against international "intervention." You're damned if you don't, and you're damned if you do. There is no doubt that in these circumstances, lack of political will is a serious obstacle to preventive action.

However, not all recent situations requiring such "late prevention" have necessarily been of this very demanding sort. In most developing countries that are now facing the strains of transition, the international community is already present in the form of multiple diplomatic missions, development activities, structural adjustment programs, trade and commercial activities, military assistance, and, as we have noted, efforts to promote democracy, human rights, civil society, and so on. In other words, international actors are already engaged in these countries during the early stages of potential conflicts. It is not a matter of getting to Kenya on time; donors, diplomatic missions, NGOs, and so on *are* already in the capital city and throughout the countryside, sometimes in sizeable numbers. However, most of their activities are being carried out without much specific consciousness or scrutiny as to whether they are helping or hurting the larger process that is at stake in achieving liberalization without violence. Programs are initiated and resources allocated for many specific sectoral reasons, such as providing health services, but with little thought as to how such choices might be oriented to preventing violent conflicts and building up the peaceful capacities of these societies to navigate the perils of wrenching change.

In other words, the policies that are already at work and the resources that are already being spent in developing countries are not yet being effectively mobilized for conflict prevention purposes. In this light, the question of generating political will for conflict prevention in many instances may not typically be the heroic act of rescuing oppressed minorities from under raised machetes or adopting sanctions in response to police crackdowns. It is a more mundane but fundamental matter of reorienting the analyses and reengineering the bureaucratic rules of the many existing development and other programs and routines that are already operating in developing countries, so that they might serve conflict prevention objectives in particular—on an ongoing basis (Lund 1998a). Nor does the only hope for prevention lie solely in international action; domestic forces for peaceful change exist as well, within and outside governments, and can be enlisted. Presumably, a significant total difference could be made if these many multilateral and domestic efforts were each modified somewhat and done more concertedly. In this way, they could achieve a critical mass whose overall impact in a given country is more "conflict-smart" than is currently the case. Such an approach is not easy. But it does seem to require less political risk and fewer new resources.

CONFLICT PREVENTION EFFECTIVENESS

Adolescence implies that one is old enough to have taken some individual initiative and to have had some impact on the world. By the same token, adolescents can do damage. But with this might also come (perhaps it occurs in late adolescence) an increasing self-awareness that one needs to take responsibility for one's mistakes and to learn from them. Something like this greater accountability is emerging in the conflict prevention field.

Up until the last year or so, the conventional wisdom was "the problem is not early warning but lack of political will to respond." As suggested, this view resulted from such experiences as the Rwanda controversy and the afterthoughts raised over the necessity of the peace enforcement intervention in Kosovo. But though sufficient political will is of course still often lacking, as discussed above, now there is also a dawning realization that the problem is not merely getting *some* response to early warnings. It is also getting an *effective* response. It is no longer sufficient merely to take just any preventive action ("Do something, quick!"). Practitioners are increasingly expected to get tangible results, in both potential and postconflict situations, toward the ultimate goal of a sustainable peace.

This new pressure for more effective prevention has been stimulated by evidence that existing international policies and actions inevitably get implicated in the course of conflicts and their outcomes, and often can worsen the situation (cf. Barre et al. 1999:4). The interest in more effective action has been building for some time and is due to developments such as the following:

- Errors of judgment in prevention decisions, such as conferring diplomatic recognition on Croatia in 1991 without guaranteeing the Serbs' security, and failing to vigorously enforce aid conditionalities regarding human rights abuses in Rwanda in 1993–1994 following the Arusha Accords.
- The "Do No Harm" debate, which has raised the question of whether humanitarian aid can often abet conflicts, such as in the maintaining of Hutu *Interahamwe* militants in the refugee camps of eastern Zaire from 1994 to 1997 after their exodus from Rwanda. This debate regarding areas in crisis has spilled over into conflict prevention discussions.
- Funding agencies and foundations, wondering whether their money is being well spent, have commissioned program evaluations. The findings in some instances reveal strengths but also the serious limitations of frequently used and well-meaning types of initiatives, such as NGO "track-two" diplomacy (e.g., Serbe et al. 1997).
- Evidence that the unqualified championing of some kinds of reforms in highly polarized societies, such as promoting democracy and minority

rights through majoritarian elections, can increase the risks of violent backlash by factions who see themselves losing (e.g., Reilly 1999).

In short, recent prevention failures have involved not only lack of action but also ineffective action. Policy errors have occurred in countries where international actors are already present on the ground carrying out programs, not places where they have yet to arrive. So if prevention failure involves not only acts of omission, but also acts of commission, the challenge for the UN, EU, and other major international actors is not simply taking timely action, though timing is still crucial. The action taken must also be appropriate to and effective in the specific context where it is applied. These actors not only need to respond toward incipient conflict situations more promptly, they also must respond more intelligently. The problem is not only political will, but also political *wisdom*.

In essence, the question of conflict prevention effectiveness is: What methods, programs, policies, and actions can achieve peaceful transition toward a more liberal form of social order—and under what conditions? In response to the growth of conflict prevention activity, several researchers began already in the early 1990s to gather policy-relevant lessons from actual prevention experience through applying methods of quantitative, case study, and evaluation research. More recently, donors and other funders are beginning to take an interest in "learning lessons" and identifying "best practices." However, the findings from the accumulating research studies have been scattered and diverse, so they have not been consolidated or disseminated to the decisionmakers who might apply them. Supply and demand have yet to meet in any significant way. But there are lessons on the shelf.

The Multiple Levels of Preventive Action in the International System

One reason for the gap between the existing knowledge and its utilization is the lack of a framework in which to classify the accumulating findings so they can be referenced by decisionmakers, as well as further cumulated by researchers. Governmental and nongovernmental policies that are impacting positively or negatively on conflict prevention and peace building are being carried out at several levels: global, regional, national, and local. Examples of potential conflict prevention action at these four levels would be, respectively: (1) the international criminal court, and the international regulation of illicit small arms; (2) a regional embargo on arms traffic or regional economic sanctions; (3) a national political debate, a preventive deployment; and (4) a rural village development project. Because preventive action takes place at all of these differing levels, the question "What is effective?" also needs to be raised and answered at each of these levels.

A few overarching "lessons" may apply to the world as a whole, such as the one developed above about balancing change and stability during periods of transition. But these are very general, and some tend toward obvious platitudes that provide little specific guidance ("Act early!" "Listen to those involved in the conflict!"). But other more concrete lessons relate specifically to different regions, individual states, and substate communities in the international system at which prevention activity is being carried out as well as to the sectoral or other units of collective, potentially preventive, activity that are operating at the different levels. Busy practitioners may want researchers to provide them with, say, *the* five lessons to be learned in conflict prevention—"1, 2, 3, 4, 5." However, there may be several sets of such lessons about what is effective or ineffective, depending on the level and type of the activity examined.

Actually, the practitioners who are potential consumers of prevention lessons will quickly recognize that they play varied roles at and across each of these different levels. Headquarters-level officials and planners tend to set general policy and oversee agency operations, desk officers monitor specific country-level developments, country-level administrators run programs, and project managers operate activities in local communities. Given their particular stations, practitioners will tend to take an interest in the results of prevention actions that are within their control, and thus in lessons that focus on their particular level for preventive action.

In sum, to learn from the existing experience in conflict prevention, more needs to be done to codify lessons in a unified classification scheme that indicates where they apply in terms of the many levels and types of activities. Such an indexed catalogue enables the many differing actors who can influence a conflict situation to find prevention guidance that applies to *them*.

Major Levels of Preventive Action for Lesson Learning

We can begin to describe such a learning framework by charting the terrain of conflict prevention activity. The following list identifies some major levels and units of preventive action at which various prevention lessons are being gathered or can be.

A Priori International Standard Setting: Norms, Standards, Goals, or Requirements Set for Countries Globally or Regionally

This level of collective action involves worldwide or regionwide legal and normative norms and principles that define a priori standards, such as with regard to human rights, rule of law, democratic government, environment, and the like. The promulgation of these standards is aimed at encouraging or enforcing appropriate behavior by governments or other actors. The norms are agreed to mainly by states, written up in international conventions and treaties, and promoted or enforced by international bodies (e.g., the OSCE's standard setting through politically binding principles, international human rights conventions, the accession criteria of the EU for prospective member countries, and the EU's Lomé Convention's goals for democracy in the signatory countries). The standards are not formulated for particular countries that face specific conflicts, but they may be used as a standard for judging their behavior in potential or actual conflict situations. Adherence to such rules is widely seen as effective structural conflict prevention.

Constitutional and Territorial Governance Structures

These are overall institutional arrangements that can be adopted by states in order to define the respective prerogatives of and operating relationships between the various parts of their central and local governments: federalism, autonomy, decentralization, parliamentary and presidential systems, and so on. As illustrated in several chapters in part III of this volume, these arrangements tend to persist for long periods of time and particular options are considered to channel political life in ways that can help prevent violent conflicts in certain conditions.

Preventive Interventions into Specific Situations

- *Policy instruments*: Organized usually on sectoral or functional lines, these are differing generic types of preventive interventions, or policy tools, that are applied in a time-sensitive way to particular conflicts (e.g., human rights observers, conditional aid, media professionalization, "track-two diplomacy," conflict resolution training, preventive deployment, and special envoys). Particular policy instruments may be applicable at the global, regional, national, or local levels. Policy instruments tend to embody differing kinds of incentives and disincentives, as well as other types of positive or negative inducements to influence a conflict. They may be carried out in several locations in a conflict arena and usually require several actors at several levels to implement them.[5]
- *Multi-instrument engagements* refer to the combination of interventions that a multilateral peace operation or other mission, along with NGOs, has initiated with regard to a particular potential or past

intrastate conflict setting and maintains there over a certain time period. These engagements often apply several kinds of instruments (e.g., political dialogue, police training, electoral assistance, and civil society capacity-building projects).

- *Individual programs and projects*: Some foreign or host governments and multilateral organizations, or their specific agencies, have taken an interest in how their own set of programs and projects in a developing country perform in conflict prevention terms. The unit of action and thus analysis includes single programs or groups of programs. The smallest meaningful unit of collective activity that can be intended explicitly to have its own prevention impacts would be projects (e.g., one or more radio programs developed by a peace radio studio).

Overall, the above units of prevention activity, and thus of analysis, comprise some of the parts of an overall de facto international conflict prevention universe of activities, or would-be system, that is currently affecting conflicts positively or harmfully in myriad ways. What is ultimately needed is to improve the overall efficacy of this disjointed or, at best, very loosely joined set of activities to imbue more of it with the values and criteria of the "culture of prevention."

Lessons from Country-Level Multi-Instrument Engagements

In response to the recent increase in explicit prevention activity, a number of researchers have looked at instances of intrastate potential or actual violent conflicts when several preventive efforts have been made, in order to identify some of the elements that appear to be associated with the (unheralded) "successes" and the (more publicized) "failures" (although most outcomes are not simply one or the other). These studies have focused on multi-actor, multi-instrument preventive engagements in situations such as the potentially violent conflict mentioned above. Box 8.1 pulls together some of the generalizations that are suggested by these case studies. They are presented in a structured outline in which lessons can be cumulated in an ongoing database that is currently under development. In this way, case studies can provide the basis for policy guidelines to effective conflict prevention practice for would-be conflict preventers. Though based on existing systematic research, the generalizations are preliminary hypotheses that additional case studies need to test further. Thus, the database can be tested further and continuously refined, and its findings continuously disseminated to those decisionmakers who can make best use of these lessons.

Box 8.1.   Key Ingredients of Effective Multi-Instrument Country-Level Preventive Engagements

Recent case-study findings suggest that serious intrastate political tensions and issues will tend to be addressed peacefully, rather than escalate into violence, to the extent that the following ingredients are present:

Features of the Preventive Engagement Itself

When?

1. Timely, early action is taken as tensions are emerging, but before, rather than following, significant use of violence, or immediately after initial outbreaks.

2. Engagement prioritizes the various goals of preventing violence (security, "peace"), managing issue disputes, and transforming overall institutions and societies (e.g., political and social justice)—that is, both "direct" and "structural" prevention—in contextually appropriate mixes and sequences. Such prioritization generally recognizes that when behaviors and actions immediately threaten major loss of life and destruction, they need to be deterred or stopped most urgently, before more fundamental structures of power and socioeconomic advantage are addressed. But it also recognizes that short-term crisis management needs to be followed or supplemented by actions that credibly tackle those more fundamental issues.

What?

3. Early action is robust, rather than half-hearted and equivocal, by exerting vigorous positive and negative inducements specifically on the major potentially conflicting parties' leaders and their mobilized rank and file.[a]

4. Early action thus brings an appropriate mix of sufficiently vigorous (conditional) carrots, (unconditioned) support, sticks, negotiating "tables," and other modes of influence to bear on the several most important short-term and long-term sources of potential conflicts, the key "fronts" in which conflicts are being played out.

5. Early action does not solely promote the cause of the weaker parties in the conflict but also addresses the fears and insecurities of dominant parties.[b]

6. Support and protection are provided to established governing formal institutions of the state, to the extent that they incorporate the leaders of the main contending communities in power sharing in rough proportion to their distribution in the population, rather than buttressing an exclusionary governmental structure or, alternatively, an antistate political opposition. Responsible autonomous organs of the state and within the security forces are assisted to provide public services professionally. This enables the state to host a process of give-and-take politicking over policy and constitutional issues that can carry out public business that "delivers the goods" for the benefit of the general population.

(continued)

7. Opportunities for joining regional security alliances and trade cooperation also create an overall climate of support for building liberal peaceful states.[c]

8. Outside formal government, a politically active but independent and broad-based civil society is built up over time that cuts across the society's main politicized identity groups, that is not solely interested in politics, that is primarily interested in business pursuits and can generate wealth, and that thus can represent a "constituency for peace" that has a vested interest in political stability and social prosperity.[d]

9. Peaceful people-power campaigns are supported through training opposition leaders in nonviolent tactics and non-incendiary rhetoric, so they exert significant pressure on leaders to take peaceful, responsible actions.

Who?

10. Preventive engagements are implemented by a sufficient number and kind of governmental and nongovernmental actors, so as to provide the range of needed instruments (mediation, deterrence, institution building, etc.) and resources to address the leading sources of the conflict. In the process, these actors form a "critical mass" that visibly symbolizes a significant international commitment to nonviolent change.

11. The engagement is supported politically and in other ways, or at least tolerated and not blocked or undermined, by major *regional* powers and major *world* powers.

12. The engagement is generally viewed as legitimate by its being carried out under the aegis of the UN or a regional multilateral organization involving the states affected.

How?

13. The early multifaceted action is concerted and consistent among the major external actors, rather than scattered or contradictory.

Features of the Regional, National, and Local Context

Where?

14. Past relations between the politically significant groups have been peaceful in the recent past, rather than violent.

15. Moderate leaders from each of the contending communities are in positions of authority and in regular contact as they carry out the public's business, and they show some progress in carrying out public policies that benefit all communities, including providing for physical security.

16. Neighboring states and refugee communities that are adjacent or close to the immediate arena of conflict are neutral to an emerging conflict or actively promote its peaceful resolution, rather than supporting one side or another politically or militarily.

17. The diasporas of the parties to a conflict that reside in major third-party countries also support peaceful means of resolution, or at least are not highly

mobilized behind their respective countrymen's cause. Thus, they do not aid and abet coercive or violent ways to pursue the conflict and lobby their host governments to take a partisan stance toward the conflict.

Note: This synthesis draws from, among others, Miall (1992); Munuera (1994); Woodward (1995); Lund (1996); Wallensteen (1998); Lund et al. (1998); Leatherman et al. (1999); Lund (1999); and Lund (2001). Special note should also be made of an outstanding book by Barnett Rubin, *Blood on the Doorstep: The Politics of Preventive Action* (2002), which includes four case studies.

a. For example, empirical studies of the antecedents of "genocides" and "politicides" conflicts by Barbara Harff (2003) suggest that announcements of possible international preventive interventions that in fact do not happen or are half-hearted and largely symbolic may be interpreted by determined combatants as a go-ahead signal to pursue the conflict with impunity through further oppression or aggression.

b. Where needed to avoid backlash from a threatened but powerful ancien regime, such an approach seeks to keep lines out and open to moderates or other persuadable elites, rather than labeling them prematurely as irredeemable pariahs and leaving them no recourse for shifting their loyalties to join the forces of change. It looks for opportunities for quiet "constructive engagement" with existing regime leaders and their cliques, to point out the "handwriting on the wall" and conjure up historic roles for them as national invigorators. It creates opportunities for amnesty or "soft landings" to prevent existing leaders from digging in their heels. It engages and supports existing moderate elements within hegemonic regimes, to exercise transformation from within. It thus avoids a sentimental or expressive moralistic approach or Manichean "good guys" versus "bad guys" campaigns in favor of pragmatic tactics that address leaders' and other actors' specific political and economic incentives.

c. As in Eastern Europe, this may involve offering specific attractive incentives to current or alternative leaders and elites that promise that, if their national policies achieve economic and political reforms, respect minorities, and so on, they can hold power by gaining the political support of interest groups and publics who will see benefit from integration.

d. This guideline thus eschews reinforcing or coddling ethnic minority movements that tend to polarize national politics by boycotting a polity's elections and declining other opportunities to participate in and thus leaven mainstream political life. It avoids polarizing the political conflict to dangerous lengths by siding only with political oppositions in "we versus them" struggles and thus keeps international support from being a catalyst that provokes violent backlash, unless it is also prepared to protect the innocent victims of repression.

LINKING LESSONS LEARNED TO
STANDARD OPERATING PROCEDURES

Although such findings are accumulating, they have yet to be significantly recognized, boiled down, and utilized to inform decision making and thus really be "learned" by the very organizations to which they pertain. Thus, the lessons gathered from actual experience at the country level and other levels of practice need to be reconnected to the actual routines and established processes of decision making and implementation.

The first thing that is needed is a process of conflict diagnosis, selection of options and strategy development, implementation, and evaluation that allows the lessons about effective prevention to become integrated into the standard operating procedures of governmental and nongovernmental bureaucracies. Fortunately, this process of mainstreaming early-warning and prevention responses is already beginning among all major multilateral and bilateral development agencies (although less so perhaps among their colleagues in foreign ministries).[6] At headquarters level, the UN Secretariat now operates a Prevention Team that meets regularly to monitor potential trouble spots and recommend appropriate action. At the country level, the UN and every other major donor and multilateral organization have established some regular process of drawing up country-specific development assistance plans.

Some organized process is then needed that conducts the analysis above in order to apply the lessons from experience in strategies that fit particular potential conflict situations. This process should not be simply bilateral but multilateral. One of the lessons discussed above is that multiple actors and their respective policy instruments and political influence are usually needed to steer any given unstable country toward peaceful progressive change. Thus, what is ideally needed to the extent that the country situation is difficult to influence is for many actors to join others in collaborative assessments and country-specific conflict prevention strategy development and implementation. More effort is needed to link the country desk officers at the headquarters level in the differing agencies. In addition, the respective development staffs at the field level could engage informally with each other at the country level in joint analyses of each host country's conflict vulnerabilities and peace-building opportunities. Such joint analysis could over time encourage more complementary in-country programs.

So far, even among the most prevention-oriented organizations there persists an understandable, but ultimately short-sighted, tendency to ask for lessons of effective prevention that are packaged only in terms and forms that are specific to their particular organization's programs and procedures. International NGOs such as FEWER and International Alert are stepping forward to stimulate such country-level exercises in specific sites such as Georgia and Kenya, in the hopes of encouraging donors, the UN, the EC, the OSCE, host governments, and local NGOs to engage in collaborative assessment and response. Ultimately this convening function might be handled by UN resident coordinators or special representatives, EU country delegations, or key NGOs, who could take the initiative and act as conveners and facilitators.

CONCLUSION

Bringing the lessons of effective past conflict prevention, such as those listed in the section on "Conflict Prevention Effectiveness," into a multi-lateral field-level process of analysis and action, such as described in the previous section, can also help to address the two questions treated more briefly at the beginning of this chapter: conflict causation and political will. With regard to understanding conflict causes, creating a structured opportunity for relevant actors to participate in a joint process for examining the sources of conflicts, especially when done at the field level, would yield richer data regarding the sources of the conflicts in specific settings and the complex dynamic interactions of these factors. The information and nuances available to astute and sensitized local observers would also add to the generic knowledge of how conflicts arise.

With regard to the problem of political will, this joint process for engaging various actors in identifying possible effective response options could itself "co-opt" these actors into taking conflict prevention more seriously. The last several years have revealed that there is a big difference between accepting the idea of conflict prevention rhetorically and intellectually on the one hand, and focusing specifically on how to do it and doing that on the other. But having to come to terms while in direct engagement with one's peers and counterparts with how one's organization may be helping to reduce emerging conflicts, or possibly worsen them, would most likely stimulate concrete actions. Even knowing that there are plausible methods that might be tried toward potentially violent conflict situations may increase hesitant decisionmakers' levels of comfort. They may lead them to feel more confident that they can exercise political will without taking huge risks. Hence, the awareness that others are engaged in the same multilateral endeavor could also help to reduce the problem of lack of political will.

NOTES

This paper is indebted to many influences, some of which are noted. It draws also from Lund and Rasamoelina (2000).

1. What one book described a decade ago as the "emerging global watch" seems to be gradually taking some form. See Ramcharan (1991).

2. Accordingly, it includes not only avoiding violence but also the range of more fundamental changes now referred to as "peace building." Prevention can come into play both in places where conflicts have not occurred recently (i.e., prevent vertical escalation), including forestalling the spread of already active hostilities to new sites (i.e., prevent horizontal escalation), and also where recent but terminated violent conflicts could recur (i.e., prevent relapse in postconflict situations). In

short, the essence of conflict prevention is a *stance of responsiveness* to unstable, potentially violent conditions that are unfolding on the ground in particular places at particular times. Thus, despite the earlier use of the term "preventive diplomacy," conflict prevention cannot be restricted to any particular means of intervention or implementing actors, such as diplomats. In principle, it could involve the methods and means of any governmental or nongovernmental policy sector, whether labeled prevention or not (e.g., not only mediation, good offices, and the like, but also sanctions, conditional development aid, mediation, structural adjustment, humanitarian assistance, arms control, media, education, preventive military deployment, democratic institution building, private investment, trade, etc.). Of course, whether any such means are *in fact* conflict preventive (i.e., effective) is not automatic from their mere intent and application, but depends on how they are applied and the results they actually obtain. Indeed, some of these tools applied without conflict sensitivity have contributed to violent conflicts.

3. The differing stages of conflict, such as emergence, escalation, de-escalation, (re)construction, and reconciliation, are now being adopted as an organizing framework by textbooks in the conflict field, for example Kriesberg (1998) and Miall et al. (1999).

4. One might hypothesize that a certain pattern has characterized the international responses to pre-genocide Rwanda, 1993–1994; Burundi, 1993; Kosovo, 1992–1998; East Timor, 1999; and possibly other recent cases of violent intrastate conflict. The international community's sympathetic political championing of an ethnic minority's rights, such as through honoring unofficial referendums and denouncing the human rights violations of their oppressors, may tend to polarize the local political relations further by demonizing the perpetrators and emboldening the victims. This may help to catalyze violence—if the forces of violent *backlash* in those settings are tempted to preempt militarily the impending threat of political change, and the international community is not prepared to deter that reaction. Ostensible violence *prevention* then can become violence *precipitation*, for well-intentioned advocacy of human rights promotion, provision of humanitarian aid, or other international measures are advanced on behalf of a vulnerable group, and yet it puts them at greater risk by neither deterring the more powerful and better-armed forces of reaction from taking further oppressive actions or genocide nor providing adequate international provision to protect the victims.

5. A small but growing field of analysis is evaluating the impacts of such instruments and putting these assessments in forms that can be used by desk officers and other practitioners. See, for example, the brief assessments of election observers, human rights observers, and other instruments in Lund et al. (1999), which was prepared for country desk officers of the European Commission. A USAID-funded study under the Greater Horn of Africa Peacebuilding Project at Management Systems International, Inc. (MSI) conducted a preliminary evaluation of the peace and conflict impacts of three instruments (peace radio, traditional local-level peace processes, and national "track-two" political dialogues) in five countries (Lund et al. 2001). A draft manual of diverse UN "preventive measures" such as fact-finding missions, humanitarian aid, and local community economic development has been prepared for the Framework Team in the UN Secretariat (Lund et al. 2001). Earlier rudimentary efforts to apply various criteria to

evaluate the actual conflict prevention capacities and limits of nineteen prevention policy instruments are found in Creative Associates International (1997) and in Lund (1998b). The case studies organized and analyzed by Mary Anderson under the Local Capacities for Peace Project at Collaborative for Development Action, Inc. (CDA) are also very relevant here (Anderson 1999).

6. For recent developments, see Leonhardt (2000). Earlier outlines of the essential steps in developing strategies are found in Lund (1996:chapter 4) and Lund (1998c:chapter 2).

REFERENCES

Anderson, Mary. 1999. *Do No Harm: How Aid Can Support Peace or War*. Boulder, CO: Lynne Rienner.

Barre, Anton, David Shearer, and Peter Uvin. 1999. *The Limits and Scope for Use of Development Assistance Incentives and Disincentives for Influencing Conflict Situations, Case-Study: Rwanda*. Summary Report to the Development Assistance Committee (DAC), Informal Task Force on Conflict, Peace and Development Cooperation, OECD.

Creative Associates International, Inc. 1997. *Preventing and Mitigating Violent Conflicts: A Guide for Practitioners*. Washington, DC: Creative Associates International, Inc., accessed at www.caii-dc.com/ghai.

Harff, Barbara. 2003. No Lessons Learned from the Holocaust? Assessing the Risks of Genocide and Political Mass Murder since 1955. *American Political Science Review* 97 (1):57–73.

Kriesberg, Louis. 1998. *Constructive Conflicts: From Escalation to Resolution*. Lanham, MD: Rowman & Littlefield.

Leatherman, Janie, William DeMars, Patrick Gaffney, and Raimo Vayrynen. 1999. *Breaking Cycles of Violence: Conflict Prevention in Intrastate Crises*. West Hartford, CT: Kumarian Press.

Leonhardt, Manuela. 2000. Improving Capacities and Procedures for Formulating and Implementing Effective Conflict Prevention Strategies—An Overview of Recent Donor Initiatives. In *The Impact of Conflict Prevention Policy: Cases, Measures, Assessments, CPN Yearbook 1999/2000*, eds. Michael S. Lund and Guenola Rasamoelina, 89–112. Baden-Baden, Germany: Nomos.

Lund, Michael S. 1996. *Preventing Violent Conflict: A Strategy for Preventive Diplomacy*. Washington, DC: U.S. Institute of Peace.

———. 1998a. Not only When, but How: From "Early Warning" to Rolling Prevention. In *Preventing Violent Conflict: Past Record and Future Challenges*, ed. Peter Wallensteen, 155–166. Uppsala, Sweden: Uppsala University, Department of Peace and Conflict Research.

———. 1998b. Impacts of Development Aid as Incentives or Disincentives in Reducing Internal and Inter-state Conflicts: A Review of Findings from Documented Experience. Report to the Development Assistance Committee (DAC), Task Force on Peace, Conflict and Development, OECD. Unpublished manuscript.

———. 1998c. Developing Conflict Prevention and Peacebuilding Strategies from Recent Experience in Europe. In *Preventing Violent Conflict: Issues from the Baltics and the Caucasus*, ed. Gianni Bonvicini et al., 36–79. Baden-Baden, Germany: Nomos.

———. 1999. Preventive Diplomacy for Macedonia, 1992–1997: Containment Becomes Nation-Building. In *Preventive Diplomacy in the Post Cold War World: Opportunities Missed, Opportunities Seized and Lessons to Be Learned*, ed. Bruce Jentleson, 173–210. Lanham, MD: Rowman & Littlefield.

———. 2001. Why Are Some Ethnic Disputes Settled Peacefully, While Others Become Violent? Comparing Slovakia, Macedonia, and Kosovo. In *Journeys through Conflict*, ed. Hayward R. Alker et al. Lanham, MD: Rowman & Littlefield.

Lund, Michael S., Larry S. Beyna, Stacy S. Stacks, Janet Tuthill, and Patricia Vondal. 2001. *The Effectiveness of Civil Society Initiatives in Controlling Violence and Building Peace*. Washington, DC: Management Systems International, Inc. Accessed at www.usaid.gov.

Lund, Michael S., and Andreas Mehler, principal contributors; Céline Moyroud, project manager. 1999. *Peacebuilding and Conflict Prevention in Developing Countries*. Ebenhausen, Germany: Conflict Prevention Network, Stiftung Wissenschaft und Politik.

Lund, Michael S., and Guenola Rasamoelina. 2000. The Impact of Conflict Prevention Policy: Cases, Measures, Assessments. *Yearbook of the Conflict Prevention Network*, Stiftung Wissenschaft und Politik, Ebenhausen, Germany, series, ed. Michael S. Lund and Guenola Rasamoelina, 23–45. Baden-Baden, Germany: Nomos.

Lund, Michael S., Barnett Rubin, and Fabienne Hara. 1998. Learning from Burundi's Failed Democratic Transition, 1993–96: Did International Initiatives Match the Problem? In *Cases and Strategies of Preventive Action*, ed. Barnett Rubin, 47–91. New York: Century Foundation Press.

Miall, Hugh. 1992. *The Peacemakers: Peaceful Settlement of Disputes since 1945*. New York: St. Martin's Press.

Miall, Hugh, Oliver Ramsbotham, and Tom Woodhouse. 1999. *Contemporary Conflict Resolution*. Cambridge: Polity Press.

Munuera, Gabriel. 1994. *Preventing Armed Conflict in Europe*. Paris: Institute for Security Studies.

Ramcharan, B. G. 1991. *The International Law and Practice of Early Warning and Preventive Diplomacy: The Emerging Global Watch*. Dordrecht, the Netherlands: Martinus Nijhoff.

Reilly, Ben. 1999, October 17. Voting Is Good, Except When It Guarantees War. *Washington Post*, B2.

Rubin, Barnett. 2002. *Blood on the Doorstep: The Politics of Preventive Action*. New York: Century Foundation Press and the Council on Foreign Relations.

Serbe, Gunnar, Joanna Macrae, and Lennart Wohlgemuth. 1997. *NGO's in Conflict—An Evaluation of International Alert*. Bergen, Norway: Christian Michelson Institute.

Wallensteen, Peter, ed. 1998. *Preventing Violent Conflict: Past Record and Future Challenges*. Uppsala, Sweden: Uppsala University, Department of Peace and Conflict Research.

Woodward, Susan. 1995. *Balkan Tragedy: Chaos and Dissolution after the Cold War*. Washington, DC: Brookings Institution.

9

❧

Sources and Settlements of Ethnic Conflicts

I. William Zartman

In understanding and dealing with violent internal conflicts, it is important to begin with a conceptualization of their causal ingredients as a guide to a search for their solutions. While internal wars are often thought to be based on Need, Need alone is not sufficient to cause conflict; conflict occurs when Need is unevenly and unfairly distributed, allowing targeted groups to identify and mobilize (Creed) and then to compete for resources both for the resistance movement and for its political entrepreneurs (Greed).[1] Each of the three elements in the conflict in turn requires a different type of justice as a solution. These elements pose complex challenges for mediators, and underscore the importance of prevention over cure. Prevention eliminates the opportunity on which Greed and Creed feed. But once the three combine to nourish conflict, mediation becomes a tough job of uncertain entry and long duration.

NATURE OF ETHNIC CONFLICT

Perceived collective need that is denied is the basic condition for conflict. Denied Need can refer to a broad range of grievances, from relief from political repression to redress for economic deprivation. These needs can be codified as rights, but they are ultimately subjective; it is not possible to establish a hierarchy of needs, despite the claims of some need theorists (Maslow 1943; Azar 1999). Needs are flexible and are satisfied at different levels under different circumstances, needs satisfied at one time do not always remain so, and need satisfaction—like all other satisfactions—is a function of expectations, which are themselves manipulable. However, conceptualizing conflict in general terms of needs is useful, for it points to the basic dimension of grievances, and hence of solutions.

Because of its subjectivity and universality, Need alone is not the source of conflict. A frequent expression of the Need thesis seeks to identify structural causes with the claim that poverty causes conflict, but it mistakes a condition for a cause. A quick look shows that there is no correlation between poverty and violent conflict, for the poorest are not the most rebellious. Yet logic suggests some sort of relationship, and more directly a distributional relationship. In ways to be further specified, conflict tends to find its roots in differentially distributed Need. In one of the most profound generalizations of political sociology, Aristotle noted, "Inferiors become revolutionaries in order to be equals, and equals in order to be superiors" (Aristotle 1948 [330 B.C.]:242 [Vii3]), and so the cycle continues to run.

When inferiors see injustice in their position and revolt, it is because Need appears to be distributed differentially for unacceptable or unexpected reasons. There are two keys to this perception: relative deprivation and targeted deprivation. Relative deprivation is well established as a cause for revolt: People rebel when there is a sudden shortfall in their expectations, when conditions that had been improving suddenly cease to do so, for blamable reasons (Davies 1962; Gurr 1970). It is the gap between expectations and satisfactions, usually induced by a material improvement that is not sustained and whose shortfall can be attributed to a specific agency, that opens the way to conflict.

Conflict management in this situation means dealing with expectations as much as it means meeting Need per se. Absolute improvements are likely to be less important than their relative aspect in comparison with expectations. Also important is dealing with the blame assigned to the object of revolt, by diffusing blame or by taking remedial measures. Since it is the relative deprivation factor that was the cause of the conflict rather than the Need deprivation in absolute terms, readjusting expectations and deprivations tends to be the key to the removal of conflict.

When Need-based deprivation is seen to be rooted in conscious identity factors, however, the cause of conflict moves on to its next level of specificity. Targeted deprivation occurs when Need is unevenly distributed for unacceptable reasons. When people no longer see themselves as poor or deprived because "that's the way things are" or because "it's God's will," for example, or because of something that they have done as an infraction of accepted rules, but because they are singled out for deprivation as a group, then the situation becomes explosive. To the extent that people feel themselves to be collective targets of repression and deprivation for ascriptive reasons (for what they are) or for unjustified achievemental reasons (for what they have done, rightly), that discrimination becomes a cause for revolt. People may feel targeted because of their political beliefs or their social position or their ascriptive membership, or variations on these themes, but whatever the cause of the discrimination, as long as it is collective it also provides the coin of identity for the targeted party and becomes a source of solidarity among its members (Gurr 1993). While conflict can be resolved in the initial stages by taking care of grievances and expectations, such response in the middle stages may not be heard by the revolters (and particularly by the leadership) as they focus their attention on their more important challenge of building unity and solidarity behind their revolt (Zartman 1996).

These sources of a sense of discrimination can be termed Creed, referring to generalized beliefs and identity feelings. Creed itself is a "need," as all individuals need to feel some level of identity, through ascriptive belongings and/or belief systems (Staub 1989:237–238, 252). Such needs vary, according to the individual and the context, the latter being a social phenomenon of greater interest to the present discussion than the former. People have a greater need to know who they are at some times or in some circumstances than at others. Three such circumstances have a particularly important impact on the need for identity or Creed: deep change, breakdown of other identities, and discrimination.

So much has been written about these three elements that they need only be noted briefly here. Times of deep change strike at the very notion of one's identity and accentuate a need to know who one is as uncertainty swirls about. Identity at such times is not just a "taking" affair, imposing demands on others to respect or honor the requirements of one's newly (re)affirmed identity. It is also a matter of "making" and doing, imposing demands on the identity party to act in particular ways and to reaffirm particular characteristics and appropriate behavior. Creed then becomes a specific aspect of identity, as belief systems and actions give content to simple identification. Similarly, when other creeds fail, new ones arise to fill the need, often given new energy by their offensive takeover. Thus, Islamic fundamentalism burst into the Muslim world with energy to capitalize on the failure of Arab socialism, and ethnic identities gain from the failure of—or even the challenges from—nation-building (Roy 1996).

But selective, targeted deprivation is the most frequent cause of identity-based conflict. Collective needs for identity turn deprivation into discrimination. When deprivation hits identifiable parts of the population, or when those parts perceive themselves to be selective targets, they take offense, using the discrimination as a cause for solidarity. When the discrimination continues, the goals of the rebels turn from substantive grievances for redress of the deprivation to procedural demands for control of the allocation system, since redress at the hands of others is no longer trusted

(Zartman 1996). Procedural demands are harder to resolve, since they can be satisfied only by a reallocation of positions as well as benefits, providing both an additional grievance and a cause for greater solidarity. The two aspects are related since stronger grievances strengthen solidarity and vice versa, make problem solving more difficult.

Creed adds security to Need as a source of conflict. Not only do creed-based groups perceive discrimination in distribution—too few benefits or too much repression—but they also fear for their security. The fear is circular, known as the security dilemma, and lies at the basis of ethnic conflict (Posner 1993; Stedman 1996). A group (or government), feeling threatened at a low level, takes measures to ensure its security; it thereby decreases the security of the threatening group, which takes measure in its turn to ensure its security; the original targeted group then responds; and on the cycle goes. It is the security dilemma that best explains the high levels of vicious violence between groups that formerly lived in harmony together, as in Bosnia, Kosovo, Burundi, Rwanda, Congo-Brazzaville, and others. In producing the material that holds groups together and gives them solidarity, Creed creates the conditions for the security dilemma to operate in conditions not provided by Need alone.

Deprivation- and, even more, discrimination-based grievances in turn produce political entrepreneurs who articulate demands, and organize and mobilize demand-bearing groups to carry out the conflict (Zartman 1995; de Figueiredo and Weingast 1999; Brown 1996:575; Holl 1997:30). Such entrepreneurs are the ultimate element in the causation of conflict: Need and Creed can provide the tinder for the fire, but to set it ablaze, a man with a match is required. Under his leadership, the process of conflict continues its circular route: Conflict aims at relief and redress of grievances but it also establishes solidarity, which is turn is necessary for the effective pursuit of conflict and which made the redress of grievances alone less satisfying. Sometimes these leaders are merely the incarnation of group demands, selfless expressions of collective grievances. Other times, their personal position becomes a source of its own demands, separate from Need and Creed.

Such "personal need," or Greed, is the basic impetus for political entrepreneurs who turn collective need into instruments of action and solidarity. The more Greed can mask itself as general (Need) or specific (Creed) collective grievances, the more it can attract a following and hide its personal nature. Greed is often not oriented toward solutions or problem solving but toward private gain and continuation of conflict, which is its source of legitimization. Greed-based leaders of ethnic conflict include Slobodan Milošević, Charles Taylor, and Rauf Denktas, among others. For such political entrepreneurs, the relation between resources and conflict often comes to be reversed: Instead of looking for resources to sustain the conflict, Greed-animated leadership sustains conflict in order to seize more and more resources (Zartman 2004a).

JUSTICE IN SOLUTION

Justice or fairness is best regarded not as one of the issues in the conflict but as a term of analysis for the entire situation and therefore a basic way in which issues and grievances can be analyzed and resolved (Zartman et al. 1996). Need-based conflict is reduced by meeting Need in absolute terms and by meeting it fairly, according to whatever meaning of fairness is currently acceptable in society (Rawls 1971; Eckhoff 1974; Deutsch 1975; Barry 1989; Elster 1992; Kolm 1998). In broad conceptual terms, nondeprivation (or allocation) is a public good, and therefore a solution to Need-based conflict calls for unhindered access to satisfaction of grievances and expectations. In these cases, conflict management is a matter of common or equal justice, that is, restoration of equal distributions in accordance with general expectations.

In those same terms, Creed-based conflicts call for access to separate or preferential justice, that is, favored or unequal access to distributions for previously deprived groups either to redress the discrimination or to achieve preferential treatment demanded by the Creed. Particularly the latter type of demands are extremely difficult to satisfy unless one buys into the Creed itself; they call for compensatory justice or "affirmative action," positive discrimination toward the previously negatively discriminated group. Although a return to equality is a less difficult type of justice to achieve, it usually is not satisfying to the rebelling group that feels targeted for Creed, who wants compensation for past inequalities as well as prevention of future ones in procedural as well as substantive terms. Yet Creed-based subjects of discrimination, from American Blacks to Macedonian Albanians, can be enticed away from violent conflict by promises (and deliveries) of preferential justice. Such notions of justice may produce winners but it need not produce losers at the same time, if preferential justice responds to the need of groups treated as inferiors—in Aristotle's terms—to become equals.

To manage Greed-based conflict, the type of justice is even more difficult to produce. Exclusive justice is required, that is, patent inequalities that exclude others in the distribution of benefits. The leaders do not want common or equal treatment, nor are they satisfied with just preferential treatment. The nature of their conflict requires exclusive payoffs; they are the group Aristotle identifies as rebelling to become superiors. If there are winners in the outcome, there are also necessarily losers, which runs against the grain of most conflict management doctrine and notions of justice.

OBSTACLES TO MEDIATION

In most cases (two out of every three in the twentieth century), internal conflicts end in a one-sided victory rather than a both-sided negotiation, but such outcomes are notoriously unstable (Stedman 1991). Victories over ethnic rebellions tend merely to push them underground, to lick wounds, build myths, and bide time until a later moment leads to their resurgence. Furthermore, half of the negotiated solutions were achieved by mediation, where third-party efforts were necessary to bring the conflicting parties to an agreement. Negotiations, whether direct or mediated, are difficult for a number of reasons. These reasons go far to explain the duration of ethnic grievances, often referred to as protracted social conflicts (Azar 1990). They indicate that the reasons for their protracted nature lie on the tactical and situational level, and not on the inherently unresolvable nature of primordial or Need-based incompatibilities. The obstacles to mediation can be overcome, if recognized, by skilful attention to their causes (Zartman 1993).

1. *The elements of compromise are characteristically missing in ethnic conflict.* In their demands for separate or preferential justice or—all the more so—for exclusive justice, ethnic rebels seek terms that are by their nature repulsive to the other side. A formula for agreement based on a shared sense of justice is difficult to identify when separate justice is demanded, and terms of trade are hard to find because the ethnic rebellion has nothing to offer to the government except an end to the rebellion. Eritrea and Kosovo present instances where the preferential demands were not palatable to the Ethiopian and Serbian governments, respectively, and where the rebellion had nothing with which to buy its satisfaction except to call off the costly conflict. Trade-offs are difficult to find because preferential justice is not a tradable item, as the debate over the legal aspects of identity in Sudan illustrates (Deng 1995). In ethnic conflict, from Algeria to Palestine to East Timor, recognition is the top and bottom line; once it is achieved, the ethnic rebellion has won and the government lost (Zartman 1995). All these aspects make compromise, formulation, and trade-offs—the very core of a negotiated or mediated agreement—difficult to achieve in ethnic conflicts.

2. *Elements of context are also missing.* Conflicts cannot be negotiated just any time; the context must lend itself to a search for a bilateral solution. Parties—government or rebellion—who are winning or who have a hope or expectation of escalating to victory are not likely to be interested in coming to terms with the enemy. Normally, they need to find themselves in a mutually hurting stalemate (MHS)

where the hopes of victory of each side are blocked by the other and that blockage hurts (Zartman 1989, 2000b). But in internal conflicts, an MHS is the beginning of a victory for ethnic conflict since it means that the rebellion's separateness and equality are recognized. The more typical situation is usually a soft stalemate, which instead of pushing the parties to a solution is a stable, viable, bearable compromise of its own, preventing victory by either side but keeping the conflict alive. Such is the situation in the Western Sahara and in Palestine, conflicts of long duration (Mohsen-Finan 1996). In the absence of an MHS to push the parties to negotiate, a mutually enticing opportunity (MEO) may at least theoretically serve to pull them in the same direction. But, again, in internal and particularly ethnic conflicts, an MEO is unobtainable since procedural grievances and preferential justice leave little room for mutual enticements. Such has been the situation in Mountainous Karabagh (Nagorno-Karabakh) since 1994, when a cease-fire was negotiated as the result of an MHS but a stable solution has yet to be produced in the absence of an MEO (Mooradian and Druckman 1999).

3. *The elements of agency are also frequently missing.* Negotiation and mediation require a valid spokesman for both sides, yet the position of spokesman is characteristically a source of conflict within the ethnic group. This is true for all three phases of ethnic revolt. In the beginning, ethnic groups tend to be pluralistic and divided, providing several leaders who seek to deal with the government in various ways, usually splitting over the question of tactics. Later, during the consolidation period, as the leader seeks to unite his group behind him, he is in competition with other leaders for the position of supreme spokesman. Even when the struggle seems to be won and victory or negotiations are near, there is a temptation for breakaway leaders to make a separate deal for a part of the group on terms more favorable to the government than those the mainstream would offer. In all stages, the position of ethnic spokesman is under contest. Negotiation delegitimizes leaders, in a struggle to capture the hard line. The division between Ismail Rugova and the various emerging leaders of the Kosovo Liberation Army, among the various Palestinian liberation groups, among the national liberation parties in Rhodesia on the way to becoming Zimbabwe, and between the successive Er-liberation fronts are all recent instances of intramovement ethnic spokesmanship, all involving a element of de-tical Question but also an element of Greed as well '91; Stedman 1991; Iyob 1997).

les purely intraparty. Each side in the conflict gitimacy both of an Other to speak to and of a particular person to speak for them, preferring their own candidate. Thus, each side enters into the debate over the tactical question within the other side. The struggle for leadership and spokesmanship in Chechnya is an eloquent case that prolonged and renewed the conflict; Ian Smith in Rhodesia had his preferred African leaders to deal with (the "Black Smiths"); and Morocco co-opts Polisario leaders, leaving a vacuum for other more radical Sahrawis to fill (Lapidus 1999; Stedman 1991; Mohsen-Finan 1996).

4. *Furthermore, elements of third-party entry beyond the MHS are also missing* (Maundi et al. 2000). Ethnic conflicts are internal affairs in which mediation is meddling. Mediation automatically strengthens the rebels since it suggests that the government is unable to handle its own internal problems. It is therefore resisted by the government for procedural as well as substantive reasons. Third-party intervention to help a weaker side—usually the rebellion—only exacerbates the solidarity of the other—in such cases, the government. Kosovo was a case of ethnic conflict where humanitarian efforts to help the minority only intensified the justification of the repressive government.

As a result, nongovernmental organizations (NGOs) pursuing second-track diplomacy are often more likely candidates for mediation than are other governments. However, second-track diplomacy has its own weaknesses: It is unable to provide any of the constraints and inducements for a solution that official agencies can offer, and it is unable to block alternative paths or reward cooperating parties. It is therefore left to use the only remaining weapon, simple persuasion, which is only as sturdy a reed as the perceived presence of more attractive alternatives allow it to be. The Carter Center mediating in the Congo-Brazzaville dispute in 1999 suffered the same weakness as the special representative of the secretaries-general of the UN and the OAU two years before—the inability to prevent troops from Angola from offering a better alternative to one side than reconciliation with the leaders of the other, largely ethnic parties (Zartman and Vogeli 2000).

5. *Finally, identity, solidarity, and resources tend to be dependent on conflict.* Creed requires protection (separation) or assertion (superiority), which is achieved by conflict, and conflict is the way to achieve the solidarity necessary for effective action. Rebels seek resources to sustain their conflict, then when they have gotten a taste for the resources, they sustain the conflict in order to acquire resources. The longer the conflict lasts, they more it opens the rebels to splits over the Tactical Question, essentially debates over whether to adopt a tougher or a milder policy since the current policy—tough or mild—clearly is not working; splits over the Tactical Question tend to be re-

inforced by generational splits if the conflict lasts long enough, as well as simply by personal and personality rivalries. As a result, normal cost-benefit calculations on which negotiation behavior is based no longer work.

NEED FOR PREVENTIVE RATHER THAN REMEDIAL ACTION

This is a formidable list of obstacles to the mediation of ethnic conflict. While some find it so daunting that they simply write off ethnic conflicts as protracted or primordial by nature and hence beyond any remedial attention, there are many other ethnic "situations" that exist peaceably and without conflict, and, indeed, most ethnic situations at conflict at any given moment enjoyed long periods of stability and coexistence without any conflict. The protracted social conflict school cannot explain these "exceptions" or the difference between conflict and nonconflict situations, in time or place. Even in time of deep change, collapse of competing identities, and deprivation, some situations produce conflict and others do not.

Explanations for this discrepancy come from two different directions (Sambanis 2001). On one hand, the contextual conditions for conflict lead to an outburst only when political entrepreneurs are on hand to throw a match into the tinder. On the other hand, the conflicts that do not occur have been prevented by specific measures applied before the conflict broke out. The second is discussed here, involving third-party efforts to prevent creed-based conflicts from developing, for it also contains measures to prevent the first. These efforts may not usually be thought of as mediation, but that merely indicates that the usual definition needs expansion if the challenge of containing conflict is to be met. The focus is on separating Greed from Creed from Need. Drawing up a specific list of measures presents an ongoing challenge to creativity; a few suggestions that follow from the previous discussion are presented here.

Setting Standards to Meet Needs

"Mediation" by human rights groups and world fora to establish criteria and set standards for open Creed-blind opportunity, access, and allocation to meet Needs and also for avoidance of Creed-based dominance of functions is an important and expanding area of activity to prevent ethnic perceptions of discrimination and grievance. Standards alone will not ensure a removal of discrimination, to be sure, but in setting up visible normative guidelines they constitute targets and yardsticks by which actors can judge themselves and be judged (Zartman 2004b).

One of the most important of such efforts has been the Helsinki Declaration, with its basket of human rights, in turn giving rise to a European commissioner for human rights and an Organization for Security and Cooperation in Europe (OSCE). Other regions have been slow to set such standards. The Helsinki experience was adapted in the Kampala Document by the movement for a Conference on Security, Stability, Development and Cooperation in Africa (CSSDCA), which is even more explicit on standards for equitable ethnic treatment (Obasanjo 1991; Deng and Lyons 1998; Deng and Zartman 2002). Critics noted—at the time—that the World Bank, in its programs in Rwanda in the late 1980s, could have attached standards for equitable benefits to its agricultural development programs and thus helped avoid the genocide of the 1990s (Lemarchand 1982; Eriksson 1998).

Such norms and standards are not self-implementing or self-enforcing, like any other prescriptive guidelines in this world, and so to expect more from them than from others is unrealistic. But like any other norms, they trumpet an ideal, making it hard to ignore even if not to disobey. As the community of obeyers grows, the pressure is on the disobeyers (Klotz 1991). Enforcement follows, by peers and then by institutions. This is of course a long and bumpy process, but it is recalled so that consideration of norms will not be dismissed.

Preempting Need from Creed

Needs can be addressed before they become creed-based conflicts. The larger challenge is to reduce deprivations, which may be a counsel of perfection; the more manageable challenge is to reduce the inequalities in the distribution of deprivations. Studies have shown that populations accept austerity and structural adjustment if it is fully explained beforehand and if the government is persuasive in showing that it knows what it is doing (Nelson 1995); absent these conditions, "IMF riots" take place. These riots can attract targeted populations if the deprivation has been accompanied by discrimination, as in the Revolutionary United Front (RUF) rebellion in Sierra Leone in the 1990s, or if specific populations are subject to neglect at a time of rising expectations, as in the Mexican state of Chiapas in the 1990s or the Moroccan region of the Rif in the 1950s and the Algerian region of Kabylia in 1980 (Abdullah 1998; Favret 1972).

All of these creed-based rebellions could have been avoided by proper government measures of equitable distribution. However, the mediator's role is particularly difficult, since it involves convincing sovereign governments to do what they should be doing on their own and are presumably not doing for some reason. In none of the cited cases was a third-party role as clearly indicated as the role of the government itself. In

Mozambique (a spotty example, to be sure), the National Resistance Movement (ReNaMo) feeding on rural disruption and neglect was brought into dialogue with the FreLiMo (Front for the Liberation of Mozambique) government by external mediation before the resistance was able to settle down in a particular ethnic base, but the mediator benefited from an MHS, induced in part by a local drought, to bring the urgency of settlement to both parties (Msabaha 1995).

Preempting Greed from Creed and Need

The crucial role played by the pyromaniac in setting off ethnic conflagrations makes it important to separate the political entrepreneur from his potential following. The image is only figurative, since the entrepreneur is generally not known before he starts on his adventure. Therefore the focus must be on the opportunities for his appeals to take hold. These can be reduced, either by government action or by external parties. Holding federation-wide elections in Yugoslavia in the late 1980s rather than separate elections in each of the republics would have reduced the opportunity for ethnic campaigning (Woodward 1995). Reducing rent-seeking by enlisting diamond magnates to ban diamond sales from conflict areas would close the opportunity to make easy, enormous financial benefits from ethnic conflicts in Angola or Sierra Leone.[2] Some suggestions can be generic; others must be adapted to the specific situation. But in general it is better to deter entrepreneurs at the beginning of the adventure than be faced with the need to remove them at the end.

Establishing Confidence- and Security-Building Measures (CSBMs)

Confidence and security are the appropriate responses to the security dilemma; they are needed to show that the fears are foundless and to provide the needed security without arousing countermeasures. Joint patrols, dialogue sessions, and enforced laws of equal treatment are measures among others that can be used. The Turkish experience in the late 1990s is interesting: After a particularly hardline campaign against the Kurdish Labour Party (PKK), the Turks extracted a call for nonviolence from the captured leader, Abdullah Öcalan, while also benefiting from a public opinion survey that showed the PKK to have less Kurdish support for a separatist program than originally feared by the Turks (Müftüler-Baç 1999). At the same time, earthquakes in Turkey and then in Greece increased the mutual help and cooperation between the old rivals, at a time when the issue of Turkish entry into the European Union (EU) provided an occasion for an official rebuff and then an apparent reconsideration by the EU. In sum, a number of disparate events pointing in different directions appear to have broken a logjam in two sets of internal and international ethnic conflicts. These measures tend to be dependent on actions of the internal parties rather than providing opportunities for third-party intervention. However, international NGOs have been active in instituting dialogues and other CSBMs and in training nationals in conflict-prone areas in conflict management practices (Saunders 1999).

SPECIFIC POSSIBILITIES FOR MEDIATION

Successful mediation means containing, enticing, and mending (Berkovitch 1997; Touval and Zartman 2001). The mediator must be able to block the impending or escalating conflict, draw the parties away from conflicting perceptions and actions, and bring them together in a more harmonious relationship so that conflict is not only halted but is also prevented from recurring. "The mediator is in fact also a participant, a wielder of power who compels a recalcitrant party to make a compromise it does not want to make" (*Economist*, 2 April 1998, regarding Ulster). Mediation requires an ability both to create incentives for Need-based situations to receive evenhanded government attention, to open opportunities for Creed-based groups to overcome their fears, and to close possibilities for Greed-based leaders to achieve their goals by destroying other groups. Optimally, mediators need to have the power/authority to guarantee both a continued endless conflict if their solutions are not accepted and an assured implementation of an attractive solution if accepted. All this is a tall order, and requires the ability to draw power from the situation as well as from mediators' own resources; it also requires the collaboration of both official and unofficial mediators and of the government (and, for that matter, of the ethnic parties as well). A number of areas for action can be suggested.

Mediation cannot be considered as a single act or even a single extended event. It is a process that requires the establishment of relations between the mediator and the mediated parties, the opening and closing of alternatives, and the gradual withdrawal of the mediator as a vehicle of trust while building a relationship of trust between the parties. This in turn requires a mixture of strategies to both strengthen and soften the separate identities of the two (or more) sides.

The process of mediation needs to pay attention to the Need- and Creed-based grievances, both substantive and procedural, of the parties in an effort to identify difficult compromises and compensations. Once that is done, the task is not over: It must also focus on setting up mechanisms for handling future grievances as they may arise. The situation of ethnic relations in Sri Lanka was a story of measures and backtracking in the 1950s, 1960s, and 1970s until the revolt of the Tamil Tigers finally broke out in unmanageable violence (Kuchinsky 1999; Wriggins 1995); the Dayton Agreements in 1995 were followed by a year of inattention and precious lost time when monitored implementation could have moved the process forward, before finally some of the Dayton mechanisms started rolling on their own (Holbrooke 1996; O'Brien forthcoming).

Constructive ambiguity is needed for creative new solutions. Sovereignty is one of the most difficult challenges to finding solutions for ethnic conflict, because it has long been treated as a clear-cut matter—"like pregnancy," commentators have noted, "you are sovereign or you aren't." However, recent solutions have been crafted out of looser and more creative status of divisible sovereignty to break nonnegotiable dilemmas. In the 1999 Good Friday Accords in Northern Ireland, there is provision for three overlapping jurisdictions—Northern Irish, British, and Anglo-Irish; in the 1995 Dayton Accords, a Serb Republic was established alongside a Croat-Bosniac Federation within the united state of Bosnia-Herzegovina, to bring together the absolutes of separateness and unity on which the three sides variously insisted; in Tatarstan, the 1994 agreement provided all but sovereignty for Tatarstan and all but unity within Russia—a state within a state (Hopmann 2000). Not all sovereignty can be divided, but the way around stark indivisibility has been a challenge to which creativity has responded positively. Jerusalem and Southern Sudan, Western Sahara, Kosovo and Sri Lanka still await a response (Albin 1991; Deng 1995).

Communication and interaction are necessary ingredients to any attempt to end conflict and prevent its future occurrence. Left separate, communities are certain to retreat into their own myths and histories, and develop an exclusivist creed that is ready to take umbrage at any perceived slight. Dialogue groups alongside official processes are a necessary complement (Saunders 1999). The fact that areas of intense intercommunity dialogue such as Israel, Ulster, and Cyprus have not burst out into total peace and reconciliation does not obviate the fact that the situation would certainly have been worse without it (Ross and Rothman 1999). The question remains open whether personal integration, in which Creed-based groups lose their importance, or communitarian power sharing and local autonomy, in which they become consolidated, is the better solution: The second may be the temporary expedient while the first gradually works its effects, but the second impedes the emergence of the first.

Where Creed-based groups are homogeneous, contiguous, and undivided by minorities of their own, where solutions of reconciliation have been worn out, and where the conflict has gone to a point of no return, separation may be the only solution (Kaufman 1996; Zartman 1998a). Even negotiated under the best conditions with the best attention to mechanisms for handling future problems, as in the Czech-Slovak or Ethiopian-Eritrean separations, problems are certain to arise and, as in the latter case, may break out in ugly, sustained violence. The difficulty in achieving a happy divorce underscores the need to exhaust all creative solutions for cohabitation before separation is undertaken.[3] Mediation is usually necessary to achieve a satisfactory separation agreement.

PRACTICAL ADVICE

What does this have to say about Kosovo, the Sudan, Cyprus, Palestine, Congo-Kinshasa and Congo-Brazzaville, Sri Lanka, and other ethnic conflict situations that have not yet appeared on the horizon? It underscores the difficulty of mediation, but it also deals with creed-based conflict not as a permanently protracted and irresoluble incompatibility but as a situation subject to careful analysis and intervention. A few maxims for first and second as well as third parties may be useful.

1. Don't repress your minorities; they may end up being a majority in a territory you claim. Minorities can regroup geographically if they do not already inhabit contiguous territory, forming a majority in an area for which they then claim self-determination. Similarly, groups that break away with their territory in the name of self-determination may well find their homogeneity illusive and soon face self-determination claims from minorities within their own midst. Once self-determination has entered the agenda, it is in danger of becoming a runaway locomotive.

2. Get plenty of exercise to keep the circulation going, before gangrene sets in and surgery becomes necessary. Flexible solutions are needed to meet changing conditions of ethnic minorities, as ethnic awareness and identity concerns rise and fall, along with expectations and satisfactions. Ethnic relations require tending lest mending becomes necessary, and mending lest rending becomes inevitable. There is no substitute for good governance, accountable democracy, and normal politics.

3. What history has joined together, let not momentary passions put asunder. Secession is a costly event, rarely as satisfying as promised, and its demands can usually be achieved more satisfactorily by autonomy and federalism. Despite the fears of many governments, autonomy is not a down payment on secession: Cancellation of autonomy is. When minorities are granted self-government in autonomy, it gives them something to do that takes their minds off of secession and conflict and puts the emphasis on skills at governing rather than on contesting government.

4. Court-mandated counseling is preferable to divorce; if divorce is necessary, don't count on alimony. Since courts are not available to handle internal or interstate disputes, states alone and in community need to take advantage of available official and unofficial mediators to help maintain their unity and harmony. If a state does break up, the breakaway part should not count on any largesse from its former sovereign, which will be occupied restoring its torn soul and honor.

5. Find ways to ensure "I'm alright" that do not make others less alright at the same time. Both ethnic communities and their opposites, whether governments or other ethnic communities, need to adopt the unusual and perhaps uncomfortable habit of thinking of each other while they are pursuing their own calls of Creed and Need. While these are times when, characteristically, one concentrates more on self than others, they are the very times when a dual-concern strategy is most necessary (Rubin et al. 1994).

6. If you have to call out the cops, make sure they shoot the gangsters and not the victims. If ethnic conflict comes to violence and peace-keeping or peace-enforcing forces are needed, their efforts should make things better, not worse. Awareness is only now beginning to grow about how expensive remedial conflict management is compared to preventive action, both in money and in lives and productivity (Brown and Rosecrance 1999). There is often an auto-da-fé quality about measures to punish Creed-based conflict, in which the Greed-based actors are the last to feel the punishment.

NOTES

1. These categories draw on the creative work of Paul Collier at the World Bank; see Collier and Hoeffler (1999) and Collier (1999). This chapter is an expansion of Zartman (2000a); see also Zartman (1998b).

2. The idea is John Collier's.

3. Separation is a large topic worthy of its own discussion, and is not treated here in the depth it deserves, being beyond the current subject. See Farley (1986), Zartman (1998a), and Kaufman (1998).

REFERENCES

Abdullah, Ibrahim. 1998. Bush Path to Destruction. *Journal of Modern African Studies* 36 (2):203–235.

Albin, Cecilia. 1991. Negotiating Indivisible Goods: The Case of Jerusalem. *The Jerusalem Journal of International Relations* 13 (1):45–76.

Aristotle. 1948 (330 B.C.). *Politics*. Oxford: Oxford University Press.

Azar, Edward. 1990. *The Management of Protracted Social Conflicts: Theory and Cases.* Aldershot, UK: Dartmouth.

———. 1999. Protracted International Conflict: Ten Propositions. In *The Understanding and Management of Global Violence*, ed. Harvey Starr, 23–34. New York: St. Martin's Press.

Barry, Brian. 1989. *Theories of Justice.* Berkeley: University of California Press.

Berkovitch, Jacob. 1997. Mediation. In *Peacemaking in International Conflict*, ed. I. William Zartman and Lewis Rasmussen, 89–112. Washington, DC: U.S. Institute of Peace.

Brown. Michael, ed. 1996. *International Dimensions of Internal Conflict.* Cambridge, MA: MIT Press.

Brown, Michael, and Richard Rosecrance, eds. 1999. *The Costs of Conflict.* Lanham, MD: Rowman & Littlefield.

Collier, Paul. 1999. Economic Consequences of Civil War. *Oxford Economic Papers* 51:168–183.

Collier, Paul, and Anke Hoeffler. 1999. *Justice-Seeking and Loot-Seeking in Civil War.* Washington, DC: World Bank.

Davies, James. 1962. Toward a Theory of Revolution. *American Sociological Review* 27 (1):5–19.

Deng, Francis. 1995. *War of Visions.* Washington, DC: Brookings Institution.

Deng, Francis, and Terrence Lyons, eds. 1998. *African Reckoning: A Quest for Good Governance.* Washington, DC: Brookings Institution.

Deng, Francis, and I. William Zartman. 2002. *A Strategic Vision for Africa: The Kampala Movement.* Washington, DC: Brookings Institution.

Deutsch, Morton. 1975. Equity, Equality and Need. *Journal of Social Issues* 31 (3):137–149.

Eckhoff, Torstein. 1974. *Justice: Its Determinants in Social Action.* Rotterdam, the Netherlands: Rotterdam University Press.

Elster, Jon. 1992. *Local Justice: How Institutions Allocate Scarce Goods and Necessary Burdens.* New York: Russell Sage Foundation.

Eriksson, John. 1998. An Institutional Framework for Learning from Failed States. In *Evaluation and Development: The Institutional Dimension*, ed. Robert Picciotto and Eduardo Wiesner, 218–230. New Brunswick, NJ: Transaction Publishers.

Farley, Lawrence. 1986. *Plebiscites and Sovereignty: The Crisis of Political Illegitimacy.* Boulder, CO: Westview.

Favret, Jeanne. 1972. Revolt by Excess Modernization. In *Arabs and Berbers: From Tribe to Nation in North Africa*, ed. Charles Micaud and Ernest Gellner, 307–324. Lexington, MA: Lexington.

de Figueiredo, Rui, and Barry Weingast. 1999. The Rationality of Fear. In *Civil Wars, Insecurity and Intervention*, ed. Barbara Walter and Jack Snyder, 261–302. New York: Columbia University Press.

Gurr, Ted Robert. 1970. *Why Men Rebel.* Princeton, NJ: Princeton University Press.

———. 1993. *Minorities at Risk.* Washington DC: U.S. Institute of Peace.

Holbrooke, Richard. 1996. *To End a War.* New York: Random House.

Holl, Jane, ed. 1997. *Preventing Deadly Conflict: Carnegie Commission on Preventing Deadly Conflict.* New York: Carnegie Corporation.

Hopmann, P. Terrence. 2000. Disintegrating States. In *Preventive Negotiation: Avoiding Conflict Escalation*, ed. I. William Zartman, 113–164. Lanham, MD: Rowman & Littlefield.

Iyob, Ruth. 1997. *The Eritrean Struggle for Independence*. Cambridge: Cambridge University Press.

Kaufman, Chaim. 1996. Possible and Impossible Solutions to Ethnic Civil Wars. *International Security* 20 (4):136–175.

———. 1998. Intervention in Ethnic and Ideological Civil Wars. *Security Studies* 6 (1):62–100.

Klotz, Audie. 1991. *Norms in International Relations*. Ithaca, NY: Cornell University Press.

Kolm, Serge-Christophe. 1998. *Justice and Equity*. Cambridge, MA: MIT Press.

Kuchinsky, Michael. 1999. Yielding Ground: Losses and Conflict Escalation in Sri Lankan Protracted Social Conflict. In *The Understanding and Management of Global Violence: New Approaches to Theory and Research on Protracted Conflict*, ed. Harvey Starr, 201–224. Basingstoke, UK: Macmillan.

Lapidus, Gail. 1999. The War in Chechnya. In *Opportunities Missed, Opportunities Seized*, ed. Bruce Jentleson, 39–67. Lanham, MD: Rowman & Littlefield.

Lemarchand, René. 1982. *The World Bank in Rwanda*. Bloomington: University of Indiana African Studies Program.

Maslow, Abraham. 1943. A Theory of Human Motivation. *Psychological Review* 50 (3):370–396.

Maundi, Mohammed, Gilbert Khadiagala, Saadia Touval, and I. William Zartman. 2000. *Getting in the Door: Entry into Mediation*. Washington, DC: U.S. Institute of Peace.

Mohsen-Finan, Khadija. 1996. *Le Sahara Occidental*. Paris: Presses de la Fondation nationale des science politique.

Mooradian, Moorad, and Daniel Druckman. 1999. Hurting Stalemate or Mediation? The Conflict over Nagorno-Karabakh 1990–95. *Journal of Peace Research* 36 (6):709–727.

Msabaha, Ibrahim. 1995. Negotiating an End to Mozambique's Murderous Rebellion. In *Elusive Peace: Negotiating an End to Civil Wars*, ed. I. William Zartman, 204–230. Washington, DC: Brookings Institution.

Müftüler-Baç, Meltem. 1999. Addressing Kurdish Separatism in Turkey. In *Theory and Practice in Ethnic Conflict Management: Theorizing Success and Failure*, ed. Marc Howard Ross and Jay Rothman, 103–119. New York: St Martin's Press.

Nelson, Joan M. 1995. Poverty, Equity and the Politics of Adjustment. In *The Politics of Economic Adjustment*, ed. Stephen Haggard and Robert R. Kaufman, 221–268. Princeton, NJ: Princeton University Press.

Obasanjo, Olusegun. 1991. *The Kampala Document*. New York: African Leadership Forum.

O'Brien, James. Forthcoming. Negotiating Dayton. In *Peace vs Justice: Negotiating Forward- and Backward-looking Outcomes*, ed. I. William Zartman and Victor Kremenyuk. Lanham, MD: Rowman & Littlefield.

Posner, Barry. 1993. The Security Dilemma and Ethnic Conflict. In *Ethnic Conflict and International Security*, ed. Michael Brown, 103–124. Princeton, NJ: Princeton University Press.

Rawls, John. 1971. *A Theory of Justice*. Cambridge, MA: Harvard University Press.

Roy, Olivier. 1996. *The Failure of Political Islam*. Cambridge, MA: Harvard University Press.

Ross, Marc, and Jay Rothman, eds. 1999. *Theory and Practice in Ethnic Conflict Management*. New York: St. Martin's Press.

Rubin, Barry. 1991. *Revolution until Victory: Politics and History of the PLO*. Cambridge, MA: Harvard University Press.

Rubin, Jeffrey, Dean G. Pruitt, and Sung-Hee Kim. 1994. *Social Conflict*. New York: McGraw-Hill.

Sambanis, Nicholas. 2001, 7 March. *A Review of Recent Advanced and Future Directions in the Literature on Civil War*. World Bank Draft Paper.

Saunders, Harold H. 1999. *A Public Peace Process*. New York: St. Martin's Press.

Staub, Ervin. 1989. *The Roots of Evil: The Origins of Genocide and Other Group Violence*. Cambridge, MA: Cambridge University Press.

Stedman, Stephen John. 1991. *Peacemaking in Civil Wars: International Mediation in Zimbabwe 1974–1980*. Boulder, CO: Lynne Rienner.

———. 1996. Negotiation and Mediation in Internal Conflict. In *The International Dimensions of Internal Conflict*, ed. Michael Brown, 235–266. Cambridge, MA: MIT Press.

Touval, Saadia, and I. William Zartman. 2001. International Mediation in the Post-Cold War Era. In *Turbulent Peace*, ed. Chester A. Crocker, Fen Osler Hampson, and Pamela Aall, 445–461. Washington, DC: U.S. Institute of Peace.

Woodward, Susan L. 1995. *Balkan Tragedy: Chaos and Dissolution after the Cold War*. Washington, DC: Brookings Institution.

Wriggins, Howard. 1995. Sri Lanka: Negotiations in a Secessionist Conflict. In *Elusive Peace: Negotiation to End Civil Wars*, ed. I. William Zartman, 35–58. Washington, DC: Brookings Institution.

Zartman, I. William. 1989. *Ripe for Resolution: Conflict and Intervention in Africa*. Oxford: Oxford University Press.

———. 1993. The Unfinished Agenda: Negotiating Internal Conflicts. In *Stopping the Killing: How Civil Wars End*, ed. Roy Licklider, 20–35. New York: New York University Press.

———. 1998a. Putting Humpty-Dumpty Together Again. In *The International Spread of Ethnic Conflict*, ed. David Lake and Donald Rothchild, 317–336. Princeton, NJ: Princeton University Press.

———. 1998b. Managing Ethnic Conflict: The First Perlmutter Lecture. *Foreign Policy Research Institute Wire* 6 (5):1–2.

———. 2000a. Mediating Conflicts of Need, Greed, and Creed. *Orbis* 44 (2):255–266.

———. 2000b. Ripeness Revisited. In *International Conflict Resolution after the Cold War*, ed. Alexander George and Paul Stern, 225–250. Washington, DC: National Academy of Science.

———. 2004a. Need, Creed, and Greed. In *The Economics of War: The Intersection of Need, Creed, and Greed*, ed. Cynthia Arnson and I. William Zartman. Washington, DC: Woodrow Wilson Center.

———. 2004b. Early and "Early Late" Prevention. In *Making States Work*, ed. Simon Chesterman. New York: United Nations University Press.

————, ed. 1995. *Elusive Peace: Negotiating an End to Civil Wars.* Washington, DC: Brookings Institution.

————, ed. 1996. *Governance as Conflict Management: Politics and Violence in West Africa.* Washington, DC: Brookings Institution.

Zartman, I. William, Daniel Druckman, Lloyd Jensen, Dean G. Pruitt, and Peyton Young. 1996. Negotiation as a Search for Justice. *International Negotiation* 1 (1):79–98.

Zartman, I. William, and Katerina Vogeli. 2000. Prevention Gained and Prevention Collapsed: Competition and Coup in the Congo. In *Opportunities Seized, Opportunities Missed,* ed. Bruce Jentleson, 265–294. Lanham, MD: Rowman & Littlefield.

10

❦

Transforming Ethnic Conflict: Theories and Practices

Hugh Miall

W hat is the state of the art in conflict transformation theory? Does a theory of conflict transformation already exist, and if so, can it be applied to ethnic conflicts? Can practitioners rely on this theory to guide their practice? Can analysts make use of it to understand the dynamics of conflict and to assess the effects of interventions?

This chapter aims to identify what is distinctive about conflict transformation theory and practice, and to identify its key dimensions. A theory of conflict transformation is necessary in order to give an adequate basis for analyzing conflicts, devising responses to them, and evaluating the effects of these responses. The chapter argues that theories need to be continually adapted as conflicts change, and that current theories have to be adapted to take account of the globalization of conflicts and conflict interventions.

The first part distinguishes conflict transformation theory from theories of conflict management and conflict resolution. It explores some of the main conflict transformation theories, and asks whether they add up to a coherent body of theory. It then goes on to propose a move from theories of conflict to theories of conflict-in-context, arguing that in the context of globalization we need to include the social, regional, and international context in our analyses of conflict. We need to consider factors that promote peace building and factors that exacerbate conflict at these different levels over an extended time period from before violent conflict to after it. This section attempts to extend Galtung's (1996) and Azar's (1990) theories of conflict formation to theories of conflict transformation within this broader setting. It also proposes a framework of five types of

160

conflict transformation as a basis for planning and assessing interventions in conflicts.

The second part of the chapter discusses current developments in conflict transformation practice in four main kinds of practice—that of governmental and intergovernmental representatives, development agencies, nongovernmental organizations, and local parties and groups in the conflict setting. The issues involved in coordinating initiatives between these different groups are discussed.

IS THERE A THEORY OF CONFLICT TRANSFORMATION?

The foundations of a theory of conflict transformation have been laid. But a wide variety of theoretical approaches are in use among different schools of thought and practice in the field. These theories reflect different paradigms and the different types of interveners (state and nonstate, internal and external). Different authors and practitioners use basic concepts and terms in inconsistent ways. In particular, it is not agreed whether the term "conflict transformation" is intended to include the field broadly and thus to be synonymous with "conflict management" and "conflict resolution," or whether conflict transformation has distinct elements that can be differentiated from the other two approaches.

I will argue here that a distinctive theory of conflict transformation is emerging. But it draws on many of the same concepts as conflict management and conflict resolution, and rests on the same tradition of theorizing about conflict. So it is not a wholly new approach, but rather a reconceptualization of the field to make it more relevant to contemporary conflicts.

Certain crucial changes in the nature of conflict call for such a reconceptualization. First of all, the majority of contemporary violent conflicts are asymmetric, marked by inequalities of power and status. Second, many contemporary conflicts are protracted, crossing into and out of violence repeatedly and defying cyclical or bell-shaped models of conflict phases. Third, protracted conflicts warp the societies, economies, and regions in which they are situated, creating complex emergencies fueled on the one hand by local struggles and on the other by global factors such as the arms trade and support by outside states for regimes or rebels. The complexity of these situations contrasts with the simplicity of the core theories in conflict resolution, especially those based on win-win outcomes in two-party contests.

It is helpful to distinguish three schools within the overall field while recognizing the significant areas of overlap between them.

Conflict management theorists see violent conflicts as an ineradicable consequence of differences of values and interests within and between communities. The propensity to violence arises from existing institutions and historical relationships and the established distribution of power. Resolving such conflicts is seen as unrealistic. The best that can be done is to manage and contain them, and occasionally reach a historic compromise in which violence may be laid aside and normal politics resumed. Conflict management is the art of appropriate intervention to achieve political settlements, particularly by those powerful actors having the power and resources to bring pressure on the conflicting parties or induce them to settle. It is also the art of designing appropriate institutions to guide the inevitable conflict into appropriate channels. In the words of Bloomfield and Reilly (1998:18):

> Conflict management is the positive and constructive handling of difference and divergence. Rather than advocating methods for removing conflict, [it] addresses the more realistic question of managing conflict: how to deal with it in a constructive way, how to bring opposing sides together in a co-operative process, how to design a practical, achievable, co-operative system for the constructive management of difference.

Conflict resolution theorists, in contrast, reject the "power political" view of conflict, arguing that in communal and identity conflicts, people cannot compromise on their fundamental needs. However, they argue that it is possible to transcend conflicts if parties can be helped to explore, analyze, question, and reframe their positions and interests. Conflict resolution therefore emphasizes intervention by skilled but powerless third parties working unofficially with the parties to foster new thinking and new relationships. They seek to explore what the roots of the conflict really are and identify creative solutions that the parties may have missed in their commitment to entrenched positions. Conflict resolution is about how parties can move from zero-sum, destructive patterns of conflict to positive-sum, constructive outcomes. The aim is to develop "processes of conflict resolution that appear to be acceptable to parties in dispute, and effective in resolving conflict" (Azar and Burton 1986:1).

Conflict transformation theorists argue that contemporary conflicts require more than reframing positions and finding win-win outcomes. The very structure of parties and relationships may be embedded in a pattern of conflictual relationships that extends beyond the site of conflict. Conflict transformation is therefore a process of engaging with and transforming the relationships, the interests, the discourses, and, if necessary, the very constitution of society that supports the continuation of violent conflict. Constructive conflict is seen as a vital agent or catalyst of change. People inside the conflict parties, within the society or region affected, and outsiders with relevant human and material resources all have complementary roles to play in a long-term process of peace building. This suggests a comprehensive and wide-ranging approach, emphasizing support for groups within the society in conflict rather than the mediation of outsiders. It also recognizes that conflicts are transformed gradually, through a series of smaller or larger changes and steps, in which a variety of actors may play important roles. In the words of Lederach (1995):

> Conflict transformation must actively envision, include, respect, and promote the human and cultural resources from within a given setting. This involves a new set of lenses through which we do not primarily "see" the setting and the people in it as the "problem" and the outsider as the "answer." Rather, we understand the long-term goal of transformation as validating and building on people and resources within the setting. (p. 212)

CONFLICT TRANSFORMATION THEORIES

Theorists of conflict transformation draw on a variety of conceptual building blocks, some recent, some older and borrowed from the other schools. The idea of conflict formation was already present in the work of the European structural theorists who analyzed conflict formations (e.g., Senghaas 1973; Krippendorf 1973). Perhaps the most influential work has been Galtung's (brought together in Galtung 1996:70–126), which offers a rich brew of core concepts. Conflicts, he suggests, have both life-affirming and life-destroying aspects. They form out of contradictions in the structure of society. They then become manifest in attitudes and behavior. Once formed, conflicts undergo a variety of transformational processes: articulation or disarticulation, conscientization or deconscientization, complexification or simplification, polarization or depolarization, escalation or de-escalation (Galtung 1996:90). The incompatibility may be eliminated by transcending the contradiction, by compromise, by deepening or widening the conflict structure, and by associating or dissociating the actors (Galtung 1996:116). Galtung, Krippendorf, and others also emphasize the relationship between local conflicts and the larger structural cleavages in world society.

Curle's (1971) work built on Galtung's approach. He traces how asymmetric relationships can be transformed through a shift from unbalanced to balanced relationships achieved through a process of conscientization, confrontation, negotiation, and development.

Azar's (1990) work on protracted social conflicts is also an important influence on conflict transformation theory and offers an explanation for the protracted quality of contemporary conflicts. His theory covers the denial of basic needs, governance, security, and economic development and thus offers an approach that is more closely suited to contemporary conflicts in fragile states than more generic theories. Although Azar concentrates on the genesis and maintenance of protracted conflicts, his ideas can be developed as the basis for a more general theory of conflict transformation.

With some modification, Azar's model is capable of capturing both the formation and the transformation (or deformation) of this form of conflict. Azar explains how a protracted conflict forms as a result of the denial of basic human needs of access, identity, and security. If the state and communal groups choose suppression and violent rebellion as their strategies, a conflict may then become destructive. A malignant cycle is set up, whereby destructive conflict then results in a more dependent and exploitative pattern of development, a distorted pattern of governance, and a militarized form of politics. This leads to the further denial of basic needs. The result is a protracted cycle of institutional deformation and destructive conflict.

On the other hand, if there is sufficient capacity in governance and society, if politics are not too militarized, and if the international environment is supportive, states may choose accommodation and communal groups may choose political forms of confrontation. This can lead to a pattern of constructive conflict that in turn promotes legitimate decision-making capacity, strengthens autonomous development, and sustains civil rather than military politics. All these are conducive to meeting basic needs. The model is attractive because it goes beyond simple structural or behavioral models and suggests how patterns of conflict interact with the satisfaction of human needs, the adequacy of political and economic institutions, and the choices made by political actors. It also suggests how the choice of different options by the parties leads to benign or malign spirals of conflict.

Vayrynen (1991) argues for a conflict theory based on the idea of transformation rather than settlement, stressing that it is important to understand how conflicts are transformed in dynamic terms:

> The bulk of conflict theory regards the issues, actors and interests as given and on that basis makes efforts to find a solution to militate or eliminate contradictions between them. Yet the issues, actors and interests change over time as a consequence of the social, economic and political dynamics of societies. (p. 4)

Vayrynen (1991) offers a useful classification of four ways in which conflict can be transformed. "Actor transformations" involve internal transformations in parties and the appearance of new parties. "Issue transformations" involve changes in the issues in conflict and parties' positions on those issues. "Rule transformations" are changes in the norms or rules governing a conflict. "Structural transformations" involve a change in the structure of relations and power distribution of the conflict setting. This classification is primarily analytical and theoretical but is suggestive of the types of intervention that peace-builders need to think about.

Rupesinghe (1995, 1998) argues for a comprehensive, eclectic approach to conflict transformation that embraces multitrack interventions. He proposes building peace constituencies at the grassroots level and across the parties at the civil society level (where it exists) and also creating peace alliances with groups able to bring about change, such as business groups, the media, the military, and so on. He sees conflict transformation as a broad approach incorporating conflict resolution training and track-one interventions including diplomatic interventions and peacekeeping.

Lederach's (1997) work is one of the most comprehensive current statements of conflict transformation thinking for practitioners. He sees peace building as a long-term transformation of a war system into a peace system, inspired by a quest for the values of peace and justice, truth and mercy. The key dimensions are changes in the personal, structural, relational, and cultural aspects of conflict, brought about over different time periods (short, middle, and long term) and affecting different system levels (from particular issues to key relationships in conflict to subsystems and systems within which the conflict is embedded). An appropriate strategy (such as networking between middle-level leaders with links to parties across the conflict) is linked to an appropriate timeframe (such as concentrating on medium-term steps to build a peace constituency while embracing a vision of the desired future and an awareness of the current crisis). In thinking about structure, Lederach contributes the idea of the pyramid with elite leaders and decisionmakers at the top; leaders of social organizations, churches, top journalists, and the like in the middle; and grassroots community leaders at the base. A comprehensive peace process should address complementary changes at all these levels. One strength of his model is that it widens its view from the conflict and the conflict parties and suggests the scope for drawing peace-building resources from the wider society. A weakness, perhaps, is the limited attention it gives to the autonomous processes of change within the political system of the conflict-affected society.

An important issue, raised by Lederach (1997) and widely discussed by the conflict resolution school in the context of mediation, is the issue of sequencing. What sort of action or intervention is appropriate, by whom, and at what time? Glasl (1982) suggested nine stages of escalation in conflicts. He proposed that different types of intervention might be appropriate at different times. Fisher and Keashly's (1991) contingency theory built on these foundations. Their idea is that the nature of intervention should be matched to the stage of the conflict. At the early stages of conflict, they suggest, facilitation may be appropriate; but when a conflict has reached a high stage of polarization, power-based mediation (or even coercion) is required. Lederach (1997) offers another version of a contingency model based on Curle's (1971) progression of conflict, avoiding coercion.

Authors within the conflict transformation tradition also draw heavily on ideas about conflict dynamics common to all three schools. For example, conflicts sometimes develop strong tendencies toward vicious or benign spirals. The common pattern is for conflict to broaden (suck in new issues), widen (suck in new actors), and intensify (suck in new victims). But it is also possible for conflict to be transformed as parties shift positions and adopt new goals, new actors emerge, and new situations develop, allowing new relationships and changed structures.

It is evident from this brief review of approaches to conflict transformation theory that some theories are primarily analytical and interpretative, attempting to explain the formation and transformation of contemporary conflicts (e.g., Azar 1990; Vayrynen 1991). Others are prescriptive, offering peace-builders means to conceptualize the path from conflict toward desired outcomes (e.g., Curle 1971; Lederach 1997). Perhaps Galtung's (1996) comes closest to a synthesis.

FROM A THEORY OF CONFLICT TO A THEORY OF CONFLICT-IN-CONTEXT

As the practice of peacemaking has extended from prevention to post-conflict peace building, and as globalization has an increasing impact on internal conflicts, the scope of theories of conflict transformation needs to be extended. On the one hand, they need to be concerned with the factors exacerbating conflict and restraining conflict over a number of different phases (see table 10.1).

On the other hand, they have to be concerned with the interplay of causes and preventers at different levels of the international system. One can identify five different levels at which contemporary conflicts are caused: the global, regional, societal, conflict party, and at individual/

Table 10.1. Factors Exacerbating or Restraining Conflict at Different Phases

Previolence	Crisis Phase	Escalation Phase	Protracted Phase	Postsettlement
Underlying Causes	Triggers	Escalators	Deformers	Peace Breakers
Deep Preventers	Light Preventers	De-Escalators	Transformers	Peace Builders

Table 10.2.   Causes and Preventers of Violent Conflicts at Different Levels

Level	Examples of Causes	Examples of Preventers
Global	Postcolonial legacy	International minority rights
Regional	Conflict spillover in Great Lakes	OSCE conflict prevention
State/Society	State capture by ethnic groups	Cross-ethnic party voting
Conflict Party	Hutu hostility toward Tutsi	Pragmatic approach of minority
Elite/Individual	Hutu leaders launch genocide	President accepts OSCE advice

elite levels (Miall et al. 1999). Table 10.2 gives examples of causes and preventers of violent conflicts at these levels.

A weakness of conflict theories if viewed narrowly is that they tend to concentrate only on the conflict party level, focusing on parties, issues, and goals, to the exclusion of the context within which conflict is situated. It is possible to add more representation of the background, for example on to Galtung's simple triangular formulation of conflict (1996). Onto "contradiction," we can build "context"; onto "attitudes," "memory"; onto "behavior," "relationships." The meaning of a conflict depends on the context out of which it arises. The attitudes parties have toward one another are shaped by their memory of what has happened in the past, and expectations of what may happen in the future. The behavior they adopt is not purely reactive but is based on previous relationships.

The context of conflict includes the society in conflict and the wider international and regional context. Within the society, culture, governance arrangements, institutions, social roles, norms, the rules and codes in place in a society, and its path of development are crucial background aspects. As globalization proceeds, local conflicts are inevitably influenced by wider economic and political forces. These are tending to strengthen trade, investment and technological networks among some areas of the world but also to marginalize other areas (such as Africa and the former Soviet Union). The result is to weaken states and economies in these areas and in some cases to create a crisis of the state. Internal conflicts are increasingly associated with fragile states and maladaptive reactions to globalization. Relationships involve the whole fabric of relationships in the society where the conflict takes place and beyond to other societies. As Lederach argues, the relational aspects of conflict are crucial (1997). Bad relationships between groups are often a trigger to conflict and often remain a vital problem for peace building after violence is over. Memories are part of the socially constructed understanding of the situation. The way groups remember (and construct) their past is often a central part of the mobilization for conflict, and a crucial matter to address in reconciliation and cultural traditions work. Context, relationships, and memories are part of the tissue connecting the contradictions, attitudes, and behaviors in the conflict formations with the wider background in space and time.

Within this template, we can place an understanding of the types of transformation that take place. Building on Vayrynen's (1991) approach, we can identify five types of transformation, or transformers.

"Context transformations" refer to changes in the context of conflict that may radically alter the conflict situation, or the motives of the parties. The impact of the end of the Cold War on regional conflicts is a dramatic example. An example of a less far-reaching change would be the proposed change in the rules of the diamond trade to outlaw "conflict diamonds" that could have a significant impact on the conflicts in Sierra Leone and Angola.

"Structural transformations" refer to change in the basic structure of conflict, that is, the set of actors, issues and incompatible goals, and conflicting beliefs or relationships, or to the society or state within which the conflict is embedded. Asymmetric conflicts cannot be transformed without changing the unbalanced and contested relationships that lie at their roots. Such changes may take place gradually, but internal and external actors can support them. For example, Steve Biko's "Black Consciousness" movement raised awareness of the power of the poor people in the townships in South Africa, and the Anti-Apartheid Movement helped to press the case for disinvestment by foreign-owned businesses.

"Issue transformations" concern the positions that parties take on key issues at the heart of the conflict, and the way that parties redefine or reframe their positions, or reach compromises or resolutions. An example of an issue transformation was the decision by the Unionist Party in Northern Ireland to accept a delinking of the decommissioning issue from the convocation of the Northern Ireland Assembly. Another recent example is the Israeli decision to contemplate a degree of Palestinian autonomy within areas of Jerusalem. Making "progress" on issues in conflict is often agonizingly slow and subject to reversals, and of course what counts as progress is itself contentious.

"Actor transformations" include decisions by actors to change their goals or alter their approach to conflict, such as decisions to seek peace or initiate a peace process. They also include changes of leadership, which are often crucial in securing transformation in conflicts. Finally, they include changes in the situation of the public constituencies and supporters of the political leaders. This opens a number of lines for broad conflict transformation work. Those who work within a party to bring about change in that party's position are often crucial actors in a peace process and may have more influence than external track-one and track-two actors.

"Personal transformations," changes of heart or mind in individual leaders or in small groups with decision-making power at critical moments, may be crucial. Some external interveners try to reach these leaders and bring about this personal change directly (Curle 1987).

These five types of transformation can be readily related to the levels of conflict causation or prevention identified above. Context transformations come usually from the global or regional setting. Structural transformations come usually at the state/society level. Actor and issue transformations take place at the conflict party and elite levels. Personal transformations are at the individual level.

They are also directed to different parts of the conflict formation, whether this is seen in Azar's terms (1990) or Galtung's (1996). Context, structural, and issue transformations affect the context and contradictions at the heart of the conflict. Actor and personal transformations affect particularly attitudes and memory, behavior, and relationships. These in turn, of course, are interrelated.

Finally, these different types of transformation relate to the phases of conflicts and the timing of intervention. Context and structural changes tend to take place over a longer timescale, and affect the setting of the conflict; the other types of transformations tend to take place more rapidly and sequentially as part of the conflict dynamics. The sequencing of changes varies with each peace process, depending on the logic of the situation. Only in the very simplest conflicts is conflict transformation a rapid or immediate process. Usually it is slow and tortuous, with turning points followed by sticking points.

To take an example of how conflict transformation takes place in practice, consider the peace process in Northern Ireland. As one of the most intensively managed conflicts, as well as one of the more intractable conflicts, of the twentieth century, Northern Ireland offers many lessons for conflict transformation. We can find evidence of all five types of transformation at different points. The context of the conflict was changed by long-term changes in British and Irish societies, the development of the EU, and the end of the Cold War. The conflict structure changed as the pan-Nationalist coalition developed sufficient alliances and confidence to balance the asymmetric relationships. Actor transformations included changes of government in Britain, the transformation of thinking among the Sinn Féin leadership, and division and change among the Unionists. Issue transformations included the mutual agreements reached in the Good Friday Agreement to reconcile the legitimacy of the two cultural traditions and establish institutions that reinforce both Irish and British dimensions of governance. People in Northern Ireland can now hold British or Irish passports. All this could not have taken place without significant changes of mind at the individual and elite level. Even so, conflict remains and continues, and each marching season reinvokes the atmosphere of division and fear.

Northern Ireland offers a striking example of the complementarity of approaches on different tracks and of "structural" and "cultural" approaches (Bloomfield 1997). For example, the patient work of the Community

Relations Council on the ground built sufficient credibility to enable the Council to facilitate quiet dialogue with young politicians (Fitzduff 1999). Hitherto, we have not had a clear understanding of the role that "civil society" played in the peace process and in the longer-term process of healing the divisions between the communities. Cochrane (2001) provides an in-depth assessment.

These rather broad theoretical considerations suggest a framework in which we can analyze and evaluate conflict transformation practices, and consider the gaps and weaknesses in the international capacity for handling conflict.

COORDINATION AND MULTITRACK DIPLOMACY

A particular challenge for conflict transformation is how to work effectively with interventions at other tracks. At times, a good level of collaboration takes place, for example in the case of Macedonia before the Kosovo conflict, when coordination between conflict prevention activities of the OSCE, the UN, and NGOs was rather effective (Ackermann 2000).

But often internal and external actors in the various tracks are at cross-purposes. This is not surprising, given the clash between paradigms. Actions on one track can sometimes wreck efforts on another. For example, it may be difficult for an organization that strives for nonviolent resolution of conflicts to cooperate with a government that relies on coercive methods to pressure the local protagonists to accept a settlement. Conversely, foreign ministries are not universally enthusiastic about the intrusion of nongovernmental organizations into diplomacy.

Practitioners of conflict transformation activities at the nonstate level therefore have to pursue their aims with sensitivity to both the culture of the conflict area and the goals and constraints of other actors. They have to proceed knowing that they may not be able to influence other actors whose actions will affect their work. Moreover, their task may broaden when conflict transformation involves changing the policies of track-one bodies outside the conflict area. For example, it is increasingly recognized that bodies like the World Bank can have a significant impact on conflicts. Efforts to influence their policies have thus become part of the wider task of conflict transformation.

ASSESSING THE IMPACT ON ETHNIC CONFLICTS

What is the overall impact of these kinds of practice on conflict? It is still very hard to say. There are reports of significant achievements in building peace constituencies (for example, in Lederach 1997). Compilations of recent work include some impressive stories of apparent "successes" (European Platform for Conflict Prevention 1999a, 1999b). But as yet there is little systematic research. Bercovitch's research (1996) suggests that conflict management approaches, including the use of power resources, are the most effective at delivering settlements. On the other hand, these settlements often fail to transform the conflict, and the longer-term work in building relationships and capacity may be more important than reaching fragile political settlements in the long term.

The overall evidence of ending of ethnic conflicts is particularly sobering. In a study of peacefully settled conflicts in Europe, the Middle East, and Africa since 1945, I found only a few cases of ethnic conflict that were peacefully settled (these include the Åland Islands, Northern Epirus, the Saar, and South Tyrol—all cases in Europe). Recent work by Pfetsch and Rohloff (2000) identified thirteen out of 121 cases of conflicts over ethnicity, religion, or regional autonomy that were resolved through peaceful negotiation. Fifty-one remain undecided, eight were resolved by the threat of force or other forms of coercion, and forty-nine by violence. The great majority of the peaceful cases were republics of the former Soviet Union, which peacefully broke away in 1991. Indeed, despite the violent conflicts in Chechnya, Tajikistan, Nagorno-Karabakh, and elsewhere, the number of ethnic conflicts which appear to have been transformed without violence in the former Soviet Union is startling. However, avoidance of violence has not necessarily been accompanied by resolution of outstanding issues.

A useful line of work is to identify these peaceful cases and ascertain the reasons why violence has been avoided, and how ethnic and other internal conflicts have been managed or addressed. But "conflict ending" measured by the end of violence is too final and crude an indicator on which to base the planning and assessment of conflict transformation initiatives. A more fine-grained approach is needed. Indicators such as those developed in work on peace and conflict impact assessment systems offer one approach. However, if conflict transformation can be broken down into sequence of changes in the conflict structure, in the parties' goals, and in issues over time, as suggested in the theoretical part of the chapter, it may be feasible to relate interventions to particular transformations in the conflict.

CONCLUSION

This chapter has argued that a distinctive school of conflict transformation theory and practice has developed over the past decade. It can be differentiated from conflict management and conflict resolution, although all three schools rely on a shared tradition of thinking about conflict and intervention.

Conflict transformation is a comprehensive approach, addressing a range of dimensions (micro to macro issues, local to global levels, grassroots to elite actors, short-term to long-term timescales). It aims to develop capacity and support structural change, rather than facilitate outcomes or deliver settlements. It seeks to engage with conflict at the previolence and postviolence phases and with the causes and consequences of violent conflict, which usually extend beyond the site of fighting.

This chapter has argued that the ambitious prescriptive theories need to be better integrated with a more incremental and analytical approach. At the same time, the analytical theories need to be extended in timescale and scope. The chapter proposed expanding conflict theory toward conflict-in-context and suggested a theoretically informed framework for evaluation.

A number of questions and gaps in the theory remain. We still lack sufficiently precise dynamic theories to capture the emergent properties of conflict, including the formation of new actors and new issues. Most theories concentrate either on the causes and development of conflict or the creation and sustenance of peace-building capacity, and fail adequately to integrate an understanding of how the preventers and causes of conflict interact. There has been a somewhat uncritical willingness to embrace multitrack diplomacy, without an adequate conceptualization of how activity in the various tracks can fit together. We still have an inadequate understanding of the impact of conflict transformation activities on conflict, which makes them difficult to evaluate.

REFERENCES

Ackermann, Alice. 2000. *Making Peace Prevail: Preventing Violent Conflict in Macedonia*. Syracuse, NY: Syracuse University Press.

Azar, Edward E. 1990. *The Management of Protracted Social Conflict*. Aldershot, UK: Dartmouth.

Azar, Edward E., and John W. Burton. 1986. *International Conflict Resolution: Theory and Practice*. Boulder, CO: Lynne Rienner.

Bercovitch, Jacob, ed. 1996. *Resolving International Conflicts: The Theory and Practice of Mediation*. Boulder, CO: Lynne Rienner.

Bloomfield, David. 1997. *Peacemaking Strategies in Northern Ireland: Building Complementarity in Conflict Management Theory*. Basingstoke, UK: Macmillan.

Bloomfield, David, and Ben Reilly. 1998. The Changing Nature of Conflict and Conflict Management. In *Democracy and Deep-rooted Conflict*, ed. Peter Harris and Ben Reilly, 7–28. Stockholm: Institute for Democracy and Electoral Assistance (IDEA).

Cochrane, Feargal. 2001. *People Power: The Role of the Voluntary and Community Sector in the Northern Ireland Conflict*. Cork, Ireland: Cork University Press.

Curle, Adam. 1971. *Making Peace*. London: Tavistock.

———. 1987. *In the Middle: Non-official Mediation in Violent Situations*. New York: Berg.

European Platform for Conflict Prevention. 1999a. *Searching for Peace in Africa: An Overview of Conflict Prevention and Management Activities*. Utrecht, the Netherlands: European Centre for Conflict Prevention.

———. 1999b. *People Building Peace*. Utrecht, the Netherlands: European Centre for Conflict Prevention.

Fisher, R., and L. Keashly. 1991. The Potential Complementarity of Mediation and Consultation within a Contingency Model of Third-Party Intervention. *Journal of Peace Research* 28 (1):29–42.

Fitzduff, Mari. 1999. Changing History—Peace-building in Northern Ireland. In *People Building Peace*, ed. European Centre for Conflict Prevention, 87–104. Utrecht, the Netherlands: European Centre for Conflict Prevention.

Galtung, Johan. 1996. *Peace by Peaceful Means*. London: Sage.

Glasl, Friedrich. 1982. The Process of Conflict Escalation and Roles of Third Parties. In *Conflict Management and Industrial Relations*, ed. G. B. Bomers and R. B. Peterson, 119–140. Boston: Kluwer Nijhoff.

Harff, Barbara. 2003. No Lessons Learned from the Holocaust? Assessing the Risks of Genocide and Political Mass Murder since 1955. *American Political Science Review* 97(1):57–73.

Krippendorf, Ekkehart. 1973. Peace Research and the Industrial Revolution. *Journal of Peace Research* 10:185–201.

Lederach, John Paul. 1995. *Preparing for Peace: Conflict Transformation across Cultures*. New York: Syracuse University Press.

———. 1997. *Building Peace: Sustainable Reconciliation in Divided Societies*. Washington, DC: U.S. Institute of Peace Press.

Miall, Hugh, Oliver Ramsbotham, and Tom Woodhouse. 1999. *Contemporary Conflict Resolution*. Cambridge: Polity Press.

Pfetsch, Frank, and Christoph Rohloff. 2000. *National and International Conflicts 1945–1995*. London: Routledge.

Rupesinghe, Kumar. 1998. *Civil Wars, Civil Peace*. London: Pluto.

———, ed. 1995. *Conflict Transformation*. London: Macmillan.

Senghaas, Dieter. 1973. Conflict Formations in Contemporary International Society. *Journal of Peace Research* 10:163–184.

Vayrynen, Raimo. 1991 To Settle or to Transform? Perspectives on the Resolution of National and International Conflicts. In *New Directions in Conflict Theory: Conflict Resolution and Conflict Transformation*, ed. Raimo Vayrynen, 1–25. London: Sage.

11

From Resolution to Transformation: Assessing the Role and Impact of Dialogue Projects

Norbert Ropers

Dialogues are one means—if not the classical means—of dealing constructively with conflicts. As one saying goes, "As long as you're talking, you can't be shooting." What better method of resolving a contentious issue than through an honest exchange of views? And, says discourse ethics, what other way is there of finding lasting solutions to the numerous political-cum-moral conflicts in an interdependent and pluralist world than through "practical discourse between the affected parties" (Apel 1990)?

In classical diplomacy, skills in negotiation and dialogue form part of the basic repertoire of any prudent management of international relations—though in the public perception, the dialoguing skills of official, track-one diplomacy have often been forced into the background by the constraints of power politics and *Realpolitik*. Representatives of nonofficial, track-two diplomacy, by contrast, have placed communication, direct encounter, and comprehension and understanding center stage. Interest in nonofficial dialoguing initiatives of this kind has, additionally, been fostered by the "societization" of conflicts—the increase in the number of acute or potentially violent disputes, particularly ethnopolitical and protracted ones, taking place *within* a given society.

There are now countless dialogue projects—from the grassroots right up to leadership level—being used to settle, resolve, or influence conflicts. But the trend is not without its critics. What good does it do if those who are, as a rule, the moderate representatives of parties to a conflict get together round a table? Even if influential persons achieve comprehension and understanding within the framework of a workshop or series of workshops, does the success of the whole enterprise not depend on how the follow-up is managed? Last, do adherents of the dialogue method not fundamentally overestimate the importance of communication in dealing with conflicts? What disputes are actually concerned with, after all, is not stereotypical perceptions, differences of opinion, and differing cultural standards, but tangible conflicts of interest, structural factors, and the struggle for power and influence.

In this chapter, some of the core features of dialogue projects, their variations, and their implications will be examined in greater detail. The first task is to give an overview of different ideal-typical forms of dialogues and to identify basic elements of dialogue processes. Second, four concepts of dialogue work are distinguished to illustrate the practical nature of such projects. Third, dialogue projects are set in the context of various approaches of handling conflict, in order to establish criteria for measuring success. Finally, a number of "lessons learned" collected in the course of recent evaluation studies are presented.

APPROACHES TO THE SYSTEMATIZATION OF DIALOGUES

In the literature, two aspects of classifying dialogues get particular attention: the identification of ideal-typical forms of dialogues, and the differentiation of steps of interaction and communication that constitute a constructive process of dialogue.

The U.S. conflict researcher Jay Rothman (1998) has proposed classifying approaches to dialogue in intergroup conflicts into three or four ideal-typical categories:

Whether the commonest form of interchange actually merits the name "dialogue" is doubtful: In a "positional dialogue," the parties articulate their respective views—which may range from differing to diametrically opposed—as positions and attitudes that merely require acknowledgment. As in a parliamentary debate, communication serves primarily to score points as one argument is set against the other.

In the case of "human relations dialogue," the differences of opinion on the substantive issues are relegated to a secondary place, and work is instead done on the relational level and on the causes of misunderstandings and stereotypes between those involved. These kinds of dialogues are often preceded by preparatory training sessions on basic mechanisms of perception and interaction in groups. The objectives are mutual acknowledgment of the person and increased respect by each party for the other. What impact this might have in terms of the substance of the conflict is left open.

"Activist dialogue" goes one step further: The issues are sifted and analyzed to find common ground, determine how the parties might
contain their dispute through joint action, or both.

The most ambitious approach is the "problem-solving dialogue," in
which the disputants organize their communication to systematically
work through the substance of their differences. Where conflicts are
highly escalated, a dialogue such as this generally requires the presence of a third party as a co-actor—or indeed as an initiator.

These approaches are not just useful as a way of classifying dialogues
according to their prevailing forms of interaction. They also emphasize
different but complementary elements of dealing constructively with conflicts through dialogue. In a modified form, one can also conceptualize the
different types of dialogues as steps in a process of enhancing the quality
of communication and interaction between the dialogue partners. Adherents of the alternative dispute resolution (ADR) movement have put forward a scheme of four phases for responding to conflicts through communication:

1. The first phase is concerned with formulating the *differing points of
   view* of the various parties as clearly as possible, securing mutual acknowledgment of them, and identifying the substance of the conflict.
2. The focus in the second phase is *reflection* on the underlying needs
   and fears of the participating actors, their values, their experiences of
   conflict, and their hopes. Ideally, it will also be possible, in this phase,
   to develop approaches for securing personal acknowledgment of,
   and insight into, the conflictual biographies of the other side.
3. The third phase is devoted to the identification of shared *interests*
   and similar *needs and fears*. It can also be aimed at initiating practical
   cooperation on less controversial issues.
4. In most cases, the fourth phase requires a lengthy period of preparation and of personal confidence building. It involves discussing approaches and ideas for *securing understanding on the substantive issues
   in dispute*, reflecting on how these approaches and ideas might be
   implemented, and initiating practical measures.

In the case of protracted conflicts, dialogues between disputing groups
will often consist of a series of dialogue events that cover a period of
many months or even years. To conceptualize constructive developments
for such series of events, several models are used. One emphasizes the
character of the relationship between the parties and the focus of the joint
efforts as the key characteristics, and it interprets progress as a movement
of relationship building, problem solving, *and* collaborative action (Mc-

Cartney 1986): contact and confidence building, empathy for the other side, joint analysis of conflict issues, explorative problem solving, joint activities, and pre-negotiations (in case of dialogues with influentials).

Most dialogues take the form of *organized group encounters* of a size that allows face-to-face communication. They are conducted by persons below top leadership level and are therefore not official negotiations, but political preliminaries. As a rule, responsibility for the initiation, organization, and direction of the meetings is assumed by a third party. This third party need not come from outside the country; it can also consist of moderate individuals from inside the conflict region. In the case of highly escalated disputes, and in divided societies, organizing a peaceful meeting and successfully getting through the first phase are extremely difficult tasks. The other three phases always require several meetings—assuming that the participants manage to get as far as the last phase. The possibility of "slipping back" to an earlier phase is always a possibility.

The basic idea behind dialogue-based meetings is very old. It was given a considerable boost in post-1945 Europe within the framework of the "international intercultural understanding" paradigm. The prime target group then was young people. What drove the project was the conviction that increased contact and interaction could help eliminate prejudices and "enemy images," and create transfrontier loyalties. The naïve "contact hypothesis" has now been replaced by more sophisticated concepts of "intercultural learning" (Otten and Treuheit 1994).

Dialogue-based meetings that expressly deal with ethnopolitical conflicts are a more recent phenomenon, but they draw on similar beliefs. Probably the most influential school of thought is the "interactive conflict resolution" or "interactive problem-solving" movement (Mitchell and Banks 1996; Kelman 1992; Fisher 1997). Its roots go back to the 1960s, when various "scholar/practitioners" began to invite influential representatives of conflicting parties to workshops, in order either to guide them through the above-mentioned four phases of constructive dialogue in a quasi-academic exercise or to facilitate this process. Experience of the use of this approach has now been gathered from a number of different crisis regions. Despite this, there has as yet been no success in using this instrument on a systematic, broad-scale basis. The focus has, instead, been on combinations of this approach and on other methods of influencing conflicts.

DIALOGUE PROJECTS IN PRACTICE

No even remotely representative overview has so far been undertaken of practical dialogue projects in conflict regions. Debates about the usefulness of these instruments are mostly confined—depending on the milieu concerned—to specific forms of dialogue. Thus, the academic discussion concerns itself primarily with interactive conflict resolution in which the scholar/practitioners set the tone as third parties, whereas the NGO world shows a strong preference for combinations of dialogue projects and other practical schemes. Such documentation that exists on the conduct and results of dialogue projects initially related largely to the more academic approaches. In the interim, the interests of the financial sponsors have led to more extensive documentation of other projects as well.

Once again, from an ideal-typical perspective, four practical forms of dialogue project can be distinguished—by reference, in particular, to the objectives they pursue over and above the communicative purposes set out above:

- *Dialogue projects as grassroots peace building and interpersonal reconciliation*: These projects generally relate to the local or neighborhood level, to people in similar situations and/or with similar interests (e.g., young people, women, trade unionists, and members of a religion), or to persons who share an interdependent fate because of a violent past (e.g., widows and orphans of war, and children of victims and perpetrators). The central elements here are personal encounters and eliminating barriers to communication. The guiding notion is that of the human relations dialogue; the long-term objective is the duplication of encounters of this kind in order to promote peace "from below." A particular approach is that of the "to reflect and trust" (TRT) movement bringing together children of victims and perpetrators for sharing and exploring ways of integrating the violent past (Bar-On 2000). The effectiveness of such projects depends to a great extent on how far it proves possible to move beyond one-off encounters, build up longer-term personal relations, and create shared structures.
- *Dialogue projects combined with individual capacity building*: Given dialogue initiatives' explicit aim of achieving understanding, it seems obvious to also enhance participants' skills in interacting constructively with one another. Another factor in favor of this kind of combination of training and conflict management is the fact that real encounters provide an ideal setting in which to try out dialogue skills. However, such combination is not without its risks and disadvantages. The target groups for conflictive encounter and for training are not necessarily the same, and participants can become confused if it is unclear, in the course of a series of encounters, what the purpose of the given exercise is.
- *Dialogue projects combined with institution building, networking, and practical projects*: Combinations such as these are generally only possible af-

ter a longish process of confidence building, and they work on the phases of dialogue discussed above. The task in many cases is either to institutionalize the dialogue in the form of "inter-ethnic advisory bodies," "reconciliation commissions," or NGO networks; or to "build the capacity" of individual NGOs. In other cases, dialogue projects provide the starting point for practical endeavors such as income-generating schemes for population groups particularly hard hit by the conflict—unemployed young people, for example. It is generally agreed that these are good ways of enhancing the effectiveness of dialogues and of exploiting their potential to bring about structural change. What is often overlooked, one has to admit, is that these kinds of follow-up measures place different demands on those involved. Thus, although many initiatives succeed in containing macro-conflicts through dialogue, they subsequently founder on the internal meso- and micro-rivalries that surface during institution building.

Dialogue projects as pre-negotiation: The most ambitious dialogue-based undertakings are those designed to exert influence on the regulation of the conflict at the political-leadership level. This is precisely what interactive conflict resolution and "problem-solving" approaches aim to do by holding confidential workshops at which a third party shows influential members of the conflict parties how to develop insights and ideas, which it is hoped will later facilitate and inspire the official negotiations. For this latter reason, this approach is sometimes also described as forming part of the "pre-negotiation" phase. In discussions about the value of these kinds of endeavors, effects were initially only classified as either "internal" or "external"— affecting those directly involved or affecting the broader context of the conflict. Now, however, discussion on this is more nuanced.

DIALOGUE PROJECTS IN THE CONTEXT OF THEORIES OF CONFLICT MANAGEMENT: HOW IS THE "SUCCESS" OF DIALOGUE PROJECTS TO BE ASSESSED?

Chris Mitchell has proposed that the "success" of pre-negotiation dialogue projects be assessed at three levels (Mitchell 1993:82–84): impact on the people involved (changes in attitude and new patterns of behavior); output in terms of ideas, proposals, practical measures, and so on that are incorporated into the process of political goal formation; and long-term impact on the overall conflict.

Commenting on the first level still appears a relatively easy task, given that what is involved here is an established research area of social psychology and group dynamics. In practice, however, what we get is a preponderance of straightforward communication of positive opinions expressed at the end of the events. Assessments of the second and third levels are based entirely on the case studies conducted by the organizers and on the latter's contacts in the respective conflict regions. Ronald Fisher evaluated seventy-six reports relating to workshops held between 1965 and 1995, and arrived at a reported "success rate" of 84 percent (Fisher 1997:187–189). However understandable this positive self-assessment is, it tells us little about what sort of dialogue will promote what sort of impact and long-term effects, and with what sort of people, at what juncture, and on what scale it has to take place to achieve this.

This question cannot be answered only within the framework of a theory or practice of dialogue, whatever its nature. It points to the broader context of macro-political conflict management (Hoffman 1995).

Overall, theoretical investigation of intergroup conflict management is still poorly developed. In the case of many concrete questions that emerge from the practical sphere in regard to appropriate strategies to be used in actual situations of conflict, no recommendations exist of a kind based on detailed theoretical discussion and the empirical verification of this. The most high-profile approaches here are normative concepts of "interest-led dispute resolution" (Fisher and Ury 1981), comparative case studies (Zartman 1985), and empirical-cum-quantitative investigation of the characteristics of conflicts that have been settled "peacefully" (Bercovitch and Houston 1996). Explicit references to theories of social change or of conflict are the exception.

This "theory gap" becomes obvious when stipulating the yardsticks by which the success of individual measures or programs of intervention are to be measured. Because of the social complexities involved, it is extraordinarily difficult to establish a causal link between micro-measures and macro-effects. It is therefore all the more necessary that the gap should be explicitly addressed and that the unspoken assumptions underlying a large part of conflict-management practice and research should be highlighted (Kleiboer 1996; Ross and Rothman 1999). If this is not done, there is a danger that peacemaking will be equated with the stabilization of relationships of dominance (Francis 2000) or with the smoothing-over of social relations.

Recently, however, something of a rapprochement between theory and practice has been observable. Indicators of this are provided by various "state-of-the-art" reviews (Miall et al. 1999; Reychler and Paffenholz 2000; Berghof Research Center 2000–2001) and by "conflict impact assessment" studies (Lund and Rasamoelina 2000) formulating criteria for the effective use of conflict-management measures in established fields of activity such as development cooperation.

Cordula Reimann has proposed assigning both theoretical and practical approaches to conflict management to three ideal-typical categories

(Reimann 2000). Her scheme permits a more precise conceptual classification of dialogue projects and the yardsticks for measuring their success (see table 11.1). The division also makes clear that "successes" within one category cannot simply be transposed to other categories.

The conflict-settlement approach aims at securing or adjusting the political order in the face of an acute or potentially violent conflict and at achieving a viable balance between the interests of the various leadership groups that hold power. Within this framework, dialogue projects can help gauge the scope of official negotiations at the level of advisers and persons of influence. If it proves possible to get initiatives for dialogue onto a broader footing, and to elicit positive responses from at least a section of the media, these projects can also create an atmosphere conducive to negotiation at this level.

The small number of case studies examining the general setup surrounding official negotiations indicates that the results of civil-society dialogue projects are only rarely directly translated into official measures. Official politics has substantial psychological and procedural reservations in regard to this form of citizen participation. Appointing persons of trust—such as "elder statesman" Jimmy Carter—to carry out semi-official exploratory missions seems to present fewer problems. The influence exerted by dialogue projects is therefore generally indirect and takes a longish time to make itself felt. It involves the socialization of future leading figures, the creation of networks of personal relationships, and the airing of new ideas in safe forums—as shown by Kelman using the example of the preparatory measures that preceded the Israeli–Palestine accord of 1993 (Kelman 1995).

The gap between official and "unofficial" diplomacy is not just an expression of the differing legitimacy and power-political options of states and societies. To many protagonists of dialogue-based approaches, this gap also reflects a fundamentally different understanding of conflict. In their view, protracted conflicts are a sign of the failure to satisfy basic needs in regard to security, recognition, and participation, and of the need for social change (Burton 1990; Burton and Dukes 1990). *Conflict resolution* deals not only with obvious conflicts over matters of substance but also with troubled relations between parties in order to set the substantive conflicts themselves in a new context and tackle them as a shared problem.

Dialogue projects are an important instrument in the conflict-resolution approach, because the mutual clarification of perceptions and relations, and improvements in communication, are their key features. That said, most dialogue projects are brief affairs, and in many cases it is difficult, once dialogue processes have been initiated, to sustain these over a longer period. Where this *is* successfully done, however, the chances are high that the process will result in the creation of a group of people who

Table 11.1. The Role of Dialogue Projects in the Context of Different Approaches to Conflict Management

Approach to Conflict Management	Notion of Conflict	Preferred Practical Approach	Measures of Success	Role of Dialogue Projects
Conflict Settlement	Conflict as a problem of the status quo and political order	*Track 1:* Diplomacy and power politics at official leadership level	*Results-oriented:* Political settlements with stabilizing effect	• Organizing prenegotiations • Promoting a political climate of understanding
Conflict Resolution	Conflict as a catalyst of social change	*Track 2:* Direct civil-society conflict management, especially at middle-ranking leadership level	*Process-oriented:* Improved communication, interaction, and relations between parties; respect for different collective identities	• Creating a leadership class with experience of dialoguing • Workshops on communication, problem solving, and so on
Conflict Transformation	Conflict as nonviolent struggle for social justice	*Track 3:* Strengthening capacities of disadvantaged groups to act and to deal with conflict, and capacity of divided/war-traumatized societies to integrate	*Structure-oriented:* Elimination of socioeconomic inequalities between identity groups; good governance; power sharing; creation of viable civil society; building conflict-management capacities at grassroots level	• Practicing communication and interaction skills • Providing opportunities for encounter and learning between polarized groups • Empowering groups

Source: Based on Reimann (2000).

possess experience in dialoguing and have close links with the other side. The challenges with which these projects are nonetheless eventually confronted stem from the question of how the dialogue can be moved beyond joint (exploratory) problem solving to practical implementation measures.

The third approach to conflict management is based on conflict settlement and conflict resolution but additionally lays stress on the need for structural change. From the point of view of *conflict transformation*, lasting peacemaking in divided societies and societies traumatized by war requires a broad palette of measures aimed on the one hand at eliminating socioeconomic inequalities and on the other at building up political and social capacities that will enable those involved to cope with (ethnic) plurality. Within this framework, dialogue projects can also perform a bridge-building function. They must be measured, however, by the degree to which they help strengthen disadvantaged groups and create a changed dispute-settlement culture at the grassroots level.

It is clear from this classification that different measures of the "success" of dialogue projects need to be applied depending on the goals and context involved. As is generally the case in conflict management, success here is a multifaceted entity. If we accept conflict transformation's assumption that conflicts are transformed through simultaneous results-oriented, process-oriented, and structure-oriented approaches, it becomes clear that projects of this kind need to be undertaken in parallel at several levels. The model most frequently cited for this has been that of "peace constituencies" or "peace alliances" (Lederach 1997). What contribution dialogue projects in particular could or should make to the creation of peace constituencies has, however, been subjected to very little discussion so far. One route to the question is provided by the "lessons learned" and "best practice" studies that have examined individual dialogue projects in greater detail.

LESSONS LEARNED

This section provides eight lessons learned, based on a number of published and unpublished studies (Spencer 1998; Mott Foundation 1999; Haumersen et al. 2002; Wolleh 2000) and on my own experiences with problem-solving workshops on conflicts in the Caucasus. For reasons of brevity, I focus on aspects that are of relevance to projects aimed at exerting influence on the political macro-conflict, and the lessons are arranged according the straightforward principle of a dialogue process: its initial phase, the actual dialogue process, and the long-term objective of the intervention.

Before a third party implements a dialogue process, it should ensure that the preconditions for successful intervention are fulfilled, especially in respect to the time horizon available, the participants involved, and the access to the necessary material resources and organizational skills.

First of all, the ambition of a problem-solving dialogue between parties to protracted conflicts can only be achieved within the framework of a *long-term process of work and learning*. Personal confidence building, clarification of positions and perceptions, and reflection on background facts are prerequisites to any substantive discussion of the material issues. Key issues are the joint handling of crises—for example, escalatory processes within the group, and threats and other influences from outside—and the realization that all the participants have the same kinds of problems of acceptance to wrestle with at home. Another important aspect is the experience of arrangements being adhered to—for example, arrangements about the confidentiality of the talks or about the solution of practical problems. The initiating third party therefore has to consider whether it is able to ensure a long-term process such as this (in practice, this means several years). Moreover, one has to reckon with the possibility that, if there are only a few meetings or even only one, a lot will be churned up but the mistrust of the participants will ultimately be greater than before.

Second, if the dialogue process is to get off to a good start, the *choice of the initial protagonists* is crucial. For one thing, they have to be capable of getting some kind of meaningful exchange off the ground—a fact that favors moderately inclined spokespersons. Also, this first choice acts as a signal that helps decide whether the enterprise is taken seriously or whether it is dismissed as an outsiders' or traitors' venture. There is, therefore, much to be said for having a mixture of moderate and well-networked "mainstream" people involved in the initial phase. At the same time, thought should be given as to how and which hard-liners could be introduced in the medium term. "Bring in" here does not automatically imply participation in meetings; it initially means trying to open up a conversation with the hard-liners about their concerns and resistance. Those who unequivocally advocate violence would not, in any case, be suitable for involvement in a dialoguing enterprise. As far as the others are concerned, the first important point is to be able to arrive at a better appraisal of their potential for disruption and resistance.

Third, in order to prepare the meetings, representatives of the third party have to conduct various preparatory talks on both sides and, through "shuttle diplomacy," build up a consensus for the list of participants and the program. These activities are themselves part of the dialogue process in the broader sense, although they mostly take a back seat in discussions about the relevance of these approaches. Contrary to a widespread belief, the real challenge of dialogue projects lies not in mastery of facilitation methods and communication techniques during actual encounters, but in the *organizational input* required simply to finance, prepare, and conduct them. In divided societies, merely announcing one's intention to engage in such an activity will be met with mistrust and rejection, if not straightforward obstruction by those in power. Because of this, the meetings have to be conducted outside the country concerned, and this necessitates high logistical and financial inputs.

Fourth, outside parties should from the beginning be aware of their own influence and role: Any intervention, however well meaning, can have intentional or unintentional consequences. For initiators of dialogue projects, there is an *ethical responsibility* to consider the effects of their actions—especially those consequences that, though unintended or unforeseen, nevertheless are at least conceivable. First and foremost here is the task of working out and minimizing the security risks to those they invite to their meetings. In highly asymmetrical conflicts, for example, participation in the dialogue often leads to the weaker party adopting a more radical stance. Lastly, any third party acting in an acute conflict is faced with the problem of how to maintain its "multipartiality" when confronted with massive human rights violations by one or the other side.

Fifth, the selection of the appropriate method of intervention is crucial. The interactive conflict-resolution movement has developed a specific type of problem-solving workshop whose style of "facilitation" is strongly influenced by the academic-analytical, and sometimes dogmatic, world of the initiators (Fisher 1997). Given the experience that has now been gathered, there is much to be said for setting the *intervention methodology* in dialogue projects on a much broader and more flexible basis. It would, in particular, be a good idea for the fund of experience built up in adult education, intercultural learning, group dynamics, counseling, supervision, and mediation in the narrower sense to be put to use in producing an active form of dialoguing. This process begins with the question of what composition the team should have and what sort of normative message emanates from the behavior of the team when the team itself is faced with conflicts. It continues with the uncovering of "undercurrents" and "overcurrents" within the group dynamic. This is important, because resistance to rapprochement in dialogues often expresses itself subtly as an apparently sudden hardening or via the raising of new topics. Finally, the process also touches on the question of how much or how little the dialogue is guided toward the identification of concrete problem-solving strategies.

As a sixth lesson, I should like to point to the now frequently used method to encourage changes of perspective through *discussions of a similar ethnopolitical conflict*. The idea underlying this approach is that it is probably easier to see the points of view of all the parties involved, and to come to a less prejudiced appraisal of the overall situation, if you are considering a conflict other than your own. It is then possible, as in a sort of mirror, to spot new aspects in your own conflict. Ideally, the matching case is one in which work is at a more advanced stage, so that it is natural to ask which settlement aspects are also suited to your own conflict. In practice, however, the process is not as smooth as this. Participants stress the "uniqueness" of their conflict, almost as if they were being robbed of part of what gives their case its meaning. Nonetheless, in retrospect participants often cite these experiences as among the most important that they had during the dialogues.

Seventh, as explained above, the macro-political effects of dialogue projects are difficult to assess. It is therefore all the more important to take a closer look at the possible impact on the *meso-social level*; this constitutes the seventh lesson. One of the key measures of success here is undoubtedly increasing ownership of the dialogue process by the participants and their respective affinity groups or organizations. Such a development cannot be achieved simply by involving the participants more in the fashioning of the seminars. It requires that the dialogue sessions be fleshed out and complemented with additional opportunities for preliminary and follow-up activities, for more in-depth treatment of individual topics, and for skills acquisition by participants. Possible forms in which this could take place are local backup forums, workgroups, and training sessions. Another measure of success is expansion of the circle of participants, both in terms of numbers taking part and replication of similar approaches, and in terms of movement closer to the track-one level. In practice, the task is to strike a balance between achieving a solid nucleus of people who will provide new impetus for conflict resolution and continually extending this circle via outreach.

Eighth, problem-solving workshops thus have to establish a self-sustaining process. In divided societies and societies traumatized by war, dialogue projects will sooner or later be confronted with the question of how their work and the impetus they provide for practical measures can be *institutionally anchored* in bodies that will replace the forums provided by the third parties in the initial phase. Without an institutional anchorage of this kind, there is a danger that the effects of the dialogue will peter out. Institutionalization of the dialogue takes very different forms, ranging from semigovernmental inter-ethnic commissions to joint task forces to multi-ethnic NGOs.

Last, probably the most important conceptual contribution that the dialogue-project approach can make to the creation of peace constituencies or peace alliances is that of generally *promoting a dialogue-based dispute culture*. What this means is that the characteristics of interest-led constructive dialogue described at the outset should not just be used to positive effect in a handful of intergroup projects, but should become a basic paradigm of political culture. It is a hallmark of many ethnopolitical conflicts—the Middle East is a case in point—that transformation will only be possible if a constructive dialogue takes place within the parties to the conflict.

REFERENCES

Apel, Karl-Otto. 1990. *Diskurs und Verantwortung*. Frankfurt, Germany: Suhrkamp.

Bar-On, Dan. 2000. *Den Abgrund überbrücken: Mit persönlicher Geschichte politischen Feindschaften begegnen*. Hamburg, Germany: Edition Koerber.

Bercovitch, Jacob, and Allison Houston. 1996. The Study of International Mediation: Theoretical Issues and Empirical Evidence. In *Resolving International Conflicts: The Theory and Practice of Mediation*, ed. Jacob Bercovitch, 11–35. Boulder, CO: Lynne Rienner.

Berghof Research Center for Constructive Conflict Management, ed. 2000–2001. *Berghof Handbook for Conflict Transformation*. Berlin: Berghof Research Center for Constructive Conflict Management. Accessed at www.berghof-center.org.

Burton, John. 1990. *Conflict: Resolution and Prevention*. London: Macmillan.

Burton, John, and Frank Dukes, eds. 1990. *Conflict: Readings in Management & Resolution*. London: Macmillan.

Fisher, Roger, and William Ury. 1981. *Getting to Yes*. Boston: Houghton Mifflin.

Fisher, Ronald J. 1997. *Interactive Conflict Resolution*. Syracuse, NY: Syracuse University Press.

Francis, Diana. 2000. Culture, Power Asymmetries and Gender in Conflict Transformation. In *Berghof Handbook for Conflict Transformation*. Berlin: Berghof Research Center for Constructive Conflict Management, accessed at www.berghof-handbook.net/francis/final.pdf.

Haumersen, Petra, Helmolt Rademacher, and Norbert Ropers. 2002. *Konfliktbearbeitung in der Zivilgesellschaft: Die Workshop-Methode im rumänisch-ungarischen Konflikt*. Münster, Germany: LIT-Verlag.

Hoffman, Mark. 1995. Defining and Evaluating Success: Facilitative Problem-Solving Workshops in an Interconnected Context. *Paradigms* 9 (2):150–167.

Kelman, Herbert C. 1992. Informal Mediation by the Scholar/Practitioner. In *Mediation in International Relations*, ed. Jacob Bercovitch and Jeffrey Z. Rubin, 64–95. London: Macmillan.

———. 1995. Contributions of an Unofficial Conflict Resolution Effort to the Israeli–Palestinian Breakthrough. *Negotiation Journal*, January 1995, 19–27.

Kleiboer, Marieke. 1996. Understanding the Success and Failure of International Mediation. *Journal of Conflict Resolution* 40 (2):360–389.

Lederach, John Paul. 1997. *Building Peace. Sustainable Reconciliation in Divided Societies*. Washington, DC: U.S. Institute of Peace.

Lund, Michael, and Guenola Rasamoelina, eds. 2000. *The Impact of Conflict Prevention Policy: Cases, Measures, Assessments*. Baden-Baden, Germany: Nomos.

McCartney, Clem. 1986. *Human Rights Education: 11th Annual Report*. Standing Advisory Committee on Human Rights. London: HMSO.

Miall, Hugh, Oliver Ramsbotham, and Tom Woodhouse. 1999. *Contemporary Conflict Resolution*. Cambridge: Polity.

Mitchell, Christopher. 1993. Problem Solving Exercises and Theories of Conflict Resolution. In *Conflict Resolution: Theory and Practice, Integration and Application*, ed. Dennis J. D. Sandole and Hugo van der Merwe, 78–94. Manchester, UK: Manchester University Press.

Mitchell, Christopher, and Michael Banks. 1996. *Handbook of Conflict Resolution: The Analytical Problem-Solving Approach*. London: Pinter.

Mott Foundation. 1999. *Reaching for Peace: Lessons Learned from Mott Foundation's Conflict Resolution Grantmaking*. Conducted by CDR Associates and the Berghof Research Center for Constructive Conflict Management. Michigan: Charles Steward Mott Foundation.

Otten, Hendrik, and Werner Treuheit. 1994. *Interkulturelles Lernen in Theorie und Praxis: Ein Handbuch für Jugendarbeit und Weiterbildung*. Opladen, Germany: Leske und Budrich.

Reimann, Cordula. 2000. Assessing the State-of-the-Art in Conflict Transformation. In *Berghof Handbook for Conflict Transformation*. Berlin: Berghof Research Center for Constructive Conflict Management, accessed at www.berghof-center.org

Reychler, Luc, and Thania Paffenholz, eds. 2000. *Peacebuilding: A Field Manual*. Boulder, CO: Lynne Rienner.

Ross, Marc Howard, and Jay Rothman, eds. 1999. *Theory and Practice in Ethnic Conflict Management: Theorizing Success and Failure*. London: Macmillan.

Rothman, Jay. 1998. Dialogue in Conflict: Past and Future. In *The Handbook of Interethnic Coexistence*, ed. Eugene Weiner, 216–235. New York: Continuum.

Spencer, Tanya. 1998. *A Synthesis of Evaluations of Peacebuilding Activities Undertaken by Humanitarian Agencies and Conflict Resolution Organisations*. London: Overseas Development Institute.

Wolleh, Oliver. 2000. Möglichkeiten und Grenzen interner Akteure bei der Friedensbildung in geteilten Gesellschaften—Die Conflict Resolution Trainer Group in Zypern (1993–1997). Ph.D. thesis, Berghof Research Center for Constructive Conflict Management, Berlin.

Zartman, I. William. 1985. *Ripe for Resolution: Conflict and Intervention in Africa*. New York: Oxford University Press.

12

✿

Justice and Reconciliation in Fragmented Societies

Richard J. Goldstone

The history of the twentieth century has been a particularly bloody saga. But the last two decades of that century have also witnessed a contrasting turn of events—a number of nations struggling to transform from situations of oppression and systematic human rights violations to forms of democratic government. Some have failed in that quest; others appear to be on the road to recovery. As a South African, I am particularly proud that our country must be regarded as one of the success stories.

I propose in this chapter to consider some of the approaches that I believe are conducive to the reconstruction of peace in fragmented societies. I will focus on the notions of justice and reconciliation, because it is, I believe, in the interaction between justice and reconciliation that a real end to conflict may be found.

PATHS TOWARD PEACE

There is, however, a precondition that must be fulfilled before justice and reconciliation can begin to lay the foundations for a new peace. Since the end of the Cold War, it has generally been recognized that without a free and open society there can be no question of truly ending conflict. Too frequently, however, it is incorrectly assumed that a democratic form of government is a guarantee of a free and open society. That assumption is refuted by the events in recent years in the Federal Republic of Yugoslavia, where Slobodan Milošević came to power through an election. And half a century earlier, Adolf Hitler, too, came to power via the ballot box. Both of those leaders used their legally gained powers to snuff out all vestiges of an open and democratic society. I regret that the same descent from democracy to an oppressive dictatorship may be unfolding in Zimbabwe, one of South Africa's northern neighbors.

A truly democratic government, one that endorses democracy not only in form but also in substance, and thus embraces notions of the free interaction of citizens and of a society buoyed by a free media—such a government is a precondition for attaining an enduring peace. This, then, is the first goal for fractured societies. They must move away from governance that has democracy merely as a façade hiding dictatorship and criminality, to truly open and democratic societies.

As a South African, I was privileged to play a role in the journey to a genuine democracy that my country undertook between 1990 and 1994. Whether our experience has lessons for others is for the people of those societies to decide. But where South Africa's transition can, I feel, have resonance for such regions is in relation to the daunting problem that faces all nations endeavoring to move from oppression to democracy—how to address past serious violations of the human rights of their people.

Broadly, such societies have three choices:

1. Criminal prosecutions, whether national or international;
2. Truth Commissions, with or without amnesties; or
3. National amnesia—closing the book on the past—which is usually accomplished by the granting of a blanket amnesty.

The most dangerous route is the last one, which ignores the victims entirely. The problem is that victims cannot and do not forget, and in some regions of the world, attempts to efface a ravaged past have created deep wells of resentment. This, in turn, provides the kind of toxic fuel that could be ignited by evil leaders to further their own nationalistic and xenophobic policies by turning people against each other.

It is disturbingly easy to ferment such conflict when people historically harbor deep hatred, especially when such hatred is based on ethnicity. An appalling example of this is the 1994 genocide in Rwanda, when the enmity between Hutu and Tutsi was exploited by leaders now dubbed "the genocidaires," resulting in the slaughter, in a period of less than 100 days, of more than 800,000 people (around 10 percent of Rwanda's population). Equally appalling is the way in which the 600-year history of cycles of violence in the former Yugoslavia has been manipulated by evil leaders to turn the 1990s into a period of recurring genocide and mass crimes against humanity, introducing to the world a new species of international crime, euphemistically termed "ethnic cleansing."

In his foreword to the *Report of the South African Truth and Reconciliation Commission*, Archbishop Desmond Tutu acknowledges that victims of gross repression cannot simply forget. He highlights the fact that there were in South Africa some who "urged that the past should be forgotten," but he goes on to say: "This option was rightly rejected because such amnesia would have resulted in further victimisation of victims by denying their awful experiences" (*Truth and Reconciliation Commission of South Africa Report* 1998:I:7). The route chosen by South Africa to avoid the resentment bred of denial was an open and transparent truth commission, held, as Archbishop Tutu put it, "in the full glare of publicity" (*Truth and Reconciliation Commission* 1998:I:1) to adjudicate on the granting of individual amnesties in return for full disclosure of the truth.

But the route that fractured societies adopt to address a ravaged past will depend upon their own unique and pragmatic considerations. In Chile, for example, the new democratic government of President Patricio Aylwin Azócar would have preferred a comprehensive truth commission. Political considerations, however, made that impossible. General Augusto Pinochet's army, which had retained significant power, reluctantly allowed a truth commission to be established, but only subject to important conditions. Investigation was to be restricted to disappearances, excluding other forms of human rights abuse, such as torture. Furthermore, the hearings of the Chilean Truth Commission were to be held in private, and the names of perpetrators were not to be made public in its report. It is significant that notwithstanding those substantial restrictions, the report of the Commission helped the people of Chile come to terms with themselves and enabled many of them to become reconciled.

But victims have long memories. This is demonstrated by the number of requests that were made by both non-Chilean and expatriate Chilean victims in a number of European countries, seeking the extradition of General Pinochet from the United Kingdom. And, after the return of Pinochet to Chile, there was a nationwide call for him to be stripped of his immunity and for his prosecution. Those things happened—and notwithstanding his advanced age. What is remarkable is the effect of the London arrest of Pinochet on Chilean society. Although some of the barely healed fissures were reopened, the frank and intense discussion in Chile of the human rights abuses committed more than two decades ago augurs well for a more permanent healing process.

PROSECUTION AND RECONCILIATION IN SOUTH AFRICA

In South Africa, political realities were very different. The democratic government of President Nelson Mandela wished to establish a truth commission. It had quickly taken effective control of the security forces, and there were sufficient financial and human resources to enable the Truth and Reconciliation Commission to fulfil the wide and open mandate given to it by the South African Parliament. It was subject to none of the constraints imposed on its Chilean predecessor.

Interestingly, significant criminal prosecutions for alleged crimes committed during the apartheid era were also held in South Africa. Although these prosecutions related in some cases to the very same incidents that were being investigated by the Truth and Reconciliation Commission, there was no theoretical or practical contradiction. Courts on occasion postponed criminal trials where those accused had applied to the Truth and Reconciliation Commission for amnesty. If an amnesty was granted, the trial was brought to an end, and if refused, the trial would proceed. The complementary coexistence of the two different processes should come as no surprise because they served a common goal—the search for the truth.

This goal of truth finding and truth telling is, I believe, one of the most important and effective ways of reconstructing fractured societies, especially where the truth relates to crimes based on irrational, ethnically motivated prejudices. South Africa realized the importance of these processes, and the most important part of the mandate of the Truth and Reconciliation Commission was thus to establish what human rights abuses were committed during the apartheid era. In order to facilitate its task, it was considered essential to persuade perpetrators who had the facts to make them public. Hence the offer of discrete amnesties in return for information. The necessity of this was acknowledged by the deputy-president of the Constitutional Court, Justice Ismail Mahomed, when the Court was asked to adjudicate the constitutionality of the granting of amnesty. He commented:

> That truth, which the victims of repression seek so desperately to know is . . . much more likely to be forthcoming if those responsible for such monstrous misdeeds are encouraged to disclose the whole truth with the incentive that they will not receive the punishment which they undoubtedly deserve. . . . Without that incentive there is nothing to encourage such persons . . . to reveal the truth which [victims] desperately desire. With that incentive, what might unfold are objectives fundamental to the ethos of a new constitutional order (*Azanian Peoples Organisation (AZAPO) and Others v President of the Republic of South Africa and Others* 1996:para. 17).[1]

In that context, however, it was crucial that criminal prosecutions of those who did not apply for amnesty should take place, since what would be the point of an amnesty without the threat of a prosecution? As to the victims, the result of both processes was the same—important public acknowledgment of what had happened to them.

Undertaking a balanced process of amnesties and prosecutions is one of the ways in which societies can possibly move away from a fractured past. Yet it must be conceded that some victims have an understandable objection to amnesty, which denies them the satisfaction that comes from the appropriate punishment of the perpetrators. Indeed, it was just such an objection that gave rise to the judgment quoted above. As Justice Mahomed commented:

> I understand perfectly why the applicants would want to insist that those wrongdoers who abused their authority and wrongfully murdered, maimed or tortured very much loved members of their families . . . should vigorously be prosecuted and effectively be punished for their callous and inhuman conduct (*AZAPO* 1996:para. 16).

But as Jose Zalaquett, the Chilean philosopher and activist who served on the Chilean Truth Commission, said at a conference in Cape Town in 1994, before the establishment of the South African Truth Commission: "It will sometimes be necessary to choose between truth and justice. We should choose truth. Truth does not bring back the dead, but it releases them from silence" (Krog 1998:24).

Indeed, in societies seeking to move beyond a scarred past, a balance has to be struck between

> the need for justice to victims of past abuse and the need for reconciliation and rapid transition to a new future, between encouragement to wrongdoers to help in the discovery of the truth and the need for reparations for the victims of that truth, between a correction in the old and the creation of the new (*AZAPO* 1996:para. 16).

Here we find the interaction between justice and reconciliation, or, put differently, between retributive justice and restorative justice.[2]

ACKNOWLEDGING THE TRUTH

I would suggest that if there is to be a lasting peace in fractured societies, an appropriate balance will have to be found between retributive and restorative justice—a balance that ensures truth telling and truth finding, and that uses this truth, however painful, to cleanse the wounds of the past and found new societies built on respect for the human dignity of all their members.

The search for, and recording of, the truth relating to past human rights violations serves several important public interests.

1. Preventing or at least curbing false denials and revisionism;
2. Assisting such nations to guard against the repetition of such violations;

3. Allowing victims to tell their stories;
4. The likelihood that many perpetrators will be removed from public office; and
5. Averting collective guilt from being ascribed to the group from which the perpetrators come.

These beneficial consequences are, I would suggest, achieved by both prosecutions and truth commissions, but in different ways and to different degrees. In order to examine this suggestion, I will compare and contrast the two areas in which I have experienced both processes—the Balkans and South Africa.

A good example of curbing false denials is provided by the exhumation of mass graves by the International Criminal Tribunal for the former Yugoslavia. Soon after the invasion of Srebrenica by the Bosnian Serb Army under General Ratko Mladic, reports began to circulate about the rounding up and subsequent massacre of thousands of Muslim men and boys. Those reports were categorically denied by the Bosnian Serb authorities. It was many months later that Drazan Erdemovic gave a firsthand account of the massacre to the media and later to investigators from the Tribunal. The thorough investigation of his allegations enabled the precise location of the massacre site to be sent to Washington, DC. In consequence, the U.S. government took aerial photographs of the site and made them public. Again, there were denials from the Bosnian Serb authorities—any mass grave identified, they said, would contain corpses of soldiers killed in action. The graves were exhumed, and the false denials were exposed for what they were. The medical evidence was to the effect that the bodies were those only of males who had been killed by a single bullet wound to the back of the head. In most cases, the hands of the victims had been bound behind them with wire. Those false denials are no longer heard.

I have no doubt that but for the work of South Africa's Truth and Reconciliation Commission, denial of many apartheid crimes would have gained currency, particularly in the white community of our country. That a number of the most senior officials of apartheid governments were involved in the perpetration of ghastly human rights violations can no longer be denied. It is also important to remember that the liberation movements were themselves guilty of human rights abuses, albeit in pursuit of a worthy cause, and this can also no longer be denied.

The revelation of the truth, whether by way of prosecutions or truth commissions, plays a material role in preventing a repetition of such horrendous conduct. The information not only becomes part of societal memory but the new democracy is also able to identify those institutions that facilitated oppression and to put in place new institutions designed to

prevent a repetition. Today crime and corruption in South Africa, more often than not, are made public by various democratic institutions and not,
as previously, by leaks to the media by disgruntled officials or members
of the public. Past human rights violations are already recorded in some
history books and today are being taught in schools and universities.

Public truth telling also exposes politicians and political leaders who
were involved in past human rights abuses. In many cases, the consequence is their ceasing to hold public office. Indeed, some countries ensure
the removal from public office of people implicated in violations of human
rights through passing lustration laws, as was done in certain Central European nations and under the Gauck administration in Germany.

Without acknowledgment for the victims and without the disclosure of
the criminality of the perpetrators, there is the inevitable consequence that
collective guilt would be ascribed to the nation or group from which the
perpetrators come. This was one of the great fears of white South
Africans, both Afrikaans and English speaking, and was one of the bars to
reconciliation that the Truth and Reconciliation Commission hoped to remove. Notwithstanding all the revelations made by the Commission, it
will take decades before black and white South Africans will be able to
come to terms with the consequences of 350 years of racial oppression.
But the Truth Commission began an extremely important process, captured in a comment by Afrikaans writer, poet, and journalist Antjie Krog:

> For me, it's a new beginning. It is not about skin colour, culture, language,
> but about people. The personal pain puts an end to all stereotypes. Where we
> connect now has nothing to do with group or colour, we connect with our
> humanity (Krog 1998:45).

The same attempt to focus on humanity rather than ethnic or religious
grouping must be made if rival ethnic groupings in fractured societies are
not to slip back into the vicious circle of attributing to each other collective blame and guilt.

A crucial aspect of any process of moving from reciprocal blame to reconciliation is the public acknowledgment of the suffering of victims. From
my own experience and contact with victims, I have no doubt that acknowledgment is often an important element in the healing process. In
some cases, that process cannot begin without acknowledgment. Although there are many examples of this in the annals of the South African
Truth Commission, one incident is highlighted in the "Reconciliation"
chapter of its *Report*. It concerns an account given by Lukas Baba Sikwepere, a resident of Heideveld in Cape Town, of how he lost his eyesight
when he was shot in the face by the security police, and how he was subsequently severely tortured by the police. When a commissioner asked
Mr. Sikwepere how he felt after having delivered his testimony, he

replied: "I feel that what has been making me sick all the time is the fact that I couldn't tell my story. But now it feels like I got my sight back by coming here and telling you the story" (*Truth and Reconciliation Commission* 1998:V:352).

What is true for individuals is also true for a society that has been torn by past human rights abuses. Public acknowledgment helps a people to reconcile with itself and is able to proceed to build a better society for all. In South Africa, the Truth and Reconciliation Commission has made white South Africans aware of the gross unfairness that is the consequence of hundreds of years of racial oppression. An extraordinary example is recounted in a letter sent to Antjie Krog as a result of one of her radio broadcasts concerning the work of the Truth Commission. The letter was written by the wife of one of the security police who had been involved in the torture and killing of those who opposed the regime. She said:

> Yes, I have forgiven the freedom fighters for the bombs, mines and AK-47s they used so liberally. . . . I finally understood what the struggle was really about the day the Truth Commission had its first hearing. I would have done the same had I been denied everything. If my life, that of my children and my parents was strangled with legislation. If I had to watch how white people became dissatisfied with the best and still wanted better. And got it (Krog 1998:147).

Such realizations have undoubtedly facilitated programs designed to redistribute wealth that are so essential if we are to achieve substantive equality that our new Constitution promises to our people.

The Truth Commission also laid the ground for reconciliation—between the races, between the genders, between communities, and between individuals. This kind of reconciliation, as Archbishop Tutu pointed out, is "not about being cosy; it is not about pretending that things were other than they were" (*Truth and Reconciliation Commission*:I:17). The kind of reconciliation fostered by the Commission was captured in a comment by Cynthia Ngewu, the mother of one of seven activists killed in the township of Gugulethu:

> This thing called reconciliation . . . if I am understanding it correctly . . . if it means this perpetrator, this man who has killed Christopher Piet, if it means he becomes human again, this man, so that I, so that all of us, get our humanity back . . . then I agree with it, then I support it all (quoted in Krog 1998:109).

Another significant advantage of truth commissions is their wide focus. Because of the absence of the formality attached to criminal prosecutions, they are able to investigate widely and comprehensively. In South Africa, the human rights abuses over a thirty-four-year period were investigated in two and a half years. How many criminal trials would have been required to bring to light the many thousands of violations recorded in the final report of the Truth and Reconciliation Commission? Over what period of time, and at what expense? As Archbishop Tutu comments in his foreword to the *Report*, Nuremberg-type trials were not a viable option for South Africa because "our country simply could not afford the resources in time, money and personnel that we would have had to invest in such an operation." In the same vein, he continues: "The Malan trials and the Goniwe inquest have also shown us that, because such legal proceedings rely on proof beyond a reasonable doubt, the criminal justice system is not the best way to arrive at the truth."[3]

It is assumed by many people that all that truth commissions require for their efficacy is the granting of amnesties in return for information. That is not necessarily so. In South Africa, the evidence of apartheid human rights violations was clouded in secrecy, and so efficacy and success did require the trade-off of amnesties for information. However, in other situations, such as the genocide in Rwanda, human rights violations were committed openly. The former government leaders who carefully planned the genocide hid their plans neither before nor after the murder of so many thousands of their fellow citizens. In such situations, the uncovering of truth may not require the granting of amnesty to perpetrators.

South Africa's experience also illustrates that, on a national level, a truth commission and criminal prosecutions can function simultaneously in a harmonious and effective way. If one extends this to the international arena, there is no reason why national truth commissions and international tribunals cannot also complement each other.

TOWARD TRUTH COMMISSIONS IN THE BALKANS

Such a situation has been debated for the past few years in Bosnia and Herzegovina, where there has been a call from many members of civil society for a truth and reconciliation commission. That interest has been shown by Serbs, Croats, and Bosnians. In December 1999 I had the fascinating and moving experience of attending a meeting in Sarajevo of some seventy members of nongovernmental organizations who were convinced of the benefits that could come to their country from the workings of such a commission.

Such an institution could provide an important mechanism through which the victims of ethnic violence could achieve acknowledgment. It could also establish that there were victims on all sides of the conflict. If a Bosnian truth commission is set up, it will, however, be essential to ensure that it would not be used as a platform for the propagation of political invective. That could be avoided if an efficient investigation department were set up—one that would investigate and monitor the evidence sought to be given by victims. Also, the proceedings of the commission would have to be carefully organized and presided over in such a way as to create the right space for both survivors and perpetrators to come forward and tell their stories.

Should such a truth commission be set up, there is admittedly a potential for conflict with the work of the War Crimes Tribunal. For example, no international prosecutor would be happy if witnesses for a pending trial were to testify before a truth commission prior to that trial. But this could very effectively be avoided by appropriate rules recognizing the primacy of the Tribunal and providing for deference to the work of its investigators. In my opinion, it would not be difficult to ensure a positive working relationship. There is indeed the precedent in South Africa of the relationship between the respective attorneys general in various provinces and the officials of the Truth and Reconciliation Commission. It is disappointing that the debate in Bosnia and Herzegovina has not achieved a positive outcome. There appears to be a lack of political will on the part of the political leaders, and no meaningful steps have been taken to support the nongovernmental institutions that have worked so hard for the establishment of such a commission.

In Croatia, the truths that heal a fractured society are emerging in a different way. There, the democratic government that the people of that country voted in to replace the authoritarian regime of President Franjo Tudjman has begun releasing documents that reveal the corruption that accompanied the Tudjman period. The truth has unusual ways of coming to the surface. Whether these revelations will satisfy the victims and mend the society does, however, remain to be seen.

It is still premature to speak of reconstruction and healing in the Federal Republic of Yugoslavia, whether through a truth and reconciliation commission or through some other method. But the fall of Milošević is a powerful symbol, and it is hoped that a government headed by President Vojislav Kostunica will embrace the open democracy that is the precursor to truly ending conflict.

And what of the most recent site of ethnic strife to explode in the Balkans—Kosovo? Much will depend on the future status of that troubled province of the Federal Republic of Yugoslavia. The question of whether Kosovo should become independent, remain under the Federal Republic of Yugoslavia, or continue as a de facto protectorate is one that is going to stay high on the international agenda. No matter what the decision regarding future status will be, I have no doubt that the international community should set its face against implementing a system of apartheid in the former Yugoslavia and in that way rewarding the perpetrators of ethnic cleansing. The international community should insist that ways be found for Albanians, Serbs, and Roma to live together in peace in Kosovo, whether through power sharing, through constitutionally guaranteed minority rights, or through a truth commission process. Whatever solution is chosen, success will not, I believe, be possible without forms of retributive and restorative justice and truth telling.

The quest to achieve lasting peace in the Balkans also demonstrates another important element necessary for ensuring reconstruction and an end to conflict in fractured societies. It has finally been realized that true stability in the Balkans will depend very much on the relationship between its states. Open borders and open trade between them and a positive relationship with the rest of Europe are vital components of peace. A very constructive development in this regard is the Stability Pact for South Eastern Europe, an agreement entered into by the European Union, the G-8, the countries of the region, and key international organizations.[4] The importance of the Pact, launched in Sarajevo at the end of July 2000, is twofold. First, it embraces a coherent regional approach rather than conflict management in individual crisis spots. Second, the EU has assumed a leading role in implementing the Pact, and is providing a crucial political link between the process of regional security and cooperation on one hand and the prospect of European integration on the other.

Similar sorts of regional initiatives for other fractured societies are vital if true reconstruction is to be assured. Economic and political assistance from wealthier nations are also crucial to ensure the stability necessary for peace.

In conclusion, I believe that there is room for optimism when it comes to reconstructing peace in fractured societies; an optimism stemming from the internationalization of the problems of systematic human rights violations. One can also draw hope from the increasing recognition that national borders and sovereignty are no longer barriers to appropriate intervention by the international community. In this respect, it is heartening to note the arrest by the Mexican government of Ricardo Miguel Cavallo, one of the men who tortured opponents of the military junta that ruled Argentina with such brutality between 1976 and 1983. The warrant to arrest Cavallo came from across the Atlantic, in the name of Spanish citizens who suffered and died in Argentina, and was signed by the same judge, Baltasar Garzón, who tried in 1998 to extradite Augusto Pinochet, the former dictator of Chile, on charges of genocide. As the *New York Times* commented on September 11, 2000:

> Mr. Cavallo's case appears likely to create a precedent that General Pinochet's did not: the principle that the law knows no borders, that a person can reach across frontiers and back through time to seek justice for crimes against humanity (Weiner and Thompson 2000).

Indeed, these developments need to be extended into Africa, Asia, and the Middle East. Evil leaders must know that their criminal conduct will not be tolerated, and that they will either face criminal prosecution or public exposure when their deeds are unmasked by the voices of their victims. Until that happens, the death toll, the numbers of women raped, and the numbers of children, women, and men driven from their homes will continue to rise as they did during the last decade of the twentieth century, and more societies will face the nightmare of schism and fracture.

NOTES

This chapter is drawn substantially from an address I delivered for the Olof Palme International Centre at the Gothenburg Book Fair in September 2000.

1. The judgment is available at www.law.wits.ac.za/judgements/azapo.html.

2. The latter term is used by Archbishop Tutu to describe "justice which is concerned not so much with punishment as with correcting imbalances, restoring broken relationships." See *Truth and Reconciliation Commission of South Africa Report*, vols. 1 and 5 (Cape Town: Juta & Co Ltd, 1998), 9.

3. Indeed, these and other problems that attach to criminal prosecutions are reflected in many of the criticisms of the UN Tribunals for the Former Yugoslavia and Rwanda.

4. For more information, see www.stabilitypact.org.

REFERENCES

Azanian Peoples Organisation (AZAPO) and Others v President of the Republic of South Africa and Others. 1996. (8) BCLR 1015 (CC), para. 16–17, accessed at www.law .wits.ac.za/judgements/azapo.html.

Krog, Antjie. 1998. *Country of My Skull*. London: Random House.

Truth and Reconciliation Commission of South Africa Report. 1998. Volume 1. Cape Town: Juta & Co Ltd., accessed at www.truth.org.za/report /index.htm

Weiner, Tim, and Ginger Thompson. 2000, September 11. Wide Net in Argentine Torture Case. *New York Times*, 6.

III

INSTITUTIONAL REFORM

13

❦

Ethnic Pluralism: Strategies for Conflict Management

Milton J. Esman

Those who study and write about ethnic policies and the management of ethnic conflict approach the subject from one of two perspectives. The social psychological perspective focuses at the local and interpersonal levels of interaction. It attempts to foster empathy among individual members of the contending parties, establish interpersonal trust, and facilitate their disposition to reciprocity and mutual respect; these, in turn, are believed to be prerequisite to "confidence building," and negotiated compromises leading to peaceful coexistence. The alternative perspective depends on institutions, rules, policies, and political structures to shape individual and group behavior and establish terms and conditions for regulating relations between contending ethnic communities.

Social psychological approaches to conflict management make the fatal mistake of extending the logic of interpersonal dynamics to large collectivities. In Palestine, Northern Ireland, Sri Lanka, and Bosnia, well-intentioned efforts to mitigate violent inter-ethnic conflicts by cultivating understandings at the individual and small-group levels have been uniformly overwhelmed by collective violence. Some ethnic conflicts are settled by the victory of one party over the other. Others may be consensually regulated not by cultivating individual friendships across ethnic lines, but by negotiated terms of intergroup relationships that the parties accept as more satisfactory than continuing warfare. Thus, my own contribution has dealt mainly with institutional factors because of compelling evidence that interpersonal dynamics have little effect on macro-political outcomes, and because human behavior is conditioned decisively by opportunities and constraints provided by the institutions that people encounter.

The principal arenas for ethnic conflict are the territorial states into which the world is currently divided. Governments reflect the distribution of power and prestige among ethnic communities; they also influence these relationships by the policies they enact and enforce. Thus the modern state is a critical participant in inter-ethnic affairs. Within this framework ethnic communities, some claiming indigenous homeland status, others more recent arrivals; governing elites; and frequently outsiders compete to shape the strategies and the institutions that govern relations among mobilized ethnic communities and between them and the state.

I shall avoid the continuing controversy among partisans of the primordialist, constructionist, and instrumentalist persuasions; any serious student of ethnic politics can cite convincing examples of all three. Nor will I discuss the specific instrumental or symbolic issues of contention between ethnic communities. Instead, I shall assume the reality of ethnic-based conflicts and focus on three of the longer-term strategies for regulating such conflicts: (1) to depluralize society, (2) to reduce the political salience of ethnic identity, and (3) to legitimize ethnic solidarities.

DEPLURALIZING SOCIETY

This is an effort to achieve ethnic homogeneity by eliminating from a particular territory all but members of the dominant nationality. This is based on the premise that an ethnically plural society is inherently unstable and conflict prone, that minorities are vulnerable to dual loyalty and even subversion, and that the dominant ethnic community has a prior moral title to claim territory as its own. Depluralizing may be pursued by such draconian measures as genocide or by mass expulsion or forced removal. History is sadly replete with examples of these practices, including prominent contemporary cases such as the attempted genocide of the Tutsi minority by the Hutu majority in Rwanda and the brutal ethnic "cleansing" implemented by the Serb authorities in Kosovo.

The more humane approach to homogenization is the policy of assimilation by which individuals are induced (and sometimes coerced) into abandoning their original identity, accepting membership in the dominant community, and adopting its culture.[1] Education, economic life, the mass media, and agencies of government are conducted in the official language, that of the dominant community; intermarriage is encouraged; and individuals are led to understand that if they (and their children) are to prosper, they are well advised to embrace the dominant culture and language. Gradually minority ethnic communities are depleted, especially among their leadership ranks, until finally they survive mainly as nostalgic memories. Assimilation may be forced by requiring members of minority communities to change their names or by proscribing speech or writing in minority languages, but such tactics usually provoke resentment and resistance that have the effect of undermining their intended goals.

Assimilationist policies tend to be most effective with immigrants who may be classified as "nonvisible minorities," whose pigmentation and religious practices offer fewest barriers to shifts in their individual identities. Homelands peoples are more inclined to cling to their collective identities and indigenous cultures, since these are rooted in their ancestral territories, while making expedient adjustments in their language skills to enable them to participate in the national economy. For two centuries prior to the 1960s, it had been assumed that a normal "nation-state" should be the homeland of a single people, that the rulers of the state were obligated to build an integrated nation, and that members of ethnic minorities were expected to assimilate willingly into the national community. In many countries, pressures toward assimilation and other forms of depluralization have begun to relax with the recognition that political community and viable statehood are not incompatible with ethnic pluralism. The concept of human rights, until recently limited to individuals, has been extended to ethnic communities. With the decline in sentiments of state nationalism, especially in the West, the scope of human rights that states are obligated to respect now includes ethnic communities and their cultures. Multiculturalism has become official policy in Canada; Spain, Belgium, and Britain have devolved substantial powers to ethnically based regional governments. Several state elites in Asia and Africa, including India, Thailand, Nigeria, and South Africa, have concluded that legitimizing the status of ethnic minorities actually stabilizes and strengthens their regimes.[2]

REDUCING THE POLITICAL SALIENCE OF ETHNIC SOLIDARITIES

While recognizing the continuing reality of ethnic solidarities, this strategy attempts to minimize their relevance in the public sphere. Eligibility for public office, government employment, public contracts, economic opportunities, and residential choice are presumed to be available to individuals by competitive ethnic-blind and color-blind meritocratic or market criteria. Political organization and electoral appeals with ethnic overtones are proscribed either by well-understood conventions or by law. Election systems are structured to discourage candidates who promote ethnic particularism and to privilege candidates with more inclusive appeals. Explicit ethnic political messages may be regarded as punishable legal offenses. Cross-cutting, inclusive memberships in professional, recreational, and welfare associations are encouraged and facilitated. While organizations devoted to maintaining ethnic heritages are tolerated, there is no recognition for multiculturalism in public policy.

The objective of this strategy is not assimilation, but rather the eventual emergence from the melting pot of an integrated culture that transcends previous ethnic loyalties and solidarities and is somehow inclusive of them all. The difficulties with this strategy are that members of some minorities may feel that their ethnic heritage that they continue to cherish is being demeaned and suppressed by public authority in a thinly veiled effort at assimilation, and that strict meritocratic-market rules of competition, though eminently fair in principle, condemn them in fact to the status of chronic losers due to previous histories of cultural deprivation, discrimination, or neglect. Any serious effort to overcome such collective handicaps through some pattern of affirmative action would contradict the main thrust of the integrationist strategy.

LEGITIMIZING ETHNIC PLURALISM

This strategy recognizes that distinct ethnic identities and solidarities are likely to remain permanent or long-term realities in the structures of their societies and that these relationships must be regulated by public authority. There are two classes of legitimizing strategies—those based on domination, and those based on one or another version of power sharing.

Domination entails control of the state apparatus, its military and civil components, by representatives of a single ethnic community. This control enables them to distribute economic opportunity and cultural prestige as well as political power and the symbols of political authority inequitably in favor of their fellow ethnics and to relegate others to collective subordination or inferior status entirely on grounds of ethnic membership. This does not mean that all members of the dominant group benefit equally or that all members of the subordinate group are equally disadvantaged, but the pattern of preferences is evident to all and is likely to be reinforced by an official, often elaborate ideology. There is no effort to downplay or diminish the salience of ethnic differences, since the maintenance of a ranked system is essential to sustaining the social order.

By contrast, the various patterns of power sharing, while respecting the legitimacy and enduring quality of ethnic differences, attempt to ensure the security of all ethnic communities and provide for collective self-management and an equitable distribution of opportunity within the framework of a common political authority. For homelands peoples, territorial autonomy can grant a large measure of devolved self-government under federal or federal-like arrangements; the possibility that regional autonomy could be the prelude to separatism is believed to be less risky than efforts to contain a disaffected people within a unitary political system. For peoples who are not territorially concentrated, a variety of arrangements may be introduced, from consociational participation in decision-making circles in government, along with proportionality in the allocation of political and bureaucratic offices and economic opportunities, to minority rights to control and operate their own institutions, notably schools and mass media at public expense in their own language, thereby ensuring the intergenerational sustainability of their culture.

Power-sharing arrangements normally require the exercise of more sophisticated political skills than other patterns of conflict management, and acceptance by political elites and their mass constituents that their partners in power sharing, in the face of inevitable competition for status and resources, have legitimate rights and interests that must be negotiated and respected. Where territorial separation is unfeasible, power sharing has become the preferred expedient for international mediators striving to terminate ethnic violence, from Northern Ireland to Bosnia, Rwanda, Azerbaijan, and Sri Lanka. To those who favor consensual outcomes that attempt to protect the vital interests of all the contending parties, power sharing has a compelling appeal. Yet, it is perilously vulnerable to two limitations.

The first of these vulnerabilities is a consequence of the internal factionalism, divisions, and politics that afflict all ethnic communities. None is free from internal competition for leadership based on class, lineage, economic interests, or ideology and from disagreements about how to define the vital economic interests of their community. The politics of power sharing demands compromises that necessarily fall short of some of the aspirations of one or both power-sharing partners. These disappointments and charges of betrayal are likely to be taken up by the spokespersons for dissatisfied factions, hoping to enhance their support base and leadership potential by the tactic of "outbidding" the moderates who have engineered the compromises. The strains produced by outbidding, as we have witnessed in Northern Ireland and the Middle East, can threaten and even overwhelm the prudential politics of power sharing.

A second vulnerability is transnational in its source: the impact of diaspora activism. Diaspora communities do not hesitate to exert influence in their erstwhile homelands; those most inclined to intervene are frequently advocates—from the safe distance of their new home bases—of the most uncompromising definitions of their peoples' interests. They are likely to provide violent factions with funds, weapons, and political support. The Tamil Tigers of Sri Lanka, the Irish Republican Army, the Palestinian Hamas, and the Kurdish Labour Party (PKK) are among the extremist factions that have been sustained by their diasporas, while obstructing efforts to moderate conflict in their native lands. The practitioners of power sharing must be continuously on guard to counteract diaspora support for violence-prone factions that charge them with sacrificing the vital interests of their community.[3]

COMBINATIONS

These strategies are sometimes manifested in public policy in their pure form, such as the intricately complex power-sharing institutions in Belgium and the rigid enforcement of white-Afrikaner domination and exclusion by the late unlamented apartheid regime in South Africa. Frequently, however, the relationships that evolve incorporate combinations of these strategies. In Turkey the large Kurdish minority encounters severe repression and discrimination as a collectivity, but individuals are encouraged to assimilate into the Turkish mainstream. In Malaysia, Malays, despite internal conflicts, zealously guard their political and cultural hegemony, while the large body of Chinese and Indian citizens enjoys limited but significant rights to participate in government and a large measure of economic freedom. Immigrants frequently claim the right as individuals to equal opportunity for education, employment, and enjoyment of public amenities, while promoting the survival of their collectivity and the cultivation and official recognition of their distinctive culture—multiculturalism.

Such relationships are not set in stone, but may evolve with changes in political regimes, demographic proportions, ideological influences, and external pressures. During the highly centralized Franco dictatorship, political and cultural expression by the non-Castilian minorities were brutally repressed; under the successor regime, Catalans and Basques operate regional governments in their own languages, promoting their distinctive cultural and economic interests. The rights to higher education and public employment, long enjoyed by Sri Lanka's Tamil minority during the colonial era, were curtailed by a Sinhalese nationalist successor government, contributing to the Tamil-based insurrection that continues to claim thousand of lives. The revocation of autonomy status for the South precipitated renewal of apparently endless civil war in Sudan, which is being waged to determine the shape of inter-ethnic relations in that unhappy country.

CONTEXTUALITY AND PRAGMATISM

There are strong incentives among scholars who identify as social scientists to reach out for powerful explanations that can order and explain what appear on the surface to be very diverse sets of phenomena. The literature on ethnic relationships has not been immune to such efforts, often dogmatic in tone, purporting to reduce the significance of ethnic politics to such systems as Marxian class analysis, liberal individualism, constructivism, genetic nepotism, neo-Freudianism, and cynical instrumentalism, or even to dismiss ethnic solidarities as illusory or unreal, platonic shadows of some deeper reality.[4] Those who struggle with empirical evidence—with the host of variables that affect the shape of inter-ethnic and state encounters—can only react skeptically to these ambitious attempts at general theory, to contain the many expressions of ethnic politics within the confines of parsimonious conceptual systems.

Several decades of observing and reflecting on ethnic politics have persuaded me of the futility of searching for a general theory about the genesis of ethnic conflicts or for universal prescriptions for managing or resolving them. I cannot see that the conflicts between Serbs and Albanians in Kosovo, Hausa and Yoruba in Lagos, Sindi and Bihari in Karachi, Zulu and the ANC government in South Africa, and Israelis and Palestinians can be explained by the same sets of concepts or settled by the application of the same or similar formulas. The reduction of such conflicts to a limited set of classes and the recognition of alternative strategies for managing conflicts such as those that I have identified can be useful points of departure for bringing intellectual order into the complex universe of ethnic politics. They are, however, no substitute for confronting the specific complexity, the numerous variable factors, the distinctive context of each conflict. What the disciplined study of ethnic-based encounters can do—and this is no mean accomplishment—is to sensitize the student or policymaker to the particular circumstances that influence each individual conflict; to make them aware of expedients and strategies that have been attempted more or less successfully elsewhere; and to help them to tease out symbolic, institutional, and structural arrangements and flows of resources that may induce the parties to that particular conflict and their various factions to coexist on civilized terms.

All of this calls for substantial doses of caution and modesty both among academics and practitioners. Peoples that long coexisted on peaceful, even friendly terms may be converted to bitter, even lethal enmity by perceived threats from the other to their vital interests. Even when an ethnic-based conflict has been apparently settled, the parties survive with their separate collective memories and divergent perspectives and interests. Ethnic politics may slumber, but they seldom sleep. Relationships must continue to be monitored, negotiated, and adjusted, issue by issue, so that as previous arrangements come under stress they are not allowed to collapse into violence, but are succeeded by freshly negotiated understandings.

NOTES

1. See Vernon Van Dyke (1975, 1977), Jack Donnally (1989), and Hurst Hannum (1991).

2. On the utility of multiethnic electoral coalitions for managing ethnic conflicts in Africa, see James R. Scarritt (1993).

3. See Gabriel Sheffer (1986), Manus Midlarsky (1992), Milton J. Esman (1990), Esman and Telhami (1995), Stephen Ryan (1990), Paul Smith (1991), Daniel Patrick Moynihan (1993), and Astrid Suhrke and Leila G. Noble (1977).

4. For examples of the unwillingness of many social scientists to regard ethnic solidarity as a legitimate expression of politics, see Orlando Patterson (1977) and Stephen Steinberg (1981).

REFERENCES

Chazan, Naomi, ed. 1991. *Irredentism and International Politics*. Boulder, CO: Lynne Rienner.

Donnally, Jack. 1989. *Universal Human Rights in Theory and Practice*. Ithaca, NY: Cornell University Press.

Esman, Milton J. 1990. Ethnic Pluralism and International Relations. *Canadian Review of Studies in Nationalism* 17 (1–2):83–93.

———. 1994. *Ethnic Politics*. Ithaca, NY: Cornell University Press.

Esman, Milton J., and Shibley Telhami, eds. 1995. *International Organizations and Ethnic Conflict*. Ithaca, NY: Cornell University Press.

Hannum, Hurst. 1991. *Autonomy, Sovereignty, and Self-determination: The Accommodation of Conflicting Rights*. Philadelphia: University of Pennsylvania Press.

Kohn, Hans. 1965. Minorities. In *Encyclopedia Britannica* (1965 ed.), vol. 15:542–553.

Midlarsky, Manus, ed. 1992. *The Internationalization of Communal Strife*. London: Unwin and Hyman.

Moynihan, Daniel Patrick. 1993. *Pandemonium: Ethnicity in International Politics*. New York: Oxford University Press.

Patterson, Orlando. 1977. *Ethnic Chauvinism: The Reactionary Impulse*. New York: Stein and Day.

Ryan, Stephen. 1990. *Ethnic Conflict and International Relations*. Aldershot, UK: Dartmouth Press.

Scarritt, James R. 1993. Communal Conflict and Contention for Power in Africa South of the Sahara. In *Minorities at Risk: A Global View*, ed. Ted Robert Gurr, 252–289. Washington DC: U.S. Institute of Peace Press.

Sheffer, Gabriel, ed. 1986. *Modern Diasporas in International Politics*. London: Croom-Helm.

Smith, Paul, ed., in collaboration with K. Koufa and A. Suppan. 1991. *Ethnic Groups in International Relations*. New York: New York University Press.

Steinberg, Stephen. 1981. *The Ethnic Myth: Race, Ethnicity and Class in America*. New York: Atheneum.

Suhrke, Astrid, and Leila G. Noble, eds. 1977. *Ethnic Conflict in International Relations*. New York: Praeger.

Van Dyke, Vernon. 1975. Justice as Fairness: For Groups. *American Political Science Review* 69:607–614.

———. 1977. The Individual, the State, and Ethnic Communities in Political Theory. *World Politics* 29:343–369.

14

❦

External Democracy Support: Challenges and Possibilities

Angel Viñas

External assistance in support of democracy is a recent industry. It is a growing industry as well. Until the 1970s, democracy support given by foreign partners or institutions remained relatively unimportant and was, more often than not, linked to the dynamics of the Cold War. At certain moments, however, it became meaningful. German political foundations played, for instance, a critical role in strengthening democratic forces in Spain during the transition years away from the dictatorship.[1] Some years later, the Woodrow Wilson Center (1986) carried out a project on transitions from authoritarian rule, out of which a highly regarded set of five volumes evolved. Comparisons were established between the different approaches followed, both by Europeans and Americans (Whitehead 1986).

The need for this kind of support became, in any case, imperative with the collapse of the Cold War. Suddenly a number of countries, old and new, were freed from the shackles of their forced allegiance to the Soviet Union. They had to create new political systems, remold their economies, and recast their societies. External democracy assistance became an essential item in the toolbox of foreign policy operations (Diamond 1995).

The European Union has not been absent in the development of this growing industry. Its democracy support programs started before the Cold War came to an end. One of the areas where they were forthcoming was Central America (Roy 1992), when manifold efforts coalesced into an increase of the European profile in what was then perceived as a potentially important crisis area (Mertes 1985).

However, widespread democracy support became an integral part in the European Community *instrumentarium* as a result of two developments: first of all, because of the need to help rebuild societies in Central and Eastern Europe in the wake of the devastation caused by Soviet legacies; and second, because of the conceptual transformations undergone by cooperation policy toward developing countries and, more particularly, within the unique framework of the Lomé Convention.

This chapter will outline some of the problems encountered by the European Commission, as a source of ideas for the Union and as its implementing organ, in drafting and carrying out democracy-supporting policies and activities.

THE CASE OF THE EUROPEAN UNION

If I have taken this angle, it is because, unfortunately, as far as the EU is concerned very little of its activities have been noticed in one of the major recent overviews of the subject (Carothers 1999). It is a fact, however, that democracy support was progressively incorporated into the "constitutional framework" of the Union and therefore into practical policies. Thus the Maastricht Treaty explicitly characterized the respect for fundamental rights and the principles of democracy as vital elements for membership (Articles F and O) and as a basic guideline for action. It also established that Community policy in the field of development cooperation must contribute to the overall objective of consolidating democracy and the rule of law and respecting human rights and fundamental freedoms (Article 130u). In 1997, the Treaty of Amsterdam strengthened those principles both in the Community field and for the evolving Common Foreign and Security Policy (Alston 1999).

To clarify and enhance the operational nature of the concepts included in the revised Lomé Convention, the European Commission presented a Communication to set out the terms of the dialogue with the ACP countries taking into account such conceptual developments (European Commission 1998).

However, even before the Amsterdam Treaty and the revision of the Lomé Convention, the Commission had energetically assisted the activities of national, regional, and nongovernmental organizations specializing in democracy support. A significant measure to enhance such commitment was the initiative of the European Parliament in 1994 to integrate a series of thematic and geographic budget lines specifically dealing with the promotion of human rights into a single chapter (B 7-7) entitled "European Initiative for Democracy and Human Rights." Largely thanks to the European Parliament, considerable resources can nowadays be mobilized to back up policies and statements of intent. In 1991, the dedicated budget available for human rights and democracy activities was only

200,000€. In 2001 this figure had grown to nearly 100 million€, almost twice as much as the yearly budget for the UN high commissioner for human rights. If the sums available for the geographical programs are also taken into account, the amounts spent on democracy support by the Union as such turn out to be far more significant.

A NEW EU POLICY FRAMEWORK

Given these realities, two Council regulations were adopted outlining the operations in which the Community may engage in order to contribute to the general objective of developing and consolidating democracy and the rule of law as well as respecting human rights and fundamental freedoms (*Official Journal of the European Communities* 1999). In summary form, such operations are as follows:

- Activities to promote human rights and the rule of law, with a focus on:

  1. Civil and political rights
  2. Economic, social, and cultural rights
  3. Rights against poverty and social exclusion
  4. Rights of minorities, indigenous peoples, refugees, and ethnic groups
  5. Institutional development in the field of rights protection and promotion
  6. Support for specific institutions to prevent torture or ill treatment, or to rehabilitate victims
  7. Education, training, and awareness raising
  8. Human rights observation
  9. Promotion of nondiscriminatory practices, including the fight against racism and xenophobia

- Activities in support of democracy and civil society, with a focus on:

  1. Independence of the judiciary, constitutional and legislative reform, and abolition of the death penalty
  2. Separation of powers
  3. Pluralism
  4. Prevention of corruption and promotion of administrative accountability
  5. Participation in economic and political life, in particular for women
  6. Support to electoral processes
  7. Separation of civilian and military functions

- Activities in support of human rights and democratization through conflict prevention, such as by:

  1. Institutional development, in particular capacity for early warning
  2. Balancing opportunities and bridging identity-based divisions
  3. Group conciliation and confidence building
  4. Promoting humanitarian law and, in particular, the international criminal courts

Those operations refer to general objectives (for example, support for cultural rights) as well as specific ones (bridging identity-based divisions). They also contain divergent orientations (the protection of identity and reducing the saliency of identity in social dynamics, for example). However, they do provide a recognizable framework for formulating project objectives, and they complement other activities financed through geographically oriented chapters of the Union budget.

The Commission has focused on the fight against racism and xenophobia in the lead-up to the World Conference on Racism, which took place in South Africa in 2001. The aim is to support NGO participation in the preparatory process as well as the conference itself through funding to the Office of the High Commissioner for Human Rights.

The Commission attaches great importance to the promotion of women's rights as human rights and has carried out a number of activities regarding the implementation of the Beijing Platform for Action. The Beijing+5 review that was held in New York in June 2000 took stock of progress made since 1995, and helped to raise awareness of how far we still have to go.

Since the regulations were adopted, the Commission has highlighted the importance for democratization of electoral processes and of equal participation in politics. It has prioritized the development of professional methodologies, logistics, and training. Following a request from the Parliament, it prepared a communication dealing with election observation with a view toward enhancing the capacity to promote democracy through electoral support operations (European Commission 2000). The communication identified a number of ways for making Union activities more effective, and it coordinated and set down guidelines and a framework for future action in this field.

Community support has been provided for civic education projects aimed at informing citizens, especially women, about electoral participation, their rights as voters, and how to use legal instruments to defend those rights. The Commission has also financed training courses on election observation and monitoring so as to create a well-prepared pool of local election observers. Other activities have involved training for journalists and education in democratic procedures for members of the political classes. New methods of quantitative and qualitative measurement of media coverage and access to the media have been developed as well as a methodology for assessing legal frameworks and media structures.

Of course, free and fair elections will not, of themselves, make a country democratic or give it the political stability required for democracy to flourish. They must be part of a broader process. This includes ensuring that the central institutions of state, such as the legislative branch, operate in a legitimate and effective manner and have the institutional capacity to draft, implement, and supervise policies addressing the needs of the people.

Many actions supported within the European Initiative for Democracy and Human Rights aim to empower members of parliament to perform their proper democratic role. In emerging democracies, training young parliamentarians to the complex history and interdependent relations of human rights and democracy is important. Other activities have focused on the impact of international human rights instruments on national legislations (European Commission forthcoming).

THE RATIONALE FOR EU ACTION

The Commission is convinced that securing democracy is one of the best ways to ensure that political systems have the capacity and motivation to respect human rights. Democratic governments are less likely to indulge in ethnic "cleansing" or to resort to extreme forms of nationalism or violent aggression. Instead they prefer to rely on building strong and cooperative partnerships and to use imaginative diplomacy to improve their security and political environment. They have created what has occasionally been referred to, in Robert Cooper's terminology, as a postmodern order, where foreign policy is driven partly by domestic concerns about the protection of democracy and the dignity of human beings.

Democracy, in particular, provides a mechanism for the timely and transparent resolution of disputes—disputes that if allowed to fester or driven underground will sooner or later surface to poison the political atmosphere. It follows that one of the most constructive contributions that the European Union can make is to help establish democratic processes where none exists or to strengthen democracy where it is weak.

The most significant impact of Community democracy assistance has been the contribution to the growth of a lively NGO sector. This sector has been important in many countries in lobbying for political reform to correct weaknesses in both formal and substantive democracy, in providing a bulwark against the reversion to authoritarianism, in changing political culture particularly where it has not spread to the countryside, and in providing a form of critical monitoring of the evolution of democracy. What has been created with the help of European funds is a moral community in many transition countries, including groups and individuals who are essential to the construction of a democratic political culture and who press for democratic change.

Community assistance has also been important psychologically; it represents an affirmation of the value of the supported projects. It has been instrumental in raising the visibility of recipient NGOs and, in more authoritarian countries, by providing a form of protection. And it has been meaningful in practical terms, in providing training and offering a learning experience in planning, implementing, and evaluating projects.

European partnerships are important. They have allowed and speeded up the exchange of know-how between east and west and the building up of highly valuable networks.

A bottom-up approach in the selection of projects, and the fact that these projects do not have to be approved by recipient governments, has also been an extremely interesting orientation. Potential applicants are likely to have a better understanding of their own society than outsiders; their applications tend to reflect the priorities for democracy as seen from within the beneficiary societies.

To sum up, democracy support has been of considerable value for the development of civil society in the beneficiary countries. Overall, it has contributed to the good image of the European Union while the recipients constitute a valuable source of critical knowledge about their own countries that can assist policy making (ISA Consult 1997).

Supporting democracy is therefore mutually beneficial. Open and accountable governments, monitored by genuinely representative legislatures and uncensored media, are less likely to be corrupt and more likely to lay the foundations for a fair business environment (Patten 1999; Moore 1995). Thus, not only is it morally right to assist in the process of democratization but it also serves the interests of the European Union to do so.

DEMOCRACY HELPS DEVELOPMENT

Democracy, in the view of the Commission, helps development. It is true that this relationship is not a linear one. Nor has it been proven that democratic countries must grow faster than nondemocratic ones. However, there seems to be sufficient evidence that the pattern of growth is different and that democratic countries are less subject to abrupt reverses of the growth trend. We cannot trust "benevolent dictators" too much. Additionally, as underlined by some authors (e.g., Dreze and Sen 1989), not one single famine has ever happened under a democratic regime, although this is correlation and not causality. One more point: Recent research underlines that countries with better governance structures grow faster.[2]

It seems realistic to assume that in very poor countries, where the indigent are a significant share of the population, democratic systems, by giving them "voice," increase the possibility that "pro-poor" policies are implemented and that poverty is alleviated. Since reducing poverty is the *primus inter pares* of all development efforts (OECD-DAC 1996), promoting democracy should be handled in such a way that that goal can be more easily achieved.

Despite all the literature published that is casting doubts on the sustainability of democratization, and although one must recognize that several states are going toward what could be called illiberal, rather than liberal, democracy, the European Commission is of the belief that a case indeed exists for being demo-optimistic.[3] A good number of the countries that have passed from authoritarian rule to democracy are achieving very positive results in human development and respect for human rights, while the countries where the regime has become more detached from the people and more authoritarian are not performing well in either field (e.g., Zimbabwe and Ivory Coast).

The European Commission has repeatedly stated that democracy, development, and good governance, including the rule of law, are inextricably linked. This might not be a foolproof academic approach, and exceptions can indeed be found, but evidence tells us that "all good things come together."

DEMOCRACY SUPPORT AND CONFLICTS

Securing a democratic culture and free democratic institutions is not an easy or one-dimensional task. Many structural deficiencies contribute to the weakening of democracy and need to be systematically addressed in order to strengthen the system. In particular, the process requires the cultivation of a free and vigorous media with sufficient legal space to be effective in its role as a watchdog on public power, a culture and legal infrastructure of official openness, and the flourishing of a free and autonomous civil society[4] that allows for the spontaneous emergence of groups that in turn enhances the capacity of society to resist undemocratic tendencies. Often it requires mechanisms such as "Truth Commissions" that facilitate the process of reconciliation that is often so necessary in order to create a breathing space for new democratic methods to be given a chance.

The trend toward democratization, however, has encountered resistance. Internal conflicts have erupted in many countries with greater intensity than ever before. Such conflicts have also affected established states and have become inextricably enmeshed with discord about national and subnational identity, cultural and religious recognition, and competition for resources and power. It has become evident that, in a sense, the Cold War froze many potential conflicts of this kind. Unfettered now by external constraints and alignments, long-suppressed sources of internal conflict have reawakened with a vengeance.

Whatever the cause of those conflicts, one feature common to many of them has been massive violations of democratic rule. Such violations have been perpetrated by governments and also by nongovernment actors. They have been particularly intense in many cases where the structures of government have been undermined or destroyed. Comparative analyses of conflict situations in the post–Cold War period have highlighted the relevance of four major factors. The role played by political leadership is the first factor. Social cohesion (as indicated by a robust civil society with adequate mechanisms to cope with increasing tensions) is the second factor. The commitment by governments to observe multilateral standards protecting political, civic, economic, social, and cultural rights is the third factor. Finally, one should mention the level of assistance from the outside world to help channel domestic reactions into peaceful responses. All of them point to the same direction: Strengthening fledging democratic structures has become essential.

Leadership selection and replacement are solidly anchored in domestic political and social dynamics. External assistance has therefore been targeted at governments and groups favorable to democratic institutions, multilateral standards, and reasonably crafted economic and social development strategies and policies.

External democracy support plays an even more important role in countries emerging from violent or long-drawn conflicts. A crucial element of peace and democracy building is the construction of consensus regarding the role of the state, particularly in ethnically divided societies. It entails designing political institutions that can manage disputes (the essence of democratic politics) peacefully. At the root of this approach is a recognition that democracy itself operates as a conflict management mechanism, allowing social disputes to be voiced by political parties and mediated by the democratic competition in the electoral process without degenerating into violence.

Transitions to democracy in states emerging from conflict situations are particularly difficult. Violent conflicts impact negatively on almost every aspect of political and social relations: Civil society becomes weak and highly polarized, local leaders and elites are usually the same people who have been engaged in the armed conflict itself, the economy is severely damaged, and the basic governmental and other institutions have either ceased to function or face a severe crisis of legitimacy. Committed and enduring external support is vital to these societies.

It is a fact that without peace, development is not achievable. Africa provides numerous examples of this axiomatic proposition: Congo, Sierra Leone, Sudan. On the other hand, without development peace is difficult to sustain. How to square the two terms of this equation in conflict-prone situations is—and remains—an enormous challenge.

LESSONS LEARNED

In the past ten years, the European Commission has learned, sometimes painfully, a number of valuable lessons for drafting democracy support policies.

The first lesson, and perhaps the most meaningful one, is the importance of local ownership. The Commission recognizes that, at the end of the day, local people bear primary responsibility for making democracy effective. Whatever outside help is given must build on local efforts, capacities, and institutions. Assistance to local civil society is absolutely essential in this respect. Ideally, such outside help should endeavor to create an enabling environment. However, if local society is not ready to accept assistance from outside, the likelihood is that foreign endeavors will not bear great results. This experience has been made repeatedly. When entrenched powerful locals have more to gain from nondemocratic solutions, there is, at least for a while, not much foreigners can do.

The second lesson refers to the need to differentiate. Political and social evolution are seldom trouble-free. Democratization is a process that takes time. It cannot be achieved overnight. The Western experience, even in the most industrialized countries, is in this respect telling enough. In today's world, situations vary enormously. There are states that are neither committed nor willing to democratize. There are "failed" or "weak" states that lack the resources and capabilities to undertake reforms. There are states emerging from conflicts that have left behind indelible legacies, and there are states that are simply a façade for poorly performing societies in terms of democratization. All these situations require tailor-made policy initiatives. There is no all-encompassing formula to ensure success.

Willy-nilly, perhaps, the confrontation with such a variety has led the Commission to a long-term approach that focuses on some of the root causes of undemocratic situations. Although the etiology is broad, it is a fact that lack of economic resources, poorly managed economic conditions, and prevalence of poverty nourish longstanding grievances that, when exploited by skillful political demagogues, are likely to set the scene for undemocratic forms of governance.

The third lesson builds upon the need for coherence. In order to tackle undemocratic situations, a comprehensive approach is required. This is more easily said than practiced. But it means that such an approach must integrate trade, economic, political, and diplomatic instruments, among others, so as to create an enabling environment in which democracy-loving forces may flourish. The mechanistic transplantation of foreign formulae into a nonreceptive local society is a sure recipe for failure.

I am well aware that many Western, industrialized, liberal democracies, and also the European Union, have been subject to criticism because of an alleged bent to export their kind of democratic self-understanding worldwide with little consideration given to local conditions and/or traditions.

In my experience, however, democracy support cannot be considered as a form of cultural imperialism, as an imposition of so-called Western values, or as an export of ethnocentric European attitudes. Democracy is an end in itself because it provides individuals and societies with a fundamental freedom: that of choosing their own representatives. This is, from the point of view of many outside donors, a basic policy objective, even if no benefits are obtained from the exercise of such freedom or even if it is not exercised. People in the most disparate situations have proved time and again that, when they are free from intimidation and coercion, they can choose their leaders in reasoned and reasonable ways. The arguments we used to hear about a lack of "readiness" of countries or even continents to adopt democracy as a political system have turned out to be mere rationalizations of deeply felt prejudices, have been disproved by the historical record, and have always ignored the immanent need for the human being to exercise its freedom.

THE IMPORTANCE OF DEMOCRATIC CLAUSES

The question arises as to what to do when democratization is reversed. We have seen this happen in all too many cases. The automatic recourse to sanction mechanisms is not the only answer; perhaps in many cases it is not even an answer.

The European Union has followed a double track. On the one hand, it has adopted a model clause according to which the respect for democratic principles and fundamental human rights constitutes an essential element of all cooperation and partnership agreements concluded by the Union.

On the other hand, this provision is accompanied by a non-execution clause that incorporates the possibility of suspension or adopting other measures if the human rights clause is violated (Rosas 1999).

In the recent Cotonou Agreement (successor to the Lomé Convention), the ACP-EU framework has forcefully anchored the common concerns regarding democracy building:

> Respect for all human rights and fundamental freedoms, including respect for fundamental social rights, democracy based on the rule of law and transparent and accountable governance are an integral part of sustainable development.

Furthermore:

> Democratic principles are universally recognised principles underpinning the organisation of the State to ensure the legitimacy of its authority, the legality of its actions reflected in its constitutional, legislative and regulatory system, and the existence of participatory mechanisms. On the basis of universally recognised principles, each country develops its democratic culture.

The rule of law is forcefully underscored:

> The structure of government and the prerogatives of the different powers shall be founded on rule of law, which shall entail in particular effective and accessible means of legal redress, an independent legal system guaranteeing equality before the law and an executive that is fully subject to the law (European Commission, 23 June 2000).

The ACP-EC partnership must therefore be considered as a powerful instrument for supporting from the outside processes of democratization among its beneficiaries. The Cotonou Agreement will still take some time to become effective, although many of its provisions are being applied on a provisional basis. Certainly, it does not constitute an example of cultural or political imperialism. It has been freely negotiated for a long time and is one of the firmest bedrocks of European development cooperation and of its attack on world poverty.

There are, nevertheless, situations where development may be jeopardized (e.g., coups d'état and stolen elections) that require an appropriate response. The philosophy of the European Union is to use the "stick" of aid suspension as a means of last resort and to reach first for the "carrot": the maintenance of the agreement with the violating country although subjecting it to a fair amount of discussions. Article 96 establishes a consultative process in cases of alleged violation or nonfulfilment of the obligation to respect human rights, democratic principles, and the rule of law. Consultations in this regard are part and parcel of the process of political dialogue on the basis of mutually defined and agreed principles.

One could therefore assert that the Cotonou Agreement is an important achievement and a building block for strengthening the rule of law and democracy in situations where there may be a lack of it. The forces supporting democratic development cannot but be encouraged by the built-in mechanisms in the agreement against misuses of power.

CONCLUSION

Given the painful process of economic political and social transformation undergone by many developing countries still struggling with dark legacies of totalitarianism and authoritarianism, external democracy support must be progressively adapted to evolving realities. Its possibilities are almost limitless: Most of the conceptual and policy guidance teething problems it has suffered have been overcome, at least within the European Union.

Democracy support, although it has appeared late in the foreign policy toolbox, has attained an unassailable position therein. It has come to stay and it has certainly come of age.

The European Union has acquired a number of comparative advantages in dealing with the root causes of some conflicts through its renewed development strategies. However, perhaps it is not too obvious to stress that democratic deficits are not always rooted in economic causes and that for this reason economic strategies are in many occasions unlikely to deal with more than symptoms.

In certain cases, the European Union is uniquely well placed to promote democratization. This is the case, for instance, with regard to the candidate countries. If they want to join the Union, they have to comply with the political, economic, and social standards that are de rigueur in the Union. To this extent, enlargement is a massive exercise in external democracy support.

In other cases, for instance in the Western Balkans, the possibility that if developments are alright the countries concerned might be considered for future accession also acts as a powerful magnet. Through its stabilization and association agreements with some Balkan countries (Former Yugoslav Republic of Macedonia [FYROM], Albania, and Croatia), the Union is sending very important signals in that respect. If the political transformation in the Federal Republic of Yugoslavia makes further headway, it too will receive those kinds of signals.

There are even more countries, however, that will not join the Union. It is such cases that demand a creative democracy-support policy. It is impossible to make general statements when you compare countries so different as those in Central Asia, Africa, Southeast Asia, or Latin America. But one could say that it has been easier for the European Union to assist macro-economic stabilization, privatization, and the development of legislative and regulatory frameworks to promote the emergence or strengthening of liberal market economies. It has been far more difficult to open up political processes. Unfortunately, the countries that remain far short of consolidated democracies are numerous. Many political parties and legislatures are weak. Structures of power tend to be personalistic. Judicial structures remain arbitrary and are often used for political purposes. Minority rights remain problematic. There is, therefore, a wide agenda for promoting democratic ideas and practices.

Obviously no foreigner will ever design on a blank sheet the future political institutions of those countries. This is something that only the locals can do. To the extent that external democracy support does not lose sight of that fact, it will remain a useful tool. Otherwise, it will be felt by locals as a foreign imposition. It is in the nature of such exercises that alleged impositions can be demagogically exploited to achieve ends that go in the opposite direction of the one intended by well-meaning foreign partners and institutions. Here, too, modesty must remain the order of the day.

NOTES

1. Schmidt (1990) contains some indications regarding this kind of assistance. Powell (1996) deals with this subject on a more global basis.

2. Thomas et al. (2000). Reference can also be made to the learned academic discussions of the 1960s and 1970s on the nature of the Franco regime as an *Entwicklungsdiktatur*. With the benefit of hindsight, historians have demonstrated all the development lacunae of that system.

3. Borrowed from Wiseman (1999).

4. See Van Rooy (1998) for a thorough discussion of that elusive concept.

REFERENCES

Alston, Philip, ed. 1999. *The EU and Human Rights*. Oxford: Oxford University Press.

Carothers, Thomas. 1999. *Aiding Democracy Abroad: The Learning* Curve. Washington, DC: Carnegie Endowment for International Peace.

Diamond, Larry. 1995. *Promoting Democracy in the 1990s*. New York: Carnegie Corporation.

Dreze, J., and A. Sen. 1989. *Hunger and Public Action*. Oxford: Clarendon.

European Commission. 1998, March 12. *Democratisation, the Rule of Law, Respect for Human Rights and Good Governance: The Challenges of the Partnership between the European Union and the ACP States*. Brussels: COM, 146.

———. 2000, April 11. *Communication on EU Election Assistance and Observation*. Brussels: COM, 191.

———. 2000, June 23. *The Cotonou Agreement*. Accessed at http://europa.eu.int/development /body/cotonou/agreement_en.htm.

———. 2000. *Report on the Implementation of Measures Intended to Promote Observance of Human Rights and Democratic Principles in External Relations for 1996–1999.* Accessed at: http://europa.eu.int/comm/external_relations/human_rights/doc/com2000_0726en01.pdf.

ISA Consult. 1997. *Final Report: Evaluation of the Phare and Tacis Democracy Programme.* Brussels: European Commission.

Mertes, Alois. 1985. Europe's Role in Central America: A West German Christian Democratic View. In *Third World Instability: Central America as a European-American Issue,* ed. Andrew J. Pierre, 106–136. New York: Council on Foreign Relations.

Moore, Mick. 1995. Democracy and Development in Cross-National Perspective: A New Look at the Statistics. *Democratization* 2 (2):1–19.

Official Journal of the European Communities. 1999, May 8. L120, vol. 42.

OECD-DAC. 1996. *Shaping the 21st Century: The Contribution of Development Co-operation.* Paris: OECD.

Patten, Chris. 1999. *East and West.* London: Pan Books.

Powell, Charles. 1996. International Aspects of Democratization: The Case of Spain. In *The International Dimensions of Democratization European and the Americas,* ed. Laurence Whitehead, 285–314. New York: Oxford University Press.

Rosas, Allan. 1999. The Role of the Universal Declaration of Human Rights in the Treaty Relations of the European Union. In *Innovation and Inspiration: Fifty Years of the Universal Declaration of Human Rights,* ed. Peter Baehr, Cees Flinterman, and Mignon Senders, 201–209. Amsterdam: Royal Netherlands Academy of Arts and Sciences.

Roy, Joaquin, ed. 1992. *The Reconstruction of Central America: The Role of the European Community.* Miami: University of Miami North-South Center.

Schmidt, Helmut. 1990. *Die Deutschen und ihre Nachbarn.* Berlin: Siedler.

Thomas, V., et al. 2000. *The Quality of Growth.* London: Oxford University Press.

Van Rooy, Alison, ed. 1998. *Civil Society and the Aid Industry.* London: Earthscan.

Whitehead, Laurence. 1986. International Aspects of Democratisation. In *Transitions from Authoritarian Rule,* vol. 4, ed. Woodrow Wilson Center. Baltimore: Johns Hopkins University Press.

Wiseman, J. 1999. The Continuing Case for Demo-optimism in Africa. *Democratization* 6 (2):128–155.

Woodrow Wilson Center, ed. 1986. *Transitions from Authoritarian Rule: I Prospects for Democracy; II Southern Europe; III Latin America; IV Comparative Perspectives; V Tentative Conclusions about Uncertain Democracies.* Baltimore: Johns Hopkins University Press.

15

❧

Liberalism, Democracy, and Conflict Management: The African Experience

Donald Rothchild

A majoritarian vision of liberal internationalist orthodoxy that calls for individual (but not group) rights, separation of powers, party competition, and tolerance of diversity can at times also be extremely rigid and conformist. The effect is to overlook the range of choices availing to decision elites and to create an unwarranted pessimism about the relevance of democracy in Africa. I remember, after the transition election in Ghana in 1992, attending a follow-up appraisal where Western observers spoke in the most disparaging terms about the organization and administration of the election. To be sure, the process had been somewhat flawed. Yet the sharp criticisms still raise questions in my mind as to the appropriate role of foreign observers in these circumstances.

Certainly foreign donors must hold their recipients accountable for their performance in delivering on their promises of good governance (including election management), but how far is such external intervention compatible with sovereign jurisdiction? To what extent are liberal internationalists, committed in many instances to majoritarian democracy as a preferred regime type, appropriately positioned to set standards on election management or the dissemination of information in developing countries? Both the tolerant and intolerant strands of liberalism seemed present in Accra that day, as Western observers condemned continuing evidence of government manipulation and called for strict adherence to democratic norms on individual rights and free and fair party competition. The question that still lingers is whether in this instance liberal internationalists were expecting too much. Were they expecting more rapid political learning and sequential change than was warranted?

In this situation, it is important to set out the main characteristics of democracy. Democratic governance is a process for managing intrastate conflict by recruiting people to high political office through free and fair competitive elections. Conflicts remain present and ongoing, although managed peacefully within the political system (Coser 1956). Democracy (or, often more accurately, polyarchy) often involves relatively low state control over the political process and extensive participation by the members of society through political parties, civil associations (including ethnic associations), and the state's decision-making institutions. Democracy establishes a basis for legitimate and effective governance, linking active civil associations with relatively secure states. Although majoritarian democracies stand out for their ability to mobilize and articulate group demands and require governmental accountability and responsiveness, other forms of polyarchy, such as power-sharing regimes, combine a relatively high degree of state-society interaction with low to moderate levels of public participation and a moderate degree of state control (Rothchild 1997a:11). The ability of these regime types to accept and work with the reality of ethnic-based organizations is likely to prove critical to political stability in developing countries.

The lack of responsiveness of the old authoritarian order to legitimate societal claims led to a wave of group demands for regime change in Africa in the late 1980s and early 1990s. The electoral process was utilized to change sixteen regimes in the 1989–1994 period, including those in Benin, Mozambique, Namibia, Niger, Malawi, Zambia, and South Africa (Bratton and van de Walle 1997:120). In many cases, what took place in Africa was a partial liberalization of authoritarian regimes, not a full transition to democracy (Bratton and van de Walle 1997:121–122). In some cases, an ongoing process of change resulted in the expansion of democratic norms and practices, as leaders and members of the general public came to expect increasing participation, accountability, and transparency. At the same time, the appearance of what Fareed Zakaria calls "illiberal democracies"—polities that combine competitive elections with excessive centralization of power and no transfers of power—were evident in twenty-one countries in 1995 (Zakaria 1997). No competitive elections were held, moreover, in thirteen countries (Bienen and Herbst 1996:25). Thus no single trajectory emerged in Africa, and the effect of a country's transition on the strategic relations between the state and civil society (including its ethnic component) varied enormously across the continent.

THE LIBERAL INTERNATIONALIST WORLDVIEW

The liberal internationalist belief in a democratic future has been widely proclaimed. For example, A. Francis Fukuyama predicted the march of democracy across the earth. "What we may be witnessing is not just the end of the Cold War, or the passing of a particular period of postwar history," he asserted, "but the end of history as such: that is, the end point of mankind's ideological evolution and the universalisation of Western liberal democracy as the final form of human government" (Fukuyama 1989:4). Accordingly, if a society wants to be included in the emergent global reality, its choice of regime types becomes inescapably clear. No government has been more committed than the United States to promoting the cause of liberal democracy. Viewing the spread of democratic regime types as being in American interests (largely on the grounds that democracies were inclined toward peaceful relations with each other), Anthony Lake, the former national security adviser in the Clinton administration, declared, "The successor to a doctrine of commitment must be a strategy of enlargement—enlargement of the world's free community of market democracies" (Lake 1993:5).

In putting this guideline into practice, the U.S. government and various nongovernmental organizations (such as Human Rights Watch) actively pressed for democratic elections in Burundi in 1993–1994 in an effort to bring ethnic peace, only to see their policies backfire and "trigger" the onset of intergroup violence (Snyder 2000:300). As Jack Snyder concludes on this, "Democratisation in the developing world, as in other settings, is most likely to stimulate nationalist conflict when elites are threatened by rapid political change and when the expansion of political participation precedes the formation of strong civic institutions" (Snyder 2000:266). Clearly, to the extent that this preference for liberal democracy becomes an orthodoxy and fails to adjust to local realities and alternative visions, it can sometimes complicate the process of managing conflict in ethnically divided societies.

Even though the wave of democratization that took place in Africa in the 1990s was largely a response to internal demands for change, as Michael Bratton and Nicolas van de Walle contend, it was also encouraged by the pressures exerted by Western donors and by the diffusion of ideas from abroad (Bratton and van de Walle 1997:31). With respect to diffusion, a powerful country or group of countries (such as the European Community) can serve as both an example and an advocate of democratization. Such powerful actors and processes can create incentives to adopt similar regimes on the part of similarly placed countries that want to secure the benefits-enhanced reputation from being included in the democratic world. This desire for inclusion can have a positive consequence on inter-ethnic relations when it causes elites to avoid discriminating against ethnic minorities in the midst in their efforts to gain external legitimation (Lake and Rothchild 1998).

The responsiveness of ruling elites to internal and external pressures for democratization also has a calming effect. In multi-ethnic societies such as Mauritius and Botswana, where ethnic groups are recognized as legitimate and feel secure about their future, ethnic politics can be compatible with democracy. The effect of recognizing both individual and group political rights and acting with political moderation is to reassure ethnic minorities about their liberties and security, reducing the incentive for civil war, secession, and the defense of co-ethnics across their borders (Talbott 2000:160). Thus Philip Roeder finds the probability of escalation to ethnic violence to be 1 percent in democracies but 15.6 percent in autocracies (Roeder 2000:21). More specifically, on the compatibility of ethnicity with democracy, Zeric Smith's data indicate an inverse relationship between ethnic conflict and civil liberties (Smith 2000:32).

However, if ethnic interests in multi-ethnic societies can be compatible with the thrust and parry of democratic politics, it can also at times provoke destructive conflict in deeply divided societies. As Jens Meierhenrich's data on South Africa and Steven Wilkinson's data on India suggest, there is a strong relationship between competitive elections and ethnic violence in these countries (Meierhenrich 2000:64–66; Wilkinson 1998:21). Where ethnic leaders engage in uncompromising behavior and seek to advance ethnic group interests at the expense of other groups, it can lead to polarization and increased conflict as the date of the election approaches. The way that elites mobilize their supporters for collective action is critical in terms of regime outcomes. Unless democratic regimes can build on a sense of overriding societal interests as a whole, they are likely to provide a frail bulwark against parochial interests over the long term.

The task we face is to determine the policy choices best suited to achieve the goals of democratization in each country in both the short and long terms. Under what circumstances is democracy likely to establish the basis for self-sustaining and peaceful inter-ethnic relationships? What will produce legitimate authority structures and further state-society cooperation while at the same time providing decisive leadership on difficult social and economic questions? Is a minimal form of democracy (for example, competitive elections without full political rights) necessarily off the table, or can it serve as a useful first step leading to democratic consolidation? And where democracy fails in ethnically divided societies, what are the appropriate international responses? Should the international community press to restore full democratic processes, negotiate peace agreements, or call for sanctions or military intervention? In their real-world applications, the complexity of these choices may well defy straightforward answers, especially when observers are far removed from the scene.

THE BENEFITS OF DEMOCRATIZATION

Clearly, a liberal internationalist formula of majoritarian democracy can be a preferred option in a number of situations. Provided agreement exists on the rules of the political game, majoritarian solutions have the advantage of concentrating power at the political center. Such approaches can promote the search for a balance of power among executive and legislative leaders at the political center while reducing the urgency of maintaining a balance among competing ethnic forces. A consensus vision of democracy, incorporating various power-sharing arrangements, may be necessary to reassure weaker parties about their security and the protection of their interests, especially during the transition period following civil war, but they often entail undesirable political costs. The balance of power, or in Robert Wagner's terms the "complex equilibrium, implicit in power-sharing regimes tends to involve costs of negotiation and implementation" (Wagner 1993:262). The result is frequently to cause immobilism and political instability, making these power-sharing systems difficult to sustain over time.

The openness of democracies and their preparedness to accommodate demands for political rights and competitive elections can also act as incentives for inter-ethnic cooperation. Democracy ushers in a rule-based system that encourages a sense of predictability about the procedures for conciliatory behavior. Not only does this process of formalizing rules for competition and state behavior often make conflict within the state more manageable, but it can also ease the strategic interactions with other state and nonstate actors in its region. As fears for the safety of co-ethnics across the border ease or as uncertainties about the possibility of aggression subside, stable interstate relations may be more likely to follow. Nevertheless, it seems premature to push this line of analysis too far by subscribing to the widely held contention that democracies do not fight wars with each other. There may be supporting evidence for this assumption in the case of the developed Western democracies, but the research on this has brought inconclusive results as it affects developing countries. One scholar contends, for example, that the absence of wars in West Africa may be explained not by the presence of democracy across the region but by the preparedness of authoritarian regimes to maintain peaceful relations among themselves (Kacowicz 1997:384).

So long as the political elite is prepared to live by and uphold democratic rules on participation, transparency, accountability, and respect for diversity, the strong state implicit in majoritarian formulas need not be a threat to societal interests. A vibrant, educated, and well-organized civil society (e.g., trade unions, professional organizations, religious societies, and ethnic associations) may be a critical factor in a stable relationship.

Where civil society is in fact "civil" and intent upon interacting constructively with the state, it can play an important role in insisting on governmental accountability and in resisting possible violations of constitutional
rules. Thus, when a strong, responsive state and a vibrant civil society become interlinked, there is a potential present for each to feed off of the
strengths of the other.

Moreover, democratic regimes of all sorts can contribute to political stability by overcoming economic discrimination against ethnic minorities.
For Ted Robert Gurr, such economic discrimination represents the
strongest global correlation between disadvantages and economic and social grievances, and it has a significant impact on the demands for political rights globally (Gurr 1993:82–84). Because election and subsequent
legislative victories often require appeals across ethnic groups to gain a
minimum winning coalition, democracy can lead to important accommo-
dations with ethnic interests. When these minorities benefit from resource
allocation to the relatively disadvantaged groups and from policies intended to equalize income inequalities, the effects can be stabilizing.

Certainly where a number of positive conditions prevail (including a
consensus supportive of democracy, widely accepted rules on elections
and on public participation, high information, low threats to group identities and cultures, high quality of leadership, moderate societal demands,
a responsive and capable state, and expanding educational and economic
opportunities), ethnic groups may feel relatively secure and prepared to
negotiate over their interests. Nevertheless, the presence of these facilitating conditions is not a reliable predictor of democracy in and of itself;
Mali meets few of these conditions but has a political culture and leadership that is supportive of democratic governance. Such conditions may be
uncommon under the difficult circumstances of contemporary political
life in the late industrializing countries, but when they do come together,
they facilitate a common agreement on basic norms and values. The result
can be the development of a bargaining culture and broadly accepted
rules of the game that help resolve a state's political differences. Pointing
to the importance of these conditions, recent data indicate that where a
country has earlier experiences with democratic norms of bargaining and
compromise, the likelihood of a negotiated settlement of a civil war sur-
viving is greatly increased (Hartzell et al. 2001:198).

DEMOCRATIC SLIPPAGE AND REVERSAL

Although the trend toward political liberalization in Africa during the
1990s was encouraging in terms of regime change and achieving greater
transparency, accountability, and more regularized state-society relations,

the process nonetheless seemed incomplete and somewhat brittle. Successes with democratization in South Africa and Nigeria were partly offset by military coups in the late 1990s in Ivory Coast, Comoros, Guinea-Bissau, and Niger. The coup in the Ivory Coast was especially hurtful to Africa's democratic trend. It exacerbated latent religious and ethnic tensions in this relatively prosperous country, with the army benefiting particular sectional interests (in terms of recruitment and patronage practices) at the expense of others.

In part, the setbacks to democratization can be explained by the constraints placed on African governments, including an insecure political and social setting, intense conflicts (involving religious fundamentalism, ethnic nationalism, class antagonism, and resource allocation), protracted economic decline, the continuance of clientelistic networks, lack of widespread agreement on norms and values, inadequate channels of political communication, the problem of establishing responsive political institutions, and obstacles to maintaining a dynamic civil society. Because of inadequate consensus on democratic norms and values and insufficient counterpressure from civil society, democratic regimes sometimes fail to give adequate heed to abuse by elites, ethnic fears of majoritarian tyranny, corruption, and legitimate group demands for political and social rights. Even with competitive elections, the possibility remains that political and ethnic minorities will be shut out of the political process and face an insecure future. In Ghana in the 1990s, for example, the Ashanti talked despondently of having no chance of winning the presidency in forthcoming elections, a sentiment that was expressive of latent grievances and, at the time, possible violence (*Statesman* 1997). With political institutions overburdened and public demands and expectations high, it is not surprising that some African elites are examining a variety of political alternatives to full democratization—such as collective executives, federalism, regional autonomy, and autonomous group rights (Rothchild 1997b).

Even when viewed in terms of the narrow prism of competitive elections rather than the broader processes of accountability, high information, extensive participation, and equal resource distribution, the limits of constitutional engineering in Africa are apparent. Election processes, despite their emphases on individual choice and the possibility of cross-party voting, remain vulnerable to elite mobilization along ethnic lines, especially when elites play upon the latent fears that members hold about their group's security and economic well-being. Particularly in closely contested districts, the approach of elections brings heightened tensions, even the possibility of riots and disturbances (Wilkinson 1998:21–24). These problems are accentuated by the continued presence of entrenched clientelistic practices in such African countries as Ivory Coast and South Africa. In part to avoid the threat of violence, some regimes seek to manage elections. They provide for the rituals of formal competition, as in Ethiopia or Daniel arap Moi's Kenya, but deny an even playing field to rival parties. The effect of such practices is to alienate broad sections of the public, as in Ghana in 1992, thereby weakening claims to political legitimacy and generating distrust in the democratic process itself. Current evidence indicates a rise in the manipulation of election processes by ruling parties. Thus, data collected by Michael Bratton show that the quality of democratic elections declined in eleven out of twenty-three elections between 1995 and 1997 (Bratton 1998:59).

Although some of the setbacks to democratization (such as electoral manipulation) involve elements of political choice, with political elites making key decisions on the organization of institutions to reflect their preferences, other environmental and contextual conditions also work against Africa's political liberalization. I consider some of the main conditions standing in the way of political liberalization on the continent below.

First, an environment of insecurity and scarce resources complicates the process of regularized interactions and limited competition (Simons 1997:273–274). Economic decline and widespread poverty lead to a desperate search for access to resources, frequently undermining the politics of moderation and restraint so critical to a democratic order. In an environment of overriding scarcity, the rise of military rulers (General Robert Guei [1999–2000] in the Ivory Coast), warlords (Charles Taylor in Liberia, Foday Sankoh in Sierra Leone, and the militia leaders of Somalia), and state populist leaders (President Thomas Sankara in Burkina Faso, President Jerry Rawlings [1981–1983] in Ghana, and President Robert Mugabe in Zimbabwe) created insecurities that weakened democratization initiatives (Rothchild and Gyimah-Boadi 1989). These military rulers and warlords undercut existing political institutions, increased intergroup hostilities and suspicions, and misallocated scarce resources. And the state populist leaders unleashed political forces, such as the ending of class privilege and corruption and engaging in land redistribution, that would be hard to contain in the period afterwards (Mapenzauswa 2000:1). As leaders such as Mugabe became overstretched in terms of foreign military entanglements and economic capabilities, they distanced themselves from their former policies on executive power sharing, respect for the rule of law, guarantees for civil liberties, and control of the mass media. In this respect, Mugabe's support for the takeover of white-owned lands can be interpreted as less a show of strength on his part than a desperate attempt to secure marginal votes in an otherwise precarious political situation.

Second, the fragility of norms lends an element of unpredictability to the stable interrelationships essential to democracy. Successful democratization requires continuous interest-group interactions over time. As elite reciprocities and political exchanges occur and can be anticipated well into the future, the effect is to build trust among the various parties. Unfortunately, however, norms of relationship in deeply divided societies have sometimes proven brittle. When some elements of the political elite ignore the norm of moderation and engage in an effort to outbid the more accommodating leaders from within their own community, the effect is to increase ethnic tensions, particularly as elections approach and the stakes of politics rise. In apartheid South Africa, nationalist politicians were replaced by even more uncompromising political leaders, who championed ever more rigid apartheid laws than those previously in force.

Other experiences with fragile norms have been the source of minority fears regarding their future. The decision of Namibian President Sam Nujoma to seek reelection to a third term, despite constitutional limits to two 5-year terms, weakened the constitutional norm before it could become established. Such actions create uncertainty about the credibility of the organizing rules of society and complicate the consolidation of enduring relations. A more threatening case of undercutting existing norms occurred in Zambia where President Frederick Chiluba, after expressing his deep commitment to democratic values, presided over the disqualification of his main opponent, former President Kenneth Kaunda, during the 1996 elections. The effect was to cause the weaker party to become extremely apprehensive over the intentions of its main opponent. In this respect, Michael Bratton has come to view Zambia as representing "perhaps the clearest example of the trend of declining quality of second elections in the sub-Sahara region." Bratton asserts:

> The Zambian case encapsulates many of the trends evidenced in other new African multiparty regimes, including the disqualification of leading candidates, the spotty coverage of voter registration, the lack of internal democracy in ruling parties, the abuse of government resources during the campaign, and the growing hostility of governments toward watchdog groups (Bratton 1998:60).

A democratic breakdown was illustrated by the July 1996 overthrow of the elected government of President Sylvestre Ntimantunganya in Burundi, where the Tutsi-led armed forces ousted a coalition regime that included a number of moderate Hutu political leaders. After the coup, army leaders spoke critically of division within the ruling coalition and suspended parliament and the political parties. Although the army chose a "moderate," Pierre Buyoya, as president, it did little to ease international criticism; moreover, what followed in the wake of the coup was frightening in terms of the mass killings that took place on both sides of the conflict.

Third, the existence of a threatening environment and frail norms is intertwined with the pivotal constraint of state weakness. As discussed here, a weak state is one that lacks political legitimacy and is largely un-responsive to the demands of societal interests. Unlike its relatively strong counterpart (one that is characterized by social cohesion, effective public institutions, and a capacity for effective economic management), the weak state lacks the capacity to administer its laws effectively throughout the territory under its jurisdiction. As a consequence, it is often unable to en-sure that the state's regulatory and distributive functions are applied in an equitable manner throughout the country. Moreover, it is largely unable to prevent predatory behavior from occurring within the country, and, in worst-case situations, it is not effective in preventing private violence.

This weakness at the political center can be gravely threatening to mi-nority ethnic peoples, for a state that is too frail to mediate between ethnic groups can lose its ability to enforce the rules on intergroup relations in an equitable manner. Where the state is viewed as a prize in the hands of the most powerful ethnic claimants, it may be seen as protecting the interests of the relatively advantaged but leaving the weaker ethnic and other groups to fend for themselves. The effect is to create distrust and insecu-rity and to make it difficult for the state to resolve problems of credible commitment (Fearon 1995, 1998). The state's failure to abide by the rules of the constitutional contract and its inability or unpreparedness to act as a primary protector of the vulnerable leave its political legitimacy dimin-ished, perhaps fatally. Such failures lead to alienation from the state, fur-ther weakening the state's ability to stabilize the constitutional bargain.

Fourth, if civil society networks are poorly integrated and lack auton-omy from the state, they will not be well placed to press the ruling coali-tion to adhere to constitutional norms and values. Certainly, the potential for meaningful and positive counterpressure differs from context to con-text. To the extent that civil society can be mobilized to act as a counter-force to an overweening state, its associations can play an indispensable role in maintaining political stability and adherence to the political rules. They can also act creatively, encouraging ethnic and racial reconciliation after bitter confrontations, as in South Africa, or they can encourage the return and resettlement of refugees, as happened in Namibia.

Yet not all elements of civil society have a positive role to play in sus-taining democracy. If civil associations, such as the Ghana Bar Associa-tion, have proved a strong force in influencing the Rawlings administra-tion to respect the autonomy of political institutions and the civil liberties of citizens, other associations have remained quietly on the sidelines, dis-inclined to challenge the entrenched state elites. In some worst cases, civil society organizations, such as the Nazis under the Weimar Republic or contemporary neo-Nazis, have themselves acted irresponsibly toward po-litical and ethnic minorities, widening social cleavages and weakening the already frail political institutions (Berman 1997:424–425).

A responsible state is most likely (but not always) strengthened by the presence of a hardy civil society; such associations can guard against possible violations of civil liberties, corrupt practices, and glaring regional or class inequalities. However, where civil society fails to warn the state against impending encroachments and threats to the basic law, it can have serious consequences, including loss of liberty, irregular state-society interactions, and the undermining of confidence in the state itself.

Finally, as the aggregate data noted above suggest, declining GDP levels and inequitable distributions can complicate democratic consolidation and aggravate ethnic tensions. The public expects democratization to have positive economic consequences. It looks upon democratization as a means of facilitating donor support. Not only are governments in the newly industrializing countries sharing values with Western aid givers, but they are also creating the conditions in which Western nongovernmental organizations, aid agencies, and business and commercial firms can operate in an effective manner. A rising GDP, it is hoped, will provide the revenues required for countrywide infrastructural development, opening up new possibilities for more equitable regional and class distributions. The statistical data presented by Zeric Smith indicate that rising levels of GDP per capita are systematically related to low levels of ethnic conflict (Smith 2000:35). In addition, because of the political legitimacy that results from competitive elections, democracy can have a great potential for mobilizing groups for developmental purposes. As greater aggregate wealth is produced, it can be expected to have a positive effect in terms of consolidating democratic gains.

However, such expectations of the payoffs from democratization, difficult to achieve under the best of circumstances, can be disappointed for a number of reasons, including mismanagement, corruption, and biases favoring advantaged ethnic interests. They may encounter unanticipated surprises as well. An unexpected falloff in export markets, economic assistance, or foreign investment; or a sudden inflow of refugees from neighboring countries, the emergence of warlord activities, or a surfacing of identity-based war can all lead to a weakening of the domestic and international commitment to economic reform. With a narrow local tax base and a limited external concern, the political system is not in a position to absorb these new shocks. Available funds are concentrated on dealing with short-term challenges, often at the expense of long-term economic and political objectives. The cumulative effect is to raise doubts among some of Africa's leaders and academicians about the liberal internationalist vision of rapid movement toward democracy. Arguing the case for "minimalist democracy," Meddi Mugyenyi contended that, because Africa's societies lacked social cohesion, democratic politics would likely be potentially divisive and destabilizing. Concluding that "resorting to unbridled democracy prematurely can be dangerous," Mugyenyi cautiously ranked rapid economic progress before democratization (Mugyenyi 1988:187).

INTERNATIONAL INTERVENTION TO
PREVENT DEMOCRATIC COLLAPSE

If democracy is necessary to provide the basis for self-sustaining peace, can an external intervener be expected to make a critical difference in preserving it against premature collapse? External intervention is surely a last resort in preventing behavior that is destructive of a functioning democratic order and in providing for credible commitment by the parties to the contract. But can intervention be expected to compensate for a weak state, and can it prove sufficient to the task of buffering between highly distrustful ethnic-based parties?

With the successful move toward democratization in Eastern Europe, a diffusion process set in that made democracy an accepted objective among elites in many parts of the world (Hill and Rothchild 1992). The external encouragement of democracy by example (i.e., diffusion) or through conditionality is very different from the preparedness of external actors to assume the costs and risks of preventing democratic collapse in Africa. The Organization of African Unity (OAU), reacting to a recent spate of military coups in Guinea-Bissau, Niger, and Comoros, provided at the Algiers Summit in 1999 that governments that overthrew constitutionally established regimes after 1997 would be suspended from future summits. It has been slow, however, to put this ban on coup leaders into effect. And the Western powers, which have a responsibility to defend an imperiled democratically elected regime as a consequence of their enormous logistical and military capacity, have nonetheless tended to stay on the sidelines, allowing African crises to burn themselves out. Thus, France, which had long interceded in Africa's internal conflicts in an effort to maintain order, remained aloof in October 1997 as Denis Sassou-Nguesso, with support from Angola, overthrew the elected government of President Pascal Lissouba in Congo-Brazzaville. Later, in December 1999, it again watched from the sidelines as General Robert Guei's coup overthrew the ethnically unbalanced and inefficient (but nonetheless competitively elected) government of President Henri Conan Bedi in the Ivory Coast. The Western powers also resisted guaranteeing the competitively elected regimes in Burundi and Sierra Leone when they were threatened. And they displayed a marked lack of resolution as majoritarian, but illiberal, governments acted punitively toward politically exposed minorities in Zimbabwe, Sudan, and Rwanda.

While Western liberal states have hesitated to make effective use of their resources to foster and protect Africa's democratic regimes, they have, directly or through the agencies of the OAU or the United Nations, made efforts to invoke and uphold democratic principles when negotiating or implementing peace agreements. Ethnically based civil wars, as illustrated by Zimbabwe, Sudan, Rwanda, and Burundi, have involved a fury and bitterness that are difficult to overcome. Confidence-building measures become essential if the uncertainty that prevails after the fighting is to be dispelled. Such measures include overseeing the processes of demobilization and disarmament, reintegrating the armed forces, rebuilding the civil service, and retraining and extending the authority of the police.

Provision for democratic features in the new constitution may also prove critical in encouraging the warring parties to come to an agreement and to secure their credible commitment to the bargain. External mediators have often confronted complex choices when designing political institutions. Whereas the ruling coalition in Mozambique steadfastly resisted demands from foreign diplomats for power-sharing arrangements, others in Burundi, Rwanda, and Angola made cautious moves toward such formulas at one time or another. In much of Anglophone (but not Francophone) West Africa, constitution-makers stayed with first-past-the-post election systems, while those crafting peace accords in southern Africa, seeking to reassure ethnic minorities about their participation in the new political order, opted for various forms of proportional representation (Mozaffar 1998, 1999).

The extension of democratic rights and protections in the post–civil war constitutions reassured weaker parties about their future security, thereby facilitating their consent to peace agreements. Nevertheless, implementing these provisions proved very trying at times. External third parties frequently lack the determination and overwhelming military capacity to subdue opposition militias. Commenting on the hindrances that third-party enforcers face in overriding regional opponents, Stephen Stedman writes:

> Some new interventionists have insisted that the United Nations use military force to compel the Khmer Rouge to abide by the 1991 Paris Peace Accords. But why should the United Nations be expected to succeed where the Vietnamese army, one of the world's most disciplined, could not? Likewise, what would enable the United Nations to defeat Angola's UNITA when the Cuban army had failed to do so? (Stedman 1993:8)

The inept performance of UN peacekeepers in the face of Foday Sankoh's irregulars in Sierra Leone in 2000 gives further support to this argument.

Moreover, as the ruling coalition's urgency to reassure minority interests faded, and as governments turned to the hard tasks of establishing

their authority and grappling with the challenges of economic reconstruction, minority fears of being shut out of the political process resur-
faced. As a result, carefully negotiated peace agreements have unraveled,
and sometimes led to a return to intrastate violence. In fostering fidelity
to an agreement under these circumstances, the external protector can
provide necessary mediatory and oversight functions by making information available about adversary intentions, clarifying and negotiating
points in contention, insisting on the implementation of the terms of the
agreement, and bringing pressure to bear to uphold the agreement.

When these third parties act effectively to maintain the accord, as in
Mozambique and Namibia, it encourages the leaders on all sides to
convince their constituents to back the bargain. Statistical data support
this contention, indicating that when provisions exist for third-party
protection of a peace accord, the risk of agreement is reduced by an estimated 98 percent (Hartzell et al. 2001). However, given the third
party's limited preparedness to commit resources to maintaining the
peace, the prevailing level of elite ambition, and the prevalence of communal distrust following civil wars, it is not surprising that many carefully negotiated agreements fail to achieve what was promised, being
either fundamentally altered over time (e.g., Zimbabwe) or collapsing
(e.g., Angola). Clearly, external protection in the aftermath of an agreement can encourage confidence in the bargain, but it cannot guarantee
its stability or survival.

CONCLUSION: THE DILEMMAS OF POLITICAL CHOICE

The liberal internationalist paradigm, with its emphasis on achieving political stability and development through the institutionalization of full
(and preferably majoritarian) democracy, has pointed us in a hopeful direction. After the difficult period of authoritarian one-party rule in Africa
following independence, the call for a transition to regimes marked by accountability, transparency, competitive elections, and recognition of and
protections for individual and group rights held out the promise of legitimate and effective governance. In the best cases, steady progress has indeed taken place toward self-enforcing democratic systems. Thus, in such
pluralistic societies as Mauritius, Botswana, Senegal, and Namibia, elites
have managed to surmount their differences and to develop authoritative
rules on channeling state-society conflict along peaceful lines. Do these
successes indicate a trajectory leading to full democracy in the future? Or
will liberal internationalist doctrines have to be revised on a country-by-
country basis to take account of possible tensions between democratic
theory and African reality?

In a number of African cases, the liberal internationalist worldview has encountered unanticipated obstacles. On the domestic African scene, democratization faced powerful constraints—including the unpreparedness of political elites to live by democratic rules, escalating ethnic tensions prior to elections, a weak civil society, insufficient information, a state that is unresponsive to legitimate group demands, stagnant economic growth, and, above all, a political environment threatening to the security and well-being of ethnic groups. Majoritarian democracy can be perceived as imperiling the minority when norms of moderation and restraint are not respected. A minority group, unable to participate productively in the policy-making process, can be effectively shut out of decision-making activities. For all these reasons and despite its obvious benefits, democratic slippages and reversals have at times occurred, as leaders have refused to abide by democratic norms and mobilized their supporters to act aggressively toward minorities in their midst. "Bad leaders," as Michael Brown observes, "are usually the catalysts that turn potentially volatile situations into open warfare" (Brown 1996:571). To the extent that majoritarian democracy sets the conditions in which this ethnic volatility surfaces, it can, perversely, have "unforeseen" effects of a most undesirable nature (Paris 1997:56).

The international community can make an important difference in stabilizing the transition to democracy, acting as a third party to facilitate the adoption of constitutional restraints following civil war, enforcing the terms of the agreement during the precarious transition period, or interceding when internal or external forces menace democratic regimes. Various African leaders, as well as former President Clinton, Kofi Annan, and others, have all asserted the need for international intervention when state leaders act brutally toward their own subjects (Obasanjo and Mosha 1993). For sovereignty to be respected, it must be exercised responsibly (Deng et al. 1996). Although, in principle, external intercession to encourage and protect democratic transitions makes sense, in practice it is difficult to mobilize the international community for effective action on behalf of beleaguered democracies. Western countries have been parsimonious when it comes to assisting democracy building and have been extremely cautious, alone or through international organizations, in buttressing democratically elected regimes in crisis (Rothchild 2001:224). As the armed forces intervened and seized power in the Ivory Coast and Burundi, and as mass killings occurred in Rwanda, Sudan, and eastern Congo, the world's democracies stood on the sidelines, irresolute and seemingly paralyzed. It became clear by the 1990s that, despite enlightened opinion in support of humanitarian intervention, there were no reliable internal or external safety nets to protect Africa's societies against ambitious ethnoregional elites, warlords, or aspiring politicians and military officers.

It is important in these circumstances for liberal internationalists to re-examine their basic premises. They might advance their long-term goals by being prepared to be more understanding of Africa's experimentation with the design and pace of political reform (the tolerant side of liberalism) in the short term, while remaining steadfast at all times on civil liberties and separation of powers as well as true to their majoritarian, democratic aspirations in the long term. Within definite limits, the flexible side of liberalism must embrace a vision of party competition, civil rights, and greater openness that can be adjusted to include alternative schemes of state-ethnic relations within the same political space. Liberal internationalists would be wise to shun a one-form-fits-all design, accepting, wherever appropriate, the principle of African responsibility for determining local institutions.

The range of choices that might achieve developmental ends during the difficult transition to full democratization is considerable. It includes such formal variants of consensus democracy as collective executives, communal legislative chambers, reserved seats in the legislature, federalism, and regional autonomy, although it should be recognized that these institutions can result in instability in certain instances. In addition, such institutional mechanisms as group cultural and social protections (i.e., nonterritorial federalism), the list system of proportional representation with a low threshold, and rules mandating proportional resource allocation represent low-cost concessions by states adopting either a majoritarian or consensus vision that can be reassuring to minority elements while not posing a threat to majority power. A willingness on the part of those with a liberal internationalist worldview to enlarge choice by adjusting to local preferences on such alternative visions and on the phasing in of political reform (as in contemporary Senegal, Ghana, or Tanzania) might prove productive in terms of gaining long-term acceptance for democratic experimentation.

The varied circumstances of state-society relations have contributed to diverse formulas in different country contexts. While rapid steps toward a majoritarian design (that included power-sharing provisions on proportional representation) was not destabilizing in Mozambique and Namibia, in other situations, such as Colombia or South Africa after apartheid, a formal power-sharing arrangement proved useful in facilitating the transition to democracy. In the latter cases, this step-by step gradualism allowed for the sequencing of transitions and helped to overcome the problem of credible commitment. An extended time period is often essential for the development of durable democracies. As Anna Simons contends:

> It is only *through time* that structures of state prove trustworthy. Or to turn this around, only once state structures prove (largely) solvent, (largely) stable, and (largely) responsible over generations is the state likely to be credibly viewed

as *the* guarantor of security by large enough numbers of its citizens (Simons 1997:277–278).

In certain contexts, then, exerting diplomatic pressure and being more flexible regarding the timing and sequencing of change can minimize difficulties in the transition to full democratization. The process of liberalization can start slowly, especially in the aftermath of civil wars or the transition from authoritarianism. As O'Donnell and Schmitter note:

> When liberalization is attempted, the innovations initially introduced by the regime rarely go beyond highly controlled (and often indirect) consultations and the restitution of some individual rights (not extensive to social groups or opposition parties) (O'Donnell and Schmitter 1986:17).

What elites are engaged in, O'Donnell and Schmitter contend, is a learning process, where moderates within the ruling coalition come increasingly to recognize that some kind of political opening will be necessary in the period ahead (O'Donnell and Schmitter 1986:17).

Rather than insisting in all circumstances on rapid moves toward full democratization, then, it is sometimes important for liberal internationalists to be flexible in their approach and to view democracy in Africa and elsewhere as part of an unfolding process. The objectives are never totally achieved, and it seems unrealistic to expect full equality of participation, accountability, transparency, and information in Africa or elsewhere. Modern democracies, which are less than scientific in their vote-counting practices and which include hierarchical organizations of various sorts within their rule systems (bureaucracies, military, business organizations, and so forth) are imperfectly responsive to public demands. However, learning can lead to changing incentives over time. Such changes encourage elites to accept the norms of restraint and moderation and to bring about a convergence of the goals of ethnic security and democratic governance in Africa and other developing regions of the world.

NOTE

I am grateful to John Harbeson, Matthew Hoddie, Shaheen Mozaffar, Edith Rothchild, and Radhika Sainath for their helpful comments on the first draft of this chapter.

REFERENCES

Berman, Sheri. 1997. Civil Society and the Collapse of the Weimar Republic. *World Politics* 49 (3):401–429.

Bienen, Henry, and Jeffrey Herbst. 1996. The Relationship between Political and Economic Reform in Africa. *Comparative Politics* 29 (1):23–42.

Bratton, Michael. 1998. Second Elections in Africa. *Journal of Democracy* 9 (3):51–66.

Bratton, Michael, and Nicolas van de Walle. 1997. *Democratic Experiments in Africa: Regime Transitions in Comparative Perspective.* Cambridge: Cambridge University Press.

Brown, Michael E. 1996. The Causes and Regional Dimensions of Internal Conflict. In *The International Dimensions of Internal Conflict*, ed. Michael E. Brown, 571–601. Cambridge, MA: MIT Press.

Coser, Lewis A. 1956. *The Functions of Social Conflict.* New York: Free Press.

Deng, Francis, Sadikiel Kimaro, Terrence Lyons, Donald Rothchild, and I. William Zartman. 1996. *Sovereignty as Responsibility: Conflict Management in Africa.* Washington, DC: Brookings Institution Press.

Fearon, James D. 1995. Rationalist Explanations for War. *International Organization* 49 (3):379–414.

———. 1998. Commitment Problems and the Spread of Ethnic Conflict. In *The International Spread of Ethnic Conflict*, ed. David A. Lake and Donald Rothchild, 107–126. Princeton, NJ: Princeton University Press.

Fukuyama, A. Francis. 1989. The End of History? *National Interest* (16):3–18.

Gurr, Ted Robert. 1993. *Minorities at Risk: A Global View of Ethnopolitical Conflicts.* Washington, DC: U.S. Institute of Peace.

Hartzell, Caroline, Matthew Hoddie, and Donald Rothchild. 2001. Stabilizing the Peace After Civil War: An Investigation of Some Key Variables. *International Organization* 55 (1):183–208.

Hill, Stuart, and Donald Rothchild. 1992. The Impact of Regime on the Diffusion of Political Conflict. In *The Internationalization of Communal Strife*, ed. Manus I. Midlarsky, 189–206. London: Routledge.

Kacowicz, Arie M. 1997. Negative International Peace and Domestic Conflicts, West Africa, 1957–96. *Journal of Modern African Studies* 35 (3):367–385.

Lake, Anthony. 1993, September 21. *From Containment to Enlargement.* Typescript. Baltimore: School of Advanced International Studies, Johns Hopkins University, 1–14.

Lake, David A., and Donald Rothchild, eds. 1998. *The International Spread of Ethnic Conflict: Fear, Diffusion and Escalation.* Princeton, NJ: Princeton University Press.

Mapenzauswa, Stella. 2000, August 17. Zimbabwe Govt Warns Farmers not to Play Games. Reuters Newswire.

Meierhenrich, Jens. 2000. *Democratization, the State, and War.* Unpublished paper, 1–78.

Mozaffar, Shaheen. 1998. Electoral Systems and Conflict Management in Africa: A Twenty-Eight-State Comparison. In *Elections and Conflict Management in Africa*, ed. Timothy D. Sisk and Andrew Reynolds, 81–98. Washington, DC: U.S. Institute of Peace Press.

———. 1999. Cascading Interdependence, Democratization, and Ethnic Conflict Management in Africa. In *The Ethnic Entanglement: Conflict and Intervention in World Politics*, ed. John F. Stack, Jr., and Lui Hebron, 47–59. Westport, CT: Praeger.

Mugyenyi, Meddi. 1988. Development First, Democracy Second. In *Democratic Theory and Practice in Africa*, ed. Walter O. Oyugi et al., 178–190. Portsmouth, NH: Heinemann Educational Books.

Obasanjo, Olusegun, and Felix G. N. Mosha. 1993. *Africa: Rise to Challenge: Towards a Conference on Security, Stability, Development and Cooperation in Africa.* New York: Africa Leadership Forum.

O'Donnell, Guillermo, and Philippe C. Schmitter. 1986. *Transitions from Authoritarian Rule: Tentative Conclusions about Uncertain Democracies.* Baltimore: Johns Hopkins University Press.

Paris, Roland. 1997. Peacebuilding and the Limits of Liberal Internationalism. *International Security* 22 (2):54–89.

Roeder, Philip G. 2000, December 8–9. *Long-Term Stability of Power-Sharing and Divided-Power Constitutions.* Paper presented at the Conference on Power-Sharing and Peacemaking, La Jolla, CA, 1–26.

Rothchild, Donald. 1997a. *Managing Ethnic Conflict in Africa: Pressures and Incentives for Cooperation.* Washington, DC: Brookings Institution Press.

———. 1997b. Conclusion: Management of Conflict in West Africa. In *Governance as Conflict Management: Politics and Violence in West Africa*, ed. I. William Zartman, 197–241. Washington, DC: Brookings Institution Press.

———. 2001. The U.S. and Africa: Power with Limited Influence. In *Eagle Rules? Foreign Policy and American Primacy in the 21st Century*, ed. Robert J. Lieber, 214–240. Upper Saddle River, NJ: Prentice Hall.

Rothchild, Donald, and E. Gyimah-Boadi. 1989. Populism in Ghana and Burkina Faso. *Current History* 88 (538):221–224, 241–244.

Simons, Anna. 1997. Democratisation and Ethnic Conflict: The Kin Connection. *Nations and Nationalism* 3 (2):273–289.

Smith, Zeric Kay. 2000. The Impact of Political Liberalisation and Democratisation on Ethnic Conflict in Africa: An Empirical Test of Common Assumptions. *Journal of Modern African Studies* 38 (1):21–39.

Snyder, Jack. 2000. *From Voting to Violence: Democratization and Nationalist Conflict.* New York: W. W. Norton.

Statesman (Ghana). 1997, January 26. Editorial: Oh, My Poor, Poor Ashantis.

Stedman, Stephen John. 1993. The New Interventionists. *Foreign Affairs* 72 (1):1–16.

Talbott, Strobe. 2000, Spring. Self-Determination in an Interdependent World. *Foreign Policy* 118:152–163.

Wagner, Robert H. 1993. The Causes of Peace. In *Stopping the Killing: How Civil Wars End*, ed. Roy Licklider, 235–268. New York: New York University Press.

Wilkinson, Steven I. 1998, September 3–6. *The Electoral Incentives for Ethnic Violence: Hindu-Muslim Riots in India.* Paper delivered at the Annual Meeting of the American Political Science Association, Boston, MA.

Zakaria, Fareed. 1997. The Rise of Illiberal Democracy. *Foreign Affairs* 76 (6):22–43.

16

❦

Some Realism about Constitutional Engineering

Donald L. Horowitz

If peacemaking in divided societies is a term with any real content, that content must be cast in terms of institutions: structures and recurrent patterns of behavior that work to reduce conflict. The alternatives are much less reliable. Leadership, a quality often emphasized by those who participate in the making of peace, is fragile. Leaders can change their minds or have their minds changed for them by changing conditions or by upstart leaders; they can be replaced, and they can die. Leadership is overrated. Rock-solid promises can crumble, provided those who make them are willing to incur the reputational costs involved. Personal relations among participants in peacemaking, sweet at the moment of agreement, can sour as the price of peace has to be paid. "The benefits of a reform," said the late Wallace Sayre, "are immediate, but the costs are cumulative." If those costs are not to undo the peace, peace has to be embodied in a network of institutions in which the participants are entangled and that provides an ongoing raison d'être to their commitments.

What shape those institutions might take in divided societies is contested territory into which I shall venture soon enough. (I deal only with institutions in states in which partition is not an option.) Before I do, however, I want to carry on with some preliminary skepticism about some common nostrums.

THE BENEFITS OF PRECAUTIONS

The first of these nostrums concerns preventive diplomacy. By this term I certainly do not mean to restrict the subject to international efforts to foster conflict reduction in divided societies. (I shall say something later about the benefits and costs of external efforts.) There is not the slightest doubt that, in the design of accommodative institutions, earlier is better. At independence, Malaysia faced a very serious problem of inter-ethnic hostility. Few countries had more serious reasons to anticipate serious ethnic conflict. But the Malaysians had taken precautions, and their conflicts have been far less serious, or at least far less violent, after independence than they were before. By contrast, the Sri Lankans faced a relatively easy ethnic problem at independence, took no precautions against it, and ended up with a desperately serious, protracted civil war (see Horowitz 1989). Precautions pay off. As I shall suggest very soon, however, deliberate precautions can be taken only on the rarest occasions.

Among the reasons that precautions pay off is that they cost less earlier than they do later. Ethnic group representatives will settle for much less early in the history of a conflict than they will later, after violence has produced bitterness and longstanding hostilities have demonstrated their strength. Anyone who doubts this should compare what the Sri Lankan Tamils were prepared to settle for in 1957, at the time of the Bandaranaike-Chelvanayakam Pact, the first serious but abortive effort to resolve Sinhalese-Tamil differences, with what they were prepared to settle for in 1968, 1980, and, most recently, in 2000. The price has gone up each time.

Yet, as the failure to reach agreement in Sri Lanka at lower price points suggests, there are serious obstacles to early action on ethnic conflict. Myths of inter-ethnic harmony may prevail, even as ethnically based parties stake out incompatible positions on ethnic issues. These myths may be well grounded in friendly interpersonal relations between group members. Consider for a moment the case of Fiji, a society in which Fijian fear of political domination by Indians goes back at least to the 1920s and 1930s (see Scarr 1984:135, 139). By the late 1970s, very serious political differences between the two groups had emerged. Yet close students of Fijian society were denying that Fiji was an ethnically "antagonistic" society or even one characterized by "developed ethnicity" (see, respectively, Norton 1986:52; Jayawardena 1980:446). At one level, these observers were certainly not wrong. An urban survey found personal relations between Fijians and Indians remarkably easygoing. Fijians expressed more favorable attitudes toward Indians than toward any other group, save for Fijians themselves, while Indians found it easier to get on with Fijians than with any other groups, including other Indians (Mamak 1978:124–127). But the interpersonal sphere is the wrong level to measure. There is a disjunction, and sometimes a strong one, between personal inter-ethnic relations and political inter-ethnic relations.

This is not the place to trace out the complicated connections between the personal and political spheres. The point I wish to make is that it is easy to be deceived at early stages of a conflict into thinking that good personal relations between members of different groups will translate into an absence of conflict or into brakes on conflict, should it occur. The result is an undue optimism in which the probability of conflict and its costs, on the one hand, and the benefits and costs of measures to avert it, on the other, are all likely to be miscalculated. But this is a common mistake that leads to a sense that preventive measures are unnecessary.

Furthermore, preventive measures involve some form of sharing of power across group lines. Political leaders who have managed to achieve power without sharing it will need to be convinced that it is in their interest to broaden or alter the existing configuration of power holders, and this in the face of the several forces that make maximal inclusiveness a strongly disfavored outcome (see Horowitz 1999). I shall say more about motives for inter-ethnic conciliation as we proceed.

I do not mean to imply that preventive measures are never taken. At certain important decision points—independence was the obvious one for most postcolonial countries—there are opportunities and sometimes necessities for accommodating opposing forces. But the arrangements that result are more likely to be exchanges of incommensurable preferences than they are to be constitutional plans based on a cogent view of what is necessary to foster intergroup accommodation. Sometimes those arrangements produce enduring results (contrary to conventional wisdom, they did in Lebanon), but because they are based on a quid pro quo, the failure of one side or another to receive what it anticipated risks undermining the entire bargain (see Horowitz 1985:580–588). And, overall, such settlements are not common.

I make no pretence of being able to specify the exact ripe moment for accommodative measures to have appeal across group lines. Perhaps a "hurting stalemate" (Zartman 1985:232) is necessary. Perhaps the delegitimation of a sitting regime is sufficient. Perhaps random shocks can create occasions for rethinking arrangements to restore peace. All I mean to say at the outset is that, despite the advantages of preventive measures, restorative measures are far more likely.

Two consequences follow immediately from this fact. First, if the constitutional moment is produced by a crisis, the specifics of the crisis that put peacemaking on the agenda will shape the nature of the response. To take a concrete example, the best arrangements for Sri Lanka might be focused principally on the creation of multi-ethnic government in Colombo and the elimination of ethnic discrimination throughout the country, but the facts of separatist warfare mean that the emphasis will be, instead, on provisions for extensive territorial cum ethnic autonomy. Second, barring circumstances in which internal political leaders are temporarily very weak and external actors very strong, no package of innovations can be adopted unless it appeals to the palpable interests of those political leaders. This may seem such a truism that it is a waste of ink to lay it down, but it is an important constraint that skews the design of acceptable institutions. I mentioned earlier the effective precautions taken in Malaysia in the 1950s. All of them are traceable to an idiosyncratic moment at which leaders of the main Malay party were confronted with a critical challenge from a Malay leader appealing for votes across ethnic lines in a series of local elections in which Chinese and Indian votes were more abundant than Malay votes. This induced leaders of the main Malay party to form a multi-ethnic coalition and to compromise on an array of ethnic issues. "Interest," said Jeremy Bentham, "smooths the path to Faith."

Before we even approach the kind of prescription we might advocate for the peaceful development of severely divided societies, we can already see that there are serious problems of timing and motivation that bear on the likelihood of adoption. From these, we can begin to sense why so many unhappy societies go on for so long without doing anything effective to reduce their conflicts. We can also sense that what they do adopt, if and when they are ready to adopt anything, may well be far from the optimal plan. The innovations may be spotty, internally inconsistent, and only partially effective. And this is what we infer from the receptivity of the parties in conflict alone. It has nothing to do with our and their limited knowledge of what might be well adapted to reduce the conflict, not to mention limited imagination and expertise in designing appropriate institutions that will not produce a variety of unintended consequences.

THE PROBLEMATIC ROLE OF LEADERS

Many ameliorative proposals will founder at the outset on a diagnostic disagreement. In spite of several decades of serious research on ethnic conflict, there is still no consensus on an issue that ought to color the design of accommodative measures. In some studies of conflict, there is the underlying assumption, often merely implicit, that leaders are more cosmopolitan than followers and that mass antipathy toward other groups ties the hands of leaders who, if they had their own way, would find means of accommodating the interests of other groups. In other studies, there is the opposite assumption—that politicians seeking advancement manipulate the sentiments of their followers and foster intergroup hatred for their own purposes. These are not *diametrically* opposed propositions, because the second does not require that leaders entertain genuine antipathy, only that they act as if they do. Yet the two propositions point in different ameliorative directions. If, to put it bluntly, the conflict problem is just mass antagonism, then an appropriate remedy might be to empower tolerant elites by creating institutions to contain behavior based on mass hostility. If, however, the conflict problem is the untrustworthiness of elites, relying on them alone to do the work of conciliation is futile, unless the structure of incentives they confront is altered radically.

If measures to strengthen the hands of tolerant elites were sufficient to reduce ethnic conflict, some remedies along these lines might run afoul of democratic presuppositions, but the problem of inter-ethnic accommodation would be much easier than it would otherwise be. I am unable here to review decades of research on ethnic conflict, and there is no single, comparative study of the relative inter-ethnic tolerance of leaders and followers. Nevertheless, it is not difficult to piece together findings from country-specific studies that measure tolerance against social variables, including education. Using level of education as a proxy for leadership, the results do not show leaders to be generally more tolerant. In the Western world, there is, in general, a positive association between level of education and level of tolerance (see Hagendoorn and Nekuee 1999). But, even in the West, generally tolerant attitudes do not necessarily extend to particular groups, some of which may be identified as particularly troublesome sources of conflict (see, e.g., Grillo 1985:18–19). Outside the West, the findings become much more mixed. In some countries, educated people are more tolerant than less well-educated people; in some, intolerance actually rises with education, as it did formerly in the United States with social status (see MacIver 1948); and in still others, there is no clear relationship or else the relationship varies by the ethnicity of the subjects or of the targets of intolerance (the studies are summarized in Horowitz 1997:457 n. 31, 1991:140–141 nn. 44–50; see also Jasinska-Kania 1999).

It seems clear that strategies to harness the tolerant attitudes of elites to the cause of conflict reduction will founder if the elites are not significantly more tolerant than their followers. And even if there were a generally positive association between education and tolerance in a given country, there would still be plenty of leaders who do not share the prevailing elite view.

In the political life of severely divided societies, there is little to indicate that the conciliatory impulses of political leaders can be counted on to offset the hostile behavior of their followers or the ethnocentrism of those espousing more extreme positions on their flanks. J. R. Jayewardene in Sri Lanka, Tunku Abdul Rahman in Malaysia, Ratu Sir Kamisese Mara in Fiji, Kenneth Kaunda in Zambia, Félix Houphouët-Boigny in the Ivory Coast: all had their moments of inter-ethnic conciliation, but none was consistently conciliatory. All had to be concerned with political com-petition and mass sentiment, and it seems likely that they partook, in some considerable measure, of the sentiments toward other ethnic groups that prevailed in their own.

Against this background, it is worth asking what ideas for inter-ethnic conciliation are on offer, whether they can be adopted, and what results they are likely to produce. For reasons explained at the outset, I shall con-centrate on institutions; and, since this is a very large subject, I shall make no attempt to be comprehensive.

CONTRASTING APPROACHES

It should be obvious from what has already been said that ordinary democracy—that is, democracy heedless of the special needs of divided societies—is inadequate to produce inter-ethnic conciliation (see Horowitz 1993). During the entire time Sri Lanka was spiraling deeper and deeper into its protracted conflict, it enjoyed democracy, on the Sin-halese side in any event. Democratic competition was the source of the opposition to each of the proposals to propitiate disaffected Tamils, in 1957, 1968, 1980, and 2000. Specially crafted democratic institutions are re-quired to achieve conciliatory effects in such societies.

In strategic terms, there are two different ways to approach this task. One way is to reward moderation and design institutions that facilitate compromise between ethnically based parties willing to occupy the mid-dle ground against the extremes of their respective groups. The alterna-tive way is to bring all major participants together in a dispensation that provides an opportunity for all those whose discontent might prove dis-ruptive to participate in politics. Even as the first approach fosters com-promise by a moderate middle, it assumes that opposition on the flanks will constrain that compromise. It aims at multi-ethnic government within the framework of majority rule. The second approach attempts in-clusiveness and so must forgo majority rule.

If rewards are to be created for moderation on ethnic issues, the key to the first approach lies in the incentives it provides for ethnic parties to be-have moderately and to compromise on disputed ethnic issues. These in-centives are typically, although not exclusively, electoral incentives. They include the requirement contained in Nigerian constitutions of the Second and Third Republics (1978 and 1999) that, to be elected president, a can-didate must receive a plurality of votes plus support widely distributed across the states, so as to ensure that the winning candidate is moderate on ethnic issues. Another set of electoral incentives is contained in the al-ternative vote (AV), an electoral system that gives weight to voters' second preferences and makes it difficult for candidates to get elected on the votes of their own supporters' first preferences alone. The result is a powerful set of incentives for parties to compromise across group lines as they exchange second preferences (Reilly 1997a, 1997b). If devices such as these work as intended, they ought to produce multi-ethnic coalitions of the sort the Malaysians stumbled upon accidentally when they discovered an idiosyncratic need to rely on the votes of members of groups other than their own.

The inclusive approach aims to represent all groups (and presumably all representatives of all groups) in government. Its preferred coalition is not a coalition of the middle but a grand coalition. To produce such a coalition in which group strength is measured accurately, list-system proportional representation is the electoral system of choice. List PR contains no incentives for preelectoral compromise—far from it, for each list competes in a zero-sum contest with every other—but it does generally measure the first preferences of the electorate accurately.

The incentives view assumes that since politicians wish to be elected and reelected and since multi-ethnic coalitions are electorally rewarding for some participants (even as opposition on the flanks is rewarding for others), multi-ethnic coalitions that are sufficiently large to form governments will produce compromise policies on ethnic issues, and these will then reinforce the electoral prospects of the coalitions. Whereas the incentives view does not specify the content of those compromises, the inclusive view—particularly the consociational version of the inclusive view—has a clear prescription designed to put to rest certain contested issues at the outset. It requires a cabinet composed of proportionately represented members of all parties, mutual group vetoes on ethnically contentious policy issues, proportional allocations of governmental funds and positions, and group autonomy on cultural matters of concern to each group, such as language and education (Lijphart 1977). This is a constitutional program that insulates minorities from the effects of majority rule.

As such, the consociational program appeals far more to minorities seeking guarantees—for it is fundamentally a program of guarantees—than it does to majorities. For its adoption, it depends on the willingness of elites "to engage in cooperative efforts with the leaders of other segments in a spirit of moderation and compromise" (Lijphart 1977:53; see also Lijphart 1977:49–50, 168–170). If, however, elites are uncooperative or intolerant, as they often are, or if leaders of majority groups are under pressure not to concede much to minorities, adoption of this model is problematic, particularly because, at the adoption stage, it offers the prospect of electoral unpopularity without offsetting gain.

Majorities are much more inclined to agree to guarantees if minorities have something valuable to concede in exchange. Generally, there is little that minorities have that is sufficiently valuable to induce majorities to restrict majority rule. Once serious violence begins, however, this can change. Minorities may then be in a position to forswear secession or terrorism in return for guarantees. This is another reason that, while earlier may be better, later is much more likely—and later means, in this sense, after the apostles of violence have gained and displayed their power—especially for those dispensations that otherwise appear to involve only unilateral concessions.

By contrast, the incentives model offers the possibility of offsetting losses in own-group electoral support with gains in electoral support from other groups. The result, may be, as it was in Malaysia, a multiethnic center coalition opposed on the flanks by parties unable to form a competing center coalition because their respective programs are diametrically opposed.

These are the starting positions of the contending prescriptions. Perhaps it comes as no surprise that neither prescription has been adopted in full in any severely divided society in the post–World War II period. That, of course, does not make the plans irrelevant, for there has been growing interest in both prescriptions in recent years, and there have been partial adoptions of each.

Yet it remains true that to adopt either requires, at the outset, an alertness to the problems of severely divided societies, a willingness to speculate pessimistically about what could happen, a certain diagnostic intuition about one's own society, sophisticated knowledge about alternatives, willingness to depart from culturally approved or conventionally most frequently adopted or prestigious institutions, and ability to design a package of institutions apt for one's specific predicament. All of this, of course, is overlaid by the riskiness of radical departures.

Not only have most divided societies failed to adopt either of these prescriptions: When they have had the opportunity, in the course of changing regimes, to adopt new institutions, most divided societies have crafted no institutions at all to attend to their ethnic problems. In fact, some have crafted counterproductive provisions, such as Benin's presidential runoff, modeled on France's, which converted a fluid tripolar conflict into a more dangerous bipolar one, or Bulgaria's prohibition on ethnic parties, which would have disfranchised the Turkish minority had the Bulgarian Supreme Court not had the wisdom to find, contrary to the manifest evidence, that the party of the Turks was not a Turkish party. Most countries, most of the time, will do exactly nothing fundamental about their fundamental conflicts. Often doing nothing does not produce great harm. Such countries limp along with their pluralism or are coaxed and cajoled by international NGOs into ad hoc concessions to aggrieved ethnic groups. But other countries cruise right along into civil war.

PARTICIPANTS, OCCASIONS, AND INNOVATIONS

If innovations are adopted after violence, generally during a respite from crisis, it follows that their adoption may be affected by the weakness or declining legitimacy of a regime or may even occur after a regime has fallen and before a new one has been created. Nigeria at the end of military rule in 1978 and again twenty years later, Northern Ireland after a long period during which Stormont was not functioning, Indonesia after Suharto, Fiji a dozen years after a coup brought down the independence constitution, Bosnia after bitter warfare: these suggest the possibilities. In some such cases, external powers may have become involved. The Western Europeans and the Americans have been concerned with Bosnia since the early 1990s. Britain and Ireland have shared some responsibility for a settlement in Northern Ireland since 1991. Fiji created a Constitution Review Commission chaired by a New Zealander who was accorded a deciding vote. The more precarious the predicament of the regime, the more likely the involvement of outsiders in institutional choice.

This is not an altogether good thing. Most outsiders are more concerned that matters be settled, especially if those matters involve violence, than that they be settled right. It stands to reason, after all, that their concern is more with the disturbance created by, for example, a Balkan war than with the working of institutions that follow a Balkan peace. They will acquiesce in inapt institutions, provided their own objectives, including quiescence, are met.

Furthermore, the experts deployed by outsiders may very well bring to bear a variety of home-country biases that favor institutions familiar to them. If international involvement is very heavy, as it has been in Bosnia, an array of organizations answerable to several central offices of international bodies, in which divergent constellations of countries are influential, will inevitably complicate the process of constructing institutions. Bureaucratic and personal rivalries, discordant operating procedures, dissimilar patterns of local contacts and influence, and difficult relations with home-country governments are overwhelmingly likely to produce conflicting approaches to the problem of new institutions. Add to this the cultural assumptions likely to prevail in such environments, in which local recalcitrance is attributed to "stubborn Serbs" or the "stubborn Balkans" or to "stubborn Ulstermen" or the "stubborn Irish," and conditions for constructive innovation are far from propitious.

On the receiving end, the targets of international activity of this kind may tire of it rather quickly and thereby confirm their reputation for recalcitrance. If they do tire quickly, they may miss some good opportunities. An internal committee appointed in Bosnia by the High Representative in 1998 to propose a new electoral system was bombarded early on with the pet ideas of perennial proponents of certain approaches in the West (the Borda system, various forms of PR, etc.). Committee members were quickly jaded by what they saw as inappropriate, a priori conceptions of what Bosnia needed, being pushed by people who knew neither them nor their country. Once they acquired this armor, they used it to repel much more interesting ideas being advanced by the International Crisis Group, ideas developed by people who knew Bosnia and had views worth considering about what it needed (see International Crisis Group 1998, 1999). Decisionmakers who have seen a few traveling salespeople believe they have seen them all, and then, of course, those decisionmakers confirm their reputation for obduracy by actually becoming obdurate.

If the process of institutional change is not externally driven but is conducted internally, there are, of course, two possibilities. The process can be conducted after a regime has failed and power has been transferred or at least surrendered to an interim body, or it can be conducted under the auspices of an outgoing regime with declining legitimacy. There is a rather clear trade-off here between peace and the completeness of the institutional change. If the previous regime has collapsed, the slate is far more likely to be blank and the moment ripe for a rethinking. By the same token, however, the collapse of a regime in a severely divided society will, in all probability, have been precipitated by an extraordinary amount of violence. If not, the collapse itself may well precipitate that violence. If, on the other hand, new institutions are designed under the auspices of a sitting regime that manages to convince its opponents that it is committed to institutional change, the process may go off in relative peace, but the change may be far from complete. Forces discredited at the outset may rehabilitate themselves as the process unfolds. As they do, they will look out for their interests.

When the Suharto regime in Indonesia collapsed, the new president, B. J. Habibie, very quickly assumed the mantle of reformer and managed to steer a quite genuine reform that eventually produced his own rather graceful exit from politics. As Habibie adapted to the new circumstances immediately after Suharto's resignation, so, too, did other elements of the Suharto regime. Most notable among the survivors were the reformist wing of Suharto's party, Golkar, and one of the other two parties that had participated in government during the Suharto regime. The first result of this high degree of continuity was a relatively peaceful transition but also a set of institutions that, save for the genuineness of the new electoral competition, did not depart dramatically from the old institutions. It took five years of step-by-step constitutional change for the previous system to be reformed. The benefits of peaceful transition, in Indonesia or elsewhere, cannot be gainsaid, but the price of an incremental approach to institutional design may well be an insufficient public appreciation of the extent of change. Yet even the most propitious circumstances do not necessarily produce coherent plans. The Nigerian Constituent Assembly that sat in Lagos for several months in 1978 was an exceedingly deliberative body, working on the basis of a draft prepared by experts and under the aegis of a military that was eager to depart from politics. The Assembly had a good general idea of the constitution it wanted: a separation-of-powers regime that would make ethnic domination hard to achieve. As I have already mentioned, it designed an electoral system to choose a pan-ethnic president, but then it failed to design an electoral system with conciliatory incentives for the legislature. And so one set of institutions worked against another (see Horowitz 1985:601–613).

These outcomes are well within the range of normalcy. Comprehensive plans are less likely than are incremental changes; design inconsistencies can create conflicting incentives. Yet there are special times and special modes of constitutional planning that can produce more coherent outcomes, and it may also be the case that even inconsistent incentives can produce benign results.

The agreement reached in Belfast on Good Friday of 1998 is unusually coherent and unusually (albeit not perfectly) consociational. It would be tempting to think that the Northern Ireland experience is replicable, but it was the result of some very special conditions conducive to a consensus spanning party lines. To begin with, the usual resistance of majorities to consociational guarantees was absent, because Unionists have come increasingly to see themselves as a future minority in Northern Ireland and certainly in Ireland as a whole, should it come to that. Moreover, the Belfast proceedings were really a continuation of a series of meetings going back many years, from which an immanent consensus about what would work and what had not worked in Northern Ireland emerged. Those parties who had a different view of these matters had either walked out of the proceedings or played an inert role as they went on. These are conditions idiosyncratic to Northern Ireland.

What emerged in Belfast was not merely an inclusive, consociational regime but a set of maximal commitments about change in ethnic relations. Commitments were made to "parity of esteem" for the two main traditions in Northern Ireland. Parity of esteem implies a far-reaching commitment to equality in all spheres. Most conciliatory regimes in severely divided societies attempt to make progress on such contentious core issues of conflict step by painful step. The framers of the Belfast agreement committed themselves to resolving these issues at a stroke and so set themselves up for shortfalls of delivery that will disappoint Catholic participants and very likely threaten the inclusive coalition that lies at the heart of the agreement. And so the Belfast agreement is not only consociational but very risky as well. Maximal commitments are not necessarily the way to ensure democratic stability in the face of ethnic conflict.

In a sense, this is the risk of the guarantees model gone to the next step: the rights model. In a severely divided society, extensive guarantees of the rights of groups fly in the face of what the groups are contesting in the first place. It is one thing to terminate hostilities by channeling the antipathy that underlies them into peaceful political processes and quite another to purport to resolve the conflict by making firm commitments to detailed outcomes. A commitment to compromise is quite different from a commitment to the outcome of a conflict that has not been extinguished. But, as I have argued, the conditions that produced such commitments in Northern Ireland, while they may not be unique, are certainly very unusual.

Even in propitious conditions, murky compromises about institutions are more likely. The participants in the Fiji negotiations of 1997 that resulted in a new constitution for that divided society made no maximal commitments. They adopted a watered-down version of a conciliatory AV electoral system and combined it with some consociational features. Theirs was a hybrid constitution par excellence. Nevertheless, the conciliatory incentives worked. In the 1999 elections, two multi-ethnic coalitions were formed. One of them won the election and formed a government with Fiji's first Indian prime minister.

Electoral incentives were attractive to the participants in Fiji, because, as the constitutional process developed, two parties, one Fijian and one Indian, could see the electoral advantages to themselves of exchanging the second preferences the AV system made essential to victory. This point, obvious though it seems, needs underscoring: The adoption of constitutional innovations to reduce conflict is heavily dependent on the existence of powerful actors who see tangible benefits to themselves in the proposed innovations.

Ironically enough, the parties that saw the benefits of these innovations actually lost the election that followed adoption of the new constitution. When the multi-ethnic government and the constitution that had brought it to power were overthrown a year later in a coup, the disappointed Fijian party that had supported the constitution but lost the election displayed no particular support for the constitution, and it thereby aided in the success of the coup. And so, to the problems already enumerated, one more can be added: It is difficult to find an occasion for constitutional innovation, or to find parties motivated to produce such innovation, or to produce a constitutional plan in which provisions do not work against each other; and, even if these obstacles are overcome, it is also difficult to attend to a more usual problem of democracy, the problem of cultivating support for a constitution even when it produces outcomes inimical to particular interests, the problem, in short, of keeping losers attached to the regime and willing to defer their fight to another day.

REFERENCES

Grillo, R. D. 1985. *Ideologies and Institutions in Modern France: The Representation of Immigrants*. Cambridge: Cambridge University Press.

Hagendoorn, Louk, and Shervin Nekuee, eds. 1999. *Education and Racism: A Cross National Inventory of Positive Effects of Education on Ethnic Tolerance*. Aldershot, UK: Ashgate.

Horowitz, Donald L. 1985. *Ethnic Groups in Conflict*. Berkeley: University of California Press.

———. 1989. Incentives and Behaviour in the Ethnic Politics of Sri Lanka and Malaysia. *Third World Quarterly* 11 (4):18–35.

———. 1991. *A Democratic South Africa? Constitutional Engineering in a Divided Society*. Berkeley: University of California Press.

———. 1993. Democracy in Divided Societies. *Journal of Democracy* 4 (4):18–38.

———. 1997. Self-Determination: Politics, Philosophy, and Law. *NOMOS* 37:421–463.

———. 1999. Structure and Strategy in Ethnic Conflict: A Few Steps toward Synthesis. In *Annual World Bank Conference on Development of Economics*, ed. Boris Pleskovic and Joseph Stiglitz, 345–370. Washington, DC: World Bank.

International Crisis Group. 1998, March 10. *Changing the Logic of Bosnian Politics: Discussion Paper on Electoral Reform*, accessed at www.intl-crisis-group.org.

———. 1999, March 4. *Breaking the Mould: Electoral Reform in Bosnia and Herzegovina*, accessed at www.intl-crisis-group.org.

Jasinska-Kania, Aleksandra. 1999. The Impact of Education on Racism in Poland Compared with Other European Countries. In *Education and Racism: A Cross National Inventory of Positive Effects of Education on Ethnic Tolerance*, ed. Louk Hagendoorn and Shervin Nekuee, 75–92. Aldershot, UK: Ashgate.

Jayawardena, Chandra. 1980. Culture and Ethnicity in Guyana and Fiji. *Man* 15:430–450.

Lijphart, Arend. 1977. *Democracy in Plural Societies*. New Haven, CT: Yale University Press.

MacIver, Robert M. 1948. *The More Perfect Union*. New York: Macmillan.

Mamak, Alexander. 1978. *Colour, Culture and Conflict*. New York: Pergamon Press.

Norton, Robert. 1986. Colonial Fiji: Ethnic Divisions and Elite Conciliation. In *Politics in Fiji: Studies in Contemporary History*, ed. Brij V. Lal, 53–72. Honolulu, HI: Institute for Polynesian Studies.

Reilly, Ben. 1997a. Preferential Voting and Political Engineering: A Comparative Study. *Journal of Commonwealth and Comparative Politics* 35 (1):1–19.

———. 1997b. The Alternative Vote and Ethnic Accommodation: New Evidence from Papua New Guinea. *Electoral Studies* 16 (1):1–11.

Scarr, Deryk. 1984. *Fiji: A Short History*. Sydney: George Allen & Unwin.

Zartman, I. William. 1985. *Ripe for Resolution: Conflict and Intervention in Africa*. New York: Oxford University Press.

17

✺

The Politics of Electoral Systems in Transition

Andrew Ellis

This chapter describes the processes of electoral system and constitutional choices surrounding transitional elections from the vantage point of the technical adviser on the ground—perhaps therefore from the engine room rather than the ship's bridge. Making an election, which is often the largest single endeavor undertaken in a state, work is a major test of transition or of reconstruction after conflict. There are both opportunities and practical constraints. No one size fits all circumstances. There will always in practice be compromises and a lack of perfect solutions, and some answers will work and some will not, on occasion for reasons that are difficult to predict.

As illustrations, this chapter considers the complex and still unfinished transition in Indonesia, in which there are many dimensions of division both ethnic and other; some salient issues in the preparations for the general election held in Guyana in March 2001; and some recent electoral system developments in Sri Lanka. Although all three are examples where elections are held under local sovereignty, some observations may also be relevant where elections are organized by international bodies in the initial stages of state reconstruction. The chapter looks to the literature; it also, however, recognizes that political factors often operate to severely restrict the apparently available options. It introduces a further important issue, the effect of the need for perceived integrity in the counting and tabulation of elections. Finally, it poses some propositions and questions.

THE TRANSITION IN INDONESIA: 1998 TO DATE[1]

The regime of former President Suharto fell in May 1998. This system was governed by the rather vague 1945 Constitution—in practice, a system of virtually complete executive dominance. The legislature was a controlled and subservient body elected every five years. It included representatives from three political parties: the governing party Golkar, and two parties formed by the forced amalgamation by Suharto of nationalist parties (PDI [Indonesian Democracy Party]) and Islamic parties (PPP [Development Unity Party]). Elections used a proportional list system based on Indonesia's then twenty-seven provinces, with complete central party control over the choice of candidates. The number of seats for each province was based on population, but with a skew built in: The islands of Java and Bali have some 62 percent of the registered electorate, but were traditionally allocated only just over half of the elected seats because of fears of Javanese political domination.

Suharto was replaced by his vice president, B. J. Habibie, and the process of developing a new framework for democratic elections began. The lack of legitimacy of the Suharto-era legislature brought agreement that new elections were urgently required, and they were fixed for June 1999. Three significant groups of actors dominated the process:

First, the Habibie government appointed a technical team ("Tim Tujuh," or the Team of Seven) responsible for drafting the package of new electoral legislation. Much of Tim Tujuh's drafting took place before international support or involvement was available: Its only source of external technical advice was a resident Australian who volunteered help.

Second were the parties within the existing legislature: Golkar, which rapidly began its transition to a party of the new era; and PPP, which realized early that its only hope of survival was to present itself as the voice of reform within the old institutions.

Third, new parties formed outside the legislature endeavored to be voices of the reform movement. The most significant were PDI-P (Indonesian Democracy Party of Struggle) following former President Sukarno's nationalist precepts and led by his daughter Megawati Sukarnoputri; PKB (National Awakening Party), in which longstanding religious leader Abdurrachman Wahid was the most prominent figure, primarily representing the traditionalist Islam of Central and East Java; and PAN (National Mandate Party), led by prominent reform campaigner Amien Rais, which attempted to appeal both to the modernist Islamic tradition and to an urban, liberal vote.

The Development of Election Legislation for 1999

Tim Tujuh's draft legislation proposed a "mixed compensatory" system, under which most of the members would be elected from single-member districts (SMDs) using "first-past-the-post" (FPTP) elections, with the candidate polling the most votes declared elected. These would be joined by members elected through "national top-up seats"; the composition of the legislature based proportionally on the national percentage vote of each party would be calculated, and the top-up seats allocated to candidates taken from lists nominated by each party at the national level so that the overall composition of the legislature would most nearly approximate this calculation. The relative numbers of SMD seats and top-up seats can be varied in designing such systems: About eighty top-up seats were proposed in this particular instance.

This mixed compensatory system was designed to respond to reformist feeling that members should not as previously be very heavily Jakarta-based and under central party direction. However, political support for this position came not from the reformists but primarily from Golkar—who believed that they could poll 30 percent nationwide and would also benefit from heavier support away from Java and Bali, where single-member districts would have smaller electorates. Golkar also wanted to maintain significant central party input into candidate nomination. The parties outside the legislature, after failing until very late in the debate to address the issue at all because they regarded it as solely technical, insisted upon a proportional system. And PPP reconciled its own support for a single-member district system with the need to position itself as the champion of reform within the legislature by espousing the proportional system for the 1999 elections and the desirability of moving to an SMD system at a later date.

The new electoral legislation was finalized in late-night negotiations against a time deadline in late January 1999. The electoral system—a "proportional system with district characteristics"—is unique and is the clear product of incremental political negotiation. Given the positions and the power bases of the parties both inside and outside the negotiations, there was no way in practice that the system finally agreed could have been substantially different.

Less controversial but also of great significance was the provision in the political party law that requires all parties contesting the elections to be organized in at least nine provinces. It is impossible to register a specifically regional party. And while parties are required to submit nominations at the provincial level, there was a single national ballot paper for the whole country. These rules encouraged parties to run candidates as widely as possible, and the stronger ones succeeded in doing so in all provinces.

There was more scope for innovation on issues of election technicalities. However, the universal desire for a fast election left little option but to base the election administration on the previously existing machinery. Any attempt to set up a new administration would have entered the political sphere, because of Golkar's close connection with the civil service (indeed, ending the ability of civil servants to campaign was a key issue in the negotiations). But it already appears that systems, procedures, and terminology retained or installed for the transition could remain long after the political issues and agendas of 1999 have become history.[2]

The electoral system remains proportional and based on party lists at the provincial level, but the legislation is not clear on essential detail. There are two commonly used methods of converting votes cast in list systems into seats gained, "highest average" and "largest remainder," each of which themselves require some further details to specify exactly how they work: These details were never provided,[3] nor was the system for identifying which particular candidates from a party's list would take the seats gained by that party. These issues were resolved only at a very late stage. Tim Tujuh members, now serving as government representatives on the KPU (National Election Commission), followed their earlier emphasis on district links and sought local accountability of successful candidates. However, many of the forty-eight party representatives on the KPU wanted to ensure their central control of their parties.

The KPU's final regulations operate the list system by largest remainder, using, as at previous elections, the "Hare quota" (one of several standard methods for establishing the number of votes required by a party to qualify for one seat). The allocation of candidates to seats won was much more complex. Parties were required when submitting nominations to attach each candidate to a specific district. Each party's entitlement to full-quota seats in a province was established, and the candidates attached to those districts where the party had polled best were declared elected to these seats. The party leadership then filled its highest remainder seats with any candidates nominated by the party within the province, with interparty agreement on the allocation of these members to districts as yet "unrepresented." Local political factors led to exceptions in two provinces, which used a pure list PR system.

The formula was made even more complex by the late introduction of the "stembus accord," under which groups of parties could reach agreements to pool their remainders with the intention of getting more seats. This attempt at introducing preelection vote pooling was unsuccessful. Some parties discovered that given the actual votes cast, their groupings (or their parties within their grouping) would win more seats without the stembus accord than with it. The result was the retrospective abolition of all stembus accords—a further regulation being issued considerably after polling day!

The trend for power to pass back from voters and local parties to central party leaderships continued. The regulations were not changed, but effectively lasted no longer than the results of the vote count as the leaderships sought further to undermine the element of the system outside their control. At least eight candidates who should have been elected for their districts under the full-quota provisions were replaced by others on the instruction of party leaderships. Two candidates even switched provinces—a clear breach of the regulations to get the leaders of small parties into the legislature.

The 1999 Results in Comparative Context

The elections were judged both domestically and internationally to have been acceptable overall and to reflect the will of the people, despite a number of specific or localized concerns (National Democratic Institute 1999). The results demonstrated a strong continuity between support for secular nationalist parties or parties representing the two major streams of Indonesian Islam in the 1955 elections (the only previous elections generally regarded as acceptable) and support for their identifiable successor parties in 1999 (King 2000). The relative strengths of the parties, however, vary widely in the different parts of Indonesia. Under the 1999 system, the effective number of parties in the legislature (following Laakso and Taagepera 1979) is 4.72—comparable with its value in established multiparty PR-based systems such as in Finland, Italy, and the Netherlands (Lijphart 1999:76).

The sensitivity of the results to the electoral system chosen has been shown by Evans (2000), who has rerun the 1999 election under a number of systems (see table 17.1).

Gallagher (1991) has defined a measure to compare votes cast in a given election with seats won by contesting parties and candidates, the "least-squares index of disproportionality" (ID). This gives a figure of 3.26 for the 1999 results under the present system. This is comparable to the average values of Reynolds (1999) of 3.7 for six recent elections under PR systems in Southern Africa, and of 2.9 for 212 elections in established democracies between 1945 and 1990 using the data and analysis of Lijphart (1994). IDs for the rerun systems show values of 12.20 for district list PR, of at least 19.79 for FPTP, and of 20.08 for the alternative vote (AV)—an SMD system under which voters mark preferences (1, 2, 3 . . .) on their ballot papers, and members are elected with 50 percent + 1 of the vote following redistribution to successive lower preferences of the votes given to the least successful candidates. These IDs compare with average values of 11.7 for Reynolds's fourteen recent Southern African elections conducted under plurality SMD systems, and 9.8 for Lijphart's seventy-eight elected

Table 17.1.   Outcome of the Indonesian Parliamentary Elections of 1999 under Different Electoral Systems

Party	PDI-P	Golkar	PKB	PPP	PAN	PBB	42 Others	Total Elected Seats	No. of Parties Represented
National Vote %	33.7	22.4	12.6	10.7	7.1	1.9	11.6		
Electoral System	Seats								
Existing System—List PR, Provincial Units	153	120	51	58	34	13	33	462	21
List PR, One National District	156	104	58	50	33	9	52	462	35
Provincial List PR, No Bias against Java/Bali	159	112	55	58	37	12	29	462	19
District-Based List PR	198	165	44	33	21	1	0	462	6
Tim Tujuh Mixed System: FPTP with Top-Up Seats	240	134	33	28	12	3	12	462	18
Single-Member District FPTP	270	136	30	20	5	1	0	462	6
Single-Member District AV	277	56	51	48	28	1	1	462	7
Single-Member District FPTP, No Bias against Java/Bali	291	113	34	20	3	1	0	462	6

Note: This table contains minor corrections to the original calculations, which are included in Ellis (2000).

under plurality SMD systems in established democracies. Indeed, the ID value for the FPTP and AV systems is greater than that for any of Lijphart's plurality SMD electoral systems with the single exception of that used in India in 1952 and 1957. FPTP appears likely to lead to more disproportional results in Indonesia than almost anywhere else.

A short note is necessary about the use of rerun elections as an analytic tool in this way. The form of campaigns that are run by political parties is likely to vary under different electoral systems. This is both intuitively so and a reasonable a fortiori inference from the finding that performance in each part of a mixed system is affected by the other (Herron and Nishikawa 2001). The question to be answered is whether this divergence invalidates the rerunning of elections completely, or whether it is still usable as an approximating tool—and if this can be done, how sensitive the results are to the approximation made.

Political and Constitutional Debate since the 1999 Elections

The shape of the Indonesian party system should not yet be taken as completely fixed, but the major parties have demonstrated enough strength and separate identity to have remained in the same form for fifteen months following the election. There is no immediate likelihood of significant change or realignment—even more so as there is no call to relax the effective prohibition of regional parties.

Coherent government, however, has not proved easy. President Abdurrachman Wahid, elected by the legislature over Megawati Sukarnoputri although the latter led the largest single party, initially assembled a cabinet of national unity, drawing from all sides. But subsequent changes to this cabinet led to the government being able to rely in the legislature only on its own PKB support—10 percent of the members. A further reshuffled cabinet announced in August 2000 may last a full year as the dangers of removing a president in a presidential system are more widely understood, but jockeying between the president and legislature is now a key feature of day-to-day politics as both try to establish precedents.

The legislature has started a full review of the 1945 constitution. This debate covers a number of fundamental issues on which all or almost all participants say they are united, in particular the retention of the presidential system[1] and of the unitary state. Other issues remain contentious, including the key relationship between the presidency and the legislature, the possible creation of a second regionally based chamber of the legislature (with attendant discussion as to its powers), and the possible introduction of a directly elected presidency. There are associated questions as to appropriate electoral systems for both the latter. Some understanding exists that changes to the electoral system for the existing chamber—for example the possible abolition of the bias against Java and Bali—may be related to all these issues.

The review of the electoral legislation has also started, and is focused on accountability and stability. The maintenance of central party control over legislators lies not far below the surface, accompanied by calculations of party advantage. Any changes will respond to these issues in their political context, rather than seeking to solve problems of division in Indonesian society—still less tackling the specific questions of local conflict and violence in Maluku, Aceh, or West Papua (formerly Irian Jaya).

Inasmuch as such questions are being addressed, it is a result of the passage of legislation in 1999 introducing wide-ranging regional autonomy in Indonesia. This response to the strong demand for the reversal of Suharto's centralized structures has played a major role in diminishing calls for the breakup of the state, although there are still difficult and sensitive unresolved tensions and separatist calls in Aceh and West Papua. These pose a major continuing challenge to the government in its dealings both with the two provinces and with members of Jakarta elites, many of whom tend to favor a heavy-handed approach.

Possibilities for Electoral System Reform

A strong feeling remains in many quarters of the importance of a direct link between legislators and specific districts. Fifty-one percent of elected members said in a survey (Centre for Electoral Reform 2000) that they regard district links as "very important," and that given conflict, 49 percent would regard the district interest as decisive as against 31 percent for personal beliefs and 19 percent for the party group position; but the firm impression is that these figures overstate district links in practice. It can indeed be shown that single-member district systems "have a benign impact on democracy through their capacity to make representation more personal and its experience more direct" (Curtice and Shively 2002). Their proponents, however, need to reconcile this with the finding that single-member district systems are likely in themselves to be destabilizing in transitions (Birch 2003). In addition, the difficulties of establishing an acceptable district boundary definition process have not yet been considered in any depth.

"Preferential voting"—requiring voters to mark ballot papers 1, 2, 3, and so on in order of their preference for candidates[5]—has been discussed as a mechanism for improving accountability, but has not proved popular. The voting process is perceived as too difficult, although this is not easy to sustain objectively (especially as neighboring Papua New Guinea successfully used such a system for a period). There is also a serious objection. The necessity to maintain popular confidence in the integrity of the tabulation makes it imperative that the vote count takes place separately within each polling station, with results aggregated and tabulated successively at higher levels. Parties and domestic observers can therefore compare lower level result protocols with higher level tabulations and ensure that no fraudulent changes have been made. The count at the polling station is a public event, at which not only party agents and domestic observers but also many of the local community are present—and noisily involved as the vote on each ballot paper is read out. Such a system would be difficult to sustain alongside the introduction of preferential ballot papers.

The idea of "double balloting"—under which a runoff election would be held between the most popular candidates in the first ballot[6]—also does not command support. The holding of two elections across a country as large and logistically difficult as Indonesia is seen as probably impractical and certainly too expensive. This may not appear to be a clinching argument given the relative cost even of an Indonesian election to the total national budget; but it is nonetheless the natural response of almost all participants in the debate.

Dissatisfaction with the electoral system in some transitions leads to major changes at an advanced stage.[7] The desire for strong member-district links and a pure first-past-the-post system may still prevail. A mixed system with a compensatory list may also emerge in response to those who believe that FPTP could fail adequately or at all to reflect the diversity of Indonesia, and foresee severe strains on national unity if a party with 30 percent or so of the popular vote were to win an absolute legislative majority.

But it is also becoming more possible as the spirit of 1998 fades that the political deal of the 1999 electoral system, for all its complexity and despite the degree to which it was undermined and contradicted in practice, may yet survive to another general election in 2004—and then perhaps beyond.

GUYANA

Guyana is a clear example of a deeply divided society, with the two major parties, broadly linked with the two major ethnic groups, having polled 55 percent and 41 percent of the vote at the 1997 elections. Recent history includes the change of the electoral system by the departing colonial power to prevent the allegedly Marxist leadership of the larger group taking power, and a period of twenty years of dictatorship on behalf of the second group. There is thus an enormous lack of trust between the two sides.

Guyana is also a polity in which power is concentrated almost entirely at the national level: There has been only one prize worth having. The major element of the electoral system has been fifty-three list PR seats using a single national constituency, with parties able to nominate after polling which candidates on their lists would fill the seats won. In addition, there has been one indirectly elected seat for each of the ten regions, and two other seats. Although both domestic and international observers were broadly supportive of the declared results in 1997,[8] the deep political divide and serious shortcomings in the administration of the count and tabulation led to a lack of acceptance of the results by one of the two major players. Externally brokered negotiations led to the Herdmanston Agreement, under which the newly elected government would serve for three, rather than five, years, and under which a review of the constitution would take place.

The National Assembly finally completed the constitutional review in 2000. Although the issue of cross-ethnic consent and the possibility of division of power were included in submissions to the review, only limited movement in these directions was made in the finally agreed amendments. The revised constitution does not include formal power-sharing institutions. It therefore remains to be seen whether, assuming the election is well conducted and the parties accept the results, there will be any commitment by the political actors to use power in a way that will be accepted across ethnic lines without the formal establishment of consociational institutions.

The problems over the count and tabulation in 1997 had a number of causes, including apparently inexplicable delays in the transmission of polling station result protocols in some areas, and the authentication of such protocols. The necessity to rebuild confidence in the election administration's ability to conduct the count has again made the count in the polling station, using a multicopy-result protocol, an essential part of the electoral arrangements.

Fierce debate over the electoral system is not at the time of writing fully resolved. The use of list PR using the largest remainder and the Hare quota has been retained. Regional seats will be directly elected and their number increased to twenty-five. Still at issue is whether the minimum number of seats in each region should be one or two. The composition of the legislature will be completed on a compensatory basis based on the overall national vote, with forty (or, if necessary, more) extra seats filled from national party lists.

The Herdmanston provisions required a general election not later than January 2001, and active preparations for the election and discussions about donor support for the process started in March 2000. The lack of agreement over the electoral system, with no agreement reached between the two sides despite the passage of the real last technical deadline, has combined with the need to create a new generally accepted electoral register to cause postponement of the elections.

SRI LANKA

Sri Lanka's October 2000 election was conducted under open list PR, in which voters choose a party and three preferred candidates. Neither big Sinhalese party won a majority on its own. As a result, the People's Alliance (PA) formed a majority coalition. Following significant problems with the campaign environment and electoral violence, a consensus actively emerged within the opposition and relevant civil society organizations in favor of an independent election commission. The government did not disagree but saw it as part of an overall constitutional review package, as it had proposed in the run-up to the election. There has also been considerable discussion of a reform of the electoral system to a German mixed compensatory system, although the precise details—such as the number of seats elected in each section—are not clear or agreed on.

This pressure has arisen for three reasons: First, the financial and material rewards of being an MP are alleged to be a significant cause of electoral violence between campaigners and supporters of candidates of the same party. Second, individual candidates have to mount campaigns in districts of, say, 400,000 electors and regard this as impractical and beyond the resources available to most. Finally, the open list preference system generates about 5 percent spoilt papers, which is thought to be too high.

Any such change to the electoral system would require a two-thirds majority in Parliament, as it would entail constitutional amendment. If it were agreed, it would remove the one element of voter input in a party dominant system. Perhaps, however, this voter choice is in practice rather a delusion, given the strength of the provision that members of Parliament who defect from their party lose their seat—which nobody in Parliament, and few outside, are challenging.

PROPOSITIONS AND QUESTIONS

There are a number of propositions that can be drawn from the experience contained in the case studies. First, all three examples point to the electoral system as, at best, one element—and maybe not the major one—in approaching ethnic conflict resolution issues. The electoral system can help things go wrong, however—witness Sri Lanka's historical experience with first-past-the-post elections. The overall constitutional and division of powers framework, and the attitude of the parties to it, have to be considered as connected with the electoral system itself. Issues such as federalism, devolution and decentralization, bicameralism, and the extent to which the system is to be presidential or parliamentary can all have a major impact that usually makes it unwise to analyze the effects of electoral change in isolation.

On the core issues of both electoral and constitutional engineering, there will be a limited number of solutions that can be reached in practice given the inherited traditions, the political background and positions of the actors, and the importance and sensitivity of national sovereignty and ownership of the electoral or constitutional process. This is probably true both during a founding election transition and afterwards. Where elections are organized by the international community, there may appear to be more options—but the problems may be even deeper, and solutions that do not command substantial local support are unlikely to be appropriate.

The input of the international community may therefore have both a short-term and a long-term component. The short-term component should concentrate on what is acceptable within the parameters of national debate, but can be relevant to important choices given the durability of "temporary" transitional arrangements especially of a technical nature. The long-term component may consist of introducing ideas that may take root in the wider debate, with civil society actors often being most receptive to pursuing this debate over a period of time.

The framework of electoral system debate is set in practice by the perceptions of political advantage of the major players along with the need to reach an agreement that will be generally acceptable. The Indonesian agreement had to be acceptable both to the parties of the New Order holding the levers of power and to the new parties outside on the street. The Guyanese argument is in essence about numbers and consequent potential threats to the majority group's overall majority. No change to the Sri Lankan electoral system is possible without the agreement of both major Sinhalese parties. The same applies to wider connected constitutional changes, for which it is unlikely that necessary majorities will be achieved without agreement of most of the political leadership.

The pressure to establish a new legitimate government in a transitional situation means that the key decisions on electoral legislation and systems and on constitutional arrangements are almost always made under time pressure. Even where more time appears to be available, as in Guyana, the quest for political advantage is likely to drive finalization of the electoral and political arrangements to the wire. The question is how to eliminate inadvertent "rough edges" resulting from such a process.

Even if the Indonesian electoral system is viewed not as a political deal but as a brave attempt to marry the principles of list PR with the creation of an element of constituency accountability, it did not achieve this. The constituency/member link was not really created in practice. It is uncertain to what extent full enforcement of the existing regulations and legal reduction of the powers of central parties would change this.

The lack of public confidence in the electoral machinery in relation to counting and tabulation in both Indonesia and Guyana restricts possible electoral systems to those that can be counted in the polling station. Single-member district systems (including double-ballot systems) and list PR systems meet this requirement, but preferential systems, for example the alternative vote or the single transferable vote, do not readily do so. (Result protocols that record first preferences would go some way toward resolving this problem but do not do so completely.) The encouraging trend of increasing involvement of civil society in election processes worldwide through domestic observation and "quick count" operations is seen in both Indonesia and Guyana.[9] It increases the pressure for polling station counts, which can be expected to gain further prevalence.[10]

In transitional elections, list PR is often the most practical route to take.[11] It is the safe option: It can be made to work in the time available, it's administratively simple, it does not require the drawing of acceptable boundaries, it can be counted in the polling station, and it will include everyone who needs to be included in the new Parliament. This does not, however, imply either that every transitional constitution should include the full package of consociational provisions proposed by Lijphart and others, or that what is agreed for the short term is right for the longer term. For example, there has been an explosion in the use of mixed systems (some compensatory, some not) in the last ten years. The experience of such systems is only now beginning to accumulate, and needs to be compared with options such as list PR systems and SMD systems for which longer-term evidence is available.

Some designers of electoral systems in the context of societies in or emerging from conflict advocate the principle of "vote pooling," both during the first stages of transition and in the longer term. This involves the use of a preferential system under which parties and candidates need in practice to attract second- and lower-preference votes from supporters of parties or candidates across conflictual divides—thus providing electoral incentives for moderation on all sides. The advocates of vote pooling have some practical questions to answer: how to meet the requirements of perceived electoral integrity, how to handle the effect of the kind of intra-party problems that have become an issue in Sri Lanka, and the extent to which the results of elections held under such preferential systems are affected by changes in support for the participants. While democratic elections have uncertain outcomes by definition, systems in which small changes in party support have a significant possibility of generating large changes in the subsequent exercise of power may be less likely to promote stability and confidence.[12]

A transitional election such as that in Indonesia in 1999 inevitably contains a major element of "referendum on change." Golkar was seen as the party of the old system: Others were against the old system. This cleavage will become less relevant over time—as has largely already happened, for example, across Eastern Europe. But its imprint may still be visible in the institutional arrangements and procedures long after it has faded from direct political relevance.

The degree to which international donors can legitimately consider constitutional and electoral engineering issues in negotiations before transitional elections is a very delicate question. It is surely correct that donors may condition support on provisions that are necessary for the holding of acceptable "free and fair" elections or for the proper handling and accounting of donor funds. In an era in which the use of aid funds may be more subject to domestic donor scrutiny, there may be pressures to extend such conditioning toward constitutional and electoral solutions that seek to minimize the risk of future conflict. If the international community is to tread this tremendously sensitive path, it has a huge responsibility to ensure that its judgments are well founded. This may be easier said than done in an environment where the precise configuration of a large number of interdependent variables is critical[13] and where political will to commit donor support often only emerges at a late stage. In addition, the strength of embassies in countries where change is taking place is small compared with the total strength of the foreign services of donor nations. It is thus currently statistically unlikely that there will be any great degree of institutional memory in conflict resolution, democratization, and transition directly present in local donor embassies. This could pose a future challenge to foreign ministries in the design of training and support programs.

NOTES

1. Some technical aspects of the Indonesian process are described in fuller detail in Ellis (2000).

2. As seen for example in India, where the decision of the Constituent Assembly of 1946–1949 to adopt the first-past-the-post system and many of the procedures of British electoral administration as laid down in the Representation of the People Acts remains in place (Bhagat 1996).

3. While this may appear to be a technical issue only, its importance was shown in practice during the elections in Cambodia in 1998. An unremarked and inadequately publicized change to votes-into-seats provisions after their publication led when the votes were counted to a situation where the Cambodian People's Party (CPP) had won sixty-four seats out of 120 in the National Assembly under the revised formula, compared with fifty-nine under the original formula. Even before the obvious impact on eventual government formation, it was with the greatest of difficulty that the opposition parties were persuaded that manipulation of the election had not taken place and that the results of the election should be accepted.

4. Mainwaring's (1993:200) assertion that "multiparty presidentialism is more likely to produce immobilising executive/legislative deadlock than either parliamentary systems or two-party presidentialism" is thus discouraging. The presidential system holds practically universal support in Indonesia, although these words are used to describe both the "normal" presidential system exemplified by the United States or the Philippines, and the unique system laid down in the 1945 constitution, which is in conventional terms neither fully presidential nor fully parliamentary. The country's diversity and established traditions make it difficult to envisage any major reduction in the number of the stronger parties leading to a configuration of parties coherently reflecting the cleavages of Indonesian society. Any such reduction would be likely to leave significant elements of society perceiving themselves as unrepresented.

5. Horowitz (1991) advances the additional argument in support of AV that it is a mechanism to encourage vote pooling across societal divides, but note Reynolds's (1999) analysis of the effects such a system might have had in recent elections in Southern Africa.

6. A discussion of the case for the double ballot can be found in Sartori (1997).

7. For example Ukraine, described in Birch (2000), where a single-member district system used for the first posttransition parliamentary elections in 1994 was replaced by a mixed system in 1998—both because of dissatisfaction with the necessity for repeated elections that resulted from a participation threshold and, in Birch's view, because of the impact of the increasing role of parties and their wish to consolidate within the system. One effect of this change was that the 1998 election results introduced a socioeconomic dimension to the divisions represented in the legislature alongside the existing ethnic/regional dimension, which will undoubtedly bring new factors into the development of the democratic transition in Ukraine.

8. For example, Electoral Assistance Bureau Guyana, the domestic observer organization, concluded that the election represented "the collective will of the Guyanese people who cast their ballots at the election" (Electoral Assistance Bureau 1998).

9. Sri Lanka is an exception to this—the electoral machinery is well established, and its ability to conduct a fair and accurate count does not currently appear to be at issue.

10. The transitional elections of Eastern Europe (1990 onwards), Russia (1991 onwards), and Palestine (1996) are all further examples. For a more ambiguous case, see Cambodia (1998): While many participants in the elections and domestic observers supported the polling station count for transparency, one major opposition party—the Sam Rainsy Party—and some NGOs opposed it because of their fear of subsequent government retribution against polling districts with strong opposition support.

11. There are nonetheless exceptions: Palestine in 1996 used multimember FPTP and (with weak or undefined parties) elected a Legislative Council that was seen to be inclusive of all the elements that fought the election.

12. Further consideration of the choice of electoral systems in divided societies can be found in Reilly and Reynolds (1998).

13. Horowitz (1985, 1991) presents some interesting further examples.

REFERENCES

Bhagat, Anjana Kaw. 1996. Elections and Electoral Reforms in India. *Vikas* 1: 7–14.

Birch, Sarah. 2000. *Elections and Democratization in Ukraine*. Basingstoke, UK: Macmillan.

———. 2003. *Electoral Systems and Political Transformation in Post-Communist Europe*. New York: Palgrave Macmillan, 2003.

Centre for Electoral Reform (CETRO). 2000, March. Survey of 252 Legislators. Jakarta: Centre for Electoral Reform.

Curtice, John, and Phil Shively. 2002, February 1–2. *Who Represents Us Best? One Member or Many?* Paper presented at the Comportamento Eleitoral e Atitudes Políticas dos Portugueses: Numa Perspectiva Comparada conference, Institute of Social Sciences, University of Lisbon, Portugal.

Electoral Assistance Bureau Guyana (EAB). 1998. General and Regional Elections in Guyana 1997, EAB, Statement of Conclusions. Georgetown, Guyana.

Ellis, Andrew. 2000. The Politics of Electoral Systems in Transition: The 1999 Elections in Indonesia and Beyond. *Representation* 37 (3–4):241–248.

Evans, Kevin. 2000. Unpublished calculations. Jakarta: United Nations Development Programme.

Gallagher, Michael. 1991. Proportionality, Disproportionality and Electoral Systems. *Electoral Studies* (10):38–40.

Herron, Erik, and Misa Nishikawa. 2001. Contamination Effects and the Number of Parties in Mixed-Superposition Electoral Systems. *Electoral Studies* 20 (1):63–86.

Horowitz, Donald. 1985. *Ethnic Groups in Conflict*. Berkeley: University of California Press.

———. 1991. *A Democratic South Africa: Constitutional Engineering in a Divided Society*. Berkeley: University of California Press.

King, Dwight. 2000, May. *The Elections of 1955 and 1999: Similarities and Continuities*. Jakarta: The Habibie Centre.

Laakso, Markku, and Rein Taagepera. 1979. Effective Number of Parties: A Measure with Application to West Europe. *Comparative Political Studies* 12 (1):3–27.

Lijphart, Arend. 1994. *Electoral Systems and Party Systems*. Oxford: Oxford University Press.

———. 1999. *Patterns of Democracy*. New Haven, CT: Yale University Press.

Mainwaring, Scott. 1993. Presidentialism, Multipartism and Democracy: The Difficult Combination. *Comparative Political Studies* 26 (2):198–228.

National Democratic Institute for International Affairs (NDI). 1999. Reports of 23 February, 28 May and 28 November 1999 and Statements of the NDI/Carter Centre Election Observation Mission from 5 June 1999 to 26 August 1999. Washington, DC: National Democratic Institute for International Affairs.

Reilly, Ben, and Andrew Reynolds. 1998. Electoral Systems for Divided Societies: International IDEA. *Democracy and Deep-Rooted Conflict: Options for Negotiators* 4 (4):191–204.

Reynolds, Andrew. 1999. *Electoral Systems and Democratisation in Southern Africa*. Oxford: Oxford University Press.

Sartori, Giovanni. 1997. *Comparative Constitutional Engineering*. New York: New York University Press.

18

❦

Territorial Autonomy: Permanent Solution or Step toward Secession?

Hurst Hannum

In the late 1980s, it was becoming apparent that a purely individualistic approach to human rights was insufficient to respond to the demands of ethnic minorities and other groups for greater recognition of and protection for their culture and, in many cases, greater political authority over their own affairs. However, neither international human rights law nor the then-contemporary understanding of "self-determination" addressed these issues; human rights could be asserted only by individuals, and self-determination in the form of independence was available only to colonial territories.

Nonetheless, bringing together the strands of human rights, attempts to promote the rights of minorities and indigenous peoples, and movements to foster fuller participation in both economic and political development activities, I argued in a book first published in 1990 that "a new principle of international law can be discerned in the interstices of contemporary definitions of sovereignty, self-determination, and the human rights of individuals and groups" (Hannum 1990:473). Although it is doubtful that this "right to autonomy" has yet achieved the status of international law, it has become the solution of choice for many of those engaged in attempting to resolve conflicts between territorially based ethnic groups around the world.

Autonomy has been proposed or adopted as a solution in countries as diverse as Finland, Norway, Sweden, Belgium, Spain, Denmark, Hungary, Romania, Yugoslavia, Bosnia and Herzegovina, Italy, the United Kingdom, Turkey, Iraq, India, China, Sri Lanka, Papua New Guinea, Cyprus, the Philippines, Bangladesh, Russia, Georgia, Azerbaijan, the Sudan,

Senegal, Canada, the United States, Mexico, Brazil, Nicaragua, and Panama—and this is certainly not an exhaustive list. Why has this particular form of conflict resolution acquired such popularity?

ADVANTAGES

There are many advantages to "autonomy" as a solution to ethnic conflicts. Perhaps the most obvious is the flexibility of the term, which is not a term of art under international law and may therefore encompass a wide range of constitutional relationships. Thus, the "highest" degree of autonomy accorded by China to Hong Kong includes the retention by Hong Kong of a wide range of political, judicial, and economic powers, from a separate legislature and judiciary to fully independent financial authority. Autonomous entities in Bosnia and Herzegovina also have a broad range of independent authority, although autonomy in that instance was designed to maintain the façade of a unified state, rather than to integrate a new territory into an existing state. Autonomy in Belgium and the Åland Islands is expressed through territorially based powers over language, education, culture, and, in the latter case, residence.

Autonomy also may be a means of responding successfully to concerns about minority rights, particularly when minorities are territorially concentrated in significant numbers. Territorial autonomy is mentioned as a possible option in the 1990 CSCE Copenhagen Document, although its formulation is fairly minimal and reflects the sensitive nature of such proposals.[1] In 1993, the Council of Europe's Parliamentary Assembly more specifically recommended,

> In the regions where they are in a majority the persons belonging to a national minority shall have the right to have at their disposal appropriate local or autonomous authorities or to have a special status, matching the specific historical and territorial situation and in accordance with the domestic legislation of the state.[2]

Territorial autonomy is discussed in some detail in the Lund Recommendations on Effective Participation by National Minorities in Political Life, which were adopted in 1999 in conjunction with the office of the OSCE's high commissioner on national minorities (Foundation on Inter-Ethnic Relations 1999). Under the heading of "self-government," both nonterritorial and territorial arrangements are discussed. Functions that might fall under the latter include education, culture, use of minority language, environment, local planning, natural resources, economic development, local policing functions, and housing, health, and other social services (Foundation on Inter-Ethnic Relations 1999:para. 20). Noting that all democracies have arrangements for governance at different territorial levels, the Recommendations urge states to "favourably consider" territorial arrangements "where it would improve the opportunities of minorities to exercise authority over matters affecting them" (Foundation on Inter-Ethnic Relations 1999:para. 19). The Recommendations also specify that territorial self-governance institutions should be based on democratic principles rather than ethnic criteria and should respect the human rights of all persons within their jurisdiction, including minorities (Foundation on Inter-Ethnic Relations 1999:paras. 16, 20).

A third advantage of "autonomy" solutions is that, by definition, they maintain the territorial integrity of existing states. However powerful they may be, autonomous units are not sovereign on the international level and remain ultimately subject in varying degrees to the jurisdiction of the state in which they are found. This is obviously attractive to the states concerned, as well as to outsiders who fear the destabilizing effect of the proliferation of ever smaller, ethnically defined states. Autonomy thus can be seen as contributing to the stability of the existing international order.

A strong commitment to autonomy solutions within states also obviates the need to develop criteria for secession, since secession (except by mutual consent) is simply not available as an internationally sanctioned outcome. This is the approach taken by the international community thus far in Kosovo, for example—although the situation there is far from resolved, and division of the Federal Republic of Yugoslavia by consent may yet occur.

In a more theoretical sense, as the nature of the state changes, and its role as an economic mediator between individuals and transnational actors wanes, creative autonomy arrangements may provide a more appropriate means of reflecting more accurately real power relationships. Complex autonomy arrangements diminish the traditional role of the state as the holder of all important rights and de-emphasize the relevance of state boundaries. In this manner, they may offer a realistic and pragmatic response to particular situations, even though the result may confuse international lawyers and foreign relation experts. This approach can be seen in the commitment of the European Union to the principle of "subsidiarity" and in the increasing role played by substate or cross-state regions in both economic and political affairs.

Since autonomy is potentially responsive to both majority concerns—preserving the integrity of the state—and minority demands—exercising a meaningful degree of self-government—it is often seen by outside mediators as inherently feasible politically and therefore useful as a means of halting conflict. It provides an obvious compromise solution, even if its precise definition is uncertain. Promoting autonomy also permits outsiders to be perceived as maintaining an impartial position between the minority and the central government, since autonomy rarely responds entirely to the wishes of either side.

DISADVANTAGES

Perhaps inevitably, each of the advantages noted above has a corresponding disadvantage. For instance, what may appear to one observer as desirable flexibility may lead others to criticize the very vagueness of autonomy as unlikely to encourage a meaningful dialogue. Since neither minorities nor governments understand exactly what autonomy comprises, autonomy itself may end up being little more than a slogan, used by one side or the other to substitute for other, equally vague slogans such as sovereignty or self-determination. Demands for autonomy may therefore make it more difficult to identify the actual interests of the parties, such as linguistic or educational rights or a greater share in economic life.

While autonomy may respond to assertions for greater rights by an ethnic or other minority, the political elements contained within most autonomy regimes go far beyond those traditionally considered essential to protect minority cultures. Minority rights are still understood as responding primarily to those elements that define minorities themselves, that is, the need to retain control over and develop their language and culture, practice their own religion, and influence or control the education of their children. In a word, minority rights are about minority identity, not (until recently) about greater political power.

If minority rights become increasingly viewed as encompassing a right to territorial autonomy, this could encourage greater demands by aggrieved (or greedy) groups that go well beyond protection of minority identity. Territorial autonomy, when exercised by an ethnically distinct minority within the country as a whole, is intended to respond primarily to group demands rather than to individual rights to equality and nondiscrimination. However, many states are wary of subordinating individual rights to the purported needs of the group.

The countervailing position to the argument that autonomy is a means of preserving territorial integrity questions whether a slavish devotion to territorial integrity remains appropriate in today's world. Why should we assume that the frontiers that existed at the dawn of a new millennium should be maintained forever? Aren't other values—preserving cultural identity, increasing meaningful and effective participation—equally important?

An absolute commitment to preserving current borders ignores the history of Europe, in which border changes have played a notable part until the mid-twentieth century, as well as the more recent changes that have occurred in the former Soviet Union, Czechoslovakia, Yugoslavia, and Ethiopia. Such a state-centric position discourages necessary thinking about what the criteria should be for statehood and secession, precisely when such thinking should be in the forefront of international attempts to deal with internal ethnic conflicts. Continuing to deify sovereign statehood and static frontiers as the only desirable goals reduces the political and economic complexity of the twenty-first century to simplistic slogans. It ignores the deliberately "soft" frontiers being introduced by the European Union and other suprastate organizations, which are seen by many as the key to resolving regional conflicts in, for example, the Balkans, Caucasus, and even Central or South Asia.

If autonomy is seen by both parties to ethnic or secessionist conflicts as an undesirable compromise, it may be unlikely to resolve those conflicts in the long run despite its attractiveness to potential mediators. Secessionist groups see acceptance of an autonomy arrangement as a defeat, since by definition their goal is independence. Even where autonomy may ultimately be accepted (or desired), it is generally seen as valuable only if it is as "high" or broad as possible, thus substituting a demand for greater political-economic power for what may have originally been complaints about discrimination or other violations of minority rights. Minority rights themselves rapidly become viewed as woefully insufficient, as evidenced by claims from, for example, Abkhazia, Chechnya, Nagorno-Karabakh, Kosovo, Bougainville, Aceh, Kashmir, and northern Cyprus.

States, on the other hand, resist wide-ranging autonomy that has the effect of removing a part of the country from the effective control of the central government and psychologically dividing rather than integrating the country's population. In the former Yugoslavia, neither the Bosnian nor Serbian/Yugoslav governments favor the de facto partition and quasi-independence that have been given to the Republika Srpska and Kosovo, respectively, and that will be enforced for the foreseeable future by foreign occupation. Indeed, the role of NATO in Kosovo seems to be to prevent Albanians from achieving independence and to prevent Yugoslavia from controlling its own territory; it does not seem likely that such a "lose-lose" scenario will stand the test of time.

Finally, the precedent of Yugoslavia, in particular, may give rise to a perception that autonomous or federal states may be more vulnerable to secessionist pressures in the future than are unitary states. Although it adopted a somewhat more nuanced position in a later opinion, this perception was reinforced by language in a decision of the Badinter Commission, which applied the concept of *uti possidetis* to the internal boundaries of Yugoslavia.[3] Such a distinction in the international personality of a state, based on its internal constitutional arrangements, is unheard of in international law, and it is likely to discourage the kind of effective devolution of power that may well offer a solution to many ethnic conflicts within states (see generally Hannum 1993).

THE PROPER ROLE OF AUTONOMY

The counterbalancing or even contradictory arguments sketched briefly above suggest that autonomy should be seen as neither a panacea nor a provocation. Autonomy will not necessarily lead to a permanent solution that will contain all ethnic tensions, nor will it inevitably encourage demands for ever-greater political power and eventually independence. Instead, autonomy is simply one tool in the arsenal of constitutional drafters, politicians, and diplomats that must be suited to the particular task at hand.

In brief, autonomy is a means, not an end. In every case, whether or not autonomy is an appropriate tool depends on a careful identification of the goal(s) to be achieved, not all of which may be mutually compatible.

If the overriding goal is to end violent conflict, proposing autonomy as a solution will not always be a good idea. By freezing incompatible demands, one may only postpone later conflict, leaving displaced or "cleansed" persons without redress. Some divisions within states are sufficiently deep that "giving war a chance" (Luttwak 1999) and allowing a definitive settlement to occur may be the best assurance that the conflict is unlikely to recur. Barbara Walter has argued that intervening in a civil war before one side achieves victory almost always requires the presence of armed peacekeepers to enforce the resulting stalemate (Walter 1997), and the willingness of the "international community" to make such long-term commitments seems to be eroding rather than growing stronger.

It remains to be seen whether the short-term deployment of NATO troops as observers in Macedonia in 2001 will accomplish the desired goal of maintaining another ethnically divided state in the Balkans, although the minimal mandate and level of deployment to which NATO agreed would seem to reinforce the notion that intervention and enforcement—at least outside the former Yugoslavia—may become less rather than more likely in the future.

While it is true that autonomy may be a useful tool if the international community decides to maintain territorial integrity as a peremptory norm of international law (*jus cogens*), such a position begs the question of when we might be morally and politically justified in supporting a right to secession as an appropriate solution in certain circumstances. I would argue that such a right should be supported, but only under very narrow conditions. These conditions might include situations where secession is the only plausible response to continuing, massive, discriminatory human rights violations (arguably the case for Kurds in Iraq and Turkey in the 1980s, and Tibetans in China during the Cultural Revolution) or where secession might be employed retroactively as a means of punishing egregious violations of humanitarian law (as occurred in Kosovo). In such cases, any internationally recognized right to secession would depend on the actions of the recognized government, not merely on the wishes of an ethnic or other minority. But where the government of a state refuses to ease repression, recognize legitimate minority claims for respect for their identity, or conduct an antiguerrilla or antiterrorist campaign in conformity with the basic laws of armed conflict, international support for secession may be appropriate.

Even when secession cannot be supported as a matter of law, the international community should consider more fully whether applying the concept of *uti possidetis* to internal borders is likely to discourage or exacerbate violence. In the former Yugoslavia, for example, the West's insistence on keeping "trapped" Serbs within Croatia and Bosnia and Herzegovina (and trapped Croats within the latter) may have actually contributed to continuation of the violence, since peaceful means of redrawing borders seem to have been excluded. As purportedly stated by one participant in the conflict, "Why should I be a minority in your state when you could be a minority in mine?" Plebiscites and referenda are not always desirable or even possible, but some attention should be paid to the wishes of individuals caught in transitional states whose borders are in the process of changing.

If the goal of the international community is to reward those who fight by the rules and punish those who do not, assuming that autonomy is an appropriate solution (as opposed to lesser minority rights protection) may unfairly strike a middle course where the "bad guys" belong to the minority. Should we, for example, reward terrorist violence by members of aggrieved groups, even if the government offers reasonable responses to their demands? Once violence occurs, should we require fundamental constitutional changes in a state, rather than merely the guarantee of recognized rights (including minority rights) to all without discrimination? Again, perhaps the answer should depend on the actions of the respective parties in either initiating or responding to violence, not upon nebulous claims of sovereignty or ethnic self-determination.

One goal upon which all could agree is that of protecting human rights, including minority rights, and promoting democracy for all those within a state. Stated differently, these norms would include the protection and promotion of minority identity and the right of minorities to effective participation in government, and certain forms of autonomy may well respond to these goals. At the same time, however, it should not be the goal of outside advocates to resolve internal debates over the disposition of political and economic power according to their own assessment of the situation. The proper concern is rights, not policy, and fixating on autonomy as a one-size-fits-all compromise solution is unlikely to respond to the needs either of the concerned parties or the international community.

In conclusion, autonomy is not a magic bullet that can resolve all conflicts, prevent violence, or guarantee political and economic development. It cannot automatically ensure social justice or bring good things to all people. Autonomy remains a useful concept, but it will be successful only where there is a sufficiently strong willingness to live together, combined with an understanding of which purposes autonomy is—and is not—likely to serve.

NOTES

1. See *Document of the Copenhagen Meeting of the Conference on the Human Dimension of the Conference on Security and Cooperation in Europe* (1990):1305. In paragraph 35 of the document, the participating states merely "note" efforts to promote the identity of national minorities through the establishment of "local or autonomous administrations, corresponding to the specific historical and territorial circumstances of such minorities and in accordance with the policies of the State concerned."

2. Recommendation 1201 (1993) on an additional protocol on the rights of national minorities to the European Convention on Human Rights, Annex, art. 11.

3. Conference on Yugoslavia Arbitration Commission, Opinion No. 2 (1 January 1992), reprinted in *International Legal Materials* 13 (1992):1497. *Uti possidetis* is a principle that was developed during the decolonization process in Latin America and Africa, pursuant to which newly independent states agreed to maintain their colonial borders as new international frontiers. See Ratner (1996).

REFERENCES

Conference on Yugoslavia Arbitration Commission: Opinions on Questions Arising from the Dissolution of Yugoslavia. 1992, January 11 and June 4. *International Legal Materials* 13:1497.

Document of the Copenhagen Meeting of the Conference on the Human Dimension of the Conference on Security and Cooperation in Europe. Adopted 29 June 1990. Reprinted in *International Legal Materials* 29 (1990):1305.

Foundation on Inter-Ethnic Relations. 1999, June. *The Lund Recommendations on the Effective Participation of National Minorities in Public Life & Explanatory Note*. The Hague: Foundation on Inter-Ethnic Relations.

Hannum, Hurst. 1990. *Autonomy, Sovereignty, and Self-Determination: The Accommodation of Conflicting Rights*. Philadelphia: University of Pennsylvania Press.

————. 1993. Self-Determination, Yugoslavia, and Europe: Old Wine in New Bottles? *Transnational Law & Contemporary Problems* 3: 57–69.

Luttwak, Edward. 1999. Give War a Chance. *Foreign Affairs* 78 (2):36–44.

Parliamentary Assembly of the Council of Europe. 1993. Recommendation 1201 (1993) on an Additional Protocol on the Rights of National Minorities to the European Convention on Human Rights Strasbourg.

Ratner, Steven R. 1996. Drawing a Better Line: *Uti Possidetis* and the Borders of New States. *American Journal of International Law* 90:590–624.

Walter, Barbara F. 1997. The Critical Barrier to Civil War Settlement. *International Organization* 51 (3):335–364.

19

❦

Containing
Ethnonationalist
Violence

Michael Hechter

Recent years have witnessed a virtual epidemic of ethnonationalist violence in the world. As a result, much attention of late has been devoted to two questions. Can this violence be contained—say, by adopting particular institutions and policies? And if so, then what might such institutions and policies consist of? The answers to these important questions are unclear, in part because there are fundamental disagreements about the character of ethnonationalist movements. For some observers, ethnonationalism emanates from deep-seated emotions. For others, ethnonationalism results from strategic action.

Why should this dispute about the motivational wellsprings of ethnonationalism matter? The answer is simple. If ethnonationalist violence springs from emotional roots, then decisionmakers can do little, if anything, to contain it. They would have about as much luck containing the destructive forces of ethnonationalism as in blunting the effects of El Niño. If ethnonationalist violence largely springs from rational roots, however, then its course might be affected by institutions that decrease individuals' incentives to participate in it. Therefore, the prospects for containing ethnonationalist violence hinge, in the first place, on the extent to which ethnonationalists are rational and likely to respond to institutional incentives. The first section of this chapter takes up this question. It concludes that much ethnonationalist violence indeed can be regarded as the outcome of rational action.

The next five sections then consider one potential institutional remedy: the relationship between federation and ethnonationalist violence. I argue that even if ethnonationalist violence is largely strategic, this has no

necessary implications for institutional remedies. The final section concludes by summarizing the policy implications of the analysis.

IS ETHNONATIONALIST VIOLENCE RATIONAL?

Consider three examples of ethnonationalist violence culled from different parts of the world. Our itinerary begins in Sri Lanka. In the midst of a
lighthearted celebration of May Day taking place in the city of Colombo
in 1993, a man rushed through the parade toward the marching sixty-
eight-year-old President Premadasa of Sri Lanka and set off explosives
that were attached to his body. The president and his assassin were in-
stantly killed, as were at least ten other people. The government of Sri
Lanka blamed the Tamil Tigers, a rebel group that had waged a ten-year
war of secession in the country's north and east and had used suicide
bombers in the past to kill government and army officials (Gargan 1993).
Whereas such self-sacrifice in the name of an ethnonationalist cause is relatively rare, it is far from unique. For example, Irish Republican Army
hunger strikers in Northern Irish detention centers were willing to pay
the ultimate price on behalf of their own ethnonational movement.
Hamas suicide bombers in Israel effectively set the stage for the victory of
the hard-line Likud Party in the 1996 Israeli elections.

Now move on to the metropolitan heartland—England. Consider the
movie *Patriot Games*, in which two members of the Irish Republican Army
target a prominent British politician for assassination. (Luckily for the distinguished British target, Harrison Ford was lurking in the neighborhood
to make sure that the assassin's best-laid plans would go awry.) Although
this particular story is, of course, a fiction, its main outlines are all too real
(Feldman 1991).

This little tour ends—where else?—in that territory now known as The
Former Yugoslavia. In late October 1992, some of the Croatians who had
fled towns in the Krajina that had been taken by Serb forces returned to
their former homes in the company of United Nations troops. They soon
discovered that Serb gunmen had desecrated the graves of their ancestors.
Serbs had pulled the covers off Croatian tombs and machine-gunned their
remains. Surely this bizarre event must reveal great irrationality; it must
take some very odd passions to make these Serbs waste valuable ammunition on Croats who, after all, were already long dead (Fearon 1994). On
the basis of stories like these, it is no wonder that many observers regard
ethnonationalism as irrational (Birch 1989:67; Smith 1986:363; Horowitz
1985:134–135; Connor 1993:206).

Yet the claim that ethnonationalism is irrational can mean two quite different things. It is obvious that ethnonationalism can be *collectively* irra-

tional, for it is often associated with undesirable social outcomes like economic decline and civil war. Whether such outcomes are the consequence of individual irrationality, however, is questionable. Many undesirable outcomes—like rush-hour traffic, overfishing, and environmental pollution—are by-products of rational action (Kollock 1998).

For this reason, the claim that ethnonationalism may be the product of *individual* irrationality is more provocative. For anthropologist Clifford Geertz (1963:109), ethnonationalists regard congruities of blood, language, and custom as having an ineffable, and at times overpowering, coerciveness in and of themselves. One is bound to one's kinsman, one's neighbor, one's fellow believer ipso facto; as a result not merely of personal affection, practical necessity, common interest, or incurred obligation, but at least in great part by virtue of some unaccountable absolute import attributed to the very tie itself.

The hallmark of rational individual action is its instrumentality. People are rational to the extent they pursue the most efficient means available to attain their most preferred ends. These ends may be material or nonmaterial. Thus people are irrational when they pursue a course of action regardless of its consequences for their personal welfare. This need not condemn altruistic actions to the realm of the irrational if the altruist's own personal welfare is enhanced by her giving. In some circumstances, committing suicide may even be rational, for death can be preferable to a life that promises little but extreme and unremitting physical suffering. Not so, however, for political suicide: It cannot be rational to consider social ties as binding regardless of their consequences for one's own welfare.

Now let's return to the three stories. How can it be rational to knowingly die for a cause, engage in terrorism, or waste ammunition on corpses in a cemetery? Of the three, the Sri Lankan story is the only one that may qualify as unambiguously irrational. This is because at some point suicide bombers know *with certainty* that they will die in carrying out their mission.[1]

By contrast, the Irish Republican Army took pains to minimize risks for its snipers. Even ostensibly individual events like sniper attacks involve elaborate planning and the coordination of many different people—from the gunman, to support staff providing weapons, ammunition, and vehicles, to sympathetic bystanders. Security must be provided to induce rational members to undertake the risky business of carrying out an armed attack (Hechter 1995). Unlike in the Sri Lankan example, the participants here are presumed to be at least somewhat self-interested.

Fair enough, but why would a rational person ever join a treacherous organization like the Irish Republican Army? Whereas it is easy to appreciate that, in certain circumstances, ethnonationalist groups might strategically adopt violent means to attain their goals, is it a mystery to understand why individuals might bear very high risks of injury, punishment, and even death to help bring the collective good of sovereignty to their nation? Not at all.

One might surmise that the use of violent means will tend to attract members who are skilled in violence, and will discourage others who are neither skilled nor interested in it. But there is a deeper reason, as well. To the degree that members are dependent on a highly solidary group that adopts violent means, they may be willing to take great risks.[2] (Much the same can be said of membership in inner-city gangs in North America, or in the Sicilian Mafia.) Risk-taking is not irrational: Wall Street is a magnet for investors' capital, and people have always engaged in risky occupations. Although it is dangerous to build skyscrapers, or to be a police officer or a firefighter, that people can be found to fill these positions is no cause for consternation. The risk of membership in a violent ethnonationalist group is not qualitatively different.

What of the Yugoslav example? An event that on its face seems wildly irrational can also have an instrumental explanation. Fearon (1994) argues that the Serb gunners' behavior was consciously designed to heighten the salience of the boundary between Serbs and Croats. Under Tito's regime, this boundary had been downplayed, and there was considerable social integration (indicated by relatively high rates of exogamy between these two communities). In such a context, desecrating Croat cemeteries had a predictable effect: It instantaneously heightened the salience of the Serb-Croat boundary.

Whereas in the 1980s Serbs carrying symbols of Serbian iconography were treated with contempt even by many fellow Serbs, a decade later, Serbs were punished for their failure to make Serbian their primary social identity. Serbs who clung to their Yugoslav identity were subjected to harsh punishments (Glenny 1993). Serb paramilitary units that swept into multiethnic Bosnian villages first killed those *Serbian* residents who were in favor of ethnic integration. Only later did they turn their attention to non-Serbian residents (Mozjes 1994).

Spending time and effort to desecrate Croat cemeteries is strategic given the knowledge that Croats are bound to regard this behavior as highly threatening—akin to cross burning in the American South. Extremist Serbs, in turn, counted on their ability to predict how Croats would act given this provocation.

So a good deal about the kind of ethnonationalist violence that, on the face of it, seems to be irrational can be plausibly interpreted as an outcome of rational individual action. If ethnonationalist violence is largely, if not wholly, the result of rational action, this suggests that, under certain conditions, it indeed can be contained because rational actors will respond to institutional incentives. If so, then what kinds of institutions can contain it?

INSTITUTIONAL REMEDIES FOR
ETHNONATIONALIST VIOLENCE

Does social theory in general, or rational choice theory in particular, provide an answer to the question about institutional remedies? To be sure, a rational choice theorist can always say that ethnonationalism can be contained by adopting institutions that raise the costs of ethnonationalist violence, decrease its benefits, or both. But this answer is vacuous because *it does not tell us the kinds of institutions that provide the requisite incentives.*

Consider one institution that has long been discussed as a candidate to mitigate intergroup conflict in multinational states—namely, federation. By this, I merely refer to any form of governance in which central authorities incorporate regional units into their decision-making procedures on some constitutional basis. Federation is the outcome of a bargain between rulers of the central state and leaders of its territorial subunits (Riker 1964). As in all bargains, this one only works because it appeals to both parties. Federation enables the territorial subunits to attain some degree of political self-control while profiting from access to the greater resources and military protection that is afforded by membership in large polities. At the same time, the federal bargain offers central rulers a relatively cost-effective means of maintaining their state's territorial integrity.

However, recent events—including the collapse of federations in the Soviet Union, Yugoslavia, and Czechoslovakia, and the continued thirst for secession among the cultural minorities in federations like Canada and Spain—have led many scholars to question the ameliorative effects of political decentralization. These events suggest the very real possibility that, far from inhibiting ethnonationalist conflict, federation instead exacerbates it. Still other observers argue that federation has no determinate effects on ethnonationalist conflict at all. The relationship between federation and ethnonationalist conflict is highly contentious.

WHY FEDERATION COULD INTENSIFY
ETHNONATIONALIST CONFLICT

The causal mechanism responsible for this effect owes to the very nature of federation. Federation diverts some government functions—and hence resources—from the center to territorial subunits. Federation may stimulate ethnonationalist conflict because it provides potential ethnonationalist leaders with patronage and other resources that can be mobilized for ethnonationalist ends. Federation also tends to provide institutional supports for ethnonationalism (Roeder 1991; Meadwell 1993; Treisman 1997; Bunce 1999; Snyder 2000; Hale 2000). In addition to the material incentives to ethnonationalist mobilization that it may provide, federation also may have cognitive implications. When nations are given many of the accoutrements of real states, this also encourages people to think and act according to ethnonational categories (Brubaker 1996). Moreover, federation may be better suited to resolving material differences between units than cultural ones (King 1982:47–48; Watts 1999). All told, federation may provide both material and cognitive supports for ethnonationalist conflict. This view has at least one clear policy implication: *to contain ethnonationalist conflict, local leaders should be offered meaningful, substantial careers in the central government* (Laitin 1998). By this means, ethnonationalist leaders will be transformed from peripheral magnates anxious to drain power from the state into stakeholders committed to upholding it. The historical record provides ample evidence linking federation to ethnonationalist conflict. The U.S. Civil War broke out in a federation; Pakistan—another federation—lost Bangladesh. The only socialist states that dissolved following the climactic year of 1989—the Soviet Union, Czechoslovakia, and Yugoslavia—also just happened to be federations.

Similarly, the recent increase in Quebec's regional authority does not seem to have dampened the fate of the separatist political party. Despite taking over the Quebec government—and the subsequent passing of extensive language legislation protecting French and the Francophones—a near majority of Quebecois voted for separation in 1995. Nor has Spain's devolution of power to the Basque region put its separatist party (Euskadi ta Askatasuna [ETA]) out of business.

WHY FEDERATION COULD INHIBIT
ETHNONATIONALIST CONFLICT

The opposing view is also based on an intuitively appealing causal mechanism. Since federation is a form of indirect rule, it ought to reduce the demand for sovereignty (Hechter 2000). On this account, federation should also serve to mute ethnonationalist conflict.[3] Since nations are by definition culturally distinctive, individual members' values reflect (to some degree) these distinctive ethnonational values. Although members of ethnonational groups share values—minimally, those relating to the attainment of wealth, power, and prestige—in common with all the other inhabitants of a given multinational state, they also share a distinctive set of values derived from their ethnonational culture. Typically, these values include preferences to speak a distinct language and practice a distinct religion.

Governments provide a range of collective goods. Some of these goods—like defense—are universally valued by inhabitants. Others—

like education in a particular language, and state support for a particular religion—appeal to only a portion of the state's inhabitants. Whereas some universally valued goods may better be provided centrally, goods that are valued only by a segment of the society are better provided locally (Oates 1972). Local provision of these goods is superior because it increases the likelihood that the right mix of goods will be produced—the mix that is most congruent with the distinctive values of the ethnonational group.[4] As federation involves the devolution of (at least some) decision making to localities, it increases local self-governance. To the degree that at least some of the units in a federal system constitute nations, federation should have the effect of inhibiting ethnonationalism. Since sovereignty is neither more nor less than self-governance, it follows that to the degree federation increases a nation's self-governance, its demand for sovereignty must be correspondingly reduced.[5]

This reasoning implies that the less self-governance a nation has in a multinational state, the greater the possibility of ethnonationalist conflict; Gurr (2000) claims that this trend has described ethnonationalist conflict during the 1990s. Assuming that nations make up at least some of the constituent local or state subunits in a multinational polity, then the greater the powers of the central government relative to those of state and local governments, the greater the ethnonationalist conflict. A constitution that minimizes the state's control over disposable, transferable revenue and rights presents a very small target for ethnonationalists. It stands to reason that local politicians are less likely to play the ethnonationalist card when their constituents see less benefit in sovereignty. This view has quite a different policy implication: To contain ethnonationalism, *the central rulers of multinational states ought to grant political devolution to mobilized ethnonational minorities.*

In spite of the apparent failures of federation alluded to above, this argument also commands ample supportive case study evidence. Many central rulers have turned to federation as a means of reducing ethnonationalist discontent, and they continue to do so. Britain's recent offer of devolution to Scotland and Wales was welcomed by voters in both lands; further, the more thoroughgoing devolution in Scotland was more enthusiastically supported than its relatively anemic Welsh counterpart. Spain and Belgium have recently undergone significant constitutional moves from unity toward federation as a means of resolving ethnonational conflicts (Forsythe 1989), and even France—traditionally, the archetypal unitary state—has granted Corsica a certain amount of devolution (Savigear 1989). In the Spanish, Belgian, and British cases, very significant powers have been granted to the relevant subunits. Federation in Switzerland has been widely celebrated (McGarry and O'Leary 1993:31; Smith 1995: 4). Finally, the federal United States has experienced little in the way of ethnonationalist conflict since the Civil War (Glazer 1977). This evidence suggests that federation may indeed mute, if not inhibit, ethnonationalist conflict.

There is yet a third view of these matters. Some scholars claim that nothing general can be said about the effects of decentralization at all because it can occur on a practically infinite number of dimensions (King 1982). Centralization of expenditure may be the key factor, rather than political decentralization. Much depends on the precise nature of the governing institutions (Habermas 1994), especially the party system. Whereas these caveats derive from the historical record, there are also theoretical reasons why decentralization may not have a determinate effect on ethnonationalism. Instead, ethnonationalism may result from path-dependent contingencies that cumulate into "reputational cascades" (Kuran 1998). Moreover, when a cultural minority gains sovereignty from a multinational state, this may not lead to an end to ethnonational conflict. On the contrary, since few if any territories on the face of the earth are really culturally homogeneous, secession may well provoke novel ethnonationalist claims (which Hall [1993] refers to as "matrioshka ethnonationalisms") on the part of minorities in the newly constituted states (Brubaker 1998). On this third view, therefore, *neither systematic co-optation of local leaders nor devolution ought to have determinate effects on the containment of ethnonationalist conflict.*

Each of these rival views is grounded in a plausible causal mechanism and is consistent with at least some of the relevant empirical evidence. Finally, these views cannot be distinguished on purely theoretical grounds, for each can be derived from the same instrumental motivational assumptions.

Is there any relationship at all between federation and ethnonationalist conflict? If so, what might its nature be?

SOME NEW EVIDENCE

Until recently, there was no means of assessing the proposition that local decision making decreases ethnonationalist conflict. Now, however, two different sources of evidence can be merged to shed some light on the question. The first, *Minorities at Risk*, consists of a large cross-ethnonational data set based on newspaper reports of ethnonationalist conflict since 1970 (Gurr 1993). These data contain variables describing various types of collective action carried out by ethnonational groups, as well as measures of the various conditions these groups face in their host states. The second consists of a cross-ethnonational data set on *Government Finance Statistics* collected by the International Monetary Fund that documents the degree to which government revenues and expenditures are centralized in a large number of countries (International Monetary Fund, various years).

Ethnonationalist conflict is measured by two indicators of antiregime activity—*rebellion* (including political banditry, terrorist campaigns, guerrilla activity, and protracted civil war) and *protest* (including expressions of verbal opposition, symbolic rebellion, and demonstrations). These indicators characterize the mean level of rebellion and protest events for all the ethnically distinct groups in a given state.

Although there are many different types of centralization, fiscal centralization is key, for any decentralization that occurs without granting budgetary power to a subunit is well-nigh hollow. The *Government Finance Statistics* data set contains four variables that indicate the degree of fiscal centralization in each country (International Monetary Fund, various years). These indicate the revenue collected and expenditures made by each level of government in every country by year.

Using these measures, new light is cast on the relationship between decentralization and ethnonationalism (Hechter and Takahashi 1999).

- Centralization indeed does have a significant effect on ethnonationalist collective action.
- Protest and rebellion events behave quite differently in these data. Although centralization is positively associated with rebellion events, it is negatively associated with protest.

This suggests a possible reconciliation of the two opposing arguments in the literature. Whereas decentralization may provide cultural minorities with greater resources to engage in collective action leading to a rise in protest events, at the same time it may erode the demand for sovereignty. Since secession is always an uncertain prospect, and groups tend to be more averse to uncertainty than individuals, this decrease in the demand for sovereignty ought to reduce the incidence of ethnonationalist rebellion.

If ethnonationalist groups engage in violent tactics as a means of pursuing sovereignty, then rebellion should be more likely to occur among groups with the greatest opportunity to attain this end (McAdam et al. 1996). Groups concentrated in territories that already have their own governance structures—such as American states, Canadian provinces, or French *départements*—can make a more plausible demand for sovereignty than groups concentrated in regions lacking a governance structure.[6]

To determine if this logic holds, the rebellion indicators from the *Minorities at Risk* data set were reconstructed by excluding all nonspatially concentrated groups, as well as those concentrated groups whose territory does not coincide with some intermediate-level political boundary.[7] The countries in bold italic have at least one minority group that is concentrated in a region with its own governance structure, while countries in regular font lack such a group. By revealing that centralization has a positive effect on ethnonationalist rebellion, figure 19.1 suggests that federation may hold the promise of containing ethnonationalist violence.

These results should not be overinterpreted, however. Fiscal centralization is an indirect indicator of local decision making, and both the meaningfulness and comparability of measures of fiscal centralization have been questioned (Bird 1986). Further, due to data limitations, the number of countries in the analysis is relatively small. This is far from a representative sample of states. Despite these caveats, the consistency of the results is notable across three decades of recent history.

Yet two questions remain. First, since most of the violent ethnonationalism during the 1980s occurs in less developed countries—such as Uganda, the Philippines, and Indonesia—is the relationship in figure 19.1 merely an artifact of the overall level of economic development? On the one hand, people may be less inclined to take action against central governments in rich states because they have more to lose from the resulting disorder. On the other, since democracy may be associated with economic development, so, perhaps, is fiscal decentralization. Further analysis reveals, however, that the relationship holds even when each country's gross domestic product per capita is controlled (Hechter and Takahashi 1999).

Second, how robust is the relationship? There is at least one reason to wonder. Yugoslavia's placement in the extreme southwestern part of the scatterplot for the decade of the 1980s would seem to imply that this should be the country that is most *immune* to ethnonationalist rebellion. Yet in the very next decade, the country was plunged into a severe and prolonged civil war and the term "ethnic cleansing" entered the English vocabulary. If, as figure 19.1 suggests, ethnonationalism is contained by political decentralization, then how can Yugoslavia's trajectory be accounted for?

Whereas federation inhibits ethnonationalist rebellion, it stimulates ethnonationalist protest. Herein lies a quandary. Federation is a spur to mobilization among minority nations, for it places greater resources (especially government jobs) in the hands of ethnonational leaders. So long as these leaders see a benefit in remaining part of the host state, federation ought to contain ethnonationalist rebellion. If the central state implodes, however, due to military defeat or fiscal crisis, then it has less to offer peripheral leaders and the prospect of fragmentation becomes more likely. This is what happened in the Soviet Union, which split apart on ethnonational grounds in a bloodless revolution.

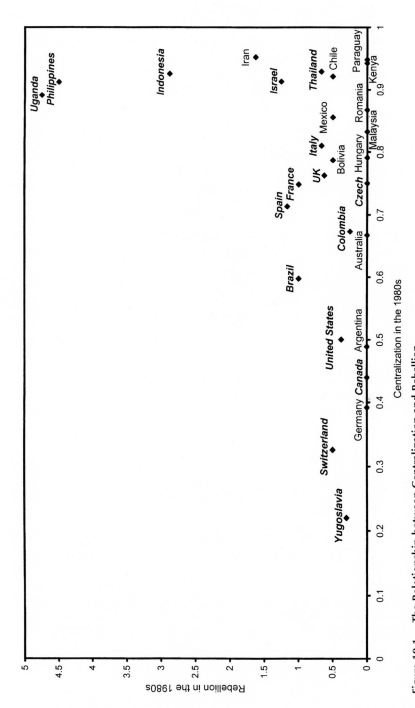

Figure 19.1. The Relationship between Centralization and Rebellion

Source: Hechter (2000).

Note: Bold-italic countries have at least one group that is concentrated in one region and "formally recognized."

The discussion of federation and ethnonationalist conflict heretofore has been based on the implicit premise that the key dynamics are endogenous to existing political boundaries. But that premise is questionable: Time and again, ethnonationalism has been strongly affected by exogenous forces. A country that decentralizes as a means of containing ethnonationalist violence is at risk of *fragmenting* when its center declines due to exogenous shocks such as military defeat or fiscal crisis. This was Yugoslavia's sorry fate.

FEDERATION AND FRAGMENTATION IN YUGOSLAVIA

From 1948 through 1991, Yugoslavia had managed to contain ethnonationalism, despite the disparate interests of its various republics (Woodward 1995). The country was held together by a constitutional order enforced by the resources of the central (federal) state that was explicitly designed to mitigate conflict between its constituent nations. This constitution aimed to provide equality among republics, as well as security for ethnonational minorities within each republic. Its goal was to prevent any single ethnonational group from gaining political dominance over the state. Federal policy depended on cooperation from republican leaders, who had the capacity to veto any decision.

All federal activities were required to take the proportional representation of individuals by constituent ethnonationality into account. Ethnonationalities were also guaranteed freedom of cultural expression. Individuals retained their ethnonational right to self-governance even if they lived outside their home nation's republic, and the choice of an ethnonational identity was voluntary. The manifestation of ethnonationalism, however, was regarded as a threat to the social order and outlawed.

As a socialist state, Yugoslavia guaranteed its citizens subsistence, and central and local governments shared responsibility for individual welfare. Public sector employment was the primary source of living standards. The economy was sustained by substantial amounts of foreign aid, largely from the United States, as well as access to foreign credit and capital markets. The basis of this exogenous support was geopolitical, and owed to the regime's neutrality during the Cold War.

During the 1980s, however, a deadly combination of exogenous economic and political shocks weakened the central government's ability to maintain this constitutional order. Yugoslavia shared in the worldwide economic recession of the 1980s. To revive economic growth, the government appealed for assistance from the International Monetary Fund and similar bodies. Some assistance was offered, but only on the basis of commitments that the central government would enact policies promoting economic privatization and cut public expenditures for welfare, public employment, and social services. The government accepted these conditions, but, as a result, living standards began to decline. Unemployment and inflation soared. By requiring constitutional revision, the debt-repayment regime turned normal disputes between central and regional governments into constitutional conflicts. The republics best able to adapt to the economic and political reforms of the debt-repayment package—Slovenia and Croatia—sought increasing autonomy from the center. Those that were disadvantaged by these reforms argued for recentralization. The upshot was a constitutional crisis that was carried out between republican leaders seeking to enhance their control over economic and political resources within their territories.

Many other countries faced austerity measures in the 1980s but did not suffer Yugoslavia's fate. Yugoslavia had the misfortune of being the only multinational state that faced another kind of exogenous shock. The central government's ability to withstand peripheral ethnonationalism was dealt a severe blow by the abrupt and unanticipated end of the Cold War. Yugoslavia had profited greatly from its neutrality in the Cold War. The demise of the Soviet Union sharply decreased the country's strategic value to the United States, however. It also ended forty years of American-backed guarantees of financial assistance and support for Yugoslav independence and integrity.

This combination of exogenous economic and political shocks so weakened the central government that its ability to contain ethnonationalism was effectively destroyed. Although the center attempted to prevent the secession of Slovenia and Croatia by force, it no longer had sufficient resources to prevail. Here, too, exogenous forces played a significant role; Germany's recognition of the sovereignty of Slovenia and Croatia spelled Yugoslavia's final chapter. Once the constitutional guarantees for minority rights were null and void, there was little to restrain intergroup violence.

At least two important lessons can be learned from the Yugoslav case. On the one hand, its complex decentralized constitutional provisions managed to contain ethnonationalism for four decades; this is no mean feat. Whereas the constitution was designed to keep the country territorially intact, its extreme decentralization made it difficult for the center to adapt to exogenous economic shifts. On the other, the Yugoslav federation relied too heavily on the country's strategic position in the Cold War. When—against all expectations—the Cold War ended, the center's resource base was substantially diminished. Clearly, decentralization can proceed so far that it courts fragmentation, which can be another source of intergroup violence. The relationship between decentralization and ethnonationalist violence, therefore, is likely to be U-shaped rather than linear. *If too little decentralization causes rebellion, then too much is likely to engender fragmentation.* To contain ethnonationalist violence, thus, a balance must be struck between peripheral regions—dependence on the center for military and economic resources, and the autonomy that allows those outside the center to pursue their own cultural and economic interests. Whereas federation is no panacea for ethnonationalist violence in relatively centralized states, it does offer substantial hope for mitigating ethnonationalism's dark side.[8]

CONCLUSION

Containing ethnonationalist violence is a pressing social issue in the contemporary world. If this kind of violence largely emerges from irrational roots, then there is little hope of containing it. I have argued, however, that the preponderance of ethnonationalist violence seems to have strategic roots, and therefore can be regarded as the outcome of individually rational action. This means that certain kinds of social institutions can provide incentives that have the potential to contain ethnonationalist violence. But what kinds of institutions will do the trick? General theory can tell us little about the answer to this key question. Theorists fundamentally disagree about the effects of federation on ethnonationalism: Some think that federation will exacerbate it, others think it will inhibit it. The best available evidence shows that whereas federation stimulates ethnonationalist political mobilization, it tends to decrease ethnonationalist violence, at least under certain conditions. Ultimately, the resort to federation in multinational states is a gamble.

- It only curbs ethnonationalist violence when central authorities retain sufficient resources to provide security and welfare to regional subunits.
- Central resources have to be deployed strategically to reward loyalty to regions that otherwise are most likely to secede.

The federal gamble, therefore, is more likely to pay off in economically developed countries than in less developed ones (figure 19.1 lends this conclusion some supportive evidence).

This suggests that to contain ethnonationalist violence in federal states, central authorities must retain sufficient resources to induce the loyalty of federal subunits.

By emphasizing belt-tightening ("structural readjustment") measures that reduce the largesse of central authorities, the fiscal policies of key third parties—like the International Monetary Fund and World Bank—

have often had the unintended effect of weakening central authorities.[9] In the past, these policies have stimulated ethnonationalist violence, and there is little reason to doubt that they will continue to do so in the future.

All told, this chapter suggests that ethnonationalist violence is subject to at least some containment by dint of proper institutional design. This is because the members of ethnonational groups have distinctive interests, and these interests can be more or less satisfied by particular governance institutions and state policies. This is an optimistic conclusion, at least for everyone interested in containing ethnonationalism's dark side.

NOTES

This chapter is a revised version of "Nationalism and Rationality," published in September 2000 in *Studies in Comparative International Development* 35 (1):3–19.

1. Can the political suicide carried out by young Tamil Tigers be considered to be a rational act? There is no hard and fast answer because there is an ongoing debate among social scientists about the status of beliefs in rational action. Some writers insist, with Pareto, that an agent must have scientifically valid beliefs to act rationally (Elster 1989). On this view, all action that owes to faith or religious belief is irrational. Since scientific research is based on metaphysical premises about the existence of an ordered universe, it too would have to be considered as irrational by a true-blue Paretian. Others hew to a more subjective conception of rational action (Boudon 1996). On this view, political suicide is rational if agents have a firm conviction that they will be adequately compensated in the hereafter. This raises other questions, however. Should we consider paranoid schizophrenics who dress like Napoleon to be rational as well? Hardly, but why not? Popper's (1994) idea that rational people must show a readiness to revise their beliefs in the face of much contrary evidence provides one possible answer. Since it is the most intellectually conservative option, in this chapter I choose to regard political suicide as irrational.

2. By definition, the members of highly solidary groups contribute a relatively high proportion of their individual resources to help further the group's ends (Hechter 1987:18).

3. Other mechanisms have also been proposed in the literature. Thus Horowitz (1985:614) argues that by moving the locus of intergroup conflict from the center to the federal subunit, ethnofederation serves to reduce ethnonationalism. The advantages that federation confers are far from costless, however; according to Breton and Scott, "The more decentralized a state is, the more the coordination or negotiation that will have to be carried on between the different jurisdictions. Therefore, the total cost of coordination increases as the degree of decentralization increases" (Breton and Scott 1980:xvi–xvii).

4. There are few empirical studies of the effect of ethnic diversity on the provision of public goods. One of the best of these analyzes variation in the provision of public goods among the American states. Although ethnically diverse jurisdictions in the United States have higher spending and deficits per capita than ethnically

homogeneous ones, these diverse jurisdictions devote lower shares of spending to core public goods like education and roads. This finding suggests that ethnically heterogeneous societies value public goods less, value patronage more, and are collectively careless about fiscal discipline (Alesina et al. 1999:1274).

5. In this respect, it should be noted that surveys indicate that federation is even popular among the inhabitants of regions that are culturally similar to state cores. Thus, popular support for sub-ethnonational governments (*Länder*) in Germany has risen steeply since their introduction in 1949, and it is on the rise in Italy (Putnam 1994:59). Despite a sharp decline in survey measures of Americans' trust in their central government in the past thirty years, trust in state and local governments has remained at high levels (Jennings 1998).

6. This contention is supported by empirical analyses of the determinants of secessionism in Russia and Eastern Europe (Beissinger 1996; Treisman 1997; Hale 2000).

7. The groups included in the analysis are Amazonian Indians in Brazil; Quebecois in Canada; indigenous peoples in Colombia; Slovaks in Czechoslovakia; Basques in France; Papuans, Chinese, and East Timorese in Indonesia; Palestinians in Israel; South Tyrolians and Sardinians in Italy; Igorots in the Philippines; Basques and Catalans in Spain; Jurassians in Switzerland; Malay-Muslims in Thailand; Acholi and Baganda in Uganda; Scots in the United Kingdom; Native Americans in the United States; and Hungarians in Yugoslavia.

8. Thus, the Russian Federation avoided further fragmentation in the early 1990s by adopting a policy of selective fiscal appeasement, which garnered electoral support for central authorities (Treisman 1999). Those territories most at risk of seceding were provided with tax breaks and other fiscal incentives; these, however, were not made available to less restive territories.

9. Structural readjustment policies have been blamed for a multitude of sins, but to my knowledge this is not one of them.

REFERENCES

Alesina, Alberto, Reza Baqir, and William Easterly. 1999. Public Goods and Ethnic Divisions. *The Quarterly Journal of Economics* 114:1243–1284.

Beissinger, Mark R. 1996. How Nationalisms Spread: Eastern Europe Adrift in the Tides and Cycles of Nationalism Contention. *Social Research* 63:97–146.

Birch, Anthony H. 1989. *Nationalism and National Integration*. London: Unwin Hyman.

Bird, R. M. 1986. On Measuring Fiscal Centralization and Fiscal Balance in Federal States. *Environment and Planning, C: Government and Policy* 4:389–404.

Boudon, Raymond. 1996. The "Cognitivist Model": A Generalized Rational-Choice Model. *Rationality and Society* 8:123–150.

Breton, Albert, and Anthony Scott. 1980. *The Design of Federations*. Montreal: The Institute for Research on Public Policy.

Brubaker, Rogers. 1996. *Nationalism Reframed: Nationhood and the National Question in the New Europe*. Cambridge: Cambridge University Press.

———. 1998. Myths and Misconceptions in the Study of Ethnonationalism. In *The State of the Nation: Ernest Gellner and the Theory of Nationalism*, ed. John A. Hall, 272–306. Cambridge: Cambridge University Press.

Bunce, Valerie. 1999. *Subversive Institutions: The Design and the Destruction of Socialism and the State*. New York: Cambridge University Press.

Connor, Walker. 1993. *Ethnonationalism*. Princeton, NJ: Princeton University Press.

Elster, Jon. 1989. *The Cement of Society*. Cambridge: Cambridge University Press.

Fearon, James D. 1994, September. *Ethnic War as a Commitment Problem*. Paper presented at the annual meeting of the American Political Science Association, New York.

Feldman, Allen. 1991. *Formations of Violence*. Chicago: University of Chicago Press.

Forsythe, Diana. 1989. German Identity and the Problem of History. In *History and Ethnicity*, ed. Elizabeth Tonkin, Malcolm Chapman, and Maryon McDonald, 137–156. London: Routledge.

Gargan, Edward A. 1993, May 2. Suicide Bomber Kills President of Sri Lanka. *New York Times*, 1.

Geertz, Clifford. 1963. The Integrative Revolution: Primordial Sentiments and Civil Politics in the New States. In *Old Societies and New States*, ed. Clifford Geertz, 105–158. Glencoe, IL: Free Press.

Glazer, Nathan. 1977. Federalism and Ethnicity: The Experience of the United States. *Publius* 7:71–87.

Glenny, Misha. 1993. *The Fall of Yugoslavia*. New York: Penguin Books.

Gurr, Ted Robert. 1993. *Minorities at Risk: A Global View of Ethnopolitical Conflicts*. Washington, DC: U.S. Institute of Peace Press.

———. 2000. Ethnic Warfare on the Wane. *Foreign Affairs* 79:52–64.

Habermas, Jürgen. 1994. Citizenship and National Identity. In *The Condition of Citizenship*, ed. Bart van Steenbergen, 20–35. London: Sage.

Hale, Henry E. 2000. The Parade of Sovereignties: Testing Theories of Secession in the Soviet Setting. *British Journal of Political Science* 30:31–56.

Hall, John A. 1993. Nationalisms: Classified and Explained. *Daedalus* 122:1–28.

Hechter, Michael. 1987. *Principles of Group Solidarity*. Berkeley: University of California Press.

———. 1995. Explaining Nationalist Violence. *Nations and Nationalism* 1:53–68.

———. 2000. *Containing Nationalism*. Oxford: Oxford University Press.

Hechter, Michael, and Nobuyuki Takahashi. 1999, August. *Political Decentralization and Nationalist Conflict*. Paper presented at the annual meeting of the American Sociological Association, Chicago.

Horowitz, Donald L. 1985. *Ethnic Groups in Conflict*. Berkeley: University of California Press.

International Monetary Fund. Various years. *Government Finance Statistics*. Washington, DC: International Monetary Fund.

Jennings, M. Kent. 1998. Political Trust and the Roots of Devolution. In *Trust and Governance*, ed. Valerie Braithwaite and Margaret Levi, 218–244. New York: Kaiser Russell Sage Foundation.

King, Preston. 1982. *Federalism and Federation*. London: Croom Helm.

Kollock, Peter. 1998. Social Dilemmas: The Anatomy of Cooperation. *Annual Review of Sociology* 24:183–214.

Kuran, Timur. 1998. Ethnic Norms and Their Transformation through Reputational Cascades. *Journal of Legal Studies* 27:623–660.

Laitin, David D. 1998. *Identity in Formation: The Russian-Speaking Populations in the Near Abroad*. Ithaca, NY: Cornell University Press.

McAdam, Doug, John D. McCarthy, and Mayer N. Zald. 1996. *Comparative Perspectives on Social Movements: Political Opportunities, Mobilizing Structures, and Cultural Framings*. Cambridge: Cambridge University Press.

McGarry, J., and Brendan O'Leary, eds. 1993. *The Politics of Ethnic Conflict Regulation*. London: Routledge.

Meadwell, Hudson. 1993. The Politics of Nationalism in Quebec. *World Politics* 45: 203–241.

Mozjes, Paul. 1994. *Yugoslavian Inferno: Ethnoreligious War in the Balkans*. New York: Continuum.

Oates, Wallace E. 1972. *Fiscal Federalism*. New York: Harcourt Brace Jovanovich.

Popper, Karl R. 1994. Models, Instruments and Truth. In *The Myth of the Framework: In Defence of Science and Rationality*, ed. Karl R. Popper, 154–184. London: Routledge.

Putnam, Robert D., with Robert Leonardi and Raffaella Y. Nanetti. 1994. *Making Democracy Work: Civic Traditions in Modern Italy*. Princeton, NJ: Princeton University Press.

Riker, William H. 1964. *Federalism: Origin, Operation, Significance*. Boston: Little-Brown.

Roeder, Philip G. 1991. Soviet Federalism and Ethnic Mobilization. *World Politics* 43: 196–233.

Savigear, Peter. 1989. Autonomy and the Unitary State: The Case of Corsica. In *Federalism and Nationalism*, ed. Murray Forsyth, 96–114. Leicester, UK: Leicester University Press.

Smith, Anthony D. 1986. *The Ethnic Origins of Nations*. Oxford: Blackwell.

Smith, Graham. 1995. Mapping the Federal Condition: Ideology, Political Practice and Social Justice. In *Federalism: The Multiethnic Challenge*, ed. Graham Smith, 1–28. London: Longman.

Snyder, Jack L. 2000. *From Voting to Violence: Democratization and Nationalist Conflict*. New York: W. W. Norton.

Treisman, Daniel S. 1997. Russia's "Ethnic Revival": The Separatist Activism of Regional Leaders in a Postcommunist Order. *World Politics* 49:212–249.

———. 1999. *After the Deluge: Regional Crises and Political Consolidation in Russia*. Ann Arbor: University of Michigan Press.

Watts, Ronald L. 1999. *Comparing Federal Systems*. Kingston, Ontario: Institute of Intergovernmental Relations, Queen's University.

Woodward, Susan L. 1995. *Balkan Tragedy: Chaos and Dissolution after the Cold War*. Washington, DC: Brookings Institution.

20

🎔

Decentralized Governance in Fragmented Societies: Solution or Cause of New Evils?

Walter Kälin

How can peace and prosperity be achieved in multi-ethnic societies where minority conflicts endanger the security of the country or even jeopardize its very existence? To what extent do federalism and other forms of decentralized governance contribute to accomplishing this goal, or are they an important cause of the problem? This short chapter attempts to answer this question first by restating the familiar thesis that in fact decentralized governance contributes in crucial ways to the resolution of minority conflicts, then by developing the antithesis that such arrangements often are the very cause of the problem, and finally by concluding with an attempt to synthesize the two positions. This is done from a constitutional law perspective, that is, from a position that focuses on basic legal principles underlying the organization and governance of a state. In this context, the concept of "decentralized governance" is used as a notion covering all forms of so-called political decentralization, that is, of organizational setups allowing for the existence of subnational units that exercise their own governmental authority over a certain territory and its population regarding specific matters and, in doing so, enjoy a certain degree of political, administrative, and fiscal autonomy. Decentralized governance, in this sense, can take many forms. It covers, for example, not only federalism in the strict sense of the word, but also arrangements like autonomous regions, districts or municipalities, and communes, but not administrative deconcentration where decision-making power is delegated to local representatives of the central government or forms of privatization.

In the following discussion, the term "minority" will be used in a specific sense: Ethnic, linguistic, and/or religious groups can be called minorities if they, on their own, are unable to dominate the rest of a population. Excluding from the definition any quantitative element such as being small or being smaller than the majority has the advantage of making the notion applicable to countries like Switzerland or Bosnia-Herzegovina, where it is difficult to define the majority in a positive sense and where everyone, to a certain extent, belongs to a minority. Minority thus denotes a specific group that is distinct from others, regardless of its absolute or relative size, if it is not dominant at the national level.

THESIS: DECENTRALIZED GOVERNANCE AS AN OPPORTUNITY IN SITUATIONS OF MINORITY CONFLICTS

Why are federalism and other forms of decentralized government important for the protection of minorities? One could argue that such solutions are not necessary where human rights are protected and democracy is alive. Strict observance of *human rights* is, in fact, of paramount importance for the protection of ethnic, linguistic, or religious minorities. Individuals have nothing to fear if they do not suffer discrimination on grounds of their origin or membership in a particular minority; if they have access to food and health services; and if they can speak their language, exercise their religion, and carry out their cultural traditions, despite the fact that others in the country use a different language or belong to a different religion and culture. If, in addition, their life and security are not threatened by the majority, there is no apparent reason for engaging in a conflict with others. However, we know that traditional concepts of human rights protection, because of their individualistic orientation, sometimes fail to respond to the specific needs of minority groups (Kymlicka 1995:35–48). Thus, for instance, members of minorities are bound by national legislation exactly like anybody else in the country and these laws may not respond to their specific needs, for example, not take into account that certain legal provisions perfectly acceptable for the majority may undermine certain cultural traditions of the minority. In addition, the effect of human rights is often limited to the duty of the state to remain passive and neutral vis-à-vis minorities and to refrain from any interference with their affairs; they do not, per se, grant effective participation in governmental affairs and access to political power.

Democratic Self-Government

This last remark explains why *democracy* is often regarded as a necessary element of human rights protection. However, there are many forms of democracy and not all of them are responsive to minorities. Traditionally, democracy is identified with the principle that the majority rules. "Majoritarian" forms of democracy rest on the assumption that majorities can change. Thus, power is limited in time: If the preferences of voters change, the political majority of yesterday becomes the minority of today and the government changes. However, there is a real risk that power resting on the will of the majority only will be abused, as those who hold the majority do not have to share their power. As pointed out by Linder, this model is detrimental to the interests of ethnic, religious, and linguistic minorities because even if there are political changes within that majority, there is little chance that they affect the predicament of the minority in a positive way (Linder 1994:170).

Where a minority is "structural" in the sense that its members cannot give up their common traits for unalterable reasons (e.g., race or history) or only at the price of losing their cultural identity (e.g., language or religion), it might suffer despite democracy. The government, regardless of the political party (or parties) in power, may disregard the specific needs and interests of structural minorities because such groups are not in a position to challenge the power of the political majority. Furthermore, the fact that structural minorities have no chance of accessing political power may alienate them from mainstream culture and majority politics and incite them to opt for separation (Linder 1994:170).

While it is true that minority conflicts are especially violent in countries ruled by undemocratic and authoritarian regimes, these two reasons explain why minority conflicts are also found in states with democratically elected governments that respect internationally guaranteed human rights to a very large extent. With this in mind, it is necessary to explore the specific advantages of federalism and other forms of decentralization for minorities.

One of the biggest advantages of decentralized governance is the possibility provided to minorities to rule themselves, at least to a certain extent. As Thürer has stressed, this transfer of "decision-making power to autonomous units . . . facilitate[s] the possibility for people belonging to minorities to identify with state institutions, to adequately express their will and to shape their way of life" and thus "to influence those matters which concern them most directly" (Thürer 1995:68). Of course, this is only true if members of a given minority have a majority on a local level. In this case, federalism and other forms of decentralization confer religious, linguistic, or political autonomy to such minorities on a territorial basis (Fleiner-Gerster 1987:407), thus granting them the right to be free as a collective and to safeguard traditions that are important for their ethnic identity (Duchacek 1979:59–69; Kälin 1993:16). The right of citizens to participate in decision-making procedures on a local level helps build a sense of community and furthers true democracy (Henkin 1987:392).

Protection of Fundamental Rights

One advantage of federalism is its role as an instrument to strengthen fundamental rights. In this regard, Henkin has correctly stated that "in many countries, the autonomy granted to local units is designed to assure self-determination and the rights of minorities and their members against abuse by national majorities" (Henkin 1987:392). The idea that subnational self-government promotes individual liberties is deeply rooted in many decentralized countries. Liberty and fundamental rights are also better protected in that the local-level administration can be more accessible for the average person and thus more "human" than a very distant and mighty central administration (Fleiner-Gerster 1987:67).

Minorities can profit from these circumstances. If they live within a specific territory, decentralization offers them the possibility of making their own decisions and fostering their own traditions. In Switzerland, for example, the federalist system has allowed for the survival of all its traditional languages and local cultural traditions. Its federalism is one of the main reasons for the cultural, economic, and political diversity of Switzerland. Federalism has also helped to overcome century-old tensions between different religious and language groups that in the past have repeatedly caused unrest and even civil wars. Similar considerations have also made decentralized government attractive as a model for formerly more centralized states that have minorities with distinct cultural or linguistic concentrations. Autonomy for Catalonians in Spain and for Bretons and Corsicans in France, for instance, has helped to reduce violent conflicts.

Decentralization in these countries offers the possibility of restoring group autonomy lost as a result of centralization (Henkin and Rosenthal 1990:20) and, at the same time, contributes to safeguarding and strengthening internal peace.

Separation of Powers

Finally, a decentralized form of government may also guarantee greater freedom and democracy because it introduces a type of control over central government: The distribution of power to different levels of government and the competition between these levels allows for a system of checks and balances that is likely to set limits on the central government if it attempts to overstep or abuse its powers. Thus, decentralized government constitutes a specific and extended expression of the basic constitutional principle of the separation of powers (Higuchi 1987:25). In federal states, this territorial separation of powers was traditionally "a means of ensuring that sub-national interests would not be subordinated to the national will . . . [and] of preventing the concentration of power in a few hands" (Paddison 1985:100). Because governmental power is distributed among several political units, no single unit can have a monopoly over the use of coercive state power.

ANTITHESIS: DECENTRALIZATION AS A DANGER IN SITUATIONS OF MINORITY CONFLICTS

Not everyone agrees that decentralized governance, per se, helps in finding appropriate solutions in situations of ethnic conflicts. Remembering the fate of such states as the former USSR, the former Yugoslavia, or even the former Czechoslovakia, which were all based on the idea of a union of constituent entities but fell apart, and recalling the many failures of federalism and other forms of decentralized governance in Africa (Basta and Ibrahim 2000), one must raise the question as to whether decentralized governance really is an answer to the challenge of multi-ethnic or multinational states. The same is true as one looks at the dire situation of such decentralized states as the present Federal Republic of Yugoslavia or Bosnia-Herzegovina. There are three important arguments that can be advanced against the cause of federalism and other forms of decentralized governance:

1. *The danger of separatism.* Giving autonomy to lower levels of the state may endanger the unity of the state. In fact, every federal state is confronted with centrifugal forces that are an integral part of federalism itself and that push toward the dissolution of the state. As the examples of the former USSR and the former Yugoslavia show, such forces may, in many cases, lead to its disintegration into many small, independent states. Similarly, "In many African countries, the word federalism is viewed with suspicion. Federalism is seen as a dangerous instrument that can be used to destroy national unity" (Basta and Ibrahim 2000:7). The basis for this fear is the fact that decentralized forms of governance not only weaken the control of the central government over all parts of the country but also grant ethnic groups and other minorities a platform and the means to organize themselves politically.
2. *Ethnic legitimatization as a source of new conflicts.* If federalism and other forms of decentralized governance are based on the idea that ethnic groups should have their own subnational governments allowed to exercise not only administrative but also political power over the population on their territory, ethnicity becomes the main factor legitimating those governments (Basta and Fleiner 1996). This creates problems especially in states that are based on the idea that not all the citizens of the particular country but only the members of

a certain national group are founders of that state. An example is provided by Serbia's 1990 Constitution, which declares in its preamble that "Serbia is the democratic State of the Serbian people" (Basta 1998:8). Where the source of legitimacy of the state is ethnicity, the introduction of regional or local governments for minority groups may cause new problems. In such a context, granting ethnic minorities autonomy and self-government must reinforce separatist tendencies because their regional or local governments will (for good reasons) argue that as a minority, they never will fully belong to that state as long as it is based on the ethnicity of the majority. Another, even more serious problem is the fact that ethnicity-based subnational governments exacerbate minority problems whenever they are unable to integrate or even tolerate persons on their territory who are of a different ethnic origin. Thus, decentralized forms of governance may become a danger for the individual rights and the possibilities of democratic participation of persons belonging to other minorities or to the ethnic group that has the majority at the national level. This is not just a question of a lack of tolerance but also a consequence of a logic based on ethnicity as the main criterion of all social interactions and political relations. Therefore, decentralized forms of governance may not solve but rather may reinforce and perpetuate the very causes of many of today's ethnic conflicts.

3. *Internal oppression.* Closely related to the issues just mentioned is the experience that autonomy and self-government for ethnic groups and similar minorities may protect them as a group, but that more freedom and democracy in their external relationships does not necessarily ensure the same for members of the group at the internal level. If, by allowing a minority to govern itself, ethnicity is recognized as the cornerstone of group identity, the danger becomes real that much pressure is exercised on those members of the group who do not share an ethnocentric worldview or who have different ideas about what constitutes the group identity. Such persons, thus, may become victims of human rights violations and nondemocratic decision making.

SYNTHESIS: NECESSARY CONDITIONS OF SUCCESSFUL FORMS OF DECENTRALIZED GOVERNANCE

General Remarks

Confronting the reasons in favor and those speaking against the use of federalism and other forms of decentralized governance as a tool for resolving ethnic and other minority conflicts, two things become clear: First, federalism and decentralization as such do not always lead to appropriate solutions. Whereas, for example, more human rights, more independence of the judiciary, or more participation automatically means better governance in most cases, this is not true for federalism and decentralization. In fact, it is necessary to analyze each specific situation in order to determine which form of governance is the most appropriate: Federalism, for example, is often not the solution to conflicts in fragmented societies. This is particularly true where ethnic, religious, or linguistic minorities are not concentrated in a particular region of a country but have their members living in many parts of the country. Here, however, other forms of decentralized governance may allow for self-government of such groups at the village or district level where they hold the majority. A language conflict, for example, can be diluted or even solved if local governments are allowed to use, as an official language besides the national language, a local idiom spoken by a majority on its territory. Furthermore, where the central state is very weak, the introduction of federalism might lead to secessionism or even to the dissolution of the country because some subnational units are strong enough to challenge the central government effectively. Here, other decentralized forms of government should be introduced to accommodate diversity without jeopardizing stability and endangering national unity.

Second, the question of the proper design of decentralized forms of governance becomes the most significant issue. How must they be framed and designed in order to be able to fulfil the promises listed in the first part of this chapter and to avoid the dangers and pitfalls mentioned in its second part? This is a very complex question whose answer can only be outlined here. Three aspects are of paramount importance: (1) Decentralized governance can take very different shapes, but some minimal elements must be in place to make decentralization work; (2) to grant local self-government to specific minorities only (asymmetrical decentralization) may be attractive on first sight, but in many situations it will further marginalize the groups concerned; and (3) decentralized forms of governance for ethnic groups become a source of new conflicts if they are undemocratic or allow for internal oppression of persons not belonging to that particular group.

Necessary Elements of Successful Decentralization

Attempts to solve conflicts by granting ethnic groups the right of self-governance at the regional or the local level will fail if such self-governance and autonomy exist only in form but not in substance. In such a case, the minority in question will be frustrated and the conflict will continue. For true decentralization, the following conditions must be fulfilled in all cases, regardless of whether or not decentralization efforts take place in the context of minority problems.

A first necessary condition for strong decentralized government is *security of existence*. Clearly, local governments cannot perform properly if their existence is in jeopardy because authorities on higher levels of government can dissolve them easily at any time. Such existence is optimally guaranteed in federal states. In other situations, secure existence requires that members of regional or local governments only be dismissed for specific, predetermined reasons and under formal procedures that require the dismissing authority to show that the dismissed person has violated the law. The fact that local government councils have been suspended for poor reasons or that their key powers have been taken over by central government has, for example, been identified as an important reason for the failure of decentralization efforts in Africa (Oluwu 1995:94). A firm constitutional base for local governments makes it more difficult for central governments to take such steps and thus enhances the chance of decentralization efforts to succeed (Kimenyi 1997:12–72).

Second, the success of decentralization efforts depends to a very large extent on the availability of *sufficient resources* and the possibility of using these resources *autonomously*. This requires, inter alia, the right of subnational governments to collect local taxes and fees and to get funds from the central government necessary for the execution of tasks transferred to them; the right to spend this money without excessive prior control by higher levels of government; the right to take decisions on local activities (including local development projects) without undue interference by line agencies; a sufficient and well-qualified local staff and, at least to a certain extent, the right to appoint and dismiss such staff; and technical support and advice from the center. There is some evidence that "[d]ecentralisation is more successful the less control the central government exerts and the more control local residents have" (Kimenyi 1997:12–68).

Full *accountability* of local governments and *transparency* of their actions are another important condition. In every organization it is of paramount importance to introduce a clear concept of accountability. At the level of subnational governments such accountability has two dimensions: (1) Making regional and local governments and their members *accountable to the people* means that the citizens can elect those who rule them and who have the possibility to assess their performance at the time of reelection. This requires transparency of governmental actions and the possibility to access relevant information such as budgets, accounts, plans, and so on. (2) Regional and local governments are also *accountable to higher levels of government*. Accountability to several authorities might create confusion and insecurity at lower levels that would be detrimental to the idea of efficient administration. Only well-defined responsibilities provide for the degree of transparency and security needed by authorities at lower levels who have to make certain decisions on their own.

Checks and balances at the local level and participation of civil society not only promote accountability much better than monopolies of power, but they also help to ensure that power at the local level is not abused by local elites with vested interests. In this regard, it is less important to duplicate specific models of democracy and separation of powers but more important to take seriously what Cohen and Peterson (1997:3) call "institutional pluralism," that is, setups "where tasks and roles are not monopolized but are shared between" a multitude of governmental and nongovernmental actors at different levels.

The success of decentralization efforts depends, to a large extent, on *central-local government partnership,* that is, the willingness of both the central and the regional and local levels to see each other as partners in an ongoing process. Where such partnership lacks, failure of decentralization plans is likely because the decentralization process, to a large extent, is a matter of power struggles between the local and the central levels with the latter often being reluctant to give up its power (see Oluwu 1995:89). Institutionally, this requires that subnational governments also can take part in the decision making at the national level, be it through formal representation as is the case in federal states (e.g., with one chamber of parliament representing the subnational entities) or through weaker mechanisms such as formal or informal procedures of consultations, which can be found in many decentralized states.

These conditions might be of a rather "technical" nature but their importance should not be underestimated. Where they are absent, decentralized forms of governance will not work and will cause new problems rather than help in finding solutions.

Mainstreaming Decentralization

Where forms of decentralized governance are only granted to specific minorities, but not those belonging to the majority population, there is the danger that these minorities will feel excluded from mainstream politics and, thus, marginalized. There is an equal danger that such asymmetric forms of decentralization will help to introduce or reinforce ethnicity as the main factor in legitimizing political action. Therefore, even in situations where minority conflicts are at the roots of efforts for more decentralization, measures aimed at granting more autonomy to regional and local levels should be generalized and applied equally all over a country. Mainstreaming decentralization excludes the danger of ethnicity becoming the foundation of subnational governments.

Democracy and Freedom within Decentralized Units

One of the major challenges of federalism and other forms of decentralized governance is the issue of democracy and freedom for all members of the group and of power sharing at the internal level. One important lesson to be learned both from history and from recent experiences is the following: Federalism and other forms of decentralized government can only further peace and stability if subnational entities as such are organized in a democratic way and national authorities do not tolerate the creation of autocratic and authoritarian forms of government on the subnational level. Experience has shown that oppression on the local level is one of the biggest dangers for federal states if the federal level remains unable to redress such human rights violations. Therefore, everything has to be done to ensure that power is not monopolized and that it is made accountable. The key to ensuring accountability is the concept of checks and balances. There are many forms of checks and balances, but they all have in common the existence of several organs and entities, each having its proper function and mandate. All of the organs and entities interact with each other, but functions and mandates are allocated in a way that avoids overlapping. It is sometimes assumed that decentralized governance in itself ensures such a separation of powers. It is true that distribution of power to different levels of government and the competition between these levels allow for a certain degree of checks and balances that is likely to set limits on the central government. However, if subnational governments are organized in a manner reinforcing power monopolies at the local level, the local population cannot benefit from these checks and balances and may fall victim to authoritarian forms of governance at the grassroots level. Therefore, it is for very good reasons that the constitutions of countries like Switzerland, Germany, and the United States provide that the constituent states must have republican forms of government.

REFERENCES

Basta, Lidija R., ed. 1998. *Constitutional Prerequisites for a Democratic Serbia.* Fribourg, Switzerland: Institut du Fédéralisme.

Basta, Lidija R., and Thomas Fleiner. 1996. *Federalism and Multiethnic States: The Case of Switzerland.* Fribourg, Switzerland: Institut du Fédéralisme.

Basta, Lidija R., and Jibrin Ibrahim. 2000. Federalism and Decentralisation in Africa—The Multicultural Challenge. In *Federalism and Decentralisation in Africa,* ed. Lidija R. Basta and Ibrahim Jibrin, 3–13. Fribourg, Switzerland: Institut du Fédéralisme.

Cohen, John M., and Stephen B. Peterson. 1997. *Administrative Decentralisation: A New Framework for Improved Governance, Accountability, and Performance.* Development Discussion Paper no. 582. Cambridge, MA: Harvard Institute for International Development.

Duchacek, Ivo D. 1979. Federalist Responses to Ethnic Demands: An Overview. In *Federalism and Political Integration*, ed. Daniel J. Elazar, 59–71. Ramat Gan, Israel: Turtledove Publishing.

Fleiner-Gerster, Thomas. 1987. The Relationship between Federalism and Rights. In *Federalism and Decentralisation: Constitutional Problems of Territorial Decentralisation in Federal and Centralized States*, vol. 2, Thomas Fleiner-Gerster and Silvan Hutter, 407–410. Fribourg, Switzerland: Editions Universitaires.

Henkin, Louis. 1987. Federalism, Decentralisation and Human Rights. In *Federalism and Decentralisation: Constitutional Problems of Territorial Decentralisation in Federal and Centralized States*, vol. 2, Thomas Fleiner-Gerster and Silvan Hutter, 291–318. Fribourg, Switzerland: Editions Universitaires.

Henkin, Louis, and Albert Rosenthal. 1990. *Constitutionalism and Rights: The Influence of the US Constitution Abroad*. New York: Columbia University Press.

Higuchi, Yoichi. 1987. La décision de la décentralisation. In *Federalism and Decentralisation: Constitutional Problems of Territorial Decentralisation in Federal and Centralized States*, vol. 2, Thomas Fleiner-Gerster and Silvan Hutter, 23–36. Fribourg, Switzerland: Editions Universitaires.

Kälin, Walter. 1993. Legal Aspects of Decentralisation. In *Workshop on the Decentralisation Process: Documentation*, vol. 2, ed. UNDP/MDP, 13–27. New York: United Nations Development Programme/Management Development Programme.

Kimenyi, Mwangi S. 1997. *Ethnic Diversity, Liberty and the State: The African Dilemma*. Cheltenham, UK: Edward Elgar.

Kymlicka, Will. 1995. *Multicultural Citizenship*. Oxford: Clarendon Press.

Linder, Wolf. 1994. *Swiss Democracy: Possible Solutions to Conflict in Multicultural Societies*. New York: St. Martin's Press.

Oluwu, Dele. 1995. The Failure of Current Decentralisation Programs in Africa. In *The Failure of the Centralized State*, ed. James S. Wunsch and Dele Owulu, 74–99. San Francisco: ICS Press.

Paddison, Ronan. 1985. *The Fragmented State*. Oxford: Basil Blackwell.

Thürer, Daniel. 1995. National Minorities: A Global, European and Swiss Perspective. *The Fletcher Forum of World Affairs* 19 (1):53–69.

IV

CONCLUSION

21

❦

Hidden Ties: Similarities between Research and Policy Approaches to Ethnic Conflicts

Ulrike Joras and Conrad Schetter

Policymakers, researchers, and the media use the term "ethnic conflict" to describe most of the intrastate conflicts that have occurred since the end of the Cold War. Such widespread usage is relatively new. True, the term "ethnicity" had appeared for the first time in the social sciences in the early 1960s (Glazer and Moynihan 1963).[1] Later on, ethnicity was used to explain violent movements in Europe (such as ETA and the IRA) and the developing world (Horowitz 1985; Waldmann 1989). Nevertheless, the term ethnicity remained little known in common political parlance and in the media until the end of the 1980s. With the collapse of the Soviet Union and the concomitant end of the Cold War world order, however, the term entered policy making and media discourses (see Allen and Seaton 1999; Rühl 2001). Karabakh, Abkhazia, Slovenia, Croatia, Somalia, Angola, Bosnia-Herzegovina, Rwanda, Chiapas, South Africa, Chechnya, Zaire, East Timor, Kosovo, Moluks, Macedonia, and Afghanistan—these are just a few of the violent conflicts that have been identified as "ethnic conflicts" in the last decade.

Despite sharing this common buzzword, many experts in this "new" field agree that researchers and policymakers do not effectively communicate with each other when it comes to ethnicity and ethnic conflicts (Bowen 1996; Schetter 2002). Fitzduff (2000), for example, argues that social science in general and the academic discourse on ethnicity and ethnic conflict in particular have little influence on policy decisions in this field. Or, in other words, the knowledge on ethnic conflict is only rarely used by policymakers, and a gulf characterizes the relationship between policymakers and researchers. In contrast, the language of journalists seems to have more currency in the world of policymakers. Their ideas are therefore more easily conveyed to the political arena. Bill Clinton, to give an example, was so impressed by Robert Kaplan's article "The Coming Anarchy," which explained current conflicts as the outcome of age-old ethnic loyalties, that he ordered his administration to take Kaplan's assessments as a basis for future policy making (see Mc Hugh 2001:54). Ahmed Rashid, the author of a journalistic book on the Taliban (2000), was invited by Tony Blair and by Joschka Fischer to explain to them the Afghan conflict.

In this chapter, we examine whether academic and policy discourses on ethnicity and ethnic conflict do indeed diverge as much as it is usually assumed. We review different explanations of ethnic conflicts as well as different conflict management strategies to see if they share certain basic understandings and definition of the conflict dynamics. We found that they do share such basic assumptions and that these can be grouped around three basic understandings of ethnic conflict. The first two approaches start from different ideas about what constitutes an "ethnic group"; while one notion emphasizes the boundedness and durability of ethnic groups, the other one accentuates variability and the changing nature of ethnicity.[2] The third approach represents a "non-ethnic" view, in which the term ethnic conflict is used interchangeably with other terms such as "civil war." Before we outline these three different approaches, we discuss in the next section the more general relationship between social sciences and policy making.

THE RESEARCH-POLICY LINK IN THE
FIELD OF ETHNIC CONFLICT

The research-policy linkage is a much-debated issue (Wagner et al. 1991). Although Western governments made increasing use of social science research in the last forty years, the relationship is still problematic. Structural problems and unrealistic expectations on both sides have led analysts to use terminology such as "two worlds" (Caplan 1979) or a "traditional dichotomy" (Cross et al. 1999:37) when describing this linkage.

If we disregard national differences here, the most common stereotypes that seem to characterize the relationship between academia and policy are that policymakers are narrow-minded and ideological, impatient and irrational in their decision making; that they do not understand research; and that they only use it to rationalize what they already decided to do. Researchers, on the other hand, are considered too slow for policy making, too self-convinced and unable to cooperate with other researchers, and lacking in common sense and the ability to comply with the needs of policymakers (OECD 1995; Fitzduff 2000). Differences in definitions, styles of argument, and expectations make social science "knowledge utilization" in policy making apparently difficult (Weiss 1977).

Perhaps because ethnic conflicts have been of comparatively little relevance for Western politicians throughout the Cold War and perhaps because researchers are reluctant to give policy advice in sensitive areas such as violent conflicts (Fitzduff 2000), the research-policy linkage in this field seems even more problematic than in most other social science disciplines. Fitzduff (2000:1) writes: "There is a fundamental divide existing between scholars, our traditional research providers, and policy-makers and practitioners, particularly in the field of conflict prevention and management"; and Cross et al. (1999) state that the majority of research in ethnic studies—although not all of it—is produced with comparatively little reference to policy. The academic discussion on the origins of ethnicity serves as an apparent example (Cross et al. 1999:110).

Notwithstanding the problematic nature of the research-policy linkage, it would be simplistic to believe that the two do not influence each other at all. Many theories thus suggest that academia may perhaps have little *direct* impact on policy decisions but influences these over the long run (e.g., the "limestone model" by Patricia Thomas 1987). Although it is often difficult to judge how this influence is asserted, or how it finds its way into policy decisions, social science arguably affects policy and vice versa more often than is recognized. Often enough, ideas of social science origin are conveyed to policymakers in think tanks such as the German Institute for International and Security Affairs or via conferences and workshops.

The purpose of the following sections is to discover argumentative convergences as well as differences between policymakers and researchers. Although we cannot explain how, and in which direction, the water of influence runs through the limestone, we found that the dividing lines in explaining and managing ethnic conflicts do not so much run between researchers and policymakers, but primarily between different schools of thoughts—or paradigms of understanding—which attract policymakers as well as researchers.

THE ETHNIC EXPLANATION

The most common explanation of ethnic conflicts among politicians, the media, and also many researchers starts from the assumption that ethnic groups are stable and clearly bounded units that may enter into hostile relationships with each other and develop self-perpetuating stereotypes and hatred. This understanding of ethnic groups, based on what Rogers Brubaker in his contribution to this volume calls "commonsense groupism," seems appropriate to explain why ethnic conflicts elude a Western, rational understanding and why such conflicts appear resistant to outside intervention. Many conflict management strategies seem to start from these assumptions: They perceive hostile feelings between ethnic groups as the root causes of the conflicts and seek to overcome them (see Schneckener 2002).

Eternal Ethnic Groups

The end of the Cold War and its bipolar world order demanded the formulation of a plausible, new political template to categorize and interpret intrastate conflicts. Researchers such as Fukuyama (1992) and Huntington (1993) seemingly had a strong influence on the popular perception of the new world order and its new political challenges. Huntington's approach, for example, offers a model for the explanation of conflicts: He divides the globe into self-contained civilizational areas, and conflicts emerge on the territorial fault lines between these cultural units. Ethnic conflicts can be easily incorporated into Huntington's view as cultural clashes of a second order. Although strongly criticized by other researchers, Huntington's explanation had arguably a strong impact on policymakers since the mid-1990s. This is, for example, demonstrated by many politicians' statements on the terrorists' attacks of September 11 (e.g., as attacks against the "civilized world"). Another example is the explanation of the Kosovo conflict by the then–U.S. president Bill Clinton, who seemed to perceive the ethnic groups in Kosovo as monolithic, clearly shaped units divided by civilizational fault lines:

> Kosovo is a very small place on a very large fault line; on the borderlands of central and eastern Europe; at the meeting place of the Islamic world and the Western and Orthodox branches of Christianity;[3] where people have settled in a complex patchwork of ethnic and religious groups; and where countless wars have been fought over faith, land and power (Clinton 1999).

Lentze (1998) showed in a comparative study that such a perception of ethnic conflicts is common not only in public parlance or among policymakers who—so the stereotype goes—"depend" on simple models of explanation, but also within academia. Many theories of ethnicity such as those developed by Ted Gurr (1993), Eric Hobsbawm (1992), Rita Jalali and Seymour M. Lipset (1992–1993), Walker Connor (1994), Dieter Senghaas (1993), Christian Scherrer (1994), and Anthony Smith (1981, 1995) either do not question the dynamics of ethnic group formation (and dissolution) at all or do not consistently adhere to their own line of argumentation. They take, in other words, the existence of ethnic groups for granted. Ethnic conflicts are thus interpreted as conflicts between apparently preexisting ethnic entities. Others seem not to be fully consistent in their argumentation and fall into an "ethnic trap." Ted Gurr (1993), for instance, argues in his theoretical explanations that ethnic identities and ethnic groups are modifiable, and their salience depends on contextual factors and historical circumstances. Yet, he later on enumerates more than 200 ethnic groups and subgroups that are represented as constant, unchangeable entities.

"Groupist" models offer a plausible explanation for the apparent rise of ethnic conflicts after the end of the Cold War. Benjamin Barber (1992), in his influential publication "Jihad vs. McWorld," for example, suggests that ancient hatred between ethnic groups was preserved under the pressure of authoritarian rule and has (re-)erupted with the collapse of the Soviet system.[4] This "defrosting theory" coincides with the explanation of ethnic conflicts stated by many policymakers such as Bill Clinton (1999), Benita Ferrero-Waldner (2000), or Netherlands Prime Minister Ruud Lubbers, as the following quotation illustrates:

> And yet, while the urgent work of democracy-building and market reform moves forward, some see in freedom's triumph a bitter harvest. In this view, *the collapse of communism has thrown open a Pandora's Box of ancient ethnic hatreds, resentment, and even revenge.* Some fear democracy's new freedoms will be used not to build new trust but to settle old scores (Lubbers 1991; emphasis added).

Irrationality of Ethnic Conflicts

One corollary of the ancient hatred hypothesis is that ethnic conflicts are not rationally comprehensible (see the citations above). Fear of ethnic others is bequeathed from one generation to the next, and forms a core aspect of group identity. The causes of a conflict are projected into an unclear past, which the present actor cannot control rationally. In other words, someone fights an ethnic conflict because of "irrational," nonresolvable causes rooted in century-old history. This perception offers an evident explanation for acts of extreme violence, such as the massacre of Srebrenica or the genocides in Rwanda: "Ancient ethnic, racial and religious hatred" (Clinton 1999) is stressed, in a virtually apologizing way, to explain these genocides (see Kaplan 1993; Eagleburger quoted in Holbrooke 1998:28.). Warren Christopher, the former U.S. secretary of state, expounded on the collapse of Yugoslavia in almost the same manner:

> The death of President Tito and the end of the communist domination of the former Yugoslavia raised the lid on the cauldron of *ancient ethnic hatreds*. This is the land where at least three religions and half-dozen ethnic groups have

vied across the centuries. It was the birthplace of World War I. It has long been a cradle of European conflict, and it remains so today (quoted in Turton 1997:33; emphasis added).

And John O'Shea, head of the Irish aid agency Goal, comments on the conflict in Rwanda in the following way:

> Two groups are bent on destroying each other. . . . The dispute is ethnic. Last April, the Hutu tribe turned on their Tutsi neighbours and butchered 800.000 of them. . . . There is *out-and-out hatred between the two groups*. . . . The Tutsi are now bent on revenge (quoted in Storey: 1997:63; emphasis added).

This interpretation of ethnic conflicts often appears in the media as well (see Seaton 1999; Allen and Seaton 1999). Honke and Servaes (1994) looked at the German press's reporting on the conflict in Rwanda. They showed that irrationalizing or prejudicing terms such as "blood thirst," "tribes," and "century-old hatred" often appeared in the commentary. However, even researchers that explicitly analyze the mobilization of ethnic movements and resist the groupist fallacy tend to link ethnic conflicts with irrationality. Walker Connor writes in his contribution to this book:

> But it should be emphasized that convictions concerning one's ethnic identity are predicated not upon chronological or factual history but upon sentient or felt history. And because its roots lie in the subconscious, rather than in reason, the conviction that one's nation was somehow created sui generis and remained essentially unadulterated down to the present is immunized against contrary fact.

Due to this alleged irrationality, ethnic conflicts have been described as a "new barbarism" (Richards 1996). Especially because of its outstanding emotional binding power, ethnicity, which makes ethnic groups as closely knit as "extended families" (Connor, in this volume), seems to provide a smooth explanation for irrational actions and a specific quality of violence—as reflected in the unquestionable idiomatic expression "Blood is thicker than water."

The Ethnic Apology

The explanation of ethnic violence as caused by "ancient hatred" lends legitimacy to non-intervention by the international community. Ethnic conflicts appear as necessary, non-influenceable events, which lack any leverage point for an outside intervention. The inaction of the international community in Rwanda, for instance, is often interpreted as resignation regarding a "centuries-old history of tribal warfare and deep distrust of outside intervention" (*New York Times* editorial, 15 April 1994, quoted in

Storey 1997:64). In the case of Bosnia, similar arguments have been made. Douglas Hurd, the former British foreign secretary, rejected intervention in Bosnia with reference to the "atavistic and endemic nature of conflicts" (Gallagher 1997:69). Toal (2001) demonstrates with respect to the Bosnian conflict that the European Union as well as the United States ruled out a military engagement in Bosnia due to the ethnic dimension of the conflict until May 1992. Leading policymakers such as Lord Carrington (quoted in Toal 2001) or Lawrence Eagleburger (1993) repeatedly pointed to the high complexity of the Bosnian conflict, caused by "blind ethnic hatred."

Conforming to the stereotype that policymakers only use academic explanations in order to justify what they had already planned to do, politicians only seem to cherish the "ethnic explanation" when they do not want to intervene in a conflict. However, in many instances the lack of strategic interest was directly cited as the main rationale to stay on the sidelines, such as in Rwanda, Sudan, Sri Lanka, Kurdistan, or Afghanistan until September 11. George W. Bush stated in rare clarity in January 23, 2000:

> We should not send our troops to end ethnic cleansings or genocides in nations which are outside our strategic interests (quoted in McManis 2000).[5]

Ethnic-Sensitive Policies

Several strategies of active conflict management also use the concept of ethnic groups as bounded stable units, albeit with entirely different policy implications and intentions.

In the mediation approach of Volkan (1997, 1999), for example, ethnic conflicts are defined as conflicts about "ethnic identities." If ethnic identities are threatened by another ethnic group, violent conflicts may erupt. Volkan assumes that ethnic identities are not chosen consciously but are shaped in early childhood and define personal identity from then on. He identifies the reason for the emergence of violent conflicts as emotional. Accordingly, his mediation approach, as applied by the Center for the Study of Mind and Human Interaction (CSMHI) in dialogues between Estonians and Russians, Arabs and Israelis, Turks and Greeks, or Croats, Serbs, and Bosnians, intends to reduce ethnic tensions by overcoming ethnic prejudices and stereotypes in open dialogues between political and social leaders. Several conflict management strategies that focus on the institutional level (e.g., territorial autonomy and power-sharing arrangements) implicitly assume that

1. ethnic identities are the predominant structural characteristics of a given society,
2. claims for ethnic sovereignty or autonomy are the predominant causes of the conflict, and

3. ethnic groups are socially (and regarding territorial solutions also spatially) clearly defined units.[6]

Territorial solutions, as well as power-sharing arrangements, intend to offer ethnic minorities the opportunity to realize their specific interests by peaceful means and to establish in the long run a culture of dialogue between the warring factions. Their goal is to avoid a situation whereby the state and its resources are only accessible and controlled by the members of a single ethnic group.

Territorial autonomy regimes, as presented in this volume by Hurst Hannum and Walter Kälin, encompass a wide spectrum of different strategies—such as the foundation of new states; federalism; regional or local autonomy over language, religion, education, or economic development; as well as other types of political decentralization that provide lower administrative levels with a greater range of competencies (see Schneckener 2002; Coakley 2003). These territorial approaches are based on the idea that the population of a modern political unit should coincide with a single ethnic group. This assumption is most clearly reflected in conflict resolution strategies that include the foundation of new states. However, thinking in terms of such ethnoterritorial principles also guided the politicians that developed the Vance-Owen Plan or the previously designed Canton Model in the case of Bosnia-Herzegovina, or those recommending ethnofederalism in Ethiopia and Nigeria.

Unlike autonomy strategies, power-sharing arrangements do not presume spatial contiguity. They include a great number of political instruments (see Sisk 1996): consociationalism, fixed quotas for minorities in parliament and the state administration, minority rights, or institutions such as schools and media for minorities, as recently discussed for the case of Afghanistan. All such power-sharing arrangements rest on the assumption that the population is clearly divided along ethnic lines and that these ethnic blocs form the relevant political entities for democratic politics.

VARIABILITY APPROACH

The "variability approach" assumes, like the previous one, that ethnic conflicts have a specific quality. However, ethnic groups are not conceived as stable units, and ethnic conflicts are not conflicts beyond rational understanding. This approach has attracted mainly the interest of many researchers, yet, increasingly, policymakers or journalists have also taken it up, if less so than the ethnic explanation. This may be due to the high complexity of the variability approach, to be outlined in the following sections.

Instability of Ethnic Groups

In contrast to the perception that ethnic groups are solid, clearly defined units that have existed since time immemorial, a growing number of researchers argue that ethnic groups have been invented and categorized in the course of the colonization and the subsequent nation-state–building experiences of the nineteenth and twentieth centuries (Elwert 1989). Assisted by ethnologists, colonial and national administrations created and classified the population into ethnic and tribal categories using existing social and cultural terms. Where these attempts at colonial ethnogenesis were successful, the fact that for instance the terms "Hutu" and "Tutsi" originally described farmers and cattle breeders and not ethnic groups, or that "Tajik" was originally an anti-ethnic term, used for people without an origin, sank into oblivion. The variability approach thus starts from the assumption that many ethnic identities have been created only recently. The deep historical roots of hostilities between ethnic groups do, more often than not, correspond to political mythologies rather than historical fact.

Researchers such as Brubaker (in this volume), Kössler and Schiel (1993), and Schetter (1999) argue that it is important to distinguish between ethnic categories and groups. Only individuals that are bound by joint acting, common identity, and organization are defined as groups. Individuals who share the same cultural characteristics are defined as categories. Thus, an ethnic party usually announces its claims in the name of all members of an ethnic category. The differentiation between category and group stands against unsound generalizations: In the Basque conflict not all Basques, but certainly the ETA, are fighting against the Spanish government; and in Sri Lanka, not all Tamils support the Tamil Tigers.

Boundaries between ethnic groups may fluctuate and vary from context to context, depending on whether language, religion, or other markers of group differences are stressed. Furthermore, many individuals who speak several languages or harbor various religious beliefs "belong" to various ethnic categories. Hence, ethnic categories are rarely as unambiguous as described by outside observers, and ethnic boundaries are often fuzzy and blurred: Hutu and Tutsi can only be distinguished by the entry in their identity cards. Kurds cannot be defined by language, religion, or any other cultural attributes: Kurds are Sunnites as well as Shiites; many Kurds, especially in Turkey, often do not speak a word of Kurdish (Schetter 2002). Field researchers are aware that for many individuals, their ethnic identity is only of subordinate importance in daily life. For example, for the inhabitants of former Yugoslavia, ethnic identity ranked behind socioeconomic identities such as profession, class, or education until the 1980s. In Moldavia, Georgia, or Sri Lanka, interethnic marriages were common until the breakout of violent conflicts.

Dominance of National Thinking

Other researchers (e.g., Callhoun 1997; Wimmer 1997, 2002) connect the distinctiveness of ethnic conflicts to the political framework—especially the fact that the global political system is made up of nation-states. The starting point for this approach is the direct conjunction of the emergence of ethnic movements with the establishment and spread of nation-states and the corresponding principles of political legitimacy: A modern state should be representative for one nation and be ruled by members of that same national group (Wimmer 2002). Taking into account that ethnic and political-territorial boundaries rarely coincide, an ethnic homogenous state is hard to realize. Therefore, ethnic conflicts can be seen as rivalries over how the nation should be defined, which symbols represent the nation, and who receives access to the public goods of the state (see Kaufman 2001; Wimmer 2002). The ethnic definition of the "titular nation" inevitably gives rise to "ethnic minorities," who deviate from the national norm regarding their cultural patterns. These minorities possess a high conflict potential because they challenge the ideal of the homogenous nation state. The state tends to exclude or to suppress minorities, which leads them to claim specific rights—from the recognition of their cultural identity to political autonomy—and equal access to the services and goods of the modern state. In other words, ethnicity is not salient because it provides the fundament of political solidarity by the sheer force of emotional binding power, but because modern state building politicizes ethnonational differences and may stir up conflicts along these lines. Violence may then be used by extremists to reinforce these dividing lines and to portray themselves as protectors of everybody in their ethnic category from the violence committed by others. This pattern of interpretation of ethnic conflicts becomes increasingly important among policymakers, as the following citations of Richard Holbrooke and Max van der Stoel underline:

> What happened in Rwanda and Bosnia was not the spontaneous result of some sort of genetic predisposition for genocide of "ancient ethnic hatreds." Such judgments do nothing but allow people to justify their own inaction. The atrocities carried out in Rwanda were done so by a small group of murderers intent on using hate to preserve their hold on power. These were political acts, plain and simple (Holbrooke 2000).

> Ethnic conflicts are the result of extremist politics, as well as the basis for future rehearsals of political extremists (van der Stoel 1999:40).

> Extreme nationalists often stick to their guns (sometimes literally) because compromise would undermine vested interests that often have nothing to do with ethnicity. National or ethnic arguments often mask interests of power, prestige, and resources (van der Stoel, in this volume).

The creation of myths and ethnic stereotypes as well as the symbolic strengthening of ethnic boundaries are part of the power politics of ethnic mobilization and conflict (Kaufman 2001). The ethnic other is mystified as being a threat to the existence of one's ethnic group and its annihilation is perceived as the sole strategy of survival. The ethnic group, politicians try to suggest, is the last bastion to provide security in times of pervasive violence and war (Posen 1993; Lake and Rothchild 1996).

Ethnicity may then indeed play the role attributed to it by the first approach discussed above. Group solidarity may rise, ethnic stereotypes become entrenched, and boundaries are drawn sharply. Varshney's (2002) suggestion that building up non-ethnic parties, labor unions, or associations to bridge ethnic cleavages and to depoliticize ethnic grievances, therefore, seems rather naïve. Already, Waldmann (1989) demonstrated that such civil society institutions may get undermined by a process of ethnicization. This is also the main problem of the non-ethnic approach, to be discussed in the following.

THE NON-ETHNIC EXPLANATION

A multitude of publications dealing with violent intrastate conflicts do not deal with the ethnic aspects of these conflicts. Either the term is used—by researchers and policymakers alike—as a substitute for more general expressions such as "violent quarrels," "intrastate conflicts," or "fragmented societies," or it is seen as a distinct, yet not determining, aspect of the civil wars of the contemporary world. This latter approach is exemplified by the "greed explanation" that recently has gained considerable influence in academia and policy making. Both variants are discussed separately in what follows.

Juggling with Words

Policymakers and researchers often avoid giving a precise definition of the conflict they deal with. Waldmann, for example (in this volume), abstains from formulating a precise definition of ethnicity because he develops a model of escalation and de-escalation dealing with all kinds of violent conflicts. Policymakers especially tend to leave the description of conflicts very vague. Two influential UN publications, the *Agenda for Peace* (1992) and the *Brahimi Report* (2000a), were written when intrastate conflicts were increasingly perceived as threats to security worldwide. Both reports, as well as many others dealing with civil wars, do not explicitly highlight the ethnic dimension as a central theme. The ethnic dimension appears as an interchangeable variable among others:

> At the same time, however, fierce new assertions of nationalism and sovereignty spring up, and the cohesion of State is threatened by brutal *ethnic, religious, social, cultural* or *linguistic* strife (United Nations 1992:2; emphasis added).
>
> Internal conflicts stemming from *religious, ethnic, economic* or *political* disputes will remain at current levels or even increase in number (Central Intelligence Agency 2000; emphasis added).

The Triumphal Procession of the Greed Explanation

The second type of non-ethnic explanation is well represented by Paul Collier and Anke Hoeffler's (2001) influential research. The central argument is that violent conflicts—although destructive for the majority of the war-affected population—can be economically profitable for some. Civil wars are statistically more often driven by the economic greed of a few than by the grievance of many. Other factors that are usually considered as causes of violent conflict have, according to their quantitative analysis, little or no influence on the probability of civil wars. Ethnolinguistic fractionalization was found statistically significant, but more fractionalized societies are not more prone to violent conflict than ethnically homogeneous countries (Collier and Hoeffler 1998). Ethnic grievance and hatred are deliberately stimulated by rebel organizations in order to mobilize and motivate their fighters. It is not the original cause of violent conflicts but represents a manufactured emotional anchor, similar to other such anchors derived from religious belief or regional identities. The real driving force is the greed for lootable resources (Collier 2000).

The idea that economic factors matter in violent conflicts had an unquestionable influence on policy making. The United Nations, for example, stated in the *Millennium Report*:

> Often driven by political ambition or greed, these wars have preyed on ethnic and religious differences, they are often sustained by external economic interests, and they are fed by a hyperactive and in large part illicit global arms market (United Nations 2000b:43).

Other examples abound. The Swedish Action Plan *Preventing Violent Conflict* (Swedish Ministry for Foreign Affairs 1999) acknowledges the importance of economic factors for the design of conflict management strategies. Lakhdar Brahimi, in his official review of UN peace operations, identifies the existence of illicit goods (such as drugs) as one of the main perpetuating factors of civil wars. Governmental and nongovernmental aid organizations all over the world undertake "peace and conflict impact assessments," while trying to ignore that their humanitarian aid is turned by clever rebel groups into cash and then into weapons. The RUF rebels were granted, in the Lomé peace accord of 1999, access to the Sierra Leonian diamond fields. And "smart UN sanctions" against war-ridden countries implicitly seek to impede trade with those commodities that represent the bone of contention of violent conflict.

CONCLUSION

The intention of this chapter was to explore one possible way to group policymakers and researchers' understanding of ethnic conflict. We distinguished between two different concepts of ethnic group and a third approach in which ethnic politics is only of minor relevance. We found that in contrast to the widespread assumption that academia and policy form "two worlds" that have little in common with, and little to say to, each other, the borders between the "worlds" may not run so much between practitioners and researchers, but rather between different understandings of ethnicity. In each of the three approaches outlined above, we find researchers as well as policymakers that share the same perspective. Evidently, the ethnic explanation is better accepted within the policymaker community, and the variability approach finds more approval among researchers. The non-ethnic explanation is widely acknowledged in the policy as well as academic arenas, especially in recent years.

As there is little previous research to build upon (but see Mack 2002), this chapter necessarily remains sketchy and somewhat inconclusive. Yet we believe that our hypothesis is worth following up. A range of essential questions remains open. It is clear that policymakers and academics who share the same basic perspective on ethnic conflicts do *not* necessarily advocate similar interventions in ethnic conflicts—the ethnic explanation, to give an example, is both compatible with advocating separate statehood plus population exchange and a federalist model in the style of Dayton. The similarities seem to be driven by shared basic understandings of what holds a society together: culture and identity, such as in the ethnic explanation; an arena of competing interests, such as in the variability approach; or production and markets, such as seen by advocates of the non-ethnic explanation. It remains to be seen whether these different outlooks also relate to shared political convictions (such as multiculturalism versus liberalism).

A second interesting avenue to pursue would be to look more closely at how research and policy making influence each other and whether shared basic assumptions help to foster a communication and exchange. An alternative hypothesis to explore would be that research commissioned by policymakers has a better chance to influence decision-making processes than research that primarily addresses an academic audience, independent of the general approach to ethnicity that underlies them. The work of Collier and Hoeffler (1998, 2001), which they undertook for the World Bank, had clearly a greater impact on the policy field than the research results of Reno (1995), Keen (1998), and Duffield (2001), who arrived nearly simultaneously at similar conclusions. In any case, a sociology of knowledge focused on the field of conflict studies is just at its beginning.

NOTES

We thank Andreas Wimmer for substantial support in developing this chapter's argument as well as for editing the text.

1. In the discipline of anthropology, the discussion about ethnic groups dates back to Clifford Geertz (1963) and Fredrik Barth (1969). In sociology, Max Weber (1921) first discussed the term "ethnic group" at the beginning of the twentieth century.

2. It is important to emphasize that our approach focuses solely on the use of the term ethnic group. Therewith, we do not discuss the established academic differentiation between primordialist and constructivist approaches. These concepts are much more complex than our concentration on different definitions of the notion of groupness.

3. Remarkable is the mixing up of culture and religion. Furthermore, Clinton equates the Catholic and Protestant confessions.

4. See also the speech of Bill Clinton at the American Society of Newspaper Editors (1999); and Stofft and Guertner (1995).

5. George W. Bush, *ABC News*, 23 January 2000; cited in Doyle McManis (2000).

6. For an overview of such strategies, see Sisk (1996) and Schneckener (2002).

REFERENCES

Allen, Tim, and Jean Seaton, eds. 1999. *The Media of Conflict: War Reporting and Representation of Ethnic Violence*. New York: Zed Books.

Barber, Benjamin. 1992. Jihad vs. McWorld. *The Atlantic Monthly* 269 (3):53–65.

Barth, Fredrik, ed. 1969. *Ethnic Groups and Boundaries: The Social Organization of Culture Difference*. Bergen, Norway: Univ. Forlaget.

Bowen, John R. 1996. The Myth of Global Ethnic Conflict. *Journal of Democracy* 7 (4):3–14.

Callhoun, Craig. 1997. *Nationalism*. Minneapolis: University of Minnesota Press.

Caplan, N. 1979. The Two Communities: Theory and Knowledge Utilization. *American Behavioural Scientist* 22 (3):459–470.

Central Intelligence Agency. 2000. *Report: The World in 2015: Current Trends to Be Aware Of*, accessed at www.ascotadvisory.com/Incorporations_Directory/CIA .html.

Clinton, Bill. 1999, April 16. Speech to the American Society of Newspaper Editors, accessed at wysiwyg//31/http://www.asne.org/99reporter/Friday/transcript.htm.

Coakley, John, ed. 2003. *The Territorial Management of Ethnic Conflict*. London: Frank Cass.

Collier, Paul. 2000. *Economic Causes of Civil Conflict and Their Implication for Policy*. Washington, DC: World Bank.

Collier, Paul, and Anke Hoeffler. 1998. On Economic Causes of Civil War. *Oxford Economic Papers* 50:563–573.

———. 2001. *Greed and Grievance in Civil War*. Washington, DC: World Bank. Accessed at www.worldbank.org/research/conflict/papers/greedgrievance_23oct.pdf.

Connor, Walker. 1994. *Ethnonationalism: The Quest for Understanding*. Princeton, NJ: Princeton University Press.

Cross, Malcolm, Roger Henke, Philippe Oberknezev, and Katarina Pouliasi. 1999. Building Bridges: Towards Effective Means of Linking Scientific Research and Public Policy: Migrants in European Cities. Utrecht, the Netherlands: Research Paper of the Netherlands School for Social and Economic Policy Research.

Duffield, Mark. 2001. *Global Governance and the New Wars: The Merging of Development and Security*. New York: Zed Books.

Eagleburger, Lawrence. 1993, January 7. Charting the Course: U.S. Foreign Policy in a Time of Transition. Address before the Council on Foreign Relations, Washington, DC.

Elwert, Georg. 1989. *Ethnizität und Nationalismus: Über die Bildung von Wir-Gruppen*. Ethnizität und Gesellschaft: Occasional Papers 22. Berlin: Das Arabische Buch.

Ferrero-Waldner, Benita. 2000, November. *Rede beim Achten Ministerrat der OSZE*. Vienna: 27.

Fitzduff, M. 2000, December. From Shelf to Field—Functional Knowledge for Conflict Management. Paper presented at conference for Facing Ethnic Conflicts: Perspectives from Research and Policy-Making, Bonn, Germany.

Fukuyama, Francis. 1992. *The End of History and the Last Man*. New York: Free Press.

Gallagher, Tom. 1997. My Neighbour, My Enemy: The Manipulation of Ethnic Identity and the Origins and Conduct of War in Yugoslavia. In *War and Ethnicity: Global Connections and Local Violence*, ed. David Turton, 47–75. San Marino: University of Rochester Press.

Geertz, Clifford. 1963. The Integrative Revolution. Primordial Sentiments and Civil Politics in the New State. In *Old Societies and New States: The Quest for Modernity in Asia and Africa*, ed. Geertz Clifford, 105–157. London: Free Press.

Glazer, Nathan, and Daniel Moynihan, eds. 1963. *Ethnicity: Theory and Experience*. Cambridge, MA: Harvard University Press.

Gurr, Ted R. 1993. *Minorities at Risk: A Global View of Ethnopolitical Conflict*. Washington, DC: U.S. Institute of Peace Press.

Hobsbawm, Eric. 1992. *Nations and Nationalism since 1780: Programme, Myth, Reality*. Cambridge: Cambridge University Press.

Holbrooke, Richard. 1998. *To End a War*. New York: Random House.

———. 2000, April 14. *Statement in the Security Council of the United Nations on Rwanda*, accessed at www.un.int/usa/00_048.htm.

Honke, Gudrun, and Sylvia Servaes. 1994. Vom Stammeskrieg zum Völkermord: Die Rwanda-Berichterstattung der deutschen Presse von April bis September 2004. In *Ein Volk verlässt sein Land: Krieg und Völkermord in Ruanda*, ed. Hildegard Schürings, 229–238. Cologne: Neuer ISP Verlag.

Horowitz, Donald L. 1985. *Ethnic Groups in Conflict*. Berkeley: University of California Press.

Huntington, Samuel. 1993. The Clash of Civilization? *Foreign Affairs* 72 (3):22–50.

Jalali, Rita, and Seymour Martin Lipset. 1992–1993. Racial and Ethnic Conflicts: A Global Perspective. *Political Science Quarterly* 107 (4):585–606.

Kaplan, Robert. 1993. *Balkan Ghosts: A Journey through History*. New York: Vintage Departures.

Kaufman, Stuart J. 2001. *Modern Hatreds: The Symbolic Politics of Ethnic War*. Ithaca, NY: Cornell University Press.

Keen, David. 1998. *The Economic Functions of Violence in Civil Wars*. Adelphi paper no 320. London: Oxford University Press.

Kössler, Reinhart, and Tilman Schiel. 1993. Modernisierung, Ethnizität und Nationalstaat. In *Die Dritte Welt und wir. Bilanz und Perspektiven für Wissenschaft und Praxis*, ed. Mohssen Massarrat et al., 346–354. Freiburg im Breisgau, Germany: Informationszentrum Dritte Welt.

Lake, David A., and Donald Rothchild. 1996. Containing Fear: The Origins and Management of Ethnic Conflict. *International Security* 21 (2):41–75.

Lentze, Matthias. 1998. *Ethnizität in der Konfliktforschung. Eine Untersuchung zur theoretischen Fundierung und praktischen Anwendung des Begriffs „ethnischer Konflikt."* University of Hamburg, Research Unit War, Armament, and Development, Working Paper no. 1.

Lubbers, Ruud. 1991, November 9. Remarks at a luncheon, the Hague, accessed at http://bushlibrary.tamu.edu/papers/1991/91110901.html.

Mack, Andrew. 2002. Civil War: Academic Research and the Policy Community. *Journal of Peace Research* 39 (5):515–525.

Mc Hugh, Heather S. 2001. USAID and Ethnic Conflict: An Epiphany? In *Carrots, Sticks, and Ethnic Conflict: Rethinking Development Assistance*, ed. Milton Esman, 49–89. Ann Arbor: University of Michigan Press.

McManis, Doyle. 2000, April 21. Lacking a '90s Doctrine, U.S. Foreign Policy Drifts. *Detroit News*. Accessed at www.detnews.com/2000/nation/0004/21/a11-40270.htm.

OECD. 1995. *Education Research and Development: Austria, Germany, Switzerland*. Paris: OECD.

Posen, Barry R. 1993. The Security Dilemma and Ethnic Conflict. *Survival* 35 (1):27–47.

Reno, William. 1995. *Corruption and State Politics in Sierra Leone*. Cambridge: Cambridge University Press.

Rashid, Ahmed. 2000. *Taliban: Militant Islam, Oil and Fundamentalism in Central Asia*. New Haven, CT: Yale University Press.

Richards, Paul. 1996. *Fighting for the Rain Forest: War, Youth and Resources in Sierra Leone.* London: James Currey.

Rühl, Lothar. 2001. Die NATO und ethnische Konflikte. *Aus Politik und Zeitgeschichte* B 29:3–5.

Scherrer, Christian. 1994. *Ethno-Nationalismus als globales Phänomen: Zur Krise der Staaten in der Dritten Welt und der früheren UdSSR.* INEF-Report 6. Dusiburg, Germany: Institut für Entwicklung und Frieden der Universität-GH-Duisburg.

Schetter, Conrad. 1999. Ethnizität als Ressource der Kriegführung. In *Afghanistan in Geschichte und Gegenwart,* ed. Conrad Schetter and Almut Wieland-Karimi, 91–108. Frankfurt am Main, Germany: IKO-Verlag.

———. 2002. Das Zeitalter ethnischer Konflikte. *Blätter für deutsche und internationale Politik* 4:473–481.

Schneckener, Ulrich. 2002. *Auswege aus dem Bürgerkrieg: Modelle zur Regulierung ethno-nationalistischer Konflikte in Europa.* Frankfurt am Main, Germany: Suhrkamp.

Seaton, Jean. 1999. Why Do We Think the Serbs Do It? New "Ethnic" Wars and the Media. *The Political Quarterly* 70 (3):254–270.

Senghaas, Dieter. 1993. Ethnische Konflikte oder die Wiederkehr der Nationalismen. In *Friedliche Streitbeilegung als Gesellschaftsaufgabe,* ed. Jörg Calliess and Christine Merkel. *Loccumer Protokolle* 7(93): 61–81.

Sisk, Timothy D. 1996. *Power Sharing and International Mediation in Ethnic Conflicts.* Washington, DC: U.S. Institute of Peace Press.

Smith, Anthony D. 1981. *The Ethnic Revival.* Cambridge: Cambridge University Press.

———. 1995. *Nations and Nationalism in a Global Era.* Cambridge: Polity Press.

Stofft, William A., and Garry L. Guertner. 1995, Spring. Ethnic Conflict: The Perils of Military Intervention. *Parameters*:30–42.

Storey, Andy. 1997. Misunderstanding Ethnicity: Ancient Hatreds, False Consciousness and Rational Choice. *Irish Journal of Anthropology* 2: 63–68.

Swedish Ministry for Foreign Affairs. 1999. *Preventing Violent Conflict: A Swedish Action Plan.* Stockholm: Printing Works of the Government Offices.

Thomas, Patricia. 1987. The Use of Social Research: Myths and Models. In *Social Science Research and Government: Comparative Essays on Britain and the United States,* ed. Martin Bulmer, 51–60. Cambridge: Cambridge University Press.

Toal, Gerard. 2001. Theorizing Practical Geopolitical Reasoning: The Case of the United States' Response to the War in Bosnia. Unpublished manuscript.

Turton, David. 1997. War and Ethnicity. In *War and Ethnicity: Global Connections and Local Violence,* ed. David Turton, 1–45. Rochester, NY: University of Rochester Press.

United Nations. 1992, June 17. *An Agenda for Peace. Preventive Diplomacy, Peacemaking and Peace-keeping* (A/47/277—S/24111). New York: United Nations.

———. 2000a. *Brahimi Report.* New York: United Nations. Accessed at www.un.org/peace/reports.

———. 2000b. *Millennium Report* (A1542). New York: United Nations.

Van der Stoel, Max. 1999. *Peace and Stability through Human and Minority Rights: Speeches by the OSCE High Commissioner on National Minorities.* Baden-Baden, Germany: Nomos Verlagsgesellschaft.

Varshney, Ashutosh. 2002. *Ethnic Conflict and Civil Life: Hindus and Muslims in India*. New Haven, CT: Yale University Press.

Volkan, Vamık. 1997. *Bloodlines: From Ethnic Pride to Ethnic Terrorism*. New York: Farrar, Straus & Giroux.

———. 1999. *Das Versagen der Diplomatie: Zur Psychoanalyse nationaler, ethnischer und religiöser Konflikte*. Giessen, Germany: Psychologischer Verlag.

Wagner, Peter, Carol Hirschon Weiss, Bjvrn Wittrock, and Hellmut Wollmann. 1991. *Social Sciences and Modern States*. Cambridge: Cambridge University Press.

Waldmann, Peter. 1989. *Ethnischer Radikalismus: Ursachen und Folgen gewaltsamer Minderheitenkonflikte am Beispiel des Baskenlandes, Nordirlands und Quebecs*. Opladen, Germany: Westdeutscher Verlag.

Weber, Max. 1921. *Wirtschaft und Gesellschaft*. Tübingen, Germany: J.C.B. Mohr.

Weiss, Carol. 1977. *Using Social Research in Public Policy Making*. Lexington, MA: Lexington Books.

Wimmer, Andreas. 1997. Who Owns the State? Understanding Ethnic Conflict in Post-Colonial Societies. *Nations and Nationalism* 3 (4):631–665.

———. 2002. *Nationalist Exclusion and Ethnic Conflict: Shadows of Modernity*. Cambridge: Cambridge University Press.

22

❧

Toward a New Realism

Andreas Wimmer

The major lines of debate and controversy on how to understand and face ethnic conflicts, as they have developed over the past decades, also run through the chapters of this book. Some of the positions are reformulated in new ways and with renewed precision, others are stated in ways already well known from the literature, and still other chapters open new fields of inquiry and suggest promising lines of future research. I should first like to outline, in an illustrative way and with no claim to comprehensiveness, a few such controversial issues. However, my main aim is to show that, between the lines of these debates, a new consensus has emerged. This consensus has a "thin" quality and does not manifest itself in strong, hypothesis-like propositions defended by all these authors in the different fields of controversy. Rather, it is a shared perspective, sometimes expressed in clarity, sometimes only implicitly acknowledged—a certain way of looking at ethnic conflicts and of evaluating possibilities for prevention, intervention, and institutional design. This perspective can best be described as a new realism, based on five fundamental insights: on the complexities involved in ethnic conflicts; on the individual character of each case; on the fundamental nature of these conflicts; on their self-sustaining character and longevity; and, finally, on the interests and ideas that bind outside mediators to the institutions they represent. Each of these aspects of the new realism will be discussed in a separate section.

For the sake of clarity, it should be noted that I do not see this "new realism" as opposed to the "old realism" of international relations theory (Krasner 1986), which aimed at describing foreign policy in a less abstract and formalized way than did rational choice theories associated with the "liberal school" of international relations. Rather, the new realism sets itself apart from an overly optimistic, at times even naïve belief in the manageability of ethnic conflict that had developed at the end of the Cold War. It then seemed that the West, victoriously released from its wrestling competition with communism, would have hands free to sort out the messy constellations of conflicts that had appeared, over the past decades, in the developing world—and would have the political will to do so, since the "new world order" promised peace, democracy, stability, and rule of law to those parts of the word still plagued by wars, autocracies, and political turmoil.

The realistic perspective shared by the authors of this volume also sets them apart from the cynics, according to whom it is unrealistic to try to prevent or stop ethnic conflicts since these are driven by irreconcilable "ancient hatreds" (Staub 1989; Kaplan 1993; cf. Bowman 1994) or incompatible claims to sovereignty that cannot be resolved by negotiated give-and-take agreements. Benevolent attempts at peacemaking and mediation from the outside therefore may prolong the fighting and prevent a more secure peace following a clear-cut military victory of one of the sides. Against the pessimism of such a "hands-off" approach, the authors of this volume—along with others (Jentleson 2001; Miall et al. 2001)—continue to believe that ethnic conflicts are driven by political interests and are therefore open to negotiation and compromise. Before I outline this shared ground of a realistic optimism, I should hint toward some of the more salient points of disagreement.

CONTROVERSIES

It comes as no surprise that in a collection of chapters by such a wide range of authors with different professional backgrounds, disciplinary orientations, and regional expertise, there should be considerable disagreement on how to understand ethnic conflicts and what the appropriate strategy for intervention would look like. Walker Connor and Valery Tishkov, to mention an obvious pair of discord, sharply diverge in how they see relations between ethnic groups and the state. Valery Tishkov privileges the view from the top (the central state) and finds that ethnic minorities claim self-determination because foreign powers aiming at weakening the central state spread minority discourses and encourage ambitious local leaders to adopt them—and not because of a genuine sense of community and drive for cultural autonomy. Walker Connor, by contrast, develops a perspective from below and emphasizes the subjective reality of feelings of ethnic (or, as he prefers, national) belonging, even if these feelings are nurtured by histories of shared origin and perceptions of cultural difference that do not stand the test of historical or anthropological scrutiny. These different points of view may be related to different terminology: What comprises an "ethnic conflict," the terminological heir of the colonial tribalism discourse, from a state-centric perspective may be described as a "national liberation struggle" (e.g., by the authors in Berberoglu 1995) or as a fight for "multicultural justice" (Stavenhager 1991) by those taking sides with ethnonational minorities.

This latter perspective implies that ethnic conflicts are about culture, identity, and deep-rooted feelings of belonging that may conflict with other groups' culture, identity, and deep-rooted feelings of belonging—a view that underlies, implicitly or explicitly, much of the mediation work of NGOs and professionals discussed by Norbert Ropers, as well as the idea of reducing conflict by introducing minority rights, as advocated by Max van der Stoel.

Other authors, most forcefully Rogers Brubaker, point out that these cultures, identities, and feelings of belonging are consequences, not causes, of a conflict. "Ethnic groups" therefore do not necessarily represent actors with a common political purpose or cultural project, but sometimes a mere category with little political content. They are transformed into groups only if political leaders are able to convince their constituencies that the ethnic is indeed the most pertinent political cleavage. They often succeed in such mobilization by using violence and terror in a strategic way, as Michael Hechter and Peter Waldmann show.

This intellectual stance is reflected in attempts to depoliticize ethnicity and de-ethnicize politics through appropriate institutions that make it more costly for political entrepreneurs to play the ethnic game,[1] such as vote-pooling electoral systems (see Donald Horowitz) or fostering trans-ethnic civil society organizations (compare Donald Rothchild or Angel Viñas). Thus, seemingly academic issues turn out to be intimately connected to major policy debates: Different definitions of what an ethnic conflict is all about can lead to contrasting political strategies of intervention, as Conrad Schetter and Ulrike Joras argue in more detail in the previous chapter.

Other such poles of opposition map the field of debate. While some authors, notably Milton Esman and Donald Horowitz, advocate institutional designs that reduce incentives for conflictual behavior, others think that only a previous change of attitude, the overcoming of entrenched concepts of friend and foe, will make such institutional change feasible (compare Norbert Ropers). Some think that massive

violence can only be stopped by the threat of massive violence (a point
raised by Peter Waldmann), while others believe that violence has to be
overcome by empowering the peaceful sectors of society (see again
Norbert Ropers).

Most of these differences are well known in the debate about ethnic
conflicts and have structured the field for some time now. This is the case
for the opposition between an ethnosymbolist perspective, where the
political power of ethnic identities and cultures is emphasized, and an
instrumentalist, constructivist, or rational-choice perspective that sees
ethnicity as only one among other bases of political loyalty. The difference
between a sociopsychological approach privileging attitudinal changes
and a political and legal approach advocating institutional reform is also
well known from the literature—and not limited to the study of ethnic
conflict, but also prominent in discussions on gender equality, the
ecology, and so on.

The same holds true for the more obviously political divisions that
became apparent during the conference on which this volume is based:
Advocates of military interventions (usually to be found in defense
ministries) oppose a peace movement largely composed of "civil
society" organizations. Those believing in diplomatic tour de force
enterprises, such as those leading to the Dayton or Good Friday
agreement (usually well represented in foreign ministries), are known to
disagree with those advocating a bottom-up community mediation
approach.

It is not the intention of this volume to "solve" these issues, since
much of this variance is related, I believe, to fundamentally different
ways of looking at the political world—to paradigmatic differences in
the sense of Thomas Kuhn—that are hardly bridgeable or negotiable.
Either you believe, to give an example, that the political world is
composed of rational individuals using violence for precise strategic
reasons or you believe that it is made up of groups who resort to
violence as an emotional valve for deep-rooted collective traumata. As
in one of the famous trompe l'oeils by M. C. Escher, where you see the
stairs either from above or from below, you cannot take both
perspectives at the same time—and both reveal different, equally "true"
views of the world.

Rather than point to possible bridges across these divides, I would like
to discover the common ground on which these different opinions are
based—focusing on the fact that we all see a stairway and not a ladder, to
remain in the iconographic language. And, indeed, despite differing
starting points and different analytical lenses, many authors share,
sometimes implicitly and sometimes explicitly, certain basic insights
about the character of ethnic conflicts and the lessons learned so far in

dealing with them. And this shared ground entails more, as I will now show, than a set of truisms. Rather, we can point to five points of substantive convergence, to be discussed one by one in what follows.

COMPLEXITY

Various authors emphasize the complexity of ethnic conflicts and highlight the consequences both for explaining and for preventing, negotiating, or institutionally taming them. Four related aspects are discussed: the interlocking of institutions, the number and variety of actors, their interrelatedness, and, finally, the transnational dimensions of the conflict.

Most conflicts touch a whole set of interlocking political, legal, and economic institutions, and are thus not easily restricted to one single political arena, as is the case for example in labor conflicts. The system of government, the electoral system, the separation of powers, and the power distribution among different levels of government all influence the political behavior of leaders and followers and thus have to be addressed in their totality in order to provide the necessary institutional incentives for accommodation and compromise. This point is explicitly made in the contributions of Andrew Ellis on electoral systems, Donald Horowitz on power sharing, Michael Lund on prevention, and Walter Kälin on federalism.

Second, researchers as well as policymakers realized that it is erroneous to deal with an ethnic group in the singular, as if we were dealing with "the government of Russia" or "the trade union X or Y"—a point made by Rogers Brubaker and William Zartman. Members of ethnic categories are also women or men, peasants or bankers, townspeople or rural folks, voters or nonvoters, and so on. The internal heterogeneity of interests and the existence of cross-cutting identities are often reflected in a set of competing leaders and continuous infighting over what the "true" group interests are and who more adequately represents them. For policymakers designing strategies of prevention, intervention, or institutional channeling of conflicts, this represents a considerable challenge, since it makes the identification of possible partners a delicate task. Some experiences with "representative" ethnic organizations during the past decade have been rather bitter, both for outside policymakers struggling to find negotiation partners as well as for leaders of such organizations themselves when their representativity was tested at the ballots.

A third element of complexity arises from the relatedness of different actors, as Hugh Miall explains in some detail. Entrepreneurs of violence—warlords, gang leaders, underground organizations, and the like—are linked through networks of friendship, patronage, and political alliance with nonviolent actors and organizations. A conflict such as the one in Northern Ireland involves, in one form or another, almost the entire fabric of social relations. It is not an easily identifiable or, in surgical terms, easy-to-insulate trouble spot that can be acted upon without taking into account the encompassing political context. This makes intervention from the outside—and conscious conflict transformation from the inside—a much more difficult endeavor than what many analysts and policymakers had thought of when extrapolating from other experiences of conflict resolution.

In addition, we now pay more systematic attention to the fact that the conflicts do not end at the borders of national states.[2] The world is nowadays more interconnected than it might have appeared some decades ago. More important, the fact that almost every nation-state in the world contains ethnic minorities that also live in neighboring states, where they may form the dominant majority and control the state apparatus, gives ethnic conflicts very often a trans-border character— more so than is the case with other types of conflict.[3] Policymakers have learned that regional powers often hold the key to the solution of protracted conflicts.[4] Adding to the international dimension, international actors and institutions, each following their own policy agenda, have gained influence and importance after the end of the Cold War. Many of them are already present before the conflict turns violent, as Michael Lund emphasizes, and influence the course of events from the start, not as "outside" mediators but as actors in a complex power field. Hugh Miall's chapter elaborates how these global, regional, national, and local actors and factors are interlocking in producing a dynamic constellation of conflict that does not follow a linear progression from one clearly patterned stage to the next.

Rather, the sheer complexity resulting from the combination of various institutional logics moving different actors into different directions gives these conflicts a chaotic nature (Ricigliano 2001). René Lemarchand's chapter on the "road to hell in the Great Lakes region" unmistakably shows, on an empirical level, how the conflicts in Burundi, Rwanda, Congo, Angola, and the Sudan are historically related to each other—developments in one country spurring events and processes in other countries, which in turn feed back on the original development—a truly complex network of interlocking relationships and event flows across state boundaries. Realizing that a one-conflict/one-country/one-action approach is not adequate was a slow process, spurred by experience with the Rwandan drama, but also with other complexly interrelated conflicts.

We still lack an adequate language to describe and analyze these complexities. Most authors in this volume would perhaps agree that game theory or other prominent rational choice models—despite promising advances over the past years (Azam 2002; Fearon and Laitin 1996)—is still not adequately refined to tackle the multileveled and interrelated nature of ethnic conflict. To adequately represent the situation around the Great Lakes, for example, as the consequence of a series of prisoner-dilemma games with multiple plays and players seems an insurmountable task. Accordingly, we are still a far cry from having any true prognostic capacities—despite several serious attempts at developing such tools by researchers (Szayna 2000; Alker et al. 2001; Harff 2003) and NGOs such as International Alert or the Forum on Early Warning and Early Response. Early warning may point to a fire where it is already simmering, but no one can tell whether and when the winds that fan the flames will blow.

Acknowledging complexity leads, on the policy side, to important insights that are shared by the authors of this volume and beyond (see Sandole 1999 and the chapters in Crocker et al. 2001). Most important, a certain modesty about the possibilities of intervention is in order for several reasons. First, the sheer complexity of a political constellation makes it impossible to hold all intervening factors constant and to act on just one dimension or level. Bringing all leaders around a table and having them sign an agreement will not help in everyday politics, if among the rank and file there is no support for such an agreement. Complexity, in other words, "absorbs" the effects of an intervention, an insight that stands in opposition to the more technocratic notion, still prevalent in the early 1990s, of "managing" ethnic conflicts.[5]

Second, as Donald Horowitz shows, intervening agents as well as the actors themselves cannot possibly have an overview of the situation, let alone be knowledgeable about the consequences and side effects of their actions in a midterm perspective. Having the flexibility, both in organizational terms and in the strategic outlook chosen, to react to new developments and unforeseen changes of alliances is thus advisable, as some authors emphasized. One could add that enhancing the institutional learning capacities and skills of "knowledge management," to use a buzzword much *en vogue* in the consultancy community, should have a high priority in departments of foreign affairs and international organizations.

Third, the ideal conditions for a successful intervention are rarely given, because the complexity of such conflicts implies that there are too many variables in the equation that would have to be "controlled" at the same time. This conclusion is not drawn in an explicit way by the authors of this volume. However, a look at the chapters that specify the conditions for a successful implementation of one or the other conflict-reducing measure reveals that these conditions are only very rarely given.

Consider the ingredients for a successful prevention of ethnic violence that Michael Lund has identified. Such prevention includes, among many other things, the consistent and timely focus on both short-term conflicts as well as structural roots (such as power imbalances); draws international and regional powers into an alliance for peace; and builds up a trans-ethnic civil society, including a network of businesspeople. Successful prevention can count on the support of moderate leaders in all communities involved and is facilitated by a recent history of peaceful relations between communities.

Walter Kälin has analyzed the conditions under which federalism reduces rather than exacerbates ethnic strife. Decentralization has to be effective and involve real autonomy and transfer of resources while at the same time establishing cooperative relationships between central and provincial elites. The entire country should be federalized in order to avoid making federalism appear to be a privilege of minorities and in order to reduce the incentive for separatism. Finally, federalism should be combined with effective democracy on the national as well as the regional level, in order to avoid ethnocratic abuse of power and human rights violations.

A third example is provided by Donald Rothchild's discussion of democracy's effects on ethnic conflict. To reduce the propensity to violence that the democratic competition for power entails, several reforms should be undertaken simultaneously: A strong civil society independent of the state should emerge; a culture of political moderation and compromise should arise; a strong state that is capable of distributing its benefits on a universalistic, nonclientelist, and noncorrupt basis is to be built; and economic growth should keep up with the expectations raised by democratization.

INDIVIDUALITY

The complexity involved in ethnic conflicts leads our authors to a second important insight, most explicitly and forcefully expressed by Milton Esman, Hurst Hannum, Michael Lund, and Angel Viñas: that no case can be analyzed or "treated" like any other. While this sounds like a truism, it is nevertheless of considerable importance for the new realism among both the academic and policy-making communities. Researchers now are skeptical about the possibility of a general theory of ethnic and nationalist conflicts. This is especially remarkable for those who, after decades of analyzing the general mechanisms driving these conflicts, now seem to confine themselves to describing patterns, the various constellations that can be understood on a case-by-case basis. Paralleling general developments in the social sciences, the ideal of a single master scheme not historically or contextually specified that would explain why ethnicity does not matter in Switzerland while it does in Belgium, why ethnic relations are stable and remain low profile in Cameroon while they do not in Nigeria, seems to have been lost from sight. Instead, contextual and historical factors are highlighted: the history of ethnic relations in colonial times (Chris Bakwesegha and René Lemarchand) or the uniqueness of each constellation of power that informs decisions about institutional reform (Andrew Ellis).

When it comes to policy recommendations, this means that a solution has to be carefully tailored to the characteristics of each individual conflict, as Michael Lund and Angel Viñas emphasize. More specifically, the discussion on which electoral system is most apt to reduce the propensity to violence has ended in a plead for a case-to-case approach: Donald Horowitz and Andrew Ellis both conclude that the constellations of power in a national arena and the precise ethnodemographic relations determine whether systems with incentives to catch votes across ethnic boundaries or systems in which parties compete largely within ethnic constituencies are more adequate.

A similar conclusion is reached in the debate over the optimum division of power between the national center and subnational units. Walter Kälin, Hurst Hannum, and Michael Hechter maintain that no general recommendation can be made and that federalism and autonomy can either exacerbate or reduce violent ethnic conflict, depending on the resources that the center is capable of providing to the federal units, the degree of overlap between the political interests of federal and central elites, and the political culture allowing for moderation and compromise in what Michael Hechter calls "the federal gamble."[6] This is, again, a much more differentiated view than the one that prevailed a decade ago, when federalism was considered a catchall solution for ethnic conflicts, because it allows for a compromise between demands for self-rule and fears of losing territorial integrity.[7]

A third area where a case-by-case approach is explicitly advocated is the question whether retributive or restorative justice is more helpful in overcoming the schisms created by past violence. According to Richard Goldstone, truth commissions are a useful instrument where at least a large part of the population is not aware of the injustices of the past. It does not make sense where everybody knew what was going on and where violence was announced and committed in broad daylight, such as in Rwanda. In such cases, criminal prosecution may be the more adequate strategy. In others, such as in South Africa or potentially also in the Balkans, a combination of both may help to lay the ground for a new beginning.

The tailor approach also guides us to look for solutions that run contrary to what Western academics, experts, and policymakers cherish as the best possible institutional design. Outside experts systematically prefer, to give an example, "civic" over "ethnic" models; that is, they think that ethnicity- and color-blind institutions are morally and politically superior to institutions based on the compartmentalization of society along ethnic or racial lines. But this may run against the perceptions and goals of the political class of entire regions and represent a major obstacle to finding a solution with a sustainable chance of implementation, as the difficulties of Bosnian democracy after the Dayton agreement show (Pugh and Cobble 2001). In a similar vein, Hurst Hannum maintains that, in the long run, the quasi-sacrosanct status of international boundaries may be a major obstacle to finding lasting solutions for many entrenched ethnic conflicts. He opts for including boundary corrections and secession in the policy arsenal.[8]

Following Peter Waldmann, a territorial separation of conflicting parties and their respective constituencies should not always be opposed but arranged for in a nonviolent way because, according to his analysis of the self-sustaining and self-amplifying logic of violence, this may be the only means of giving the forces of peace a chance (see also Kaufmann 1998). He does not discuss, however, the political implications, such as the incentives for ethnic cleansings, of such a return to the "population exchange" model of the League of Nations. Donald Rothchild convincingly argues that Western governments should support or even encourage institutional solutions that accommodate the specific political realities of individual African countries, even if such solutions deviate from standard models of majoritarian democracy. He mentions reserved parliament seats for minority groups, communal legislative chambers, consultative bodies, and other nonmajoritarian forms of political participation usually banned from the list of "good" democratic practices.

DEPTH

Differentiating between individual cases and tailored solutions does not mean that no generalizations about the dynamics of ethnic conflicts can be made. The general trend reflected in this volume is to see such conflicts as *deeply and closely related to the basic political institutions*. This comes as no surprise to the veterans of ethnic conflict research. It is a "new" insight, however, for those who have recently shifted their research and policy interest to the field. As Rogers Brubaker, Walker Connor, Milton Esman, and others have noted, this group of authors soon realized that ethnonational conflicts are not merely about resource distribution or the balance of power between political parties. Conformingly, there are specific difficulties in negotiating peace that international relations specialists find surprising. William Zartman describes these specificities in his contribution: A zero-sum attitude prevails when it comes to questions of sovereignty or recognition of a group as a nationality; negotiations and calls for outside mediators are avoided because they would mean recognizing the enemy as a legitimate representative of such a group; and solidarity along ethnic or national lines perdures only as long as the conflict goes on—which again creates a vested interest in *not* arriving at a negotiated agreement.

These three difficulties in negotiating peace already hint toward the specific nature of such conflicts. Many authors note that they directly relate to the fundamental institutions of a nation-state, in other words, to the distribution of power and the structure of its political and legal systems. This position is reflected in various shadings and colorings in a number of chapters. René Lemarchand shows that it is the systematic and institutionalized discrimination against certain ethnic groups that provides the fuel for the conflicts in the Great Lakes region. More precisely, the monopolization of the modern state apparatus and the tailoring of its legal and political systems to the interests and needs of one particular group—either Hutu or Tutsi—set the spiral of mobilization and repression in motion.

For Milton Esman, the way the state elites define the relationship between themselves, as members of the core "national" group, and other ethnic groups explains much of the dynamics of accommodation and conflict. His typology of state-ethnicity relations, including assimilationism, meritocracy, and multiculturalism, makes clear that ethnic conflicts may arise in all three models, depending on how the state is perceived in ethnonational terms and how power is distributed among such groups.

Chris Bakwesegha too maintains that preferentialism, nepotism, and clientelism along ethnic lines are at the heart of ethnic conflicts. Such practices of bad governance are a legacy of colonial times, when ethnic preferentialism was part and parcel of the politics of divide and rule.[9] William Zartman elaborates the same theme in another conceptual language. He finds that discrimination along ethnic lines produces a mixture between interest-driven demands (greed) and issues of identity and dignity (grievances) that is difficult to resolve. Ethnic conflicts thus exemplify the more general point that when identities come into play and structure the perception of one's own interests, to paraphrase Max Weber's famous dictum (Weber 1920:252), the resulting amalgam may powerfully direct the choice of political strategies. It also explains why these conflicts may appear, at least on the surface, to be entirely driven by questions of identity and culture, as Walker Connor states in his caveat against overstating the economic and political side of the Weberian equation.

In summary, there seems to be agreement that (1) ethnic conflicts are directly related to fundamental structures of inclusion and exclusion of modern nation-states, or, more precisely, they are the effects of ethnic clientelism, favoritism, and corresponding forms of discrimination along ethnonational lines.[10] I am happy to note that this largely conforms to my own theoretical positions and research findings (Wimmer 2002). (2) They characteristically produce a mixture of ideas (identity) and interests (control of the state) that have to be taken seriously both analytically and in the search for adequate policy options. Finally, (3) the interlocking of identity and interests often make standard negotiating techniques fail and may put a "rational deal" out of reach of those sitting at the negotiating tables (cf. Byman 2002:chapter 8).

There are important policy implications that derive from what we may call, in experts' jargon, the deep-seated nature of the "root causes." First, only a multistranded approach will help to overcome violent ethnic conflicts. Official negotiations at roundtables—which may address major issues such as power sharing, the restructuring of security forces, and the redesign of state institutions—will have to be combined with "unofficial" efforts of negotiating around kitchen tables, mediating between leaders of civil society organizations, and reconciling victims of terror and violence. Given the deep-seated character of ethnic conflicts, it has become clear that such a combination of approaches is necessary for a durable and encompassing transformation of the conflict. The belief in "multitrack" diplomacy, as the technical jargon puts it, seems to have achieved an almost hegemonic status among both scholars and professional negotiators, notwithstanding some cautious remarks, for example, by Hugh Miall. This new orthodoxy was repeatedly evoked during the Bonn conference (see also Crocker et al. 2001). In this volume, the main arguments are summarized by Michael Lund.

Second and perhaps more important, negotiating peace more often than not touches upon the most vital interests of powerful actors and the fundamental rules of the political game. This entails two consequences. First, which agreement or institutional design has a chance of being adopted depends on the constellation of forces and the balance of power between the different players. While this, again, is certainly not an entirely new insight (see Nordlinger 1972:chapter 3), its recent spread provided an important caveat against the technocratic utopia, quite widespread in the early 1990s, that the "best solution" designed by experienced international experts will be adopted by policymakers in the national arena. Andrew Ellis shows that the geometry of power between national parties, the army, and other important actors at specific historical junctures determined which electoral system was adopted in Indonesia, Sri Lanka, and Guyana. Experience taught him a sober realism with regard to the possibility of outside intervention and consulting. In the short run, he argues, outside consultants and experts may have to find "best solutions" within the rather narrow horizon of established local political traditions and existing parameters of power. In a long-term perspective, alternative institutional models can be introduced to the national debate and perhaps one day be adopted.

Other examples, such as the Guatemaltecan case that Angela Kane discussed at the conference, show that even the most carefully mediated and drafted institutional designs meant to overcome ethnic discrimination and exclusion, including a reform of the educational system and a solution to the thorny issue of recognizing official languages (Kane 2001), have no chance in a democratic process—often simultaneously promoted by the same international forces as part of a peace agreement—if they do not conform to the perceived interests of the majority of voters. The new constitution was rejected by a narrow but significant majority in a popular referendum in 1999.

Second, we arrive at a caveat against an overly enthusiastic and mechanistic promotion of minority rights regimes and power-sharing formulas by outside forces: To be adopted, such steps toward a more inclusive power balance have to appeal to the most powerful actors, including ruling state elites or, under conditions of concomitant democratization as was the case in Guatemala, of powerful voting blocs. The promotion of minority rights, power-sharing arrangements, autonomous regions or provinces, and so on may appeal to the leaders of ethnonationalist movements. Without taking into account the perceived interests of majority and state governments, support for such proposals by the international community may quickly lead to a dead end or even exacerbate the very conflicts that these proposals are meant to overcome, as Michael Lund observes.

PERSISTENCE AND DURABILITY

While the basic structures of the political system are at the heart of violent ethnic conflicts, recent scholarship has also drawn attention to the self-sustaining logic of violence, once it has been set in motion. Additional factors and dynamics, not directly related to those accounting for the emergence of a conflict in the first place, come to influence the chain of events and transform the interests of actors. Peter Waldmann offers a fine-grained analysis of the power disequilibria between those actors who choose violence over those who prefer peaceful strategies of pursuing political ends. These disequilibria stem from the well-known security dilemma (counting on the enemy's worst intentions pays), the logic of revenge and the culture of violence that emerge over time, as well as the tendency for violence to draw ever more actors and resources into a conflict.[11]

William Zartman points to the importance of war economies for both understanding and intervening in ethnic conflicts—a topic that has received much attention, not so much in this volume but in the broader literature on civil wars. The debate was set in motion with Collier and Hoeffler, who argued that it is "greed" for diamonds, gold, and other lootable resources rather than "grievances" about social injustice that motivates civil wars in the developing world (Collier and Hoeffler 2000). For other researchers, claims for ethnic justice, minority rights, and power sharing are less important in explaining ethnic wars than a territory for rebels to retreat, a government too weak to repress guerrilla forces effectively, and so on (Fearon and Laitin 2003). However, this does not explain why rebels bother at all to frame their demands in the language of ethnonational justice—instead of posing simply as bandits or warlords.[12] We are perhaps well advised *not* to take such aspects of military-technical feasibility as original driving forces for ethnic conflicts, but as factors explaining their reproduction and perpetuation. After all, this important strand of research has taught us that more realism and less idealism are in place when assessing the motives of minority rebels and guerillas.

"Markets of violence" (Elwert 1999) indeed create their own dynamics, not necessarily related to the fundamental political issues that led to the politicization of ethnicity. The seizure of lootable raw materials (such as the much-discussed "blood diamonds"), the recruitment of fighters, their provision with looted property or international aid packages—none of these warlord strategies is feasible any longer if a peaceful settlement of the conflict is reached. Thus, violence creates its own environment conducive to further violence and to a political economy of looting and war, with a new structure of incentives and interests difficult to address at the negotiation table.

This adds to the points already made at the end of the preceding section: It may be good advice, as Peter Waldmann points out, to have a special eye on the entrepreneurs of violence who can sabotage a negotiated agreement.[13] As Aldo Ajello, special representative of the European Union to the Great Lakes region, made clear during his keynote speech at the conference, it is necessary to give economic incentives not only to warlords and guerrilla leaders, but also to the rank and file of armed men who have no other skills than fighting and looting. Thus, a durable solution for a war-torn society has to address those economic motives and incentives, especially where war has led to the implosion of state institutions and to political devolution into a series of fiefdoms and small tributary states.

On a yet more general level, it has become clear by now that the deep-rooted character and the tenacity of these conflicts imply that they are phenomena of a long-term nature.[14] Such conflicts do not erupt in a single decade and most of them will not be settled in a single decade. Their life cycle often spans generations, as Walker Connor argues in his contribution. Sometimes, he says, the conflict recedes into the background—as was the case with the Basque conflict or Northern Ireland. Networks of personal relations across community divides may be mistaken as signs of a sustainable peace, as Donald Horowitz notes. As long as the state continues to exclude sections of the population along ethnonational lines, however, the potential for rekindling the fire is always there, awaiting political entrepreneurs capable of formulating a discourse of injustice and of organizing a following.

With regard to policy making, both the persistence and the durability of ethnic conflicts demand much staying power from outside mediators. This is made clear by many authors of this volume, including a good number of persons with firsthand experience in conflict prevention, intervention, and institutional design (Andrew Ellis, Hugh Miall, Norbert Ropers, Donald Rothchild, and Angel Viñas). This again may seem obvious, especially to the veterans of ethnic conflict research, but for the conflict management community it represents a considerable step forward toward a more realistic assessment of the time horizon necessary for conflict transformation. In the field of mediation, to give an example, sociopsychological concepts of small-group conflicts were transferred to the large and heavily politicized field of ethnic conflict, a move initially accompanied by an overly optimistic and entrepreneurial assessment of the potential for overcoming deeply entrenched conflicts through dialogue workshops and seminars. Now it seems to be generally recognized, as many of the above-mentioned authors make clear, that even such necessarily localized projects involving a few dozen people may often need a time span of several years to achieve results. When it comes to the more structural and institutional issues of building up a democratic culture of moderation and compromise, a civil society with trans-ethnic networks, and so on, time is counted in decades, not in years.

BOUNDED MEDIATORS

Who has so much time? Politicians in Western democracies certainly do not, although they may be well aware of the time dimensions involved in conflict resolution. Costly and politically risky endeavors, such as organizing a new round of negotiations in a protracted conflict, let alone sending one's own troops on peace-enforcing or peacekeeping missions, have to promise an immediate payback, otherwise the incentives for intervention are too weak. This brings me to the last element of a more realistic assessment of prevention, peaceful settlement, or institutional channeling of ethnic conflict: the growing awareness that outside generals, diplomats, consultants, and peace activists are bound by their own interests and ideas. The institutional constraints that shape their action and that influence peace building and maintenance both positively and negatively are addressed by several authors of this book, focusing on various types of organizations from IGOs to NGOs.[15]

Donald Horowitz argues that due to the characteristically short time horizon of democratic politics, crisis managers are principally interested in a quick settlement and solution of crises that have gained international media attention. The optimal long-term solution to a conflict is not their business. They represent the firefighters rather than the construction engineer: They want to put out fires before running cameras, rather than construct fireproof buildings.[16]

In his contribution to the conference, Joseph Montville showed which institutional constraints effectively limit government capacities for early action and prevention: First, since they already face too many burning conflicts, the energy and time for prevention are simply in too short supply. Second, prevention is politically risky because nobody can tell whether, without prevention, a conflict would indeed have erupted. Third, early action implies recognizing the failure of earlier assessments and policy choices—and thus runs against the laws of path-dependent action typical of large bureaucracies (Montville 2001).

It may be argued that some of these difficulties can be overcome through the creation of specialized institutions with different incentive structures. The chapter by Max van der Stoel shows that an office like the OSCE high commissioner for minorities, whose mandate is entirely focused on prevention and behind-the-scenes negotiations before a conflict gains international media attention, can indeed be effective. Compromise solutions, including minority rights, ombudsmen, or consultative bodies to discuss minority grievances, may be accepted by moderate forces on both sides at an early stage of the conflict when pragmatism still prevails and compromise is still possible. Ethnic discrimination may thus gradually be reduced and the core of the state opened for minorities hitherto excluded.

Different sorts of constraints are faced by NGOs. One could argue that they are in the same way as specialized departments in governments and international organizations, subject to Parson's law of institutional growth and therefore have an intrinsic interest in discovering "ethnic conflicts" in need of mediation and reconciliation. They may thus play an important role in framing conflicts as ethnic—in the sense of Rogers Brubaker—and therefore may have contributed to what Conrad Schetter and Ulrike Joras describe as a shift in public perceptions of older conflicts, formerly perceived along Cold War lines and then reclassified as "ethnic." Norbert Ropers shows, in a somewhat different context, how difficult it is to measure the effectiveness of NGOs' performance, since the evaluation obviously depends on the goals set and is hampered by the fact that successful prevention remains invisible.[17] He also notices that solid evaluation started only recently and has not, so far, become a routine part of NGOs' operations—which would certainly help to overcome some of the difficulties mentioned.

Another and surely more controversial point refers to the models that outside mediators recommend as solutions to ethnic conflicts. In recent years, skepticism has grown about the liberal belief, strongly reinforced after the end of the Cold War, that all good things go together in life: that the fostering of good governance, democratization, and the introduction of minority rights will automatically lead a country to follow the paths of political moderation on which established Western democracies seem to travel. Some authors in this volume even maintain that what is usually considered a cure for ethnic conflicts may well be their cause: Democratization, the introduction of the idea of minority "rights," the notion of discrimination-free good governance, and a "just" distribution of the benefits of development may destabilize established ethnoracial hierarchies and start a cycle of political mobilization, repression, and violence.

There are several variants, stronger and weaker, of this thesis.[18] Following Donald Horowitz and Walter Kälin, democracy pure and simple is not enough to avoid an escalation of ethnic tensions or the violation of the human rights of members of minority groups. The competitive politics and election campaigning of majoritarian democracy may exacerbate conflicts and lead to a radicalization of positions, as was the case for example in Sri Lanka, if no precautions are built into the democratic institutions (Donald Horowitz). Walter Kälin argues that unitarian democracy without federal provisions may lead to the violation of human and minority rights.

Michael Lund takes a slightly broader view on the issue. According to him, democratic representation, special protection and rights for minorities, and a nondiscriminatory delivery of public services may destabilize taken-for-granted ethnic hierarchies, in which a particular ethnonational group legitimately "owns" the state while deference and silence are taken as appropriate behaviors for members of "ethnic minorities."[19] The liberalizing dynamics of democracy and accountable government lead, at least in the short run, to a politicization of ethnic inequalities and may lead into a spiral of escalating demands for justice and provoke counterreactions aimed at safeguarding the privileged positions of ethnocratic elites.

This is more or less in line with the position that Donald Rothchild elaborates in his chapter on Africa. According to his review of the literature, stable and established democracies tend to handle ethnic conflicts peacefully, but *democratization* in the developing world often stirs up such conflicts. A strong civil society, independent of the state and of outside donor support, and an equally strong state administration capable of resisting the gravitation of ethnic nepotism and clientelism are among the conditions that may help to avoid the destabilizing effects of democratization. These conditions, it should be recalled, were absent in much of Western Europe throughout the first half of the twentieth century (Snyder 2000). The spiral of nationalist mobilizations in an environment of rapid democratization played an important role in the events that led to World War I and to the major genocides of the twentieth century (Mann 1999). While more research is needed to fully understand the relationship between democratization and ethnic violence, this volume documents the skepticism that has arisen over the last decade against assessing democracy's potential to solve the ethnic issue in an overly optimistic way.

Several policy implications flow from this. First, fostering democratization as a foreign policy and long-term security goal in itself—a position emphatically stated by EU official Angel Viñas—may conflict with the goal of preventing ethnic conflict and violence in the short run. There is no easy solution to this dilemma. Both Michael Lund and Donald Rothchild recommend allowing democratization and political modernization to proceed at a speed geared to the effective capacities of the political system and the society at large to absorb the conflicts that a dynamized political arena produces.[20] For outside forces this implies, as both point out, more tolerance if not active support for nonmajoritarian forms of political participation and, as Donald Rothchild repeatedly emphasizes, for what he calls a minimal democracy with competitive elections but no full political rights.

Second and perhaps less controversial, democratization, the introduction of minority rights, or power-sharing arrangements have to be supported by powerful local actors if they are going to be sustainable and effectively reduce the potential for violence and conflict. As Angel Viñas—who, at the time of writing his chapter, was responsible for the European Union's 100-billion-euro democratization-support program— makes clear, this was a lesson that still had to be learned in the early

1990s. Consequently, the European Union's program now focuses on bringing about the political environment for sustainable democratization through the support of civil society organizations. Such an approach, I should like to add, also changes the relationship between outside democracy support and local forces—rather than one between enforcement agency and object of action, it will be one of partners for a common goal: to help democracy work out its potential for domesticating political competition and to reduce its propensity to exacerbate tension between ethnic communities.

SUMMARY

Five elements of a new realism emerge from the pages of this book. Each includes research-based analysis and experience-based policy lessons. Acknowledging the complexity of ethnic conflicts, we are well advised to expect modest effects—and not always in the direction intended—even of forceful interventions and to advocate for more flexibility and a culture of learning within intervening organizations. Knowing about the individuality of each conflict reinforces the case-by-case approach, especially in the domain of institutional design. Ethnic conflicts are about access to and control over the nation-state and therefore involve a large section of the population and touch upon their fundamental political interests. This deep-seated nature of ethnic conflicts demands a multistranded approach for intervention and conflict transformation, one taking into account the specific constellations of power and the interests of all the major actors. The deep-seated nature of ethnic conflicts explains why they seem to be so perdurable,[21] why they often span entire generations, not years. In addition, ethnic conflicts are especially tenacious when an economy of war and a market of violence have flourished in their shadow. The policy recommendations that follow from this are to take these economic factors seriously when trying to broker a settlement and to develop a long-term framework even for shorter-term programs. The institutional and ideological constraints on intervening organizations have become clearer in the last decade, and it seems that creating the right institutional incentives and broadening the range of political options may help to overcome some of these limitations. Box 22.1 provides a more detailed summary of these five elements.

Looking back, the end of the Cold War brought not only a reshifting of the political lines of conflict, but also a heightened capacity and propensity for intervention in such conflict. In parallel, the technocratic utopia of nineteenth-century positivism and of the developmentalist

Box 22.1.   Five Elements of a New Realism Facing Ethnic Conflicts

Elements of Analysis	Policy Elements
Complexity • Institutional interlocking • Internal heterogeneity of groups • Interrelatedness of actors • Transnational connections	Modesty about the possibilities of prevention and intervention because • complexity limits effects of prevention and intervention; • overview and knowledge of long-term consequences are lacking; and • multiple conditions for success are rarely given. Organizational response could include • enhancing flexibility and adaptability of intervening organizations; and • heightening learning capacities of intervening organizations.
Individuality	Case-by-case approach, for example with regard to • electoral systems, • autonomy and federalist arrangements, and • mixture between retributive and restorative justice.
Depth • Ethnic conflicts are about participation and exclusion from state power. • Interpenetration of political interests and cultural identities is characteristic. • Standard negotiation strategies don't work.	A multistranded approach is necessary (multitrack diplomacy, encompassing conflict-transformation approach, and the like) for prevention, intervention, and institutional channeling of ethnic conflicts. Proposals from the outside have to take into account • the constellation of power at a given historical moment; and • interests and perceptions of major actors, including voting majorities and government elites.
Durability • Ethnic conflicts are long-term phenomena. Persistence • Violence has a self-sustaining character. • War economies transform incentive structures.	Long-time horizon is necessary for successful intervention. Economic interests of conflict parties (including entrepreneurs of violence and rank-and-file fighters) have to be taken into account in negotiating durable peace.

| Mediators are bound by institutional interests and constraints. | Modifying organizational structures and proceedings through:
• creation of adequate institutions with different incentive structures; and
• systematic evaluations. |
| Mediators are bound by their own political models and ideals, usually not taking into account that
• democratization, introducing minority rights, and so on may exacerbate rather than reduce ethnic violence.
• local actors may consistently aim for other models of state and democracy (e.g., a unitarian and homogenous nation state). | Broaden the approach by considering:
• democratization with carefully designed incentives for moderation of ethnic claims;
• allowing democratization to proceed according to local capacities of conflict absorption and management; and
• new options (secession, minimal democracy, nonmajoritarian forms of democracy, ethnonational federalism). |

community of the postwar era was revived. Democracy, rule of law, federalism, and minority rights seemed to be the formulas that would bring peace and stability to conflict-torn societies. Mediation, reconciliation, and dialogue would overcome community divides and enable people to discover the human other in their former enemies.

The debate has entered the stage of adulthood now, with a more realistic assessment of the possibilities of prevention, intervention, and institutional design—paralleled by a more realistic view of the potential to influence the policy agenda of the powerful through sound research. This second dimension of realism, not discussed in this volume, was greatly enhanced by the recent rise of the doctrine of preventive war in the U.S. administration and consecutively among many regional powers across the world, with at best uncertain consequences for the prospects of peaceful settlement of ethnic conflicts. A "disinterested" approach to civil wars in the developing world, one not driven primarily by perceived national security interests but by a broader concern with stability and peace, is no longer a shared vision of the majority of Western governments. The hope for a new world order, in which governments, NGOs, and researchers would jointly work toward "managing" and "solving" ethnic conflicts around the word by spreading multicultural justice and democratic participation, has evaporated. However, the lessons learnt during the past decade remain valid for the future, even under the modified geopolitical circumstances that the events of September 11 have brought about. Realism remains the best ally of sustainable optimism, for it saves from false judgments and subsequent disappointments. I hope, perhaps rather unrealistically, that this volume will provide a renewed impetus to search for more adequate ways of understanding and dealing with what remains one of the most salient problems of the contemporary world.

NOTES

1. Jabri (1996) provides a general critique of traditional conflict resolution approaches. She takes them to task for merely reproducing institutionalized dividing lines and discourses of difference, instead of analyzing their origin and providing alternatives.

2. For earlier treatments of the international aspects of ethnic conflict, see Shiels (1984), Boucher et al. (1987), Heraclides (1991), Moynihan (1993), and Ryan (1990). Carment (1994) gives an overview.

3. Discussion of the possible cross-border "contagious effects" of ethnic conflicts are provided by Lake and Rothchild (1998), Saideman (2001), and Lobell and Mauceri (2004); Gurr (1993b:181) and Gleditsch (2003) find statistical evidence; and Horowitz (1985:267–270, 278f.) gives examples of secessionist chain reactions.

4. Crocker et al. (2001) notice a "return of geopolitics" in American discussions on peacemaking, contrasting with the one-country approach at the beginning of the 1990s.

5. Some empirical evidence for the limited effects of intervention is provided, with regard to UN interventions, by Carment (1998).

6. For an excellent comparative evaluation, on the basis of a large number of case studies, of the conditions for sustainable federalization, see McGarry and O'Leary (2003).

7. Some of this optimism can still be seen in Scherrer (2002) or a recent article of Gurr (2000), for whom the decline in the number of ethnic conflicts in the second half of the 1990s results from, among other things, the successful implementation of autonomy regulations.

8. See also the recent discussion in Byman (2002:chapter 7).

9. In concordance with this approach, a quantitative analysis found that French and British colonialism implied different legacies of ethnic stratification and therefore have left different propensities and frequencies of ethnic conflict; see Blanton et al. (2001).

10. See the empirical research in Horowitz (1985:194), Hyden and Williams (1994), and Grodeland et al. (2000).

11. For an earlier statement along these lines, see Kuper (1977).

12. See the critique of Collier and Hoeffler and other microeconomic approaches by Cramer (2002). His call for a "liberation struggle" against "economic imperialism" risks diverting attention from his otherwise well-taken points of criticism.

13. On the importance of neutralizing "spoilers" to a peace agreement, see the empirical evidence derived from case study comparisons by Stedman (2001).

14. In Gurr's analysis of 227 politically mobilized ethnic groups, the strongest statistical correlation shows that groups already mobilized and involved in conflict in the 1970s found themselves still in a similar situation in the 1980s (Gurr 1993b:182, 186).

15. Recently, a literature has developed around the role of development cooperation in preventing or promoting ethnic conflict. See Muscat (2002), Esman and Herring (2001), and Esman and Telhami (1995).

16. According to quantitative research, it is not the neutrality of mediators in a specific conflict but their power on a global scale that explains how often they have been intervening in ongoing conflicts (Bercovitch and Schneider 2000). International conflict management may thus be seen as part of global and regional hegemonic structures rather than as an exercise in disinterested peacemaking.

Richard K. Betts has a different take on this issue and sees partiality as a *condition* for successful intervention. According to him, it is a delusion to believe that a successful intervention can be neutral and at the same time limited in its extent. When intervention is limited militarily and politically, only "taking sides" with one of the parties in conflict will end the stalemate (Betts 2001). Similarly, Stephen Stedman concludes, on the basis of studying sixteen peacemaking efforts, that success depends whether the great powers or regional hegemons support a UN intervention (Stedman 2001).

17. See the special issue of the *Journal of Peace Research*, introduced by Pearson (2001). The difficulties for measuring NGO effectiveness are also noted by Aall (2001).

18. For statistical evidence, see Gurr (1994) and Yalcin Mousseau (2001).

19. The fact that ethnic inequality does not automatically lead to political mobilization and rebellion explains why researchers find no strong correlation between inequality and ethnic conflict in cross-national research (Gurr 1993a; Majstorovic 1995; Fearon and Laitin 2003). Active political discrimination against an ethnic group is even detrimental to a rebellion, as Gurr (1993a:28) finds, probably because the costs of repression are higher in such a situation. This repeats, evidently, a point that has been made with regard to income and wealth inequalities since Alexis de Tocqueville. Cramer (2003) gives a full account, from a political economy perspective, of the complex interrelations between inequality and conflict.

20. A strong argument in favor of enhancing conflict regulation capacities *before* democratization is presented by Paris (2001). For a review of the debate in the United States, see Baker (2001).

21. For statistical evidence, see Gurr (1994) and Fearon and Laitin (2003).

REFERENCES

Aall, Pamela. 2001. What Do NGOs Bring to Peacemaking? In *Turbulent Peace: The Challenges of Managing International Conflict*, ed. Chester A. Crocker, Fen Osler Hampson, and Pamela Aall, 365–383. Washington, DC: U.S. Institute for Peace Press.

Alker, Hayward R., Ted Robert Gurr, and Kumar Rupesinghe, eds. 2001. *Journeys through Conflict: Narratives and Lessons*. Lanham, Md.: Rowman & Littlefield.

Azam, Jean-Paul. 2002. Looting and Conflict between Ethnoregional Groups: Lessons for State Formation in Africa. *Journal of Conflict Resolution* 46 (1):131–153.

Baker, Pauline H. 2001. Conflict Resolution versus Democratic Governance: Divergent Paths to Peace? In *Turbulent Peace: The Challenges of Managing International Conflict*, ed. Chester A. Crocker, Fen Osler Hampson, and Pamela Aall, 753–764. Washington, DC: U.S. Institute for Peace Press.

Berberoglu, Berch, ed. 1995. *The National Question: Nationalism, Ethnic Conflict, and Self-Determination in the 20th Century*. Philadelphia: Temple University Press.

Bercovitch, Jacob, and Gerald Schneider. 2000. Who Mediates? The Political Economy of International Conflict Management. *Journal of Peace Research* 37 (2):145–165.

Betts, Richard K. 2001. The Delusion of Impartial Intervention. In *Turbulent Peace: The Challenges of Managing International Conflict*, ed. Chester A. Crocker, Fen Osler Hampson, and Pamela Aall, 285–294. Washington, DC: U.S. Institute for Peace Press.

Blanton, Robert, David T. Mason, and Brian Athow. 2001. Colonial Style and Post-Colonial Ethnic Conflict in Africa. *Journal of Peace Research* 38 (4):473–491.

Boucher, Jerry, Dan Landis, and Karen Clark. 1987. *Ethnic Conflict: International Perspectives*. Newbury Park, CA: Sage.

Bowman, Glen. 1994. Xenophobia, Fantasy and the Nation: The Logic of Ethnic Violence in former Yugoslavia. In *The Anthropology of Europe. Identities and Boundaries in Conflict*, ed. Victoria A. Goddard, Joseph Llobera, and Cris Shore. London: Berg.

Byman, Daniel L. 2002. *Lasting Solutions to Ethnic Conflict*. Baltimore: Johns Hopkins University Press.

Carment, David. 1994. The Ethnic Dimension in World Politics: Theory, Policy and Early Warning. *Third World Quarterly* 15 (4):551–582.

———. 1998. The United Nations at 50: Managing Ethnic Crises—Past and Present. *Journal of Peace Research* 35 (1):61–82.

Collier, Paul, and Anke Hoeffler. 2000. *Greed and Grievance in Civil War*. Washington, DC: World Bank Development Research Group.

Cramer, Christopher. 2002. *Homo Economicus* Goes to War: Methodological Individualism, Rational Choice and the Political Economy of War. *World Development* 30 (11): 1845–1864.

———. 2003. Does Inequality Cause Conflict? *Journal of International Development* 15:397–412.

Crocker, Chester A., Fen Osler Hampson, and Pamela Aall. 2001. Introduction. In *Turbulent Peace: The Challenges of Managing International Conflict*, ed. Chester A. Crocker, Fen Osler Hampson, and Pamela Aall, 15–25. Washington, DC: U.S. Institute for Peace Press.

Elwert, Georg. 1999. Markets of Violence. In *Dynamics of Violence: Processes of Escalation and Deescalation of Violent Group Conflicts*, ed. Georg Elwert, Stephan Feuchtwang, and Dieter Neubert, 85–102. Berlin: Duncker & Humboldt.

Esman, Milton J., and Ronald J. Herring, eds. 2001. *Carrots, Sticks, and Ethnic Conflict: Rethinking Development Assistance*. Lansing: University of Michigan Press.

Esman, Milton J., and Shibley Telhami, eds. 1995. *International Organizations and Ethnic Conflict*. Ithaca, NY: Cornell University Press.

Fearon, James D., and David D. Laitin. 1996. Explaining Interethnic Cooperation. *American Political Science Review* 90 (4):715–735.

———. 2003. Ethnicity, Insurgency, and Civil War. *American Political Science Review* 97 (1):1–16.

Gleditsch, Kristian S. 2003. *Transnational Dimensions of Civil War*. Unpublished manuscript. University of California, San Diego.

Grodeland, Ase B., William L. Miller, and Tatyana Y. Koshechkina. 2000. The Ethnic Dimension to Bureaucratic Encounters in Postcommunist Europe: Perceptions and Experience. *Nations and Nationalism* 6 (1):43–66.

Gurr, Ted R. 1993a. *Minorities at Risk: A Global View of Ethnopolitical Conflict*. Washington, DC: U.S. Institute of Peace Press.

———. 1993b. Why Minorities Rebel: A Global Analysis of Communal Mobilization and Conflict since 1945. *International Political Science Review* 14 (2):161–201.

———. 1994. Peoples against the State: Ethnopolitical Conflict in the Changing World System. *International Studies Quarterly* 38:347–377.

———. 2000. Ethnic Warfare on the Wane. *Foreign Affairs* 79 (3):52–64.

Harff, Barbara. 2003. No Lessons Learned from the Holocaust? Assessing the Risks of Genocide and Political Mass Murder since 1955. *American Political Science Review* 97(1):57–73.

Heraclides, Alexis. 1991. *The Self-Determination of Minorities in International Politics*. London: Frank Cass.

Horowitz, Donald L. 1985. *Ethnic Groups in Conflict*. Berkeley: University of California Press.

Hyden, Goran, and Donald C. Williams. 1994. A Community Model of African Politics: Illustrations from Nigeria and Tanzania. *Comparative Studies in Society and History* 26 (1):68–96.

Jabri, Vivienne. 1996. *Discourses on Violence: Conflict Analysis Reconsidered*. Manchester, UK: Manchester University Press.

Jentleson, Bruce W. 2001. Preventive Statecraft: A Realist Strategy for the Post-Cold War Era. In *Turbulent Peace: The Challenges of Managing International Conflict*, ed. Chester A. Crocker, Fen Osler Hampson, and Pamela Aall, 249–264. Washington, DC: U.S. Institute of Peace Press.

Kane, Angela. 2001, December. *Negotiating Peace and Ethnic Equality: The Guatemalan Experience*. Paper presented at the conference Facing Ethnic Conflicts, Bonn, Germany.

Kaplan, Robert. 1993. *Balkan Ghosts: A Journey through History*. New York: St. Martin's Press.

Kaufmann, Chaim. 1998. When All Else Fails: Separation as a Remedy for Ethnic Conflicts, Ethnic Partitions and Population Transfers in the Twentieth Century. *International Security* 23 (2):120–156.

Krasner, Stephen. 1986. *International Regimes*. Ithaca, NY: Cornell University Press.

Kuper, Leo. 1977. *The Pity of It All: Polarization of Racial and Ethnic Relations*. Minneapolis: University of Minnesota Press.

Lake, David A., and Donald Rothchild, eds. 1998. *The International Spread of Ethnic Conflict*. Princeton, NJ: Princeton University Press.

Lobell, Steven E., and Philip Mauceri, eds. 2004. *Ethnic Conflict and International Politics: Explaining Diffusion and Escalation*. Houndsmill, UK: Palgrave Macmillan.

Majstorovic, Steven. 1995. Politicized Ethnicity and Economic Inequality: A Subjective Perspective and a Cross-National Examination. *Nationalism and Ethnic Politics* 1 (1):33–53.

Mann, Michael. 1999. The Dark Side of Democracy: The Modern Tradition of Ethnic and Political Cleansing. *New Left Review* 235:18–45.

McGarry, John, and Brendan O'Leary. 2003, September. *Federalism, Conflict-Regulation and Ethnic Power-Sharing*. Paper presented at the Annual Meeting of the American Political Science Association, Philadelphia.

Miall, Hugh, Oliver Ramsbotham, and Tom Woodhouse. 2001. *Contemporary Conflict Resolution: The Prevention, Management and Transformation of Deadly Conflicts*. Cambridge: Polity Press.

Montville, Joseph. 2001, December. *Strategic Planning in Preventive Diplomacy*. Paper presented at the conference Facing Ethnic Conflicts, Bonn, Germany.

Moynihan, Daniel Patrick. 1993. *Pandaemonium: Ethnicity and International Politics*. Oxford: Oxford University Press.

Muscat, Robert J. 2002. *Investing in Peace: How Development Aid Can Prevent or Promote Conflict*. Armonk, NY: M.E. Sharpe.

Nordlinger, Eric A. 1972. *Conflict Regulation in Divided Societies*. Cambridge, MA: Center for International Affairs of Harvard University.

Paris, Roland. 2001. Wilson's Ghost: The Faulty Assumptions of Postconflict Peacebuilding. In *Turbulent Peace: The Challenges of Managing International Conflict*, ed. Chester A. Crocker, Fen Osler Hampson, and Pamela Aall, 765–784. Washington, DC: U.S. Institute of Peace Press.

Pearson, Frederic S. 2001. Dimension of Conflict Resolution in Ethnopolitical Disputes. *Journal of Peace Research* 38 (3):275–287.

Pugh, Michael, and Margaret Cobble. 2001. Non-Nationalist Voting in Bosnian Municipal Elections: Implications for Democracy and Peace-Building. *Journal of Peace Research* 38 (1):27–47.

Ricigliano, Robert. 2001, December. *The Chaordic Peace Process*. Paper presented at the conference Facing Ethnic Conflicts, Bonn, Germany.

Ryan, Stephen. 1990. *Ethnic Conflict in International Relations*. Aldershot, UK: Dartmouth.

Saideman, Stephen M. 2001. *The Ties that Divide. Ethnic Politics, Foreign Policy, and International Conflict*. New York: Columbia University Press.

Sandole, Dennis J. D. 1999. *Capturing the Complexity of Conflict: Dealing with Violent Ethnic Conflicts in the Post-Cold War Era*. London: Pinter.

Scherrer, Christian. 2002. *Structural Prevention of Ethnic Violence*. Houndsmill, UK: Palgrave.

Shiels, Frederick. 1984. *Ethnic Separatism and World Politics*. Lanham, MD: University Press of America.

Snyder, Jack. 2000. *From Voting to Violence: Democratization and Nationalist Violence*. New York: W. W. Norton.

Stavenhagen, Rodolfo. 1991. *The Ethnic Question: Conflicts, Development, and Human Rights*. Tokyo: United Nations Press.

Staub, Ervin. 1989. *The Roots of Evil: The Origins of Genocide and Other Group Violence*. Cambridge: Cambridge University Press.

Stedman, Stephen John. 2001. International Implementation of Peace Agreements in Civil Wars: Findings from a Study of Sixteen Cases. In *Turbulent Peace: The Challenges of Managing International Conflict*, ed. Chester A. Crocker, Fen Osler Hampson, and Pamela Aall, 737–752. Washington, DC: U.S. Institute of Peace Press.

Szayna, Thomas S. 2000. *Identifying Potential Ethnic Conflict: Application of a Process Model*. Santa Monica: Rand Corporation.

Weber, Max. 1920. Die Wirtschaftsethik der Weltreligionen. In Max Weber, *Gesammelte Aufsätze zur Religionssoziologie*. Tübingen, Germany: Mohr.

Wimmer, Andreas. 2002. *Nationalist Exclusion and Ethnic Conflict: Shadows of Modernity*. Cambridge: Cambridge University Press.

Yalcin Mousseau, Demet. 2001. Democratizing with Ethnic Divisions: A Source of Conflict? *Journal of Peace Research* 38 (5):547–567.

Index

About the Editors
and Contributors

Christopher J. Bakwesegha is former project management team leader in the Conflict Management Center of the Organization of African Unity (OAU). He has wide experience in the field of conflict prevention, management, and resolution—for example, by covering United Nations Security Council sessions on peace, security, and stability in Africa—and he has undertaken field missions in close to fifty OAU member states. He has consulted for government authorities, has worked as an election observer, and has delivered numerous public lectures on peace, security, and development. Bakwesegha is professor at the Faculty of Law, Makerere University, Kampala.

Rogers Brubaker is professor of sociology at the University of California, Los Angeles. Brubaker has written widely on social theory, immigration, citizenship, and nationalism. His publications include *Citizenship and Nationhood in France and Germany* (1992); *Nationalism Reframed: Nationhood and the National Question in the New Europe* (1996); and *Ethnicity without Groups* (forthcoming 2004). He is currently working on an ethnographic study of ethnicity and nationalism in everyday life among minority Hungarians and majority Romanians in the Transylvanian Romanian town of Cluj.

Walker Connor is Distinguished Visiting Professor of Political Science at Middlebury College, Middlebury, Vermont. He has held resident appointments at Harvard, the London School of Economics, Oxford, and Cambridge. The University of Nevada named him Distinguished United States Humanist of 1991–1992, and the University of Vermont named him

Distinguished United States Political Scientist of 1997. He has published widely on the comparative study of nationalism. A second edition of his *Ethnonationalism: The Quest for Understanding* (1994) is in preparation.

Andrew Ellis is expert technical adviser on electoral and constitutional processes and head of the participation and election processes team of the International Institute for Democracy and Electoral Assistance (IDEA). Ellis worked as a senior adviser to the National Democratic Institute (NDI), Indonesia, giving support to the parliamentary constitutional review committee and designing training schemes for the implementation of regional autonomy currently taking place. His previous assignments include acting as chief technical adviser to the Palestinian Election Commission; the design and planning of European Commission electoral assistance programs in Cambodia, Surinam, and Guyana; and coordinator for the OSCE Office for Democratic Institutions and Human Rights for the observation of registration of electors for the local elections in Bosnia and Herzegovina.

Milton J. Esman is John S. Knight Professor of International Studies, emeritus, and professor of government, emeritus, at Cornell University. He is a veteran student of the politics of ethnic pluralism. Among his more recent writings on this subject are *Ethnic Politics* (1994); *International Organizations and Ethnic Conflict* (edited with Shibley Telhami, 1995); and *Carrots, Sticks and Ethnic Conflicts: Rethinking Development Assistance* (edited with Ronald Herring, 2001).

Richard J. Goldstone was justice of the Constitutional Court of South Africa until 2001, and former chief prosecutor of the UN Criminal Tribunal for the Former Yugoslavia. From 1991 to 1994 he served as chairperson of the Commission of Inquiry regarding Public Violence and Intimidation, which came to be known as the Goldstone Commission. Since 1999 he has been the chairperson of the International Independent Inquiry on Kosovo. The many awards he has received include the International Human Rights Award of the American Bar Association and Honorary Doctorates of Law from numerous national and international universities. Most recently, Goldstone has served on the International Task Force on Terrorism, established by the International Bar Association.

Hurst Hannum is professor of international law and codirector of the Center for Human Rights and Conflict Resolution, The Fletcher School of Law and Diplomacy, Tufts University, Medford, Massachusetts. Hannum has served as counsel in cases before European and Inter-American human rights bodies and the United Nations, and has been a consultant to the UN and other organizations on issues related to minority rights and self-determination. Hannum is author or editor of numerous publications in the field of human rights, including *Autonomy, Sovereignty, and Self-Determination: The Accommodation of Conflicting Rights* (1996); *International Human Rights: Problems of Law, Policy and Process* (with Richard Lillich, 1995); and *Guide to International Human Rights Practice* (2004).

Michael Hechter is professor of sociology, University of Washington. His major fields of interest are political sociology, sociological theory, intergroup relations, and nationalism. His major book publications are *Internal Colonialism: The Celtic Fringe in British National Development 1536–1966* (1975, 1999); *Principles of Group Solidarity* (1987); and *Containing Nationalism* (2000).

Donald L. Horowitz is James B. Duke Professor of Law and Political Science at Duke Law School, Durham, North Carolina. In addition to his academic work, he has been consulted widely on the problems of divided societies and on policies to reduce ethnic conflict in various locations. Horowitz's major book publications are *Ethnic Groups in Conflict* (1985; reissued 2000); *A Democratic South Africa? Constitutional Engineering in a Divided Society* (1991); and *The Deadly Ethnic Riot* (2001).

Ulrike Joras is associate program officer for the United Nations Fund for International Partnerships, New York. Her research focuses on the role of the private business sector in conflict transformation. She is a former staff member of the Center for Development Research (ZEF) of the University of Bonn.

Walter Kälin is professor of constitutional and international law, University of Bern. His major areas of interest are refugee law, human rights law, and legal aspects of decentralization. Among his publications are *Human Rights in Times of Occupation* (with Lara Gabriel, 1994); *Grundrechte im Kulturkonflikt* (2000); *Guiding Principles on Internal Displacement: Annotations* (2000); and *Schweizerische Aussenwirtschaftshilfe und Menschenrechtspolitik—Konflikte und Konvergenzen?* (with Erika Schläppi, 2001). In addition to his academic work, Kälin has served as expert adviser on decentralization, on minority and human rights problems for Swiss Development Cooperation (SDC), for other branches of the Swiss federal administration, for cantonal and communal governments, and for the United Nations. He is currently a member of the United Nations Human Rights Committee.

René Lemarchand is professor of political science, emeritus, at the University of Florida, and was recently visiting professor at the University of California, Berkeley. He has written extensively on the Congo, Rwanda, and

Burundi. His major book publications are *Rwanda and Burundi* (1970); and *Burundi: Ethnic Conflict and Genocide* (1995). Lemarchand also served as a regional consultant on governance and democracy for the United States Agency for International Development (USAID) in Ivory Coast and Ghana.

Michael S. Lund is senior associate at the Center for Strategic and International Studies (CSIS) and Management Systems International, Inc. (MSI), and professorial lecturer in conflict management at the School of Advanced International Studies (SAIS) at the Johns Hopkins University, Washington, D.C. He holds a Ph.D. in political science from the University of Chicago. Lund's work has focused on conceptualizing, researching, and operationalizing the field of conflict prevention. Lund is author of *Preventing Violent Conflicts* (1996); *Preventing and Mitigating Conflict: A Guide for Practitioners* (with John Prendergast, 1997); and *Peacebuilding and Conflict Prevention in Developing Countries: A Practical Guide* (with Andreas Mehler, 1999).

Hugh Miall is reader in peace and conflict research and director of the Richardson Institute at Lancaster University. He is author of *The Peacemakers: Peaceful Settlement of Disputes since 1945* (1992), and *Contemporary Conflict Resolution: The Prevention, Management and Transformations of Deadly Conflicts* (with Oliver Ramsbotham and Tom Woodhouse, 1999); and he edited *Redefining Europe: New Patterns of Conflict and Cooperation*, and *Minority Rights in Europe* (both 1994). Miall received a Ph.D. in peace and conflict research from Lancaster University.

Norbert Ropers is director of the Berghof Research Center for Constructive Conflict Management, a Berlin-based nongovernmental institution dedicated to developing and testing constructive models for dealing with ethnopolitical conflicts and to creating peace constituencies in crisis zones. Currently, he is on leave from this function to facilitate the establishment of a Resource Network for Conflict Studies and Transformation in Sri Lanka. His main areas of interest are the contribution of civil society actors and development agencies to peace building, and the interlinking of "track-one" and "track-two" approaches to conflict resolution. Ropers particularly dealt with East-West relations in Europe, security policy, and the OSCE. His publications include *Friedliche Einmischung: Strukturen, Prozesse und Strategien zur konstruktiven Bearbeitung ethnopolitischer Konflikte* (1995). Ropers holds a Ph.D. in social science, international relations, and conflict studies.

Donald Rothchild is professor of political science at the University of California, Davis. Rothchild's current research interests are state building, ethnic conflict, and conflict resolution in Africa. Rothchild has published widely on African and ethnic politics. Among his recent book publications are *The International Spread of Ethnic Conflict: Fear, Diffusion, and Escalation* (coedited with David A. Lake, 1998); *Managing Ethnic Conflict in Africa: Pressures and Incentives for Cooperation* (1997); and *Sovereignty as Responsibility: Conflict Management in Africa* (coauthored with Francis M. Deng, Sadikiel Kimaro, Terrence Lyons, and I. William Zartman, 1996).

Conrad Schetter is research fellow at the Center for Development Research (ZEF), University of Bonn. His major areas of interest are ethnic movements, war economy, and the question of space and power. Schetter is the author of *Ethnizität und ethnische Konflikte in Afghanistan* (2003), and he was coeditor of *Afghanistan in Geschichte und Gegenwart* (with Almut Wieland-Karimi, 1999) and *Afghanistan—A Country without a State* (with Christine Noelle-Karimi and Reinhard Schlagintweit, 2001).

Valery A. Tishkov is director of the Institute of Ethnology and Anthropology of the Russian Academy of Science, Moscow, and former chairman of the State Committee for Nationalities Affairs, minister of the Russian Federation. His recent book publications include *Nationalities and Conflicting Ethnicity in Post-Communist Russian* (1993); *Ethnicity and Power in Multiethnic States* (1995, in Russian); *Ethnicity, Nationalism and Conflicts in and after the Soviet Union: The Mind Aflame* (1997); and *The War-Torn Society: Ethnography of the Chechen War* (2001, in Russian).

Max van der Stoel has been special adviser to Javier Solana, the European high representative for the common foreign and security policy, since 2001. Between 1993 and 2001, he was OSCE high commissioner on national minorities. Previously, he was minister for foreign affairs of the Netherlands, permanent representative of the Netherlands to the UN, and rapporteur on Iraq (UN Human Rights Commission). Van der Stoel holds several honorary doctorates from a number of universities and numerous distinctions from governments.

Angel Viñas is professor of political economy. He has held chairs at several Spanish universities, most recently at the Universidad Complutense, Madrid. Until 2000 he was director for Multilateral Relations and Human Rights in the External Relations Directorate General of the European Commission.

Peter Waldmann is professor of sociology, emeritus, at the University of Augsburg, Germany. Among his central areas of research are minority problems, ethnic conflicts, nationalism, possibilities and social consequences for the regulation of civil wars, repressive dictatorships in international comparison, political resistance, terrorism, and protest and violent rebellion. His major book publications are *Ethnischer Radikalismus: Ursachen und Folgen gewaltsamer Minderheitenkonflikte am Beispiel des Baskenlandes, Nordirlands und Quebecs* (1992); *Terrorismus: Provokation der Macht* (1998); *Der Anomische Staat* (2002); and *Terrorismus und Bürgerkrieg: Der Staat in Bedrängnis* (2003).

Andreas Wimmer is professor at the Department of Sociology, University of California, Los Angeles. He is the former director of the Department of Political and Cultural Change, Center for Development Research (ZEF), University of Bonn. Wimmer's current research topics are ethnicity and nationalism and political development. His recent book publications include *Transformationen: Sozialer Wandel im indianischen Mittelamerika* (1995); *Nation and National Identity: The European Experience in Perspective* (edited with Hans-Peter Kriesi, Klaus Armigeon, and Hannes Siegrist, 1999); and *Nationalist Exclusion and Ethnic Conflicts: Shadows of Modernity* (2002).

I. William Zartman is director of the Conflict Management Program and Jacob Blaustein Professor of International Organization and Conflict Resolution at the Nitze School of Advanced International Studies of Johns Hopkins University, Washington. Zartman's major areas of interest are African studies, conflict resolution, and political economy. Among his book publications are *Ripe for Resolution: Conflict and Intervention in Africa* (1989); *Peacemaking in International Conflict: Methods and Techniques* (edited with Lewis Rasmussen, 1998); *Elusive Peace: Negotiating an End to Civil Wars* (1998); *Power and Negotiation* (edited with Jeffrey Z. Rubin, 2000); and *Preventive Negotiation: Avoiding Conflict Escalation* (2001). Zartman has been mediating the civil war in Congo-Brazzaville for the Carter Center.